New World
Third Edition
HISTORY & GEOGRAPHY
in Christian Perspective

NEW WORLD

Third Edition

HISTORY & GEOGRAPHY

in Christian Perspective

A Beka Book® Pensacola, FL 32523-9100
a ministry of PENSACOLA CHRISTIAN COLLEGE

New World History and Geography **Map Studies & Reviews
is coordinated with this text. In order for students
to get a complete study of Western Hemisphere
geography, it is essential that they have the Map
Studies and Reviews book.**

New World History & Geography
Third Edition

Correlated Materials
New World History & Geography Teacher Edition
New World History & Geography Tests and Key
New World History & Geography Quizzes and Key
New World History & Geography Map Studies/Reviews and Key
History and Geography 6 Curriculum

Staff Credits
Editors: Elizabeth Berry, Marion Hedquist
Contributors: Laurel Hicks, Judy Hull Moore, Julie Lostroh, Brian Ashbaugh, Laura Snider, Catherine Pendley, Kelley Chunn
Consultants: Michael Lowman, D.A., Kevin Hozey, M.S.
Designer: Mark Whitcher
Production Artists: Stan Shimmin, Joe Digangi, Andrew Macarthur

Copyright © 2001, 1992, 1982 Pensacola Christian College
All rights reserved. Printed in U.S.A. 2002/2 C02

No part of this publication may be reproduced or transmitted in any form or by any means, electronic or mechanical, including photocopy, recording, or any information storage and retrieval system, or by license from any collective or licensing body, without permission in writing from the publisher.

A Beka Book, a Christian textbook ministry of Pensacola Christian College, is designed to meet the need for Christian textbooks and teaching aids. The purpose of this publishing ministry is to help Christian schools reach children and young people for the Lord and train them in the Christian way of life.

Credits are listed on inside back cover which is an extension of this copyright page.

Cataloging Data
Hicks, Laurel E. (Laurel Elizabeth)
    New world history and geography / Laurel Hicks. -- 3rd. ed.
  --- p.: col. ill., maps; 26 cm. (A Beka Book history and geography series in Christian perspective)
    1. America -- History -- Study and teaching (Elementary) 2. America -- Discovery and exploration. 3. United States -- History -- Study and teaching (Elementary) IV. A Beka Book, Inc.
Library of Congress: E18 .H55 2001
Dewey System: 970

Contents

1 The First Americans and the Land They Found 2
- 1.1 The Greatest Migration in History *2*
- 1.2 The Land the Americans Settled *4*
- 1.3 How the American Indians Lived *9*

North America

2 Cold Lands to the North 14
- 2.1 A Trip to the North Ptole *14*
- 2.2 The Tundra *16*
- 2.3 The People of the Tundra *18*
- 2.4 The Northern Woodlands *21*
- 2.5 The Indians of the Far North *24*

3 Canada: the Second Largest Country 26
- 3.1 Vast Land to the North *26*
- 3.2 Highlights of Canadian History *31*
- 3.3 The Maritime Provinces *35*
- 3.4 Quebec and Ontario *37*
- 3.5 The Prairie Provinces *40*
- 3.6 British Columbia and the Territories *42*
- 3.7 People, Resources, and Industry *44*
- 3.8 Canadian Government *48*

4 The Eastern United States 50
- 4.1 The Eastern Coasts and Mountains *50*
- 4.2 The Atlantic Ocean *53*
- 4.3 Woodland Animals *55*
- 4.4 Indians of the Eastern Woodlands *57*
- 4.5 Missionaries to the American Indians *60*
- 4.6 Famous Woodland Indians *62*

5 The North American Plains 64
- 5.1 The World's Largest Prairie *64*
- 5.2 Animals of the Prairies *65*
- 5.3 Special Features of the Land *68*
- 5.4 Plains Indians *70*

6 The American West 72
- 6.1 The Rocky Mountains *72*
- 6.2 Animals of the Rockies *76*
- 6.3 The Intermountain Region *78*
- 6.4 Desert Flora and Fauna *82*
- 6.5 The Pacific Coast *85*
- 6.6 Indians of the West *88*

Atlas 94
- A1 World—Political *94*
- A2 Western Hemisphere—Physical *96*
- A3 United States—Physical/Political *98*
- A4 Canada—Physical/Political *100*
- A5 Middle America—Political/Physical *102*
- A6 South America—Political/Physical *104*

7 The Colonial Heritage 106

- 7.1 The English Colonize America *106*
- 7.2 The Pilgrims: Lovers of Religious Freedom *112*
- 7.3 The New England Colonies *116*
- 7.4 The Middle Colonies *121*
- 7.5 The Southern Colonies *125*
- 7.6 The Great Awakening *131*

8 George Washington and the New World's First Republic 136

- 8.1 Young Hero of the French and Indian War *136*
- 8.2 Threats to American Freedoms *140*
- 8.3 The Fight for Independence *145*
- 8.4 Independence for America *149*
- 8.5 Building a New Nation *152*

9 Expansion and Evangelism 160

- 9.1 Pioneers Push Farther West *160*
- 9.2 Revival and Missions *165*
- 9.3 Christianity among Black Americans *169*
- 9.4 From the Gulf of Mexico to the Rocky Mountains *172*
- 9.5 From Sea to Shining Sea *177*
- 9.6 New Friends in Japan *179*

10 Division and Reunion 182

- 10.1 Slavery, Compromise, and States' Rights *182*
- 10.2 The Civil War Begins *186*
- 10.3 Important Civil War Battles *190*
- 10.4 Other Events of Civil War Times *192*
- 10.5 Rebuilding the South *195*

11 The Nation Grows and Prospers 198

- 11.1 The Western Frontier *198*
- 11.2 Immigration, Revival, and Industry *204*
- 11.3 Inventions: New Ways to Do Things *208*
- 11.4 New Frontiers *215*

12 Into the Twentieth Century 218

- 12.1 Our Country in 1900 *218*
- 12.2 President Theodore Roosevelt *226*
- 12.3 World War I *230*
- 12.4 Between the World Wars *233*

13 No Substitute for Victory 238

- 13.1 The World between the Wars *238*
- 13.2 World War II *241*
- 13.3 The United States Enters World War II *243*
- 13.4 Continuing World Problems *250*

14 Time for Freedom and Responsibility 254

- 14.1 Years of Prosperity and Opportunity *254*
- 14.2 Preserving Freedom in an Age of Big Government *261*
- 14.3 Return to Peace through Strength *266*
- 14.4 Advances for Freedom *270*
- 14.5 Into the Next Millennium *273*

15 MEXICO AND CENTRAL AMERICA 276
- **15.1** Middle America *276*
- **15.2** Mexico: Land of the Aztecs *277*
- **15.3** Central America: Land in between *285*
- **15.4** Countries of Central America *288*

16 WEST INDIES: ISLANDS OF THE CARIBBEAN 292
- **16.1** Land of Discovery *292*
- **16.2** Exploring the West Indies *296*
- **16.3** People and Islands *299*
- **16.4** Cuba: Country under Communist Dictatorship *306*

SOUTH AMERICA

17 SOUTH AMERICA: CONTINENT OF NATURAL RESOURCES 316
- **17.1** Exploring South America *316*
- **17.2** The Amazon and Its Peoples *321*
- **17.3** Highlights of South American History *321*

18 NATIONS OF SOUTH AMERICA 328
- **18.1** Peru, Ecuador, and Bolivia *328*
- **18.2** Colombia, Venezuela, and the Three Guianas *331*
- **18.3** Brazil: Giant of the South *334*
- **18.4** Argentina, Chile, Paraguay, and Uruguay *337*

Document Study 342
1. The American's Creed *342*
2. The Declaration of Independence *343*
3. Preamble to the Constitution *344*
4. First Amendment to the Constitution *344*
5. The Rights of Americans *344*
6. Lincoln's Gettysburg Address *345*
7. States and Capitals *346–347*
8. United States Presidents *348–349*

Dictionary of Geographical Terms 350

Index *353*
Credits *363*

Special Features

Of Special Interest
- Greenland **16**
- The Spanish Language **279**
- The Miracle of Tierra del Fuego **339**

Events in History
- The Gettysburg Address **191**
- The *Titanic* **229**
- Paricutín **282**
- The Panama Canal **290**

Missionary Heroes
- David Brainerd **61**
- Marcus and Narcissa Whitman **90**
- Adoniram Judson **168**
- Jim Eliot **322**

Concepts to Consider
- Using Dates and Timelines **108**
- Civil Government **153**
- A Study in Contrasts between Free and Communist Countries **312**

People in History
- Phillis Wheatley **133**
- Benjamin Banneker **158**
- Catherine Ferguson **171**
- James A. Garfield **203**
- Mary McLeod Bethune **221**
- Calvin Coolidge **234**
- The Nisei **245**
- Colonel Benjamin O. Davis, Jr., and the Fighting Red Tails **246**
- Huber Matos **260**
- Balboa's Discovery of the Pacific Ocean **294**

chapter 1
The First Americans
and the Land They Found

History is the record of what has happened to mankind. It is the true story of what man has done with the time and other resources God has given him. **Geography** is the study of the earth, including all the continents, islands, oceans, rivers, mountains, and plains that God created. The study of animals and their habitats, as well as people and their cultures, is also part of geography. Learning about our planet's history and geography helps us to understand what is happening around us.

During this study we will be learning about the **New World**—the continents and islands of the **Western Hemisphere** [hĕm′ĭ·sfîr]. North America, South America, and the many islands rising up out of the Caribbean Sea are all part of the New World.

1.1 The Greatest Migration in History

Over four thousand years ago, after the great Flood of Noah's day, God caused the people of the world to speak many different languages and scattered them from the Tower of Babel "upon the face of all the earth."

Some people stayed in the **Middle East,** near the site of the Tower of Babel. Others journeyed west and south into **Africa,** north and west into **Europe,** or east into **Asia.** Some went southeast and eventually reached what is today called **Australia.**

The ancestors of the native Americans (who would eventually speak around 1,000 different languages) left the Tower of Babel to begin what was the greatest migration in history. (A **migration** is the movement of a group of people or animals from one part of the world to another.) They eventually arrived in **North America** and **South America,** the area of the earth that we call the Western Hemisphere, or the New World. During their great migration, these Indians probably became the first people to discover America.

A Land Bridge

How did these Indians get to America? Most people think that they walked over from Asia! This may be surprising if you look at a map or globe and see the lands of the Western Hemisphere separated from Asia by the Pacific Ocean. But if you look more closely, you can

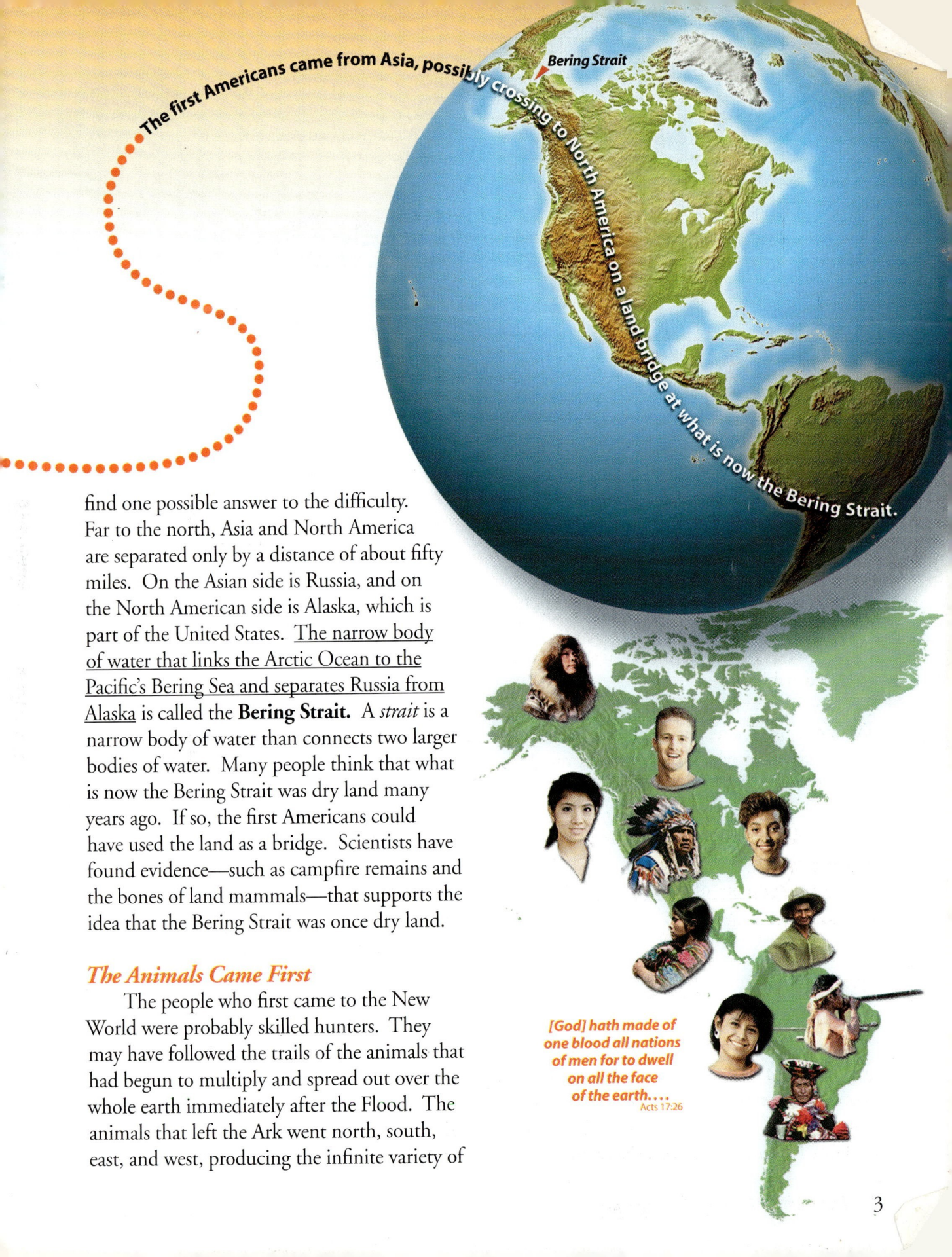

The first Americans came from Asia, possibly crossing to North America on a land bridge at what is now the Bering Strait.

Bering Strait

find one possible answer to the difficulty. Far to the north, Asia and North America are separated only by a distance of about fifty miles. On the Asian side is Russia, and on the North American side is Alaska, which is part of the United States. <u>The narrow body of water that links the Arctic Ocean to the Pacific's Bering Sea and separates Russia from Alaska</u> is called the **Bering Strait.** A *strait* is a narrow body of water than connects two larger bodies of water. Many people think that what is now the Bering Strait was dry land many years ago. If so, the first Americans could have used the land as a bridge. Scientists have found evidence—such as campfire remains and the bones of land mammals—that supports the idea that the Bering Strait was once dry land.

The Animals Came First

The people who first came to the New World were probably skilled hunters. They may have followed the trails of the animals that had begun to multiply and spread out over the whole earth immediately after the Flood. The animals that left the Ark went north, south, east, and west, producing the infinite variety of

[God] hath made of one blood all nations of men for to dwell on all the face of the earth....
Acts 17:26

3

animal life that now exists on the earth's continents. Some probably traveled east across the vast Asian continent and the Bering Strait as they made their way to North America. Many of these animals, drawn by strong instincts, were not content to stay in the north. They continued their migration until they reached Mexico, Central America, or South America, where the climate was suited to their physical characteristics and habits.

Other animals that left the Ark may have walked, galloped, trotted, slithered, crept, or run west across the African continent to South America. It might have taken many generations to complete the migration. How could they have walked from Africa to South America? They could not today, because 2,000 miles of ocean separate the two continents. Some people believe, however, that South America and Africa were at one time a single landmass. If you check a world map, you can see how the two continents could have fit together almost like pieces of a puzzle. The continents could have been divided during the days of Noah's great-great-great grandson Peleg, who was born 101 years after the Flood. Peleg's name means "divided," and the Bible says that in his days the earth was divided (Gen. 10:25).

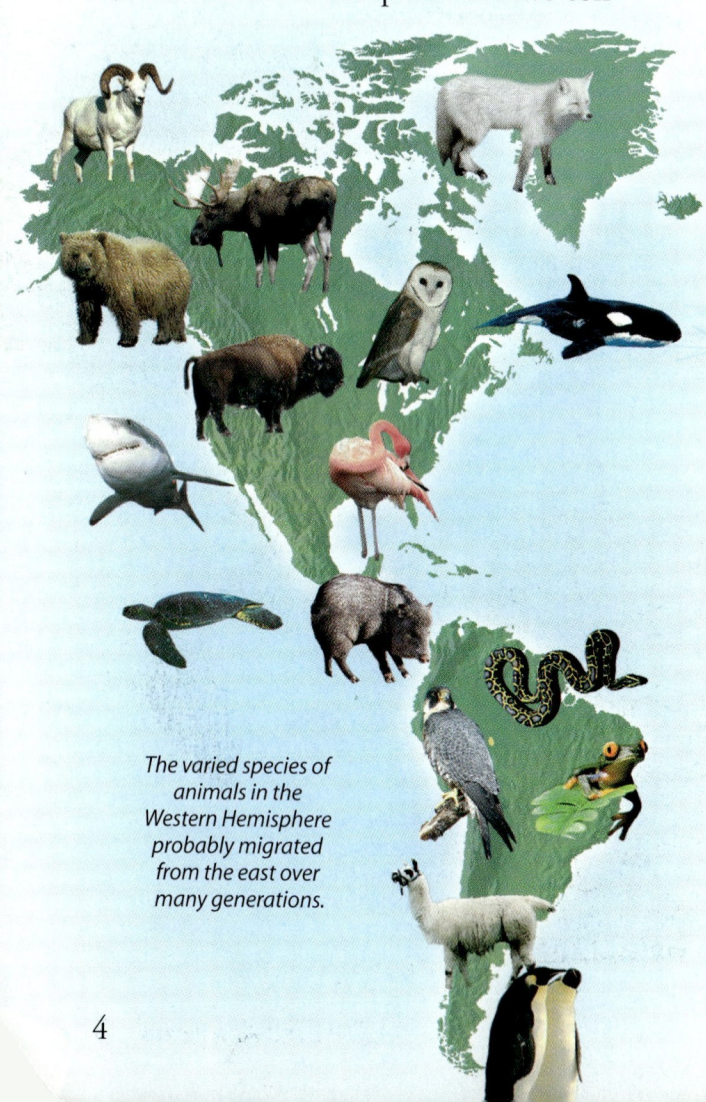

Today, South America has the widest variety of animals on any continent. The continent has nearly every type of climate and **habitat** [hăb′ĭ·tăt], or setting in which certain types of plants and animals thrive. South America's large, lush rain forests provide the perfect habitat for hundreds of thousands of mammals, reptiles, birds, and insects.

The varied species of animals in the Western Hemisphere probably migrated from the east over many generations.

Comprehension Check 1A

1. The movement of a group of people or animals from one part of the world to another is called a(n) ? .
2. What narrow body of water links the Arctic Ocean to the Bering Sea? What two countries does it separate?
3. A ? is a setting in which certain types of plants and animals thrive.

1.2 THE LAND THE AMERICANS SETTLED
Two Vast Continents

The two huge continents that the Indians settled were lands of vast resources and amazing beauty. The Native American tribes spread out; members of each family, language group, and nation moved to a different area until they reached every corner of the New World—from near the **Arctic Ocean** of North America to the

4

southern tip of **South America.** These people were spread from the **Pacific Ocean** in the west to the **Atlantic Ocean** in the east. Each tribe or group created its own unique **culture,** or <u>way of life</u>. The way the Indians lived—by hunting, fishing, raising animals, farming, and so on—depended largely on the part of America to which they migrated.

North America: Land of Plenty

Many Indians stayed in **North America,** <u>the third largest continent</u>. North America is over nine million square miles in area and extends over 5,000 miles from north to south. This massive continent was connected to South America by a narrow strip of land called the Isthmus of Panama. The isthmus is the narrowest part of the Americas—at one place it is only about 30 miles wide!

North America is noted for its high **Rocky Mountains** in the west, the low **Appalachian** [ăp′ə·lā′chē·ən] **Mountains** in the east, and the **Great Plains** that lie between. Alaska's **Mt. McKinley,** <u>the highest peak in North America,</u>

The different American Indian cultures spread to all corners of the New World.

The Rocky Mountains are North America's most prominent mountain range, stretching from Canada to Mexico.

The First Americans 5

Crops flourish in the volcanic landscape of Guatemala in Central America.

A beach on Martinique, a French island in the West Indies

has an altitude of 20,320 feet above sea level. East of the Rocky Mountains, the *plains* region lies well above sea level and yet it is very flat. Gently and gradually, the plains slope down toward the east until they reach two great lowland areas, one around cold **Hudson Bay** in the north and the other around the warm **Gulf of Mexico** in the south. Hudson Bay is the world's largest bay, and the Gulf of Mexico is the world's largest gulf. The **Mississippi River,** North America's longest river, provides hundreds of miles of waterway from its beginnings near the Canadian-American border to its mouth at the Gulf of Mexico.

Greenland, the world's largest island, lies northeast of the continent between the frigid North Atlantic and the Arctic Ocean. Greenland is about one third the size of Australia, the smallest continent, and it is almost completely covered by ice.

The farther south one travels in North America, the warmer the weather becomes. South of what is now the United States, across the Rio Grande ("large river"), some of the Indians settled in **Mexico,** a land marked by mountains, canyons, a high central plateau, and two large peninsulas (**Baja** [Lower] **California** and the **Yucatán** [yōō′kə·tăn′]). Mexico has deserts, tropical rain forests, cold mountain areas, and everything in between. The most famous Indians who lived in Mexico were the **Aztecs.**

Central America: A Narrow Bridge

The Indians who continued to migrate southward eventually reached Central America. **Central America,** which is actually a part of North America, is a narrow bridge of land that connects North America to South America and divides the Atlantic's **Caribbean Sea** from the Pacific Ocean. High in the Central American mountains, the weather is cool. Volcanic eruptions and violent earthquakes frequently shake the region. The coastal areas are hot and steamy; monkeys and colorful parrots play in the jungles along the Caribbean coast. The people of one of the most advanced early civili-

6 *New World History & Geography*

zations of the Western Hemisphere, the **Maya** [mä′yə] **Indians,** made their home in Central America.

West Indies: Islands of the Caribbean

Some Indians made their way to the **West Indies,** a 2,000-mile-long chain of mountainous islands in the Caribbean Sea. There are thousands of islands in the West Indies, including the Bahamas [bə·hä′məz], Cuba, Jamaica [jə·mā′kə], Puerto Rico [pwĕr′tə rē′kō], and the Virgin Islands. The climate in the West Indies is pleasant most of the year, and tropical forests cover many of the islands.

In 1492, Christopher Columbus landed in the West Indies and claimed them for Spain. Columbus called the land he discovered the Indies because he thought it was part of the Indies islands of Asia. He called the native Americans "Indians" because he thought they were natives of the Indies in Asia. Columbus's discovery of the West Indies led to lasting contact between the Old World and the New World.

The First Americans 7

Native villagers use canoes on the Amazon River for transportation.

South America: Land of the Amazon

South America is the fourth largest continent. The people who journeyed down to South America discovered a land whose features were similar to that of North America—they found high mountains (the **Andes Mountains**) in the west, low mountains in the east, and plains in the middle. The climate of much of the continent is warmer than that of North America because the equator—where the sun's rays are the strongest—passes through the northern part of South America. If you look at a map of the continent you can see that most of the land lies within the tropics. The mighty **Amazon River,** which flows just south of the equator, runs from the Andes Mountains in the west to the Atlantic Ocean in the east. The Amazon is the second longest river and also the largest river in the world in terms of the amount of water it contains.

South America's **Atacama** [ä′tä·kä′mä] **Desert** is one of the driest places on earth.

Indian tribes migrated to all parts of South America. Many of the people settled in the Andes, including the **Incas** [ĭng′kəz], the most famous South American Indians, who established a great empire. Some Indians went all the way to **Tierra del Fuego** [tĭ·ĕr′ə dĕl′ fwā′gō], an *archipelago* [är′kə·pĕl′ə·gō: group of islands] off the southern tip of South America. Much of the archipelago is separated from the mainland of South America by the **Strait of Magellan.** The southernmost point in the Americas is **Cape Horn,** which is on Hornos Island.

Comprehension Check 1B

1. A ? is a people's unique way of life.
2. Name three Indian groups that lived south of what is now the United States.
3.   ?   America is a narrow bridge of land that connects North America to South America.

8 *New World History & Geography*

1.3 How the American Indians Lived

God provided well for the people who migrated to North and South America. The land, plants, and animals that they discovered were more than sufficient to meet their needs for food, clothing, and shelter, and God was faithful in keeping the promise He gave to all mankind after the Flood:

> While the earth remaineth, seedtime and harvest, and cold and heat, and summer and winter, and day and night shall not cease.
> —Genesis 8:22

No matter where the new Americans settled—whether in the frozen north or in the deserts, in the mountains or along the seashores, on the prairies or in the forests—all nature bore witness to them of the faithfulness of their Creator. The Western Hemisphere Indians developed different cultures depending on where they settled. Although there were many differences among the tribes, in many ways they were much alike.

Education

The children of most Indian tribes did not go to school. Instead, the girls were taught to be good housekeepers, food gatherers, and mothers, and the boys were trained to be brave, strong warriors. The boys learned how to fish, hunt animals for food, and use weapons such as the bow and arrow and the **tomahawk** (type of light ax). When a boy was about thirteen or fourteen, his strength and bravery were tested. If he passed the test, he was considered an adult. Some Indians, such as the Maya and Aztecs, did have schools. The priests taught subjects such as mathematics, history, astronomy, language, and religion. The educated people developed calendars, systems of writing, and impressive building techniques.

Food, Clothing, and Shelter

Because the Indians were excellent hunters, meat was a main food. The people ate deer, buffalo, antelope, turkeys, rabbits, and guinea pigs, and those who lived near water caught fish and dug for clams. The land also provided many edible plants, from which the Indians gathered berries, nuts, roots, and seeds. Sassafras [săs′ə·frăs] roots and wintergreen berries were used to make tea. Many tribes raised crops such as **maize** [māz: corn], beans, and squash.

There were no horses, cattle, hogs, chickens, or metal tools in the Americas until

A Navajo woman stands at the door of her hogan, a round dwelling which has been used by some Indian cultures for centuries.

The First Americans 9

the Europeans introduced these things in the 1500s. The Indians taught the white men who began coming to America to make **snowshoes, toboggans** (long, runnerless sleds), and **canoes** and to grow such native American crops as **corn, peanuts, potatoes, squash, tomatoes,** and **peppers.**

The Indians used the skins of animals for clothing. Deerskins, buffalo hides, and rabbit furs were made into shirts, **leggings** (leather coverings that protect the legs), robes, sandals, and moccasins. Tribes in North America sometimes used tree bark and woven grasses for clothing.

Some Indians lived in **tepees** [tē′pēz], which were made by sewing as many as twenty buffalo hides together and stretching the hides around a frame of poles. Others lived in **wigwams** (dome-shaped buildings covered with leaves and bark), lodges, **hogans** (circular dwellings made with logs and mud), mud or adobe huts, stone houses, and other kinds of homes.

Recreation

Indians enjoyed playing games and competing in sports. Men ran footraces and tested their accuracy in **archery** (shooting with bows and arrows), and both men and women played several kinds of ball games. In winter months, people rode toboggans and probably had snowball fights. Guessing games were very popular for indoor entertainment.

Religion

Indians have a long heritage that goes all the way back to our first parents, Adam and Eve. Like all people everywhere, the Indians were made in the image of God, and after

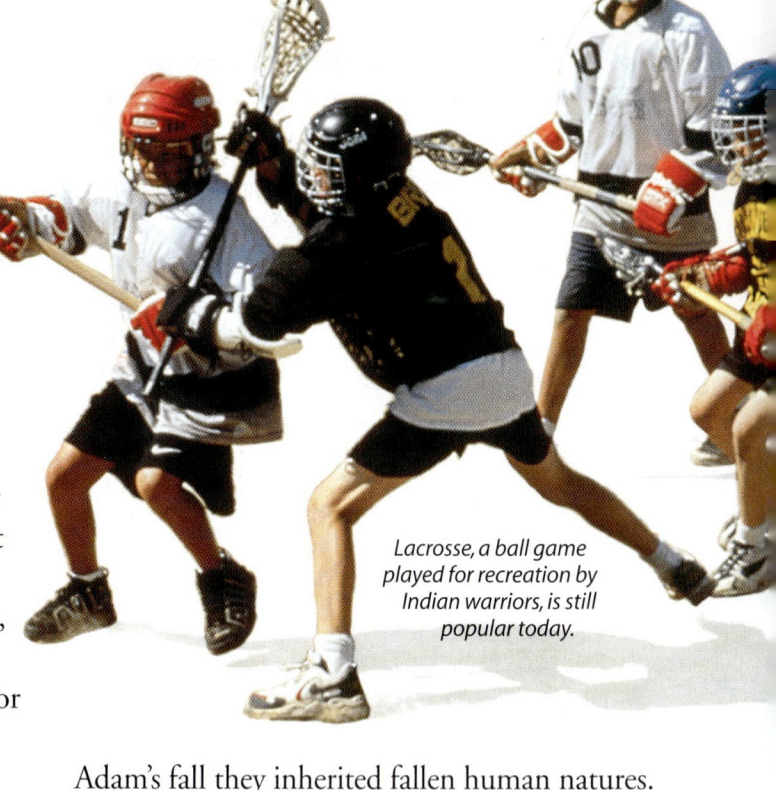

Lacrosse, a ball game played for recreation by Indian warriors, is still popular today.

Adam's fall they inherited fallen human natures. All are in need of Christ as their Savior. Some of the best friends of the Indians have been missionaries, including Christian Indians who have taken the gospel message to their own peoples.

The early Americans, like most other early peoples, forsook the things they once knew about God. Although they still told stories about the Creation and the Flood, they turned

Mayan temple at Tikal, Guatemala

away from the truth and their accounts of these events were not accurate.

The Indians were not foolish enough to be *atheists* [ā′thē·ĭsts: people who say there is no God]. They knew that there is a God Who made the world and all that is in it, but they did not know what He is like. They thought there was one Great Spirit who ruled over many other gods or spirits. Their ignorance of God's nature led them to the evils of idolatry.

Rather than worshiping the God Who made the mountains, plains, valleys, rivers, oceans, people, animals, and everything else, the Indians worshiped the spirits that they said lived in the mountains, trees, water, animals, plants, and other parts of nature. This spirit worship caused the Indians to live in fear of nature rather than to conquer it as God told man to do (Gen. 1:28).

Certain Indian groups, such as the Aztecs, the Mayas, and the Incas, built impressive civilizations that lasted for a time, but their false religions and fallen natures caused them to turn to great wickedness, and thus their civilizations crumbled. The same thing happened to the great civilizations of the Old World, such as Egypt, Babylon, Greece, and Rome, and it continues to happen even today.

Native Americans Today

Modern Indians are very proud of being the descendants of the first settlers of the New World. They are also proud to be citizens of the United States, Canada, and other American countries. Many have served faithfully in the armed forces and fought bravely in international wars; others have held high positions in business and government. **Jim Thorpe,** who was from Oklahoma, was one of America's greatest athletes. **Will Rogers,** who has been called "America's Greatest Storyteller" was part Indian. He liked to remind Americans, "My ancestors didn't come over on the *Mayflower,* but they met the boat."

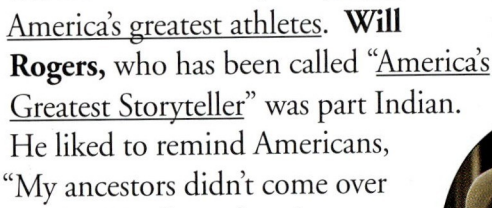

Jim Thorpe

Will Rogers

Comprehension Check 1C

1. What kinds of animals did the American Indians hunt and eat?
2. Name four kinds of shelters the Indians made.

Chapter 1 Checkup

I. *Tell why these* **people** *are important.*
- Aztecs
- Incas
- Mayas
- Jim Thorpe
- Will Rogers

II. *Define these* **terms.**

history	strait	North America
geography	Bering Strait	Mt. McKinley
Western Hemisphere	habitat	Hudson Bay
migration	culture	Gulf of Mexico

III. *Identify the locations on* **Map Masteries 1–3.***

*Found in New World History and Geography *Map Studies and Reviews.*

The First Americans

ARCTIC OCEAN

Eskimo

Mt. McKinley

walrus

elk

grizzly bear

grain elevator

PACIFIC OCEAN

CANADA

bald eagle

Canadian goose

totem pole

hockey

Toronto, Ontario

Old Faithful

Mt. Rushmore

corn field

Niagara Falls

Great Salt Lake

UNITED STATES

Golden Gate Bridge

Cowboy

St. Louis, Missouri

Grand Canyon

Mexican señorita

The Alamo

Blue Angels

Pyramid of Kukulkan Chichén Itzá, Yucatan

MEXICO

Cabo San Lucas

Mexico City

CENTRAL AMERICA

- Mt. McKinley in Alaska is the highest peak in North America.
- North America's most famous waterfall found on the U.S.-Canadian border is Niagara Falls, 167 feet high. However, California's Yosemite Falls is the highest with falls of 2,425 feet.
- Utah's Great Salt Lake is 4 to 7 times saltier than the ocean.
- The world's smallest tree is in Canada's tundra region. The arctic willow grows to be only 1 to 2 inches tall.
- Old Faithful in Yellowstone National Park erupts, on an average, every 65 minutes, shooting streams of boiling water over 100 feet in the air.
- Paricutin took only 9 years to grow from a corn field to a small mountain 1,345 feet tall. The volcano is located outside of Mexico City, Mexico.
- Mt. Rushmore took 14 years to complete. It shows the faces of 4 great American presidents—George Washington, Thomas Jefferson, Abraham Lincoln, and Theodore Roosevelt. Washington's head is as high as a 5-story building.

NORTH AMERICA

seaman

Portland Head Light

Statue of Liberty

Washington, D.C.

ATLANTIC OCEAN

fishing boat

Kennedy Space Center

dolphins

West Indies

underwater diving Cayman Island

chapter 2
COLD LANDS to the NORTH

2.1 A Trip to the North Pole

The North Pole is one of the strangest places on earth. Unlike the South Pole, which is on the continent of Antarctica, the North Pole is not located on land. Instead, it is in the middle of the ice-covered Arctic Ocean.

The North Pole and the surrounding area lie within the **Arctic.** The farther north a place is within the Arctic, the more days it has in which the sun does not set or rise. At the North Pole, the sun never completely sets for six months at a time; during the next six months, the sun never completely rises.

The Arctic is the area between the North Pole and the northern timberline of North America, Europe, and Asia. The **timberline** is the point beyond which trees cannot grow because of the extreme cold, type of soil, and other factors.

In the far north, the **aurora borealis** [ô·rôr′ə bôr′ē·ăl′ĭs], or **northern lights,** sometimes light up the night sky. The beautiful northern lights can often be seen as far south as the northern part of the United States.

Although no one actually lives at the North Pole, some Eskimo and Inuit people do live in areas very close to it. Their way of life has been greatly influenced by the cold polar climate and the hardy plants and animals that share their icy surroundings.

The Arctic Ocean

Around the North Pole is the ice-covered Arctic Ocean, the smallest and coldest ocean on earth. Only a small portion of the Arctic Ocean is kept open by water drifting from the warmer parts of the Atlantic Ocean. **Glaciers,**

14 *New World History & Geography*

Aurora borealis, a spectacular lighting of the northern night sky, is caused by particles from the sun that are drawn to the North Pole.

which are large masses of ice that flow slowly over land, break off into the water to form huge icebergs. An **iceberg** is a piece of a glacier that has moved down a mountain or across a polar region and broken off into the sea. The visible part of an iceberg is only a small fraction of its total size—there is at least six times as much ice under the water as there is above the surface.

Temperatures near the Arctic Ocean do not rise much above the freezing point in summer, and in winter they can be 40°F. below zero and even lower. Very little rain or snow can fall in these freezing temperatures. There is some precipitation in the summer, but no more than what some of the large tropical deserts receive.

God designed certain animals to be able to live near the frozen North Pole. Many tiny plants and animals called **plankton** [plăngk′-tən] thrive in the Arctic waters. Fish such as cod, halibut, and arctic trout eat the plankton, and these fish are then eaten by seals, walruses, whales, and **narwhals** [när′wĕlz], which are small whales whose males have a single spiraled tusk. **Polar bears,** some of the world's largest carnivores, live on the ice and hunt the seals. **Puffins** are strange-looking birds who spend their time swimming and diving for fish in the Arctic Ocean's icy waters. These birds are sometimes called sea parrots because of their brightly colored beaks and feet.

Fur seals are well equipped for living in the cold northern waters. These seals all have coarse, frost-proof hair and a thick layer of fat called **blubber** that helps keep them warm and a dense coat of fur that keeps water from penetrating to their skin. Some of the people who live close to the Arctic Ocean depend on the seal for much of their food, clothing, light, and heat. They eat the seal meat, burn the fat for warmth and light, and make leather from the skin.

Comprehension Check 2A

1. What is another name for the northern lights?
2. What are glaciers? From where do most of the Northern Hemisphere's icebergs come?
3. Why is the fur seal an important animal to the people of the Arctic?

Of Special Interest
Greenland: The World's Largest Island

Greenland lies within the frigid waters of the North Atlantic and Arctic oceans. This huge island is over three times as large as the state of Texas. Most of the island is covered by a layer of ice which is an average of about one mile thick; in some places the ice is over two miles thick. Snow that falls onto this glacier is packed into ice and moves outward to the ocean, where chunks break off to form icebergs. Western Greenland is the main source of the Northern Hemisphere's icebergs; approximately 10,000 break off from the glacier every year. Many of these icebergs, which range from the size of a refrigerator to a ten-story building, travel down into the Atlantic and become dangerous to ships. Scientists estimate that if Greenland's ice melted all at once, the world's sea level would rise nearly twenty feet!

Erik the Red, a Viking from Norway, founded the island's first European settlement about five hundred years before Columbus discovered the New World. Hoping to attract more settlers, he gave the island its misleading name. Today, Greenland belongs to Denmark, although the island has a fair amount of independence. Most of the people live in small villages along the twisting coastline, and fishing, food processing, and mining provide many of these people with jobs.

2.2 The Tundra

The treeless Arctic plains north of the timberline form a region called the **tundra.** Most of the tundra is north of the Arctic Circle, in the north **Frigid Zone.** (The Frigid Zones are the coldest regions of the earth.) The tundra of North America includes part of Alaska, Canada, Greenland, and a large number of islands in the Arctic Ocean and the Bering Sea. (In the Eastern Hemisphere, the northernmost parts of Norway, Sweden, Finland, and Russia are also tundra regions.)

As winter approaches, the tundra's nights gradually grow longer and the temperatures get colder. Snow and ice blanket the earth and the ground freezes solid. With the approach of summer, the land warms up as the sun shines during the long Arctic days. Eventually, the sun shines all day and all night, giving the tundra region the nickname **"Land of the Midnight Sun."** The sun heats the top layer of soil, making it marshy (soft and wet). Even during the warmest days of summer, however, the ground underneath the top layer of soil remains frozen. This permanently frozen ground is called **permafrost.** Because of the permafrost, most houses, stores, and other buildings in the tundra have to be set upon special posts to keep them off the ground. If a building were placed directly on the ground it would thaw the permafrost and sink down into the marshy ground.

Hardy plants. Winters are long and bitterly cold on the tundra, but the short, cool summers have many hours of sunshine each day to melt the ice and snow. In the summer, the tundra is dotted by many lakes,

In early fall, the tundra foliage becomes vibrant with color.

Ptarmigan molting its summer plumage.

16 New World History & Geography

ponds, and marshes. Low shrubs, mosses, and **lichens** [lĭk′ənz] grow. Lichens, which are actually two kinds of plants—fungi and algae—growing together, are some of the hardiest plants on earth. They are an important source of food for the animals of the tundra. For a few short weeks during the summer, flowers such as poppies and bluebells blanket the land with color.

Since the tundra is above the timberline, there are no large trees. A few types of trees do manage to survive on the windswept plains, including the tiny **arctic willow,** the world's smallest tree. In some places, the arctic willow grows to a height of only two inches. Other trees grow a little taller, but all of them are dwarfed and shrubby.

Unusual animals. God designed some animals to thrive in the cold, harsh climate of the Arctic. Musk oxen, caribou, arctic wolves, and arctic foxes roam the tundra. The Arctic shore area is also the breeding place for the **arctic tern,** a sea bird that migrates farther than any other bird, flying 22,000 miles a year from the Arctic to Antarctica and back. Another arctic bird, the **ptarmigan** [tär′mĭ·gən], has on its feet a mat of short feathers that serve as snowshoes to help it travel across the snow. The ptarmigan is pure white, like the snow, in winter and brown, gray, or reddish brown during the summer. Other birds that live on the tundra are the **snowy owl,** several kinds of **gulls,** the **snow goose,** and the **Canada goose.**

Musk oxen, which roam the frigid northern tundra, are large cattlelike mammals that stand about five feet high. They feed mostly on grasses, lichens, and patches of arctic willow, often pawing through the snow to find their meals. When wolves threaten a herd of musk oxen, the larger animals arrange themselves in a circle around the younger, weaker ones, their sharp horns facing outward to meet the foe. Few enemies can get inside the ferocious circle to attack the weak of the herd.

Great herds of **caribou** [kăr′ə·bōō], North American reindeer, travel hundreds of miles across the tundra each year in search of food. In the Arctic areas, they feed on lichens, moss, and swamp grass, and in the woodlands farther to the south they eat the tender branches of shrubs. They have been one of the most valuable of all land animals to the people of the tundra. Caribou provided a principal source of food for the Eskimos, Inuits, and the American Indians of the north, especially those who did not live near the ocean. The people ate the meat of the caribou, made soup from their bone marrow, and used the hides for clothing, tents, and dog harnesses. They used caribou bones for needles and knives, their tendons for thread, and their horns for fishhooks, spears, and spoons.

The big, shaggy **arctic wolf** is a member of the dog family. It hunts wild birds in the short Arctic summer and musk oxen, caribou, and other large animals during the long winter. Arctic wolves live in family packs; only one female in a pack has babies, but all the adults help to raise and feed the hungry cubs.

arctic willow, the world's smallest tree ▼

Cold Lands to the North

The little **arctic fox** often travels more than a thousand miles in search of food, making it one of the widest ranging land mammals. Its small body, short legs and muzzle (snout), and rounded ears help it conserve body heat. Its long coat is brown or gray in summer and thick, white, and fluffy in winter, allowing the fox to blend in with its background. In winter, it keeps itself warm by ruffling up its fur to trap its body heat in an insulating jacket of warm air.

One of the most important sources of food for the meat-eating animals of the tundra are the **lemmings**—little rodents four or five inches long that look like fat, round mice. At times, the lemmings increase in number so rapidly that the tundra becomes crowded with them. At these times, owls, sea gulls, arctic foxes, and arctic wolves, which usually have to search for the lemmings, easily snatch the little creatures from the tundra. So many lemmings are eaten or die of hunger that the animal almost disappears for a while, causing some of the other tundra animals to starve until the lemming population starts increasing again. In some years, the lemmings become so packed that they leave their homes in great hordes, migrating in all directions. Those that reach the sea will plunge in and swim until they eventually tire and drown. This strange behavior has given rise to a legend that every ten years the lemmings all leave their homes and rush into the ocean to commit suicide. The legend is not true, but the unusual facts about lemming overpopulation are true.

Comprehension Check 2B

1. Why is the tundra called the "Land of the Midnight Sun"?
2. What is the name used for permanently frozen ground?

lemming

2.3 THE PEOPLE OF THE TUNDRA

The ancestors of the people of the Far North migrated long ago from eastern Asia to North America. The people of northern Alaska are known as the **Eskimos,** an Indian word which was once thought to mean "eaters of raw meat" but is now believed to refer to snowshoes. In Greenland and Arctic Canada, the people prefer to be called **Inuits,** a word which means "the people."

The people of the Far North had no tribes or chiefs, and most of them lived in small family groups scattered across the tundra. They are remarkably inventive and have been able to think of clever ways of adapting to their harsh environment. Until the 1900s, they still lived in their traditional ways. When the animals they hunted began to grow scarce, many Eskimos and Inuits had to find jobs in towns. They have adapted to town life as easily as they adapted to the wilds.

Traditional Life

Food. Because the Eskimos could not grow crops in the ice and snow, meat was their main food source. **Seal** and **caribou** were the most common meats. The Eskimos ate the seal meat and used the blubber for cooking, light, and heat. They also ate the flesh of fish, whales, birds, musk oxen, walruses, and polar bears. For dinnerware, they made forks of polar bear bone, and knives of caribou bone. They used musk oxen horns for drinking cups. Cooking pots and lamps were made from a soft rock called soapstone.

Clothing. Freezing temperatures forced the Eskimos and Inuits to wear heavy clothing almost year around. In winter, they had to wear two layers of clothes—two jackets and two pairs of trousers, socks, and gloves. Much of it was made from the light, warm skin of the caribou and the long, soft, shaggy

18 *New World History & Geography*

brown hair of the musk ox. The people also made clothes from the skins of seals, polar bears, and arctic foxes. They made waterproof raincoats from seal intestines and **mukluks** (boots) from sealskins. Their **parkas** were long, hooded jackets made of different types of fur. The fur helped to keep their bodies warm and the furry hoods helped protect their faces. A woman's parka had an extra hood in which a mother could place her baby to keep him warm and close to her. To protect themselves from the glare of the sun shining on the snow, they invented snow goggles, wood or bone eye covers with narrow slits that allowed only part of the sunlight to come through.

traditional snow igloo

young Eskimo mother carrying her sleeping child on her back

Shelter. In summer, the Eskimos and Inuits lived in tents made of caribou skins, and in winter, they lived in stone and sod-block houses that were built mostly underground. (Sod is a layer of earth held together by grass and roots.) Some made winter homes from blocks of snow, especially if they needed a temporary shelter when they were traveling. They called both the snow houses and the sod houses **igloos.** The snow igloos were so well designed that two people working together could build one in less than two hours. They cut the blocks in such a way that the blocks could be laid in a gradually rising spiral, thus keeping the snow house from caving in before it was completed. Igloos could be built to house an entire family, and they could also be connected together to form multiple rooms. Some snow igloos even had windows made from seal gut that allowed sunlight to filter in. The people kept their snow houses warm by lining the walls and floors with furs.

Transportation. **Dog sleds** gave the inhabitants of the Arctic a good way to travel long distances over ice and snow. The people made the sleds of wood when it was available; otherwise they used whale jawbones, frozen animal skins, or even frozen meat. The dog was the only kind of animal that was domesti-

Cold Lands to the North 19

This Eskimo is practicing throwing his harpoon for hunting narwhal.

cated (tamed), and the people could keep only as many as they were able to feed. Today, many Eskimos and Inuits use **snowmobiles** rather than dogs to pull their sleds.

For water travel, the people invented two kinds of boats. The **kayak** [kī′ăk/] was a one-man boat constructed of sealskin stretched over a frame. There was a hole in the skin just big enough for a man to stick his legs through and sit down. The *umiak* [o͞o′mē·ăk/], a large open boat also made of skins stretched over a frame, was used for long hunting trips. It seated about a dozen people. Both types of boats were propelled by paddling.

Hunting. Until European traders brought rifles to the tundra in the nineteenth century, the people of the Arctic used wooden and bone **harpoons** for hunting. A harpoon had a barbed head attached to a long shaft and the hunters could attach some kind of cord to the shaft. After a hunter had thrown his spearlike weapon at his target, he could retrieve the animal by pulling on the cord connected to the harpoon. If wood was not available for harpoon shafts, long narwhal horns were sometimes used. The Eskimos and Inuits also designed spears and arrows that are admired even today for their outstanding craftsmanship. A skilled hunter could creep up on sleeping seals and polar bears without waking them. To capture his dinner, a hunter would often sit by a hole in the ice, waiting for a fish to bite a hook or for a seal to come up for air.

Language. There are many Eskimo and Inuit languages and dialects. Words were often made by stringing several short words together. For instance, when the people heard about the telegraph in the 1880s, they gave it a "one-word" name that was something like "that-by-which-one-communicates-habitually-in-a-hurry." Until relatively recently, the language had no written form. Thus the people had no books before the 1700s, when missionaries put their language into writing and gave them the Bible and other books in their own tongue. Many of the people now speak English, Danish, and other languages, but some of them still use the languages of their ancestors. In Greenland, the native language is still spoken in the schools and churches and on the radio.

Modern Eskimos

Today, there are well over 100,000 Eskimos and Inuits living in Alaska, Canada, Greenland, Denmark, and Siberia. Because of improved living conditions and better health care, their population is growing. Many have moved into towns and villages because there are not enough animals left on the tun-

20 *New World History & Geography*

dra for them to hunt to support themselves. Many have become commercial fishermen or construction workers, and their mechanical minds have enabled them to quickly learn how to use and repair modern machinery. Some work in Alaska's oil fields and mines.

Missionaries and traders have set up churches, trading posts, missions, and schools near the villages, and many people have heard the gospel since the time the white men came. For years, visitors to the villages around Hudson Bay were entertained by the singing of hymns. The people loved to sing, and one of their favorites was "What a Friend We Have in Jesus" sung in their native language. Perhaps the most famous missionary to the Canadian Inuits and their neighbors was **Sir Wilfred Grenfell** of England.

In recent years, the governments of Canada, the United States, and Greenland have taken over many of the services that the missionaries used to provide for the people. These governments have also begun to do many things for the Eskimos and Inuits that they used to do for themselves, taking away their traditional self-reliance. The government cannot teach them the Bible; thus many of them are also missing out on the valuable religious training their parents and grandparents had. The greatest need of the modern people of the Arctic is for more Christians to go to them with the Word of God.

Comprehension Check 2C

1. What are the people of northern Alaska called? What about the people of Greenland and northern Canada?
2. How did people travel over snow and ice? What kinds of boats did they use?
3. Why have many Eskimos moved into towns and villages today?
4. Name the famous missionary who went to the Canadian Inuits and their neighbors.

2.4 THE NORTHERN WOODLANDS

South of the tundra, a vast evergreen forest stretches for three thousand miles to cover much of Canada and parts of Alaska. These cold northern woods are sometimes called the **taiga** [tī′gə], which is a Russian word meaning "forest"; another common term for these woods is the **boreal forests.** (*Boreal* means "northern.") During the long, hard winter months, the woods are blanketed with heavy snows and the multitude of ponds, lakes, rivers, and streams that drain the region are often frozen. The largest forests in the world are these boreal forests of North America, as well as the ones in Sweden, Finland, and Siberia in the Eastern Hemisphere.

Land of Tall Trees

Conifers. The main trees of the taiga are conifers (cone-bearers), <u>the oldest and largest trees in the world</u>. They have needle-shaped leaves and woody cones that contain seeds. Most of these coniferous trees are **evergreens,** <u>trees that keep their leaves all year</u>.

Many varieties of **spruce,** which are valued for their wood, grow in the taiga. They vary in height from twenty to two hundred feet. They often grow so abundantly and so closely together that a man can hardly squeeze between them. Spruce are some of the few conifers that grow in the very cold areas near the Arctic Circle.

In the more southern areas of the taiga, **pines** and **firs** grow as well. The **balsam fir** has needles that give off a fragrant aroma as they dry. Its beautiful shape makes it a favorite for Christmas trees. The resin (gummy substance) that comes from the blisters on its bark is called *Canada balsam* and is used in medicine and art.

Broadleaf trees. Broadleaf trees grow in the open areas of the boreal forests around

evergreen forest along the Bow River in Alberta, Canada

lakes and rivers. The broadleaf trees are the most numerous and varied trees in the world. They have regular broad, flat leaves rather than needles, and those in the temperate zones are *deciduous,* which means they lose their leaves in the fall. They are often called *hardwoods* because many of them have tough, hard wood; these trees are excellent for making furniture. In the northern woods, aspens and birches are the most common, but there are also beeches, alders, tamaracks, and maples. The **paper birch,** or canoe birch, is distinguished by its brown to whitish bark which can be easily peeled from the tree in thin layers. The Indians used birch bark for canoes and baskets, and very thin strips of it have sometimes been used as a substitute for paper.

Animals of the Woodlands

The many lakes and streams that dot the region are filled with huge fish (perch, bass, salmon, trout, and others) designed to thrive in cold water. A multitude of animals—caribou, moose, deer, foxes, wolves, squirrels, beavers, porcupines, bears, weasels, hares, and many others—make their homes in the woods. In the summer, many kinds of birds—crows, ravens, sparrows, ducks, geese, pheasants, cranes, gulls, eagles, hawks, and owls—come from the lands farther south.

The deer family. Large members of the deer family, the caribou, the moose, and the wapiti [wŏp′ĭ·tē], were especially valuable to the Indians of the northern forests for their meat, hides, and antlers. At one time, millions of **woodland caribou** roamed throughout the area, but their numbers have been greatly reduced. They are similar to the tundra caribou, but woodland caribou feed on the tender branches of shrubs and young trees not available in the tundra. **Moose,** the largest member of the deer family, also range through the woods. These animals, which tend to be solitary except in winter, are distinguished by the "bell," or flap of skin hanging from their neck and the huge, broad antlers of the males. They were named *Musse,* or "wood eater," by the Algonquian [ăl·gŏng′kwē·ən] Indians.

Fur-bearing animals. Millions of small fur-bearing animals live in the boreal forests. The hard-working **beaver,** North America's largest rodent, feeds on berries, leaves, and bark. It gnaws through branches and trunks with

22 *New World History & Geography*

its four strong front teeth for materials to build its dams and lodges. The Indians ate beaver meat, used their furs for clothing and decoration, and made knives with their teeth. Through their endless dam building and ditch digging, beavers have done more than any other animal to shape the landscape of the North American continent.

The long, slender **weasel** is an active, hungry predator that feeds on various rodents and other prey. One type of weasel, the **ermine,** sheds its summer coat of chocolate brown for a winter coat of white. This molting is caused by seasonal changes of day length. Other weasel-like mammals include the fierce little **wolverine.** The wolverine, sometimes called "skunk-bear" because of its appearance, is one of the strongest mammals of its size. Its broad feet support it well in the snow. The **marten** has furry feet that allow it to walk on top of the snow. It also tunnels under the snow and climbs trees, hunting for hares, shrews, chipmunks, eggs, and blueberries to eat. Because of its intense curiosity, the marten is easily trapped by man. The **mink,** another weasel-like animal, has a luxurious fur coat that makes it especially sought after by man. After Europeans came to North America, many of them earned their living by trapping the fur-bearing animals of the taiga or trading with the Indians for furs.

Birds. The **raven,** a large black bird (about twenty-six inches long) that resembles a crow, is common in the northern forests. Another common bird is the **crow,** which is about eighteen inches long and one of the world's most intelligent birds. Other birds include the distinctive-looking loons and gannets.

Perhaps the most majestic birds of North America are the eagles. Eagles are among the largest and most powerful birds in the world. The **golden eagle** gets its name from the crown of golden feathers around its head and neck. The rest of its feathers are dark brown. Because of its fierce, proud appearance and the graceful way it soars high above trees and hills in search of food, the golden eagle has been called "king of the birds." The **bald eagle** is not bald; the feathers on its head are white. (*Bald* originally meant "white-headed.") Eagles soar high in the air and use their keen eyesight to hunt rabbits, hares, ground squirrels, birds, fish, and other small animals. Their flying speed is between 20–60 miles per hour, but when they dive, they can go faster than 100 miles per hour. They make huge nests of sticks high up on cliffs or on the tops of tall trees. One gigantic nest measured 10 feet wide, 20 feet deep, and weighed about two tons!

Comprehension Check 2D

1. What two terms are used for the vast forest that covers much of northern Canada and Alaska?
2. How did the Indians use the paper birch?
3. Which animal has done the most to shape the landscape of North America?

23

2.5 THE INDIANS OF THE FAR NORTH

American Indian tribes of the Far North included the Cree [krē], Ottawa [ŏt′ə·wə], Yellowknife, Beaver, and Ojibwa [ō·jĭb′wā′] tribes, as well as many others. There were very few Indians in the region, however, compared with the vast land area, and they moved around quite a bit in search of food.

Food and travel. Because the growing season was too short for much farming, the Indians relied mainly on hunting and on gathering wild plants, berries, and nuts for food. Using bows and arrows and knives made of stone, beaver teeth, or bones, the Indians hunted bear, elk, deer, moose, caribou, and buffalo. They also fished the many inland lakes and streams. During the summer, they used birch bark canoes to travel. When winter came and the water froze over, they used **snowshoes** and **toboggans** (long, runnerless sleds) to travel over the deep snow and ice. For traveling food for long trips, they made **pemmican** [pĕm′ĭ·kən], a mixture of dried meat pounded together with fat and berries.

Clothing. The Indians made their clothes out of the skins of moose and caribou. Sometimes the people would decorate their clothing with porcupine quills, embroidery, or paint made from colorful earth. The men wore long shirts, breechcloths, leggings, and **moccasins** (soft leather shoes). The women wore longer shirts and shorter leggings. For the cold winters, robes, mittens, and fur caps were worn by men, women, and children alike. It is thought that the **Ojibwa** people might have received their tribal name because of the way a certain seam on their moccasins puckered. When the white man tried to pronounce the name it came out *"Chippeway."* Soon even some of the Indians were calling themselves that. Over the years, they have often been called the **Chippewa** [chĭp′ə·wâ] Indian tribe, although they still prefer the name Ojibwa.

Homes. The Indians of the taiga made several kinds of dwellings. Permanent winter houses were made of spruce, tamarack, and other kinds of wood covered with bark, brush, or animal skins. When they were out traveling, the Indians made wigwams, tepees, and simple lean-tos.

Religion. The various tribes of the northern forests worshiped many different gods and spirits. Rituals and superstitious practices played an important part in the everyday lives of the people. For example, some of the people believed that if certain animal bones were not properly disposed of, their hunts would not be successful.

When missionaries began sharing the Good News of the gospel, many Indians turned to the God of the Bible. Wanting to know more about Heaven, a Yellowknife Indian named Saltatha asked the following question:

Is it more beautiful than the country of the musk ox in summer, where sometimes the mist blows over the lakes, and sometimes the water is blue, and the loons

young Chippewa boy in traditional costume

24 New World History & Geography

modern Native American building Ojibwa-style birch bark canoe

cry very often? That is beautiful; and if Heaven is still more beautiful, my heart will be glad, and I shall be content to rest there till I am very old.

Before they ate, some of the Naskapi [năs′kə·pē] Indians of the region said this prayer:

> Thank you, Creator, for sending the caribou;
> Thank you, Caribou, for being obedient and coming;
> And thank you, Cook, for preparing it so well.

Children. The children of the taiga had no chance to learn reading, writing, and arithmetic, for there were no books or schools.

Instead, their parents taught them how to survive in the wilderness. The boys were taught to be watchful, peaceable, self-reliant hunters and to keep their emotions under control. They learned many skills by observing the examples set by the men. Girls learned from the example of the women. A mother might ask her daughter to make tea, and the little girl would try her best to gather roots and herbs and fix tea the way she had seen her mother do it so many times before. If children stole, lied, or disobeyed, the parents were careful to punish them. Parents did what they could to train their children to do things on their own as soon as possible. A baby's first tooth, a boy's first success at hunting, and other important firsts were occasions for feasts and celebrations.

Modern Life. Today, there is a big variety in the ways that the Indians of the northern forests live. Many of the native people of this region have changed their manner of life, moving to towns and working at various jobs. Others, however, desire to continue living the way their ancestors did.

Comprehension Check 2E

1. Name five American Indian tribes of the Far North.
2. How did the children of the people of the Far North learn how to survive?

Chapter 2 Checkup

I. Tell why these **people** are important.

    Erik the Red   Inuits   Eskimos   Sir Wilfred Grenfell

II. Define these **terms**.

Arctic	glacier	tundra	igloo	boreal forest	deciduous
timberline	iceberg	Frigid Zone	kayak	conifer	toboggan
northern lights	blubber	permafrost	harpoon	evergreen	pemmican
Arctic Ocean	Greenland	parka	taiga	broadleaf	moccasins

III. Give the noted (significant) fact about these **animals**.

    fur seal   caribou   beaver   bald eagle
    arctic tern   lemming   golden eagle

IV. Identify the locations in **Map Mastery 3**.

Chapter 3
CANADA the SECOND LARGEST COUNTRY

3.1 VAST LAND TO THE NORTH

From Sea to Sea

The name *Canada* comes from the Iroquois [ir′ə·kwoi′] Indian word *kanata,* which means *a group of huts.* Although the name may bring a small, cozy Indian village to mind, Canada is actually the second largest country in the world. It is larger than Europe and covers about forty percent of North America, one fifteenth of the land area of the earth. It extends from the Atlantic Ocean to the Pacific Ocean and from the Arctic Ocean to the northern border of the United States. (Canada is one of the few countries that borders on three oceans.) The country's official motto, "From sea to sea," was taken from the verse "he shall have dominion also from sea to sea, and from the river unto the ends of the earth" (Psalm 72:8).

Sparsely Settled

The cold climate and poor soil conditions of this huge land of tundra, forests, and high, snowcapped mountains have left much of the country sparsely populated. The Canadian North (the tundra and boreal forests) is one of the least used and most deserted areas in the world. One area of dense population is southern Ontario.

Large Islands

Many islands decorate the Canadian coastline. The largest of these are Canada's *Arctic islands.* Located north of the mainland, almost all of these islands lie within the Arctic Circle. The Arctic islands are characterized by either tundra or an icecap climate. Cold temperatures prevent most tree growth. Isolated trading posts along the coasts have been founded by Inuit, weathermen, and missionaries. The Arctic islands include three of the world's largest islands—**Baffin Island, Victoria Island,** and **Ellesmere Island.** The most northerly settlement of North America, the military base of Alert, is located on Ellesmere Island. This settlement, which was started as a weather station, is only about 500 miles from the North Pole!

The islands off Canada's east and west coasts are more densely populated. **Newfoundland** [noo′fən·lənd], is off the east coast in the northern Atlantic. In the Pacific lies

26 *New World History & Geography*

*Banff National Park
Alberta, Canada*

Vancouver Island, the largest island on North America's west coast. This island was named for the British explorer, **Captain George Vancouver** [văn·kōō′vər]. The island has one of the mildest climates in all of Canada. The warm ocean currents that keep ice from ever forming in the surrounding straits also keep the air temperature moderate. Victoria, the capital of British Columbia, is located on the southeastern tip of the island.

Hudson Bay and the Canadian Shield

Canada has the longest coastline of any country in the world. Gulfs, bays, and countless inlets indent its rugged coast. More than half of Canada's coastline lies along the Arctic Ocean.

Hudson Bay, the world's largest bay, lies entirely within Canada. The bay opens into the icy arctic waters of the Hudson Strait. English explorer Henry Hudson sailed through this strait to discover the bay in 1610. Many of the Inuit and American Indians who live around the bay make their living by hunting and fishing. Because ice covers much of the bay for several months each year, ships may visit certain ports in the region only during the summer months. The shores of the bay border upon the provinces of Quebec, Ontario, and Manitoba, as well as the territory Nunavut [nōō′nə·vōōt′].

Hudson Bay is nearly surrounded by the **Canadian Shield,** a horseshoe-shaped region that covers about half of the nation, from Labrador in the northeast to the Arctic Ocean in the northwest. (When seen from above, this range of hills resembles a shield.) The hills, which cover much of the Shield, are made up of hard rock (granite and gneiss) covered by little or no soil; the shield is the source of much of Canada's mineral wealth. The Canadian Shield is Canada's largest and most sparsely populated land area.

The St. Lawrence Seaway

St. Lawrence River. When the early explorers sailed beyond the islands of Newfoundland and Nova Scotia, they discovered an inland sea—the **Gulf of St. Lawrence**—between the islands and the mainland. They also discovered the **St. Lawrence River,** which they followed as a highway into the continent. This

Canada: the Second Largest Country

broad and deep river holds a great deal of water, making it easy for ships to navigate. It is one of Canada's major rivers; some think it is second only to the Amazon in the amount of water it holds. From its headwaters in Lake Ontario, it flows 800 miles (1,288 km) to the Gulf of St. Lawrence.

Paddling their canoes upstream toward the river's headwaters, the explorers came to the Great Lakes. Although the explorers had to bypass waterfalls and rapids and sometimes had to carry their canoes across stretches of land between the lakes, ships today can sail from the Atlantic all the way to Lake Superior.

Together, the Great Lakes, their connecting rivers and canals, and the St. Lawrence River make up the **St. Lawrence Seaway.** <u>This seaway is the largest inland seaway in the world.</u> Canada and the United States built the St. Lawrence Seaway in the 1950s to open the North American continent to oceangoing ships. Canals were dredged where the land interrupted the course of the waterway. Locks (huge chambers in a canal or river closed off with gates and used to control the level of the water) were built to raise and lower ships between lakes of different water levels. Water is pumped in through valves to raise a ship or drained out to lower it.

From April to December, the St. Lawrence Seaway is sufficiently ice-free for ships to travel over 2,300 miles (3,703 km) inland from the Atlantic Ocean. The seaway allows cargo ships to sail to some of North America's important industrial and agricultural centers. One of the most famous ports is at Thunder Bay, a city on the northwestern shore of Lake Superior. Hundreds of thousands of tons of grain, minerals, timber, and other goods pass through this busy port every year.

The Great Lakes and Niagara Falls

A large portion of the St. Lawrence Seaway lies in the **Great Lakes:** Lake **Superior,** Lake **Michigan,** Lake **Huron,** Lake **Erie,** and Lake **Ontario.** The Great Lakes are the largest group of freshwater *lakes* in the world. They contain approximately 1/5 of the earth's freshwater supply. An easy way to recall the lake names is to remember the word *HOMES.* Each of the letters in the word is the first letter of one of the lakes.

Lake Michigan is the only Great Lake that does not touch Canada. It is located totally within the United States border. Lake Superior, Lake Huron, Lake Erie, and Lake Ontario are shared by both the United States and Canada, and they form part of the boundary between the two countries.

Niagara Falls

The Great Lakes are at different heights above sea level. Lake Superior, which is the farthest north and west, has a higher elevation than the others. The most spectacular drop in elevation is found between Lake Erie and Lake Ontario. As the Niagara [nī·ăg′rə] River flows from Lake Erie to Lake Ontario, it divides into two streams and drops over rocky ledges to form **Niagara Falls,** one of the world's most beautiful waterfalls. Niagara Falls has two parts, one in Canada and the other in the United States. Canada's Horseshoe Falls is over 170 feet high (51 m) and well over 2,000 feet (600 m) wide. The American Falls is over 180 feet (54 m) high and about 1,000 feet (300 m) across. More water flows over Niagara Falls per second than flows over any other waterfall in the world. These falls

The Great Lakes

Lake	Depth above sea level	Depth below sea level
Lake Superior	600 ft. (183 m)	1,333 ft. (406 m)
Lake Michigan	579 ft. (176 m)	923 ft. (281 m)
Lake Huron	579 ft. (176 m)	750 ft. (229 m)
Lake Erie	570 ft. (174 m)	210 ft. (64 m)
Lake Ontario	245 ft. (75 m)	802 ft. (244 m)

Connecting waterways: Soo Canals, St. Mary's River, Straits of Mackinac, St. Clair River, Lake St. Clair, Detroit River, Niagara River, Niagara Falls, St. Lawrence River

Canada: the Second Largest Country

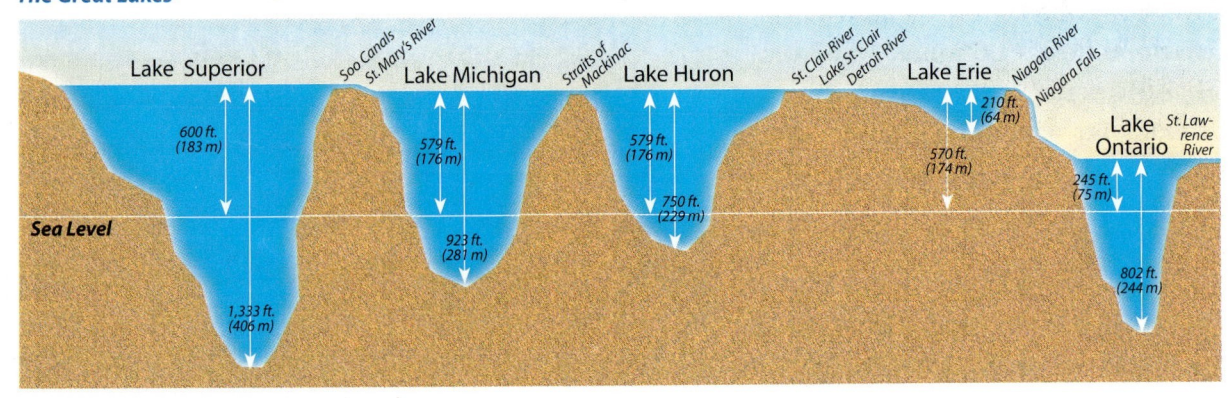

Great Bear Lake possibly got its name from the many polar bears that are found there.

are the result of the tremendous difference between the elevations of Lake Erie and the much lower Lake Ontario.

All five of the lakes are among the world's twelve largest lakes. By itself, Lake Superior, the largest freshwater lake in the world, is slightly larger than the state of South Carolina! It is also deep—with its 1,333 foot (400 m) depth, a 100-story skyscraper could be buried upright under its waters. Lake Huron and Lake Michigan are the world's third and fourth largest lakes.

Northern Lakes

Located in the Northwest Territories on the Arctic Circle is **Great Bear Lake,** the world's seventh largest freshwater lake and the largest lake entirely within Canada. It may have been named for the many bears found in the area. This lake is frozen eight months of the year.

Farther south, the world's ninth largest freshwater lake, **Great Slave Lake,** is also frozen eight months of the year. This lake was named for the Slavey Indians that lived in the area, and it is the source of the **Mackenzie River,** Canada's longest river (1,025 mi. or 1,650 km).

Majestic Mountains

Canada has mountains running along its west, east, and north coasts. The high, rugged mountains that stretch across western Canada are a part of the **Western Cordillera** [kôr′dl·yâr′ə], a mountain chain which reaches from the southern tip of South America to the Arctic Circle. *Cordillera* is a Spanish term for a group of mountain ranges. One important range in the Western Cordillera is the **Canadian Rockies.** In the east, the **Appalachian** [ăp′ə·lā′chē·ən] **Mountains** stretch from the southern United States north through the provinces of New Brunswick and Nova Scotia. Among the islands of the Arctic region are the Innuitian Mountains.

Comprehension Check 3A

1. What is the second largest country in the world? What three oceans border this country?
2. Canada's large Baffin, Victoria, and Ellesmere Islands are part of what island group?
3. What is the name of the largest inland seaway in the world?
4. Name all five of the Great Lakes. Which one is largest?

Appalachian Mountains in the fall

30 *New World History & Geography*

3.2 Highlights of Canadian History

The Vikings and Christopher Columbus

Early Exploration. Long after the first Indians, Eskimos, and Inuits arrived in Canada, European explorers began arriving on the northeast shores of North America. During the Middle Ages (A.D. 500–1500), fierce warriors called **Vikings** lived on the Scandinavian [skăn′də·nā′vē·ən] Peninsula of northern Europe. The Vikings, a tall people known for their blond hair and blue eyes, were skilled craftsmen and daring seamen. They raided many European nations and explored far out into the Atlantic Ocean.

Around the year A.D. 1000, the Viking **Leif Ericson** [lēf ěr′ĭk·sən] discovered the North American continent. It is believed that the Vikings might have started several little villages at the tip of Newfoundland, an island off Canada's Atlantic coast. Although they did not tell anyone about their discovery, the Vikings were nevertheless probably the second people to discover America. (Do you remember who the first were?)

Columbus discovers America. About 500 years later (1492), **Christopher Columbus** became the first modern explorer to discover the New World. He landed far to the south in the islands of the Caribbean Sea and began a great era of discovery.

John Cabot Claims the Land for England

Like Christopher Columbus, **John Cabot** [kăb′ət] was eager to find a sea route to the Indies. Cabot was an Italian explorer who had moved to England. "If Columbus had sailed farther north, he would have found an even shorter route to the Indies," thought Cabot. "If only I could try myself!" King Henry VII of England gave him permission. With a crew of only eighteen men, Cabot set sail from Bristol, England. In 1497, John Cabot became the first modern explorer to reach the North American mainland.

The Vikings were the first Europeans to find America.

No one knows for sure where he landed, but it was most likely in a part of what is now Canada, either Newfoundland or Nova Scotia's Cape Breton Island or on the coast of Labrador. Thinking that he, too, had reached the Far East, Cabot claimed the land for England. Although the explorer never found a route to the Indies, he did find vast schools of fish in an area now called the Grand Banks—a discovery which led to Europe's very profitable fishing industry.

Jacques Cartier Gives France a Claim

By now, both England and France were interested in finding a sea route through North America to the riches of Asia. They were so sure that such a route existed that they gave it a name—the **Northwest Passage.** As you know from your study of maps, there is no waterway through North America from east to west. In the 1500s, however, no one had yet explored and mapped the New World; it was up to explorers to find out for themselves.

Canada: the Second Largest Country 31

In 1534, a Frenchman named **Jacques Cartier** [zhäk kär·tyā′] set sail in hopes of finding the Northwest Passage and sailing on to China. If Cartier could find such a route, he would gain great wealth for the king of France.

Cartier

Cartier reached North America and sailed past the southern tip of Newfoundland, where he discovered the Gulf of St. Lawrence. During his explorations, he traded with the American Indians he met. No doubt, many Indians watched as he claimed the land for France. They probably did not understand what he was saying, but they trusted him. Although Cartier wanted their valuable furs, he did not take them. Instead, he traded colorful coats, caps, beads, knives, and other goods that the Indians wanted for the furs. Cartier made three voyages to this region and eventually traveled up the St. Lawrence River to where Quebec City now stands. Even though he never found the Northwest Passage, Cartier's explorations gave France a claim to Canada and opened the way for a valuable fur trade between the French and the Indians.

Comprehension Check 3B

1. Which Viking became one of the first Europeans to discover North America? Who was the first modern explorer to discover the New World?
2. Who was the first modern explorer to reach the North American mainland?
3. Jacques Cartier searched for what route through North America?

The French Settle Canada

The French discovered that the beautiful animal furs of North America could be sold for high prices in Europe for hats and coats. Many Indians were eager to trade their furs with the Frenchmen, who treated them as friends.

Champlain

In 1603, **Samuel de Champlain** [săm′ū·əl də shăm·plān′] arrived in what is now Canada. At that time in history, the French claims in the New World were called **"New France."** Champlain and his men explored and traded with the Indians and then sailed back to France with a valuable cargo of furs. The king of France became interested in starting a permanent settlement in North America.

Early Exploration North America

- → 1497 John Cabot
- → 1534 Jacques Cartier
- → 1535 Jacques Cartier
- → 1603–1607 Samuel de Champlain
- → 1608–1610 Samuel de Champlain

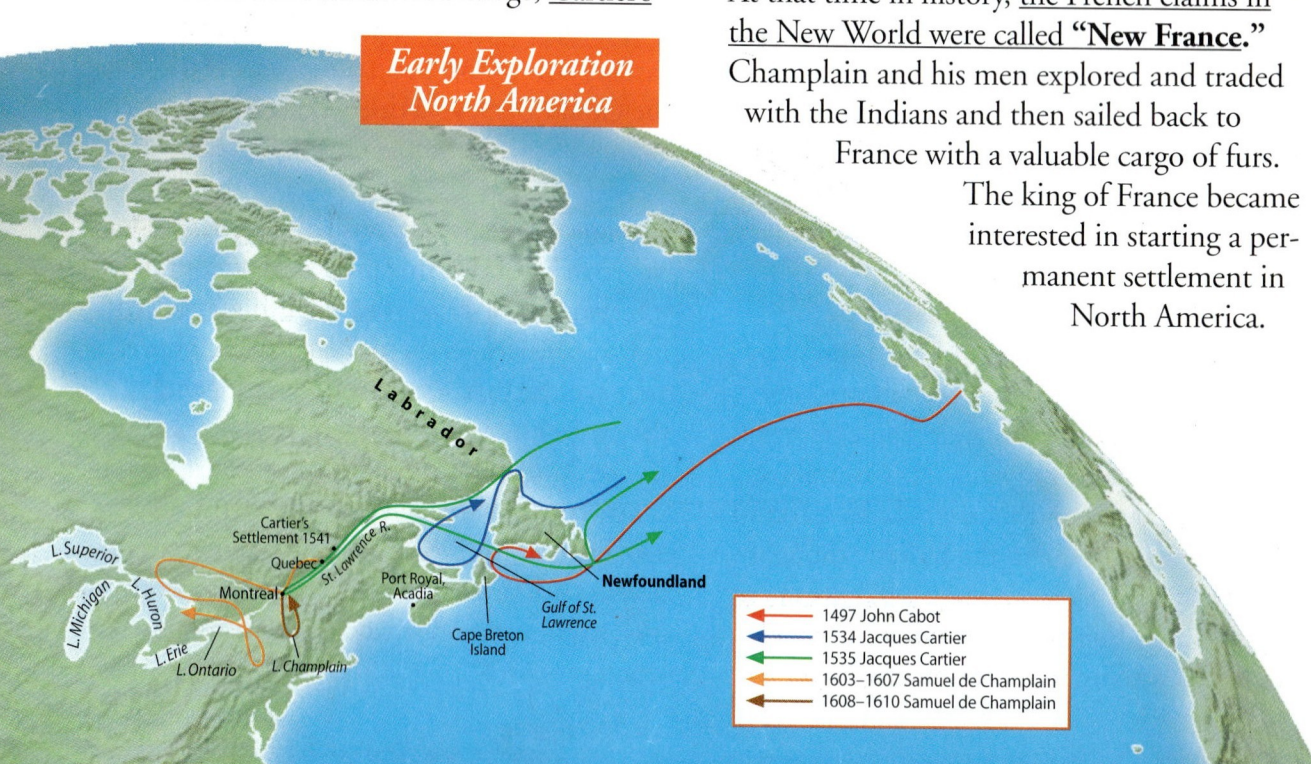

Realizing that the fur trade would be a valuable business, he decided that Frenchmen must be sent there to live. In 1604, the French established the settlement called **Port Royal, Acadia** (now Annapolis Royal, Nova Scotia).

Champlain returned to New France. This time, he explored the coastline of New England and made maps of the region. He also discovered the beautiful Lake Champlain in what is now New York state. He then returned to New France, where he helped build the first important French settlement in the New World in 1608: **Quebec.**

British Fur Traders Come to Canada

British Claims. While the French were settling parts of Canada, the British were establishing colonies farther south at Jamestown and Plymouth. The British also hired **Henry Hudson** to explore farther north. In 1610, while searching for the Northwest Passage, Henry Hudson discovered Hudson Bay. Shortly thereafter, his cold, hungry crew mutinied and set Hudson, his son, and a few loyal sailors adrift to die in the bay which was later named for him.

Hudson

Hudson's Bay Company. By the 1660s, French fur traders from the St. Lawrence settlements had heard stories of a great "North Sea" area rich in furs, but French authorities did not follow up on any plans to trade there. Three French explorers and fur traders took their plan to English merchants, who sent a ship to Hudson Bay in 1668. It returned loaded with furs. In 1670, the **Hudson's Bay Company,** Canada's oldest business, was founded in London, England. It secured trading rights in the vast land surrounding Hudson Bay and began building trading posts. Soon, the French traders had a serious rival for the Canadian fur trade. The French and British struggled over the bay for many years before England took firm control. Although Hudson's Bay Company transferred its Northwest lands to Canada in 1870, it is still in business today, operating department stores and other interests.

Key Dates in Early Exploration

c. 1000	Vikings land in the New World (c. is short for *circa,* which means "about")
1492	Christopher Columbus sails across the Atlantic
1497	John Cabot claims a part of Canada for England
1534	Cartier discovers the Gulf of St. Lawrence and makes a claim for France
1610	Henry Hudson discovers Hudson Bay

The French and Indian War

Because the boundaries of the French and English territories in North America were not clearly defined, conflicts between France and England grew over land rights until war was declared. As part of the 1763 treaty that ended the **French and Indian War** (1754–1763), France gave most of its North American possessions to England. This was important to the United States as well as to Canada because it established Britain's importance in all of North America. Later, in the Quebec Act of 1774, the English granted the French settlers rights to their own language, religion, and civil law.

Growth and Exploration

Loyalists. The colonists in Canada did not join in the American War for Independence. Many American colonists, called Loyalists, moved up to Canada during that war because they did not feel that they should

Canada: the Second Largest Country 33

fight against their king. They founded the city of St. John, New Brunswick. Other Loyalists settled in Quebec, Nova Scotia, and on the Niagara Peninsula.

Expanded boundaries. Canada's boundaries moved farther north and west as fur traders and explorers ventured into new land. The Pacific coast was explored and mapped by **Captain Cook** and **Captain Vancouver,** both of England. Much of this land was claimed for England by the Hudson's Bay Company and the North West Fur Company, another fur-trading organization.

Cook

The Dominion of Canada

Moves toward independence. In 1837, the people of Canada let it be known that they wanted a more democratic government. Britain's Lord Durham suggested in 1839 that Upper and Lower Canada (later Ontario and Quebec) be united into one colony which would be allowed to govern itself. In 1867, the **Dominion of Canada** was formed, including the provinces of Ontario, Quebec, Nova Scotia, and New Brunswick. Other provinces were added, and by 1931, Canada was a self-governing member of the British Commonwealth. Newfoundland was the last province to be added (1949).

In 1982, Canada achieved nearly complete political independence from the United Kingdom. The British monarch is still recognized as Canada's head of state, but the nation is governed by its own prime minister and Parliament.

Comprehension Check 3C

1. Who established Quebec, Canada's first permanent settlement?
2. What is the name of Canada's oldest business?
3. Which two important countries fought over land in the French and Indian War? What was an important result that affected the United States?

Canadian Provinces and Territories

Rank in Area	Province	Capital	Rank in Population
1	Quebec	Quebec City	2
2	Ontario	Toronto	1
3	British Columbia	Victoria	3
4	Alberta	Edmonton	4
5	Saskatchewan	Regina	6
6	Manitoba	Winnipeg	5
7	Newfoundland	St. John's	9
8	New Brunswick	Fredericton	8
9	Nova Scotia	Halifax	7
10	Prince Edward Island	Charlottetown	10

Territory	Capital
Northwest Territories	Yellowknife
Nunavut	Iqaluit
Yukon Territory	Whitehorse

34 *New World History & Geography*

3.3 THE MARITIME PROVINCES

Politically, Canada is divided into ten **provinces** and three **territories.** The provinces are similar to states in the United States, each having its own capital and system of government. The territories are very sparsely populated and also have capitals, but their governments are not as independent.

New Brunswick, Nova Scotia, and Prince Edward Island lie along the Atlantic Ocean and are called the Maritime Provinces, because they border the sea. When Newfoundland, farther north of the Maritime Provinces, is included, the group is called the *Atlantic Provinces.* Each province has one large city: Halifax, Nova Scotia; St. John's, Newfoundland; Fredericton, New Brunswick; and Charlottetown, Prince Edward Island.

Prince Edward Island

The smallest but most densely populated province in Canada is **Prince Edward Island.** The island, which was named in honor of Queen Victoria's father, is the only province that is completely separated from the Canadian mainland, connected by an eight-mile-long bridge. Its gently rolling plains make agriculture—especially potatoes—its main industry. Many tourists come to the island every year to enjoy the beautiful fields and seacoasts. The writer, Lucy Maud Montgomery, a native of Prince Edward Island, used the island as the setting for her famous book **Anne of Green Gables.**

Newfoundland

The island of Newfoundland and the rugged mainland region of Labrador together make up **Newfoundland,** Canada's youngest province. About 1,000 years ago, the Vikings had discovered the island and built a small settlement at L'Anse aux Meadows [lăns ō mĕd'ōz]. This small community is the oldest known European settlement in North America. Sir Wilfred Grenfell (1865–1940) of England worked as a medical missionary among the people of Labrador and helped establish several hospitals and nursing stations in the region.

Newfoundland

Prince Edward Island

35

Bay of Fundy at high tide

Bay of Fundy at low tide

St. John's, the capital of Newfoundland, is the easternmost point of Canada's main road, the Trans-Canada Highway. This highway reaches from the Atlantic to the Pacific. Today, most of Newfoundland's population lives on the island in towns and cities. Fish and shellfish are the most important natural resources in the province. Forest products and minerals are also important to the province's economy. Newfoundland's chief source of energy is her rivers. One of the world's largest hydroelectric facilities is located at Churchill Falls in Labrador.

New Brunswick

The province of **New Brunswick** is mostly forest and ranks as Canada's fourth largest timber producer. Between New Brunswick and Nova Scotia lies the **Bay of Fundy,** famous for having some of the highest tides in the world. The tide is so strong that it temporarily forces the water to run back up the Saint John River, creating a reversing waterfall! New Brunswick is Canada's largest potato exporter. Fishing is also an important resource, with lobster being the greatest catch. New Brunswick is the only officially bilingual province; two thirds of its people speak English and one third speak French. Public signs and documents in New Brunswick are written in both English and French.

Nova Scotia

New Brunswick's southeastern neighbor, **Nova Scotia,** is connected to the mainland by a thin strip of land. Nova Scotia includes **Cape Breton Island,** which is separated from the rest of the province by a narrow strait. Nova Scotia has been called "Canada's Ocean Playground" because of its ties to the sea. Halifax, the capital, has long been an important port. The province's economy depends largely on its fishery and forests. Other important resources include coal, oil, natural gas, salt, gypsum, and minerals. Seven national parks, numerous museums and historical sites, and cozy fishing villages make Nova Scotia a favorite tourist area. The Cajuns of Louisiana are descendants of the French settlers called **Acadians** who settled around the Bay of Fundy. The Acadians

36 *New World History & Geography*

refused to pledge their loyalty to the British when the British took control of the Atlantic region and were driven from their homes as a result. The American poet Henry Wadsworth Longfellow wrote about the Acadians in his beautiful poem *Evangeline.*

Missionary to the black community. After the American War for Independence, many American missionaries traveled northward to Canada. **David George,** a black man from Virginia, was one such missionary. He organized a Baptist church in Nova Scotia and ministered to the blacks in the area.

Apostle of Nova Scotia. When **Henry Alline** was twelve years old, in 1760, he moved with his family from Rhode Island to Nova Scotia, where he helped his father on the family farm. Some years later, while reading his Bible, Henry came to know Christ as his personal Savior. This experience was so wonderful to him that he wanted others to know the Lord too. After learning more about God's Word, Alline started traveling all over the Maritime Provinces, preaching the gospel in almost every town. He traveled by horse or boat and in winter on snowshoes. He started churches, wrote hymns, and led many people to Christ. Although Henry Alline died of tuberculosis when he was only thirty-six years old, he was so effective for Christ during his short lifetime that people put the following epitaph on his tombstone: "He was a burning and shining light, and was justly esteemed the apostle of Nova Scotia."

Comprehension Check 3D

1. Name each of the Atlantic Provinces with its capital.
2. For what is New Brunswick's Bay of Fundy known?
3. Which two languages are officially used in New Brunswick?
4. What was the name of the French settlers whose descendants were the Cajuns of Louisiana?

3.4 QUEBEC AND ONTARIO

Quebec

The fertile St. Lawrence Valley in the province of Quebec is dotted with small farms and towns in which the people still preserve the ways and language of the early French settlers. In fact, the official language of Quebec is French. Also in this fertile lowland area are two of Canada's great cities: **Quebec City,** Canada's oldest large city, and **Montreal,** Canada's second largest city. The rest of Quebec province is part of the rocky and forested Canadian Shield. *Quebec is Canada's largest province in land area and second largest in population.*

Quebec City. In 1608, the French explorer Samuel de Champlain established a permanent village along the St. Lawrence River and named it Quebec after the Algonquian Indian word which meant *where the river narrows.* Ownership of Quebec City shifted back and forth between France and Great Britain until 1763, when much of Canada was ceded to Britain. In 1867, when the British

a view of Quebec City showing the wall and the hotel Chateau de Frontenac

Canada: the Second Largest Country

tulips at Ottawa

established the Dominion of Canada, Quebec City became the capital of the province of Quebec. Today, Quebec City is the second largest city in the province, and its people are of mostly French ancestry. It is known as the cradle of French civilization in North America. Besides being the oldest large city in Canada, it is also the only walled city in Canada or the United States. It is divided into *Upper Town* and *Lower Town* sections. Quebec City is a major center for mining, papermaking, and manufacturing. Its location on the St. Lawrence Seaway allows many large oceangoing ships to pass through its harbor.

Montreal. Montreal, the second largest city in Canada, is located on the Island of Montreal where the St. Lawrence and Ottawa Rivers join. Its ideal location has allowed Montreal to become one of the world's largest inland ports.

Montreal is the only city in North America that is built around a mountain. In 1535, Jacques Cartier became the first European to visit this area. He claimed the area for France and named this mountain Mont Réal, or Mount Royal in English. Later the city built there also took the name Montreal. Language plays a very important role in Montreal. Some of the residents speak only French while others speak only English. With its millions of people, Montreal boasts that it is the second largest French-speaking city (after Paris).

Ontario

West of the province of Quebec is Ontario, Canada's most populous province. The population lives primarily on the fertile lowland area between Lake Huron and Lakes Erie and Ontario. **Ottawa,** Canada's capital, and **Toronto,** Canada's largest city, are both located in this prosperous region.

The winds from the Great Lakes warm the land, and the many streams flowing from the Canadian Shield provide unlimited water power. Niagara Falls also provides power that is used to generate electricity.

Ottawa. Ottawa is **the capital of Canada** and the country's fourth largest city. The name *Ottawa* is the English version of the Algonquian word *adawe,* which means "to trade." In 1613, a Frenchman explored the land and discovered that it had many fur-bearing animals. Soon many other European fur traders arrived in the area. In 1857, Queen Victoria of Great Britain was asked to choose a capital city for Canada because the Canadians could not agree on one. She chose Ottawa for its beauty and its distance from the United States. Ten years later, Ottawa became the official capital of the Dominion of Canada.

Modern Ottawa has developed into a beautiful capital city, known for the tulips that bloom there each year. While Queen Juliana of the Netherlands was still a princess, during World War II, she was forced to flee her home and live in Ottawa while German soldiers occupied her country. When it was finally safe

38 *New World History & Geography*

for her to return home, Princess Juliana sent 100,000 tulip bulbs to the city of Ottawa to show her appreciation for the hospitality she enjoyed. Every year since then, the Netherlands has continued to send over 10,000 more bulbs. Today, over three million tulips spring to life each year in the city, and the annual **Canadian Tulip Festival** is held as a testimony of the friendship between the two countries.

Toronto. During the early 1700s, the French established a mission on the northern shore of Lake Ontario in Iroquois Indian territory. Soon a fur trading post and a fort were also included. However, in 1763, the Treaty of Paris gave all of the land to England. In 1793, John Graves Simcoe, the lieutenant governor of part of Canada, established a settlement, which he named **York,** in this same area along Lake Ontario. This was the site chosen to become the new capital of Upper Canada, the region in which the St. Lawrence River begins its northward course. (Lower Canada was actually north of Upper Canada, from the Ottawa River to the mouth of the St. Lawrence River.) During the War of 1812, United States troops stormed the village of York and burned it. (In retaliation, the British burned Washington, D.C.) The Canadians rebuilt the city and years later renamed it Toronto.

Today, Toronto is the capital of Ontario and Canada's largest city. It is also the major center of industry and banking in Canada and one of the nation's busiest ports. Food processing, printing, and publishing are Toronto's major industries. Canada's first subway was built under the streets of Toronto in 1954. The slender CN (Canadian National) Tower, the world's tallest free-standing structure (553 m or 1,815 ft.), can be seen from almost anywhere in the city. Visitors to Toronto can ride glass elevators to a revolving restaurant high in the tower for a spectacular view of the city.

Comprehension Check 3E

1. What is Canada's largest province? What is its most populous province?
2. What city is both the oldest city in Canada and the capital of the province of Quebec?
3. What city is the capital of Canada? Who chose this city to be the capital? What festival demonstrates the friendship between Canada and the Netherlands?
4. What is Canada's largest city?

CN Tower dominates the Toronto skyline.

3.5 THE PRAIRIE PROVINCES

Alberta, Saskatchewan, and **Manitoba** [măn′ĭ·tō′bə] are called the **Prairie Provinces.** More than three fourths of Canada's farmland is located in the south of these provinces on the flat, treeless plain that lies west of the Canadian Shield and east of the Canadian Rockies. This area provides most of Canada's cattle and grain. The Prairie Provinces border on the states of Minnesota, North Dakota, and Montana.

Manitoba

About half the people of Manitoba live in Winnipeg, which is the main transportation center linking eastern and western Canada. The Assiniboin [ə·sĭn′ə·boin] and Cree Indians used to hunt and fish where the city now stands. They named the area *win nipee,* which means "muddy water." Today, **Winnipeg** is Canada's leading grain market and an important cultural, financial, and industrial center. The city's location, sixty miles (96 km) north of the Canada-United States border and approximately halfway between the east and west coasts, makes it a main trading center and has earned it the nickname "Gateway to the West." Another interesting city is **Churchill,** called the "Polar Bear Capital of the World." Hundreds of polar bears gather here each fall and winter to hunt for seals in the ice-covered Hudson Bay.

Lake Winnipeg, one of the world's largest lakes, is located in central Manitoba, stretching from the plains in the south to the forests of the Canadian Shield. Dams built on the rivers flowing in and out of Lake Winnipeg help produce much electricity. Another lake in Manitoba has one of the world's longest names—Pakwachnamaykoskwaskwaypinwanik!

Teacher and translator. When settlers began moving to areas west of the Great Lakes, missionaries joined them to start churches and to teach the American Indians. One of the pioneer missionaries was **James Evans** (1801–1846). After working among the Indians in Ontario, he moved west to begin a work among the Cree Indians living on a northern outlet of Lake Winnipeg. There he developed a system of symbols for reading and writing the Cree language. The Cree Indians quickly learned how to write messages on materials they had available, and Evans became known as "the man who made birchbark talk." Evans built his own printing press and used it to print literature in the Indians' native tongue.

Scottish minister. **James Robertson** (1839–1902), a Presbyterian missionary from Scotland, moved to Ontario with his family when he was sixteen. After traveling west on an expedition, he became pastor of a church in Winnipeg. He also helped establish a college and served as the superintendent of Presbyterian Missions for Manitoba and the Northwest. Because of James Robertson, thousands of dollars were raised for Canadian home missions, hundreds of churches were erected, and many new missionaries were recruited.

Farmers harvest wheat in Saskatchewan.

New World History & Geography

hikers enjoying the trails at Banff National Park, Alberta

Saskatchewan

The province of **Saskatchewan** is one of the greatest wheat-growing regions in North America. More than half of Canada's wheat comes from this province, which is nicknamed "Canada's Breadbasket." In most parts of Saskatchewan, wheat fields can be seen in all directions and tall grain elevators rise from the towns and villages that dot the prairies. Saskatchewan is also a leading oil producer in North America. It is bordered on the east by Manitoba and on the west by Alberta. The Saskatchewan River, which flows through the area, gave the province of Saskatchewan its name. *Saskatchewan* comes from the name the Cree Indians gave to the mighty river—a name which means "rapid river."

Alberta

Alberta is bordered on the east by Saskatchewan and on the west by British Columbia. This western province contains rich mines and large oil reserves. Many fossil remains have been found in the badlands of southeastern Alberta. Like Saskatchewan, Alberta has prime land in the south for raising crops and livestock. Calgary, a city in southwestern Alberta, is an important trading center for cattle, grains, lumber, and oil. Every year in July, the Calgary Stampede, a ten-day rodeo, attracts cowboys from all over North America. **Edmonton,** located on Alberta's prairie, is the capital city. West Edmonton Mall, the world's largest shopping mall, is a favorite attraction. Alberta is not all prairies. The Rocky Mountains rise along the province's southwestern border with British Columbia. Tourists to this area enjoy beautiful national parks, such as Banff and Jasper.

Comprehension Check 3F

1. Manitoba, Saskatchewan, and Alberta make up the ? Provinces.
2. Name two missionaries who served in Manitoba.
3. Saskatchewan is known especially for what crop? This crop helped give the province what nickname?

Canada: the Second Largest Country 41

3.6 BRITISH COLUMBIA AND THE TERRITORIES

British Columbia

British Columbia, Canada's third largest province, is the only province that borders the Pacific Ocean. It includes hundreds of coastal islands, including the large Queen Charlotte Islands and Vancouver Island. The southwestern corner of the province, where most of the people live, has a milder climate than most of Canada because of the warm waters brought in by the North Pacific Drift, the ocean current which also warms the states of Washington and Oregon. Farther north, the land is covered with forests, tundra, and glaciers. Many mountain ranges run up and down the province. British Columbia shares a long border with the state of Washington and short borders with Idaho and Montana.

The first white men to settle in British Columbia were trappers searching for beaver and other furs. Later, the discovery of gold brought settlers who labored as farmers, woodsmen, trappers, and traders. British Columbia is popular for its mild climate and good living conditions, and many immigrants still come to the province. The plentiful rainfall and mild temperatures encourage the rapid growth of trees; thus many British Columbians work in forests or sawmills. Salmon are the most valuable fruits of the sea to the fisheries of this province, although the salmon population has decreased in recent years, reducing the fishing industry. Vancouver and Victoria are British Columbia's two largest cities.

Victoria, the capital of British Columbia, was founded as a trading post in 1843 by the Hudson's Bay Company. They named it after Queen Victoria of Great Britain. Located on Vancouver Island, Victoria is very scenic and "British" in appearance, attracting over two million tourists each year. The tourism industry employs many of Victoria's residents.

The city of **Vancouver** is called "Canada's Gateway to the Pacific." It is the third largest city in Canada and one of the busiest seaports on North America's Pacific coast. It is also Canada's most important industrial center in the west and the western stopping point of

Scenic Victoria attracts millions of tourists each year.

Canada's two transcontinental railroads. Food processing and the manufacture of wood and wood products are important industries of the city. Many Canadians from all over the country retire in Vancouver because of its beauty, culture, and mild weather.

The Territories

The northern third of Canada is divided into three large territories—the **Yukon,** the **Northwest Territories,** and **Nunavut.** The territorial governments have been given limited powers, but they do not have the same status that the provinces have. Canada's northern region is characterized by arctic and subarctic conditions, including tundra, ice fields, and permafrost. Few people live in the territories.

The Yukon. Located in the extreme northwest corner of Canada, the Yukon territory covers over 186,661 square miles (485,319 sq. km) and is shaped like a triangle. It was named after the Yukon River, <u>Canada's second longest river</u>, which drains the territory. The Yukon is rich in minerals, such as coal, copper, gold, lead, nickel, silver, and zinc. The territory first became <u>famous because of the great Klondike Gold Rush</u> in 1897. Thousands of people rushed to the territory in hopes of finding gold in the Klondike's rivers and rocks. Although mining towns boomed and tens of thousands of people lived in the area at one time, the population dwindled as prospectors either gave up or struck it rich and left to spend their new-found wealth. <u>Mining and tourism are main sources of income for the Yukon</u>.

The thick forests that cover the region provide homes for a large variety of animals that are trapped for their hides and furs. Fishing has also become an important industry in the Yukon. **Mount Logan,** <u>Canada's highest

prospectors panning for gold on the Klondike River

peak</u> (19,850 ft. or 5,955 m), is located in the southwest corner of the Yukon.

The total population of the Yukon is less than 35,000 people. **Whitehorse,** capital of the Yukon, is the largest city in the territory and is home to sixty percent of the territory's population.

The Northwest Territories. Between the Yukon and Nunavut lie the Northwest Territories, which cover 503,951 square miles (1,310,273 sq. km). Few people live in the Northwest Territories; the vast region has a population of less than 40,000 people. Small settlements populated by Indians and Inuits are scattered across the territory. **Yellowknife,** the largest city, is the capital of the Northwest Territories. **Dempster Highway,** <u>the only

Dempster Highway

Canada: the Second Largest Country 43

public highway above the Arctic Circle that is open year-round, runs through the territory. This road is vital to the people of the Northwest Territories.

Mining is the most important industry. Fur trapping is also important to the region's economy. Most of the Indian and Inuit population make their living by trapping and hunting. The fishing and forest industries also provide jobs and income for the territory. The Northwest Territories are rich in lakes and streams—the **Great Bear Lake, Great Slave Lake,** and Canada's longest river, the **Mackenzie,** are all here.

Nunavut. In 1999, Nunavut was carved out of the Northwest Territories to provide a self-governing territory for the Inuits. A vast area, Nunavut covers 818,959 square miles (2,129,293 sq. km) and is the largest of the three territories. The name of the territory means "Our Land," and the majority of the people who live in this Arctic climate are Inuits. Nunavut's small population totals about 27,692 people with most of the people living in small coastal settlements. The main industries are mining and trapping. Nunavut is made up of the Canadian Shield around Hudson's Bay and many of the Arctic islands, including the large Baffin and Ellesmere Islands. **Iqaluit** [ĭ·kăl′ōō·ĭt], on Baffin Island, is the capital city.

Comprehension Check 3G

1. Canada's province that borders the Pacific Ocean is named what? What is its capital and where is it located?
2. What city is known as the "Gateway to the Pacific"?
3. What event brought thousands of people to the Yukon in 1897?
4. What two large lakes are found in the Northwest Territories? What is the name of Canada's longest river?

3.7 PEOPLE, RESOURCES, AND INDUSTRY

The Canadian People

Population. Canada has few people for its size—about one eighth the population of the United States. The country has just over thirty million people, which averages only eight people per square mile! Of course, southern Canada, with its large cities and towns, averages many more people per square mile, but much of northern Canada is uninhabited. The vast majority of Canadians live within two hundred miles (322 km) of the United States border. About ninety percent of all Canadians live on 12 percent of the land in the southern part of the country.

Many backgrounds. Most Canadians are of European background, especially British and French. Others come from other parts of Europe, including Scandinavia, the Ukraine, Germany, Poland, Italy, and the Netherlands. Many recent immigrants have come from Asian countries such as China. Although the Indians and Inuits are a distinct minority in Canada, in places such as the Northwest Territories and Nunavut, they are in the majority.

Two languages. Canada has two official languages, English and French. Many advertisements, signs, and public documents are printed in both languages. English and French are printed on all Canadian stamps and money.

Canadian contributions. Canadians have made many important contributions to science. **Sir William Osler** was one of the greatest figures of modern medicine. He worked and taught at hospitals and medical schools in Canada, Great Britain, and the United States and strongly influenced medical progress. In the early 1920s, two Canadian researchers, **Frederick G. Banting** and **Charles H. Best,** discovered and prepared insulin for the treatment of diabetes. As a result of this medical breakthrough, the lives of thousands of diabetics around the world have been saved. Canadians led the way in using cobalt in radiation therapy to treat cancer. Through the years, the country has worked closely with the U.S. space program. In 1962, the first Canadian satellite was launched by the United States. Canadian scientists designed a robotic arm called the **Canadarm** for the U.S. space shuttle *Challenger* in 1981. In 1984, Marc Garneau [gärn′nō′] became the first Canadian to enter space when he accompanied the *Challenger* on a research mission.

Canadian missionaries and pastors have made great spiritual contributions to the peoples of the world. **Jonathan Goforth,** an Ontario farmboy, became a much-loved missionary to China. Readers around the world have come to love the writings of **Isobel Kuhn.** Her books tell of the work that she and her husband had among the remote Lisu [lē′sōō] villages in the mountains near the China/Burma border. **T. T. Shields,** a great fundamentalist pastor, is known for his brave defense of the Bible against liberalism. When his church association expelled him for opposing its false teachings, T. T. Shields founded a new association that upheld Biblical truth. He also helped Americans found the Baptist Bible Union to fight liberalism in the United States.

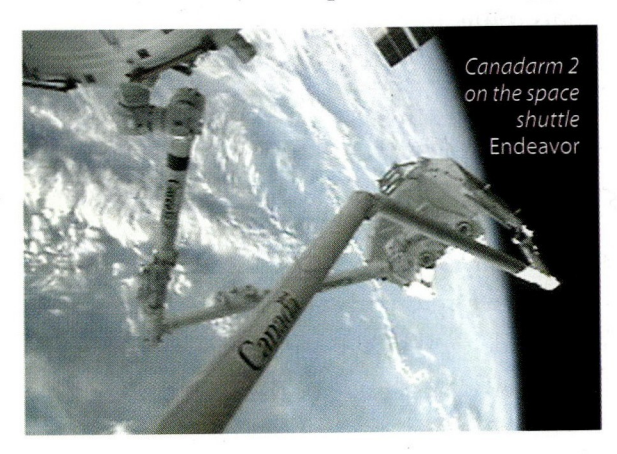

Best (pictured) was a college-aged lab assistant to Banting (portrait on wall) when together they discovered insulin.

Canadarm 2 on the space shuttle Endeavor

Climate

Cool climate. Because Canada is enormous, it has a varied climate. Areas farthest from open waters are coldest in the winter and warmest in the summer. About three fourths of Canada experiences very cold winters; mild winters are common on the Pacific coast. In the north, the brief, cool summers often make the growing season too short for most crops, but the longer summers in the south make farming possible. In the winter, heavy snowfalls in the east can bring up to one hundred inches (2.5 m) of snow yearly to large areas of Ontario, Quebec, New Brunswick, and Newfoundland. The deepest snow is about 240 inches (20 ft. or 6 m) in the Rocky Mountains. Permanent icecaps cover parts of the large Arctic islands.

Resources and Industry

Energy resources. Canada is rich in natural resources. Its energy resources include **water, petroleum, natural gas,** and **uranium.** (Uranium is used as fuel in nuclear power plants.) The force of Canada's swiftly moving rivers is harnessed to produce **hydroelectric power.**

Canada: the Second Largest Country

Canada is the fifth largest energy producer in the world and is a top-ranking producer of hydroelectricity.

Minerals. Canada is richly endowed with mineral resources. It is the largest world producer of nickel and zinc and is one of the world's leading ore producers. The Western Interior Plains have numerous deposits of petroleum and natural gas. Alberta is the top mineral-producing province, and Saskatchewan and Manitoba have the world's greatest potash deposits. (Potash is a chemical compound used in fertilizers.)

Canada's treasure chest of gold, silver, nickel, iron, copper, zinc, and other minerals lies in the Canadian Shield. The Shield's valuable minerals were discovered by railroad builders trying to blast through the extremely hard rock that makes up much of the terrain.

Grand forests. Enormous forests cover about one third of Canada. Only about 25 percent of the forested area is productive forest land, however, because the rest cannot be reached and used. Many kinds of trees grow in Canada, including spruce, western red cedar, sugar maple, white oak, yellow birch, jack pine, and tamarack. Along the Pacific coast, Douglas firs can grow to be as tall as a twenty-story building. The southern regions of the Canadian Shield have abundant softwood forests which supply the pulp for Canada's paper industry. The majority of Canada's lumber for building comes from British Columbia.

Fishing. Fish are one of Canada's most important natural resources. Salmon, herring, tuna, mackerel, and lobster are caught off the Pacific coast, while schools of cod, halibut, herring, haddock, and pollock are some of the fish found in the Atlantic. Canadian lakes and streams are abundantly supplied with tasty freshwater fish.

Off the southeastern coast of Newfoundland lies the **Grand Banks,** which has been one of the most heavily fished areas in the world. A *bank* is a relatively shallow area in a large body of water, and the average depth of the water in this area is only 180 feet (54 m). When John Cabot discovered the Grand Banks in 1497, he reported that the fish were so abundant that one could catch them with a basket. The cold Labrador Current meets the warmer Gulf Stream in this region to create ideal conditions for fish breeding and feeding. Consequently, fishermen from all over the world came to fish these waters. So many fish were harvested during the last century that the Canadian government had to close many of Grand Banks fisheries. It is hoped, however, that the fish population will soon increase enough to allow more commercial fishing.

The same conditions that made the Grand Banks a favorable fishing spot also make those waters dangerous. A dense fog often engulfs the area as the cold waters of the Labrador Current mix with the warmer waters of the Gulf Stream, making visibility poor. Also, icebergs frequently float down from the north to threaten the many ships. It was in this very area that the famous British steamer, the *Titanic,* collided with an iceberg and sank in 1912, killing about 1,500 people.

Agriculture. Only about five percent of Canada's vast expanse is fully suited to raising crops. The gray-brown soil of the St. Lawrence-Great Lakes Lowlands is good for agriculture. The Prairie Provinces have large farms, mostly in the south near the United States border. The rich, black soil of this area receives much rain during the summer months, making it ideal for crops of wheat. Canada is one of the world's leading wheat exporters. Grapes, peaches, and

Canadian fishermen with a large catch of herring

blue grapes from Canada

other fruits grow on the Niagara Peninsula; southern Ontario has large fields of corn; and British Columbia has many poultry farms. Although the number of farms and farmers has decreased in recent years, the production of crops and livestock has been increasing. The value of livestock and dairy products in Canada is greater than that of crops. Cattle are raised in the foothills of the Canadian Rockies and on the drier portions of the Prairie Provinces; pigs and sheep are also raised.

Leader in industry. Though Canada has been traditionally agricultural, in the late 1930s it began to emerge as one of the world's leading industrial nations. Today, Canada is one of the most prosperous nations in the world. Its location for trade has contributed greatly to its prosperity, as it is near some of the most populated areas of the world: Russia to the west, northern Europe to the east, and the United States to the south. Canada is a world leader in trade, and the United States is its chief trading partner.

Manufacturing. The manufacturing of chemicals, electrical products, and paper and wood products is of great importance to the Canadian economy. Canada is the world leader in the manufacture of newsprint, an inexpensive paper that is generally used for newspapers. **Food processing** is also a leading industry in Canada. **The fur industry,** the chief source of wealth in the 1600s and 1700s, still profits from the country's animal resources, although many of the animals are now raised on fur farms. The resourceful usage of petroleum and natural gas is important to the Canadian economy, as is the mining of valuable minerals. The **automobile industry** is also a major business in Canada.

Comprehension Check 3H

1. What are Canada's two official languages?
2. Name the two Canadians who discovered insulin treatment for diabetics.
3. What area off Newfoundland has been one of the most heavily fished areas in the world?
4. Who is Canada's chief trading partner?

Canada: the Second Largest Country

3.8 CANADIAN GOVERNMENT

Constitutional Monarchy

Canada's form of government is called a constitutional monarchy. The country is a member of the **Commonwealth of Nations,** a group of over fifty independent countries that were once under British rule. The Commonwealth today includes such countries as Australia, India, Kenya, South Africa, and New Zealand. The members of the Commonwealth maintain ties of cooperation and friendship. Like the other members, Canada recognizes the British monarch as head of state, but Canada is an independent nation that is self-governing. The national capital is Ottawa, Ontario.

Prime Minister. The leader of the nation is the **Prime Minister.** The Prime Minister's duties are similar to those of the President of the United States, but he is not elected in the same manner as the President.

Parliament. The **Parliament** is similar to the United States Congress. Parliament has two houses. The **House of Commons** consists of 301 members (in the year 2000) who are elected by the Canadian public every five or fewer years. Because its members are elected, the House of Commons is the most powerful house in Parliament. The Prime Minister usually serves as the majority party leader in the House of Commons and picks his cabinet (advisors) from among its members. The other parliamentary house, the **Senate,** consists of 105 members (in 2000) who are appointed for life by the Governor General.

Governor General. Another leader in Canada's government is the **Governor General,** the personal representative of the British monarch. The Governor General is now selected by the Prime Minister of Canada and ratified by the British monarch. The Governor General's duties are primarily exercised on the advice of the prime minister, but he does have special authority in times of emergency.

Symbols and songs. Canada has two official patriotic songs: **"O Canada"** is the national anthem, and "God Save the Queen (or King)" is the royal anthem. The **maple leaf** has long been a symbol for the country, and the **beaver** is the national animal. The national flag is a red, eleven-point maple leaf on a white field flanked by red bars on each side.

The Mounties

Canada's world-famous police force, the **Royal Canadian Mounted Police** (RCMP) was formed in 1873. The "Mounties," as they were nicknamed, were formed to stop men from the United States who were crossing over the Canadian border and causing trouble among the Canadian Indians by illegally selling whiskey to them. It took the Mounties only three months to restore law and order. The original Mounties chose a scarlet coat for their uniform because the western Indians had come to respect the red coats of the early British soldiers as a symbol of fair treatment and justice. Along with keeping law and order, the Mounties delivered mail to distant settlements, helped new settlers establish homes, and administered first aid.

Canadian Mounty

48 New World History & Geography

Today, the Royal Canadian Mounted Police enforce federal laws and serve as provincial police (similar to state police) in all provinces except Ontario and Quebec. Although they rode horses for many years, they now use motor vehicles. Their motto is "<u>Maintain the Right</u>," and their hard work and dedication to justice have earned them the saying "The Mounties always get their man."

Peaceful Neighbors

The border between Canada and the United States (including the border with Alaska) is the <u>world's longest undefended border</u>, stretching 5,527 miles (8,898 km). Canada and the United States have been peaceful neighbors for over 150 years. In 1846, the southern boundary of Canada was set by mutual agreement with the United States, as was the border of Alaska in 1903. Though the vast Arctic region of northern Canada is sparsely populated, it is nevertheless an important area for national defense: the United States and Canada have radar stations there to detect any air attacks that may come from across the Arctic Ocean. The military forces of Canada and the United States have plans for mutual defense against any attacks from foreign powers.

Comprehension Check 3I

1. The House of Commons and the Senate are the two houses of __?__.
2. What is the title of the Canadian head of government?
3. Name Canada's world-famous police force. What is the nickname for members of this force?
4. Which two countries share the longest undefended border?

Chapter 3 Checkup

I. Tell why these **people** are important.

Leif Ericson	Henry Hudson	Lucy Maud Montgomery	Christopher Columbus
Captain Cook	James Evans	James Robertson	John Cabot
Captain Vancouver	Fredrick Banting	Jacques Cartier	David George
Charles Best	Samuel de Champlain	Henry Alline	Jonathan Goforth

II. Define these **terms.**

Northwest Passage	French and Indian War	Dempster Highway	Canadarm
New France	loyalist	CN Tower	
Hudson's Bay Company	Acadians	Prime Minister	
Mounties	Klondike Gold Rush	Governor General	

III. Give the unusual characteristic of these **cities.**

St. John	Montreal	Toronto	Vancouver	Churchill
Quebec City	Ottawa	Winnipeg	Calgary	

IV. Define these **bodies of water** and **landforms.**

Arctic islands	Great Lakes	Great Slave Lake	Mt. Logan
Hudson Bay	Niagara Falls	Mackenzie River	
St. Lawrence Seaway	Great Bear Lake	Bay of Fundy	

V. Know these facts about **Canada.**

world rank (in size)	national symbol
major industries	patriotic songs
national resources	
kind of government	

VI. Know the capitals and locations of the **provinces** and **territories.**

VII. Identify the locations from **Map Mastery 4.**

Chapter 4
The Eastern United States

South of Canada lies the United States, the fourth largest country in the world. Like Canada, the U.S. stretches from the Atlantic Ocean to the Pacific. Before the first white men came to the New World, American Indians settled across the mountains, hills, plains, and deserts of this beautiful land. The United States is often divided into three regions: the *Eastern United States*, the *Middle United States*, and the *Western United States*.

4.1 The Eastern Coasts and Mountains

The Vast Eastern Forests

Before the first white men came to what is now the United States, most of the land from the Atlantic Ocean to the Mississippi River was covered by forests. Cedars, hemlocks, pines, beeches, sugar maples, white ashes, and yellow birches blanketed the lowlands around the Great Lakes and the hills and valleys of New England, protecting the land and wildlife during the long, cold winters. In the South, where the winters are short and the summers are long, hot, and humid, vast stands of pine trees and oak trees grew on the hills and coastal plains. In the areas in between, deciduous forests covered the plains and the low eastern mountains. Ashes, beeches, hickory trees, sugar maples, cherry trees, oaks, tulip trees, and many other trees that display beautifully colored foliage in the fall and lose their leaves for the winter provided the Indians of the Eastern Woodlands with food, shelter, beauty, and variety. Many trees still cover large areas of the East today, but a number of forests have been cleared away to make room for cities and farms.

The Appalachian Mountains

The most prominent landform in eastern North America is a system of low mountain ranges called the **Appalachian** [ap′ə·lā′chē·ən] **Mountains.** The Appalachians extend for nearly 2,000 miles from Canada to northern Alabama. A good number of peaks are over 6,000 feet, but most are less than 4,000 feet. They are much lower and more rounded than the mountains of the West. From north to south, the chief ranges of the Appalachians are the *Green Mountains* in Vermont, the *White*

50 *New World History & Geography*

Great Smoky Mountains

Mountains in New Hampshire and Maine, the *Catskills* and *Adirondacks* [ăd′ə·rŏn′dăks] in New York, and the *Alleghenies* [ăl′ə·gā′nēz], the *Blue Ridge Mountains,* and the *Cumberland Mountains.* Another Appalachian range is the **Great Smoky Mountains,** named for the smoky-looking haze that often envelops the range. The Appalachian region is sometimes referred to as **Appalachia** [ăp′ə·lā′chē·ə].

The central Appalachian Mountains have several *gaps,* or narrow passageways lying between mountains, and numerous valleys. Mountain gaps have been used by man as natural gateways through the mountains and have played a tremendous role in the settlement of the United States. The **Cumberland Gap,** through which pioneer families passed on their way west, is an important example. Many valleys, such as the famous *Shenandoah Valley* [shĕn′ən·dō′ə], were settled by farmers attracted to the rich soil.

Many caves are found in areas of the Appalachian Mountains where softer limestone rocks are constantly being worn away by water. The most impressive is Kentucky's **Mammoth Cave,** the largest known underground cave system in the world. Approximately 350 miles of the cave have been explored, but there is much that has still not been discovered. Within the cave the temperature stays between 55–60 °F. both summer and winter, providing the perfect habitat for the bats, colorless spiders, and eyeless fish that live in the inky darkness of the cave's chambers and rivers.

Streams, rivers, and waterfalls lace the entire area, and rainfall is abundant. Forty to sixty inches of rain fall each year across the region. The rain often falls in heavy downpours, and many areas of Appalachia are prone to flooding.

Because of its climate and low height, the Appalachian range has some of the most extensive deciduous forests in the world. About one hundred forty species of trees are found in Appalachia. Besides the coniferous trees like pine and cedar trees and the common, non-flowering deciduous trees, there are many spectacular flowering trees and shrubs. Flowering trees of the Appalachians include the redbud, hawthorne, tulip poplar, dogwood,

The Eastern United States

and locust. Some of the most noted flowering shrubs are the rhododendron, azalea, and mountain laurel.

The Piedmont

The **Piedmont Plateau** [pēd′mŏnt′ plă·tō′] slopes from the eastern edge of the Appalachians down to the Atlantic Coastal Plain. *Piedmont* means "at the foot of the mountains." Most of the land in the region is hilly and rolling. The Appalachians form a divide between the rivers that flow into the Atlantic Ocean and those that flow into the Gulf of Mexico. Most of the rivers are short and flow over the Piedmont and into the Atlantic. They include the Delaware River, the Potomac [pə·tō′mək] River, the Hudson River, and the Susquehanna River [sŭs′kwə·hăn′ə]. When they reach the eastern edge of the Piedmont, the rivers make an abrupt drop where the Piedmont Plateau borders the Atlantic Coastal Plain, which creates a *fall line*. At the fall line, the rivers descend over rocky rapids or waterfalls. Today there are many large cities along the fall line, because waterfalls are a good source of power for manufacturing and because ships cannot go farther inland than the fall line. Some of the fall line cities are Washington, D.C.; Richmond, Virginia; and Raleigh, North Carolina.

Coastal Plains

East and south of the Piedmont lie the broad coastal lowlands: the **Atlantic Coastal Plain** and the **Gulf Coastal Plain.** The Atlantic Coastal Plain is narrow to the north in New England and about 500 miles wide in the south. West of the Chesapeake Bay is a region of the coastal plain called the *Tidewater Region,* because the tides of the Atlantic Ocean flow miles inland, following the rivers up into the plains. It was on these coastal plains that the earliest European colonists settled. In the South, where the land is low and fertile, agriculture became very important. Many early settlers built their own wharves on the riverbanks where oceangoing ships could come to pick up the settlers' crops and take them to London to be sold.

In New England, the mountains and the cold weather made crops harder to grow. In-

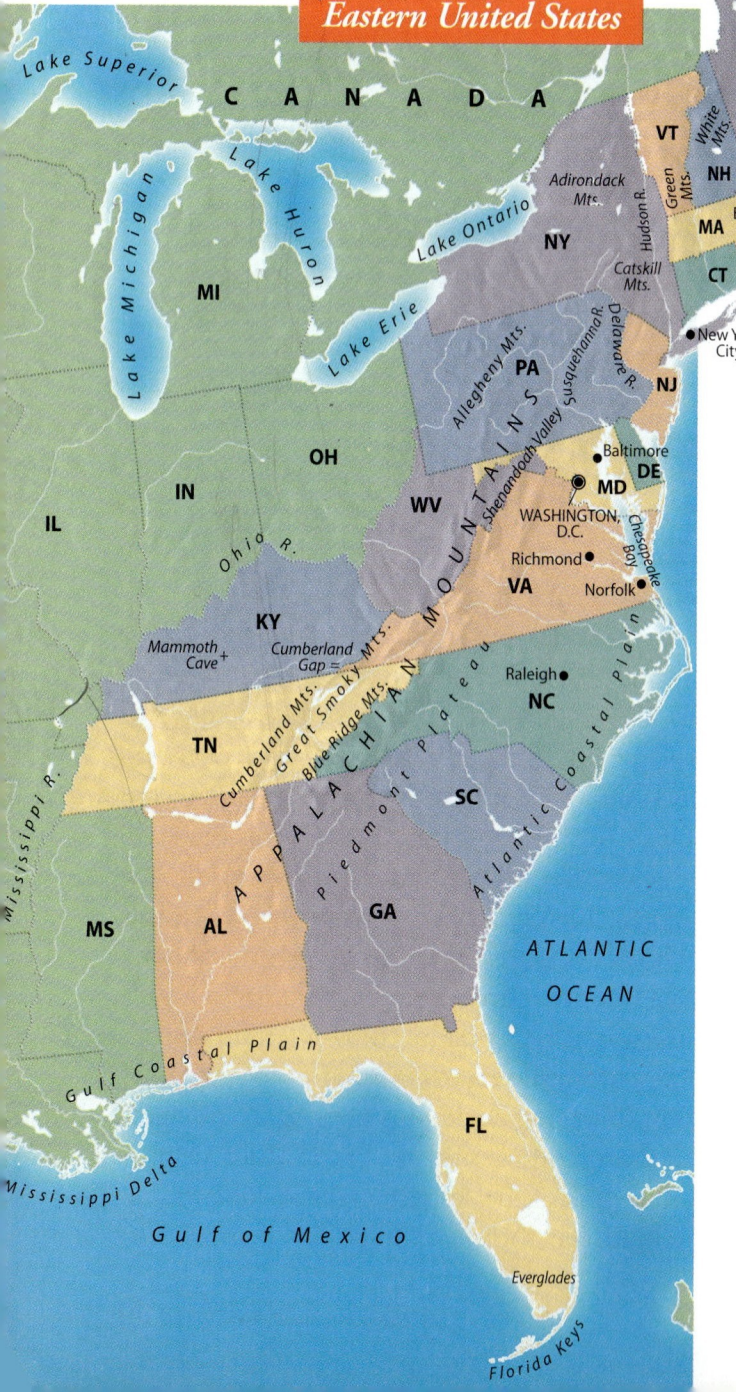

The rapids along the fall line create exciting white-water rafting.

stead, fishing and shipping became key industries. The Atlantic Coast is punctuated with many bays that make excellent *harbors*. Boston Bay, Cape Cod Bay, Chesapeake Bay, Long Island Sound, and New York Bay have long been important to our country. Some of the great *port cities* that eventually grew up beside the bays are Boston, Massachusetts; Baltimore, Maryland; New York, New York; and Norfolk, Virginia.

The Gulf Coastal Plain extends all along the Gulf of Mexico from the southern tip of Florida to Mexico. This low, flat region has hot summers and warm or cool winters. Seasonal changes in the South are not as sharp as they are in the North. Fewer trees change color in the fall, and some children in Florida have never seen snow. Many animals not found in other parts of the United States live along the Gulf Coast and in the coastal waters, such as alligators, manatees, and armadillos. Although there are some natural harbors along the Gulf Coast, engineers have dredged out sand to enlarge the existing bays for oceangoing ships.

Comprehension Check 4A

1. What is the most prominent landform in the eastern United States? Name its seven chief ranges.
2. What is Mammoth Cave's main distinction?
3. What plateau lies between the Appalachians and the coastal plain?
4. West of the Chesapeake Bay, what is the name of the area whose rivers and streams are affected by the Atlantic's tides?

4.2 THE ATLANTIC OCEAN

The Atlantic Ocean is the world's second largest body of water. Only the Pacific Ocean is larger. The Atlantic is also the saltiest ocean. Unlike the Pacific, it has few islands. Because the Atlantic separates some of the world's busiest industrial regions (Europe and North America), it has become the most important ocean for commerce (trade). The North Atlantic Ocean (north of the Equator) has been more closely studied by man than any other ocean area.

The oceans and seas of the world make up one huge body of water, covering

The Eastern United States 53

over 70 percent of the earth's surface. Thus, the Atlantic Ocean has no definite boundaries, especially in the north and south. It borders the continents of Europe and Africa on the east and North and South America on the west. It joins the Arctic Ocean in the north and meets the Pacific Ocean, the Indian Ocean, and Antarctica in the south.

The Atlantic Ocean once contained the major fishing grounds of the world. Because the waters were heavily fished for many years, restrictions have been placed on fishing and the industry has greatly declined. Fishing in the Pacific, particularly around China and Japan, now far surpasses that of the Atlantic. **Cod, herring, haddock, ocean perch, sardine, tuna,** and **hake** are just some of the fish once abundant in these waters that are now much less plentiful. **Clams, scallops, oysters, crabs, lobsters,** and **octopuses** are other useful sea creatures found in the region.

Fish and other sea animals are most abundant in water that is rich in the tiny plants that provide their food. Because these plants need sunlight to grow, they live near the surface of the water. Minerals also help plants to grow. Ocean currents from the west coast of Africa and in the far northern and far southern parts of the Atlantic carry minerals from the deep ocean floor to the surface, making sea life plentiful. Below the area where plants grow, **sperm whales** and **giant squids** wait for debris to float down to them and provide their food. These great creatures live at a depth of 600 to 3,000 feet. The deep ocean, from 3,000 to 13,200 feet, is the home of some of the most unusual and least-known fish in the world. The area is so deep that it is always dark. Almost two thirds of the deep ocean fish, including the viper fish, lantern fish, and angler fish, are able to produce their own light.

lobster fishing on the Atlantic

Water temperature is an important factor in determining where fish can live. The surface temperature of the Atlantic Ocean varies from 80°F. at the equator to 28°F. near the Arctic Ocean and Antarctica. Below the area where light penetrates, the water gets colder and colder. Near the bottom of the Atlantic, the temperature is freezing most of the time. Despite the great variations in depth and temperature, there is life of some kind in every part of the ocean.

Comprehension Check 4B

1. What is the second largest body of water on earth?
2. Give five facts about the Atlantic Ocean.
3. Why has the fishing industry in the Atlantic declined?

4.3 WOODLAND ANIMALS

The wildlife as well as the plant life of the Eastern Woodlands provided the American Indians of the region with all they needed for food, shelter, and clothing.

Fish and Shellfish

The lakes, streams, and oceans contained far more fish and shellfish than anyone could ever catch and eat. Trout swam in the many inland lakes and rivers, and cod were plentiful along the Atlantic Coast. Such shellfish as clams, oysters, shrimp, and lobsters offered a good variety in the Indians' diet. The Indians used the shells of the quahog [kwô′hŏg: a type of hard-shelled clam] to make beads called **wampum.** Wampum were often strung together and used as gifts, tokens of friendship, or money.

In the Bible, God told His people, the Jews, that they could eat fish that have fins and scales but not shellfish. Many centuries later, scientists discovered that shellfish sometimes grow in polluted water and can cause diseases if they are not checked carefully by modern scientific methods and prepared properly. The things we now know about shellfish testify to the accuracy of the unchanging Word of God.

Birds

Horned owls, barred owls, bobwhites, wood ducks, pelicans, and wild turkeys are just a few of the birds native to the Eastern Woodlands. The **wild turkey** has a heavy body and resembles a pheasant. Many centuries ago, the turkey was domesticated (tamed and bred for use by man). Wild turkeys became almost extinct for a time, but they are now thriving in North America once again. The turkey that Americans enjoy for Thanksgiving dinner is quite different from its wild ancestor. In colonial days, the wild turkey was such a strong symbol of America that Benjamin Franklin recommended it for the national bird. Despite his recommendations, the magnificent **bald eagle,** which can also be found in the Eastern Woodlands, was chosen instead.

wild turkey

Indian showing wampum to a friend

Mammals

Otters, chipmunks, squirrels, muskrats, opossums, raccoons, red foxes, porcupines, cottontail rabbits, and many other small animals live in the Eastern Woodlands. Indians hunted them for food and used their skins for clothing.

Deer were among the most important prey of the woodland Indians. The Indians ate *venison* (deer meat) and used the hides for clothing and shelter. The **white-tailed deer** has a large tail that is white underneath. When danger approaches, it raises its tail like a warning flag and bounds off into the thick underbrush. Because of the coloring God gave deer, it is difficult to see them in the woods. Fawns (baby deer) are born with white spots on their brown coat. These spots help them blend in with the forest even better.

Wapiti, sometimes called American **elk,** were also important to the Indians. Besides eating their meat and using the hide for clothing, the Indians used the large antlers for decorations and tools. Although wapiti still live in the Rocky Mountains out west, they are no longer found in the eastern United States.

One of the biggest mammals in the Eastern Woodlands is the **black bear.** Because of the skill and danger involved in the hunt, many Indian hunters earned great respect by bringing home a bear carcass. They would eat the meat and use the skins for robes or blankets. The members of some tribes used bear grease to make their hair shine more.

Comprehension Check 4C
1. What is wampum? How was it used?
2. How did the American Indians use the black bear?

white-tailed deer

black bear

56 New World History & Geography

4.4 INDIANS OF THE EASTERN WOODLANDS

Mound Builders

One of the earliest American cultures in the Eastern Woodlands was that of the **Hopewell Indians.** The people of the Hopewell culture built large mounds for the purpose of burying their dead and for worshiping false gods.

The Hopewell Indians, who lived over a large area of the eastern and central United States in very early times, built many **burial mounds.** They would bury as many as one thousand bodies in just one large mound. The mounds were built in many sizes and shapes. The Hopewell Indians were farmers, hunters, and fishermen. They raised corn and other crops. They lived in villages near lakes and streams and built houses made of sticks and covered with bark. The men wore shirts and breech cloths, and the women wore robes. Both men and women wore beautiful jewelry. The Hopewell Indians were far more advanced than many of the Indian cultures that followed them in later years.

Indian burial mound of the Hopewell culture

The League of Five Nations

During the centuries prior to the arrival of the white man, many tribes shifted to new areas, often driving existing tribes out of the land to do so. Thus wars between the tribes were common. Around A.D. 1400, five **Iroquois** [ĭr′ə·kwoi] tribes—the **Mohawk** [mō′hôk′], **Oneida** [ō·nī′də], **Onondaga** [ŏn′ən·dô′gə], **Cayuga** [kā·yōō′gə], and **Seneca** [sĕn′ə·kə] tribes—joined together and formed the **Iroquois League of Five Nations.**

The purpose of the League was to unite the tribes in common defense of their territories. Even though the League brought peace among the five members, these same members still fought with other neighboring tribes. The Iroquois League formed the largest Indian group in the eastern United States. They were among the more civilized tribes on the North American continent.

Agriculture. Each spring, the Iroquois men cleared the land for crops. The women were responsible for planting, hoeing, and harvesting the crops of maize (corn), beans, and squash. They ground the corn and often seasoned it with berries, mushrooms, or maple sugar. In fall and winter, the Iroquois men hunted, and in spring and summer they fished, using harpoons, nets, bone hooks, and lines.

The Eastern United States

a recreation of an Iroquois longhouse

Home life. The Iroquois lived in **longhouses,** which were similar to log cabins but were sometimes as much as one hundred feet long. All of the families who lived in a longhouse were related, and each family had separate living quarters within the longhouse. Down the center of each longhouse was a row of cooking fires. Two families shared each fire. They lived across from each other in the house with the small fire between them.

Mohawks. The Mohawks were the easternmost tribe of the Iroquois League. They were given the name Mohawk, which means "man-eaters," by enemy tribes. They were fierce fighters who, like all Iroquois, were known for torturing their captives or adopting them into their tribe. The Mohawks were open to the gospel, however, and by 1750, many had accepted Christianity. Notable among the Christian Mohawks was the famous chief, Joseph Brant.

Cherokees. A tribe of Iroquois Indians who were not in the League were the Cherokees [chĕr′ə·kēz′]. The Cherokees were friendly to the white settlers who came to the area around North Carolina and the Great Smoky Mountains. They helped the white men build houses and plant crops, and in return they received education and training in Christianity.

The Cherokees lived for many years in wigwams; later they started building log cabins. They hunted and farmed, raising typical Indian crops, such as corn and tobacco.

Southern Indians

Shawnees. The area we now call Kentucky, southern Illinois, and Indiana, was the home of the Shawnee [shô′nē] Indians. Shawnee means "southerners." During the summer, the Shawnees grouped their bark-covered houses into villages near the maize fields. The women planted and harvested the corn while the men hunted and skinned animals for food and clothing. When winter came, these villages broke up into small family groups that lived in hunting camps.

Creeks. The Creek Indians were a large and powerful nation who lived in parts of Tennessee, Georgia, and Alabama. Some of these people lived by a creek, and the English who met them called them the Creek Indians.

58 *New World History & Geography*

Buildings in their towns were built around plazas that were used for ceremonies and festivals.

Seminoles. The area known as Florida was the domain of the Seminole [sĕm′ə·nōl] Indians. The name *Seminole* means "runaway." This tribe was made up of runaway slaves (both Indian and black) and a mixture of Creek, Choctaw [chŏk′tô], and Chickasaw Indians, who were all fleeing the white man and the many wars.

The Seminoles lived by hunting and fishing more than by farming. Their houses consisted of thatched roofs supported by poles. Those Indians living in the **Everglades** (a low, marshy area of tall grasses and swamps in what is now southern Florida) built their houses on tall platforms. They used brightly colored strips of cloth to decorate their clothing.

The Indians the Pilgrims Knew

Wampanoag. When the Pilgrims landed at Plymouth Rock in 1620, they were met by the Wampanoag [wŏm′pə·nō′ăg] Indians. After a very harsh winter, the Pilgrims met an Indian from Maine named **Samoset** [săm′ō·sĕt]. "Much welcome Englishmen, much welcome Englishmen," Samoset cried as he entered the Pilgrims' village. He had learned to speak English from English fishermen who had earlier fished the waters off the Atlantic Coast. Samoset introduced the Pilgrims to **Massasoit** [măs′ə·soit′], the Wampanoag chief. Massasoit signed a treaty with the Pilgrims, promising that his people would not hurt the settlers. With the help of their Native American friends, the Pilgrims learned how to survive in their new land. The Wampanoag were the Indians that the Pilgrims invited to share that first Thanksgiving dinner.

Delaware. South of the Wampanoag tribe lived the Delaware, one of the most civilized

The Seminole Indians lived in thatched-roof huts.

tribes of the eastern United States. These gentle, peace-loving Indians quickly adopted the ways of the white man, although they remained a separate people. Many of the Delaware became Christians. This tribe also kept a pictorial chronicle of their history and traditions. Years after the Pilgrims settled in Massachusetts, William Penn signed treaties with the Delaware in the Pennsylvania region. Penn was careful to treat the people fairly and to pay them for the land which the king of England had granted him. The Delaware gradually moved west, driven by the fierce Iroquois and by increasing numbers of white settlers. In later years, at least one Delaware would assist the famous frontiersman "Kit" Carson as he traveled throughout the West.

Comprehension Check 4D

1. What was one of the earliest cultures in the eastern and central United States? What large structures did the people build?
2. Name the nations of the Iroquois League of Five Nations, the largest Indian group in the eastern United States.
3. Which tribe's name meant "southerners"? The tribe of runaway slaves and other Indians living in the Everglades was called what?
4. What tribe helped the Pilgrims to survive? Who introduced the Pilgrims to Chief Massasoit?

The Eastern United States 59

4.5 MISSIONARIES TO THE AMERICAN INDIANS

Many of the settlers who came to America from Europe during the colonial days were burdened for the spiritual salvation of the Indians. Some of the best-known colonial missionaries were John Eliot, John Campanius, Roger Williams, and David Brainerd.

John Eliot (1604–1690), an English Puritan, came to Boston to pastor a church. With the support of his congregation, he began preaching to the native people in the area we now call Massachusetts. (This state was named after a tribe of Indians.) He was a kind, gentle man who truly loved the Lord. The Indians grew to love him and his Lord. John Eliot organized towns for his **praying Indians,** as his four thousand Christian Indians were called. At one time, he had fourteen towns set up, each with a church and a school. Several Indians became pastors of their churches. Eliot made sure that the Indians learned trades they could use to earn a living. He translated the Bible into the Indians' native language and used this Bible to teach them to read and write. This was the first complete Bible to be printed in America.

Under the leadership of Chief Massasoit's son, King Philip, many eastern Indians joined together to fight the colonists. During the uprising that came to be called King Philip's War, the praying Indians were badly persecuted, and many villages fell to ruin, never to fully recover.

John Eliot, who became known as the **"Apostle to the Indians,"** had begun a wonderful work for God, however. Because of his unselfish desire to serve, thousands of American Indians came to know the true God.

John Campanius, a Swedish Lutheran missionary, traveled to New Sweden (the Swedish settlement on the Delaware River in the New World) to teach the American Indians. The Indians, who were generally

title page from John Eliot's Indian Bible

John Eliot preaching to Native Americans

60 New World History & Geography

friendly with the Swedes, would sometimes visit the missionary's home. Campanius's grandson wrote that his grandfather "generally succeeded in making them understand . . . how God sent upon earth his only Son, Jesus Christ" and "how He died upon the cross, and was raised again the third day." Campanius also translated Martin Luther's catechism into the language of the native people.

Roger Williams (1603?–1683), the famous founder of Rhode Island, lived and worked among the Narragansett [năr′ə·găn′sĭt] in the area we now call Rhode Island. He became a good friend of the Indians because he always treated them fairly and with love. The Narragansett were very eager to learn about the Lord because of Roger Williams's testimony among them. In addition to his work among the Native Americans, Roger Williams also founded America's first Baptist church.

David Brainerd

David Brainerd (1718–1747), a native of Connecticut, gave his life as a missionary to the native Americans. Although Brainerd contracted tuberculosis while in college, he completed his studies and became a missionary to the Indians of New York, New Jersey, and Pennsylvania. The young missionary worked tirelessly among the Indians until his strength was spent and the disease had claimed him. Brainerd died in 1747 at the age of twenty-nine.

Comprehension Check 4E

1. What "Apostle to the Indians" translated the first complete Bible to be printed in America? What nickname was given to the people for whom he organized villages?
2. What Swedish Lutheran missionary ministered to the Native Americans around his home?
3. Who founded America's first Baptist church? Where did he minister?
4. What young missionary traveled on horseback, despite pain from his illness, to share the gospel with the Indians? Who was his interpreter?

MISSIONARY HEROES
David Brainerd: MISSIONARY ON HORSEBACK

When he was fourteen years old, David Brainerd became an orphan and went to live with his older sister and her family. Because his parents had taught David the importance of reading the Bible, he continued reading God's Word and accepted Christ as his Savior at the age of nineteen.

Soon afterward, David went to Yale College to train for the ministry. There, he became ill with tuberculosis, a disease that killed many people in colonial America. But David refused to give up his studies. He believed that God was calling him to be a missionary to the American Indians, and although his disease made him very sick, David was determined to reach the Indians for Christ.

In 1744, the Presbyterian church sent David Brainerd to Indians in New York, New Jersey, and Pennsylvania. He traveled from village to village preaching in English, while a faithful Indian helper named **Tattamy** [tăt′tə·mē] interpreted his words into the Indian language. During his short ministry, the young missionary trained six Indians to preach the gospel to their own people. He traveled about one 100 miles a week on horseback, despite the increasing pain from his illness.

When he could no longer work, David reluctantly left his Indians and retired to the home of Jonathan Edwards, the famous New England preacher. There, David died in 1747, at the age of twenty-nine. David Brainerd's testimony inspired many other missionaries to preach the gospel both in the New World and across the sea.

4.6 FAMOUS WOODLAND INDIANS

After the white men came to America, a number of Woodland Indians became known for important accomplishments in language, leadership, or Christian work. Besides Samoset and Massasoit, some of the most famous are Joseph Brant, Tecumseh [tĭ·kŭm′sə], and Sequoya [sĭ·kwoi′ə].

Joseph Brant

Joseph Brant (1742–1807) was a famous Mohawk chief. His native name was Thayendanegea. Joseph, who fought for the British in the French and Indian War when he was only thirteen years old, attended a school that a missionary had started for Indian children. There he received an education and became a Christian. He later helped translate parts of the Bible and the Anglican prayer book into the Mohawk language.

Joseph Brant

During the American War for Independence, Joseph Brant and his followers again fought for the British. Because of his fighting, the American colonists named him "Monster Brant." His name and deeds were known throughout the country. After the war, Joseph and others of the Iroquois who had fought for the British were given some land on the Grand River in Ontario, Canada. Once again he returned to his work of translating Scripture into the language of his people.

Tecumseh

One well-known Shawnee chief was **Tecumseh** [1768–1813], whose name meant "shooting star." Because his father and two brothers had been killed by white settlers, Tecumseh fought to keep all white men out of Indian territory. Tecumseh spent many weeks traveling to the tribes east of the Rocky Mountains, urging them to join together to fight the white man. He joined the British soldiers in the War of 1812 with hopes that the Americans would lose and leave his land. He died in Canada in the War of 1812 while leading his Native American troops in battle.

Tecumseh

Sequoya

Sequoya [c. 1760–1843], who was half Cherokee, grew up with his Cherokee mother and never learned to read or even speak English. This did not stop him from the great work that he did for his Indian language and people, however.

Sequoya wanted his people to remain free. He thought that if his people could communicate with each other by reading and writing, then they could keep their independence of the white people. Because the Cherokees had no written language, Sequoya invented one! He first tried writing in pictures called *pictographs*. Later, he used symbols similar to English, Greek, and Hebrew letters. Each of the eighty-six symbols stood for a certain syllable of the Cherokee language. Because the symbols he invented stood for syllables rather than for individual letters, Sequoya's system was called a syllabary. He taught the syllabary to Indian children, and soon everyone in the tribe was reading and writing the Cherokee language! They even began publishing books and newspapers.

In devising a syllabary, Sequoya accomplished something that few peoples in history have ever managed to do without outside help. He was truly a genius of language. Sequoya made such an important contribution that the large redwood trees in California were named *sequoias* after him. (Notice that the trees are spelled differently from Sequoya's name.)

Modern Times

Today, most of the Eastern Woodland Indians have blended in with the white man through intermarriage, though some still remain on small reservations. Their Indian languages and crafts have been forgotten by most young Indians in favor of the English language and modern jobs.

Sequoya

Sequoya's syllabary

Comprehension Check 4F

1. Which Native American chief helped to translate parts of the Bible into the Mohawk language?
2. Who was the Shawnee chief who fought to keep European settlers out of Indian territory?
3. Who invented a written language for the Cherokee?
4. What was his system of syllable symbols called?

Chapter 4 Checkup

I. Tell why these **people** are important.

Samoset	Roger Williams	Tattamy	Tecumseh
John Eliot	David Brainerd	Joseph Brant	Sequoya
John Campanius			

II. Define these **terms.**

United States	Cumberland Gap	wampum	"Praying Indians"
Atlantic Ocean	Mammoth Cave	venison	syllabary
Appalachian Mountains	Piedmont Plateau	everglades	

III. Tell why these **Indian groups** are important.

Hopewell	Mohawks	Seminoles	Wampanoags
League of Five Nations	Shawnee	Delaware	

IV. Give the noted (significant) facts about these **animals.**

wild turkey   wapiti   white-tailed deer

V. Identify the locations from **Map Mastery 5.**

The Eastern United States

chapter 5
The NORTH AMERICAN PLAINS

5.1 THE WORLD'S LARGEST PRAIRIE

The North American Plains stretch like a wide belt across the center of the continent from the Mississippi River to the Rocky Mountains and from the Hudson Bay to the Gulf of Mexico. This great region is the world's largest **prairie.** A prairie is a plain or a hilly region within the temperate zone that is covered by grasses. Its name comes from a French word meaning "meadow." Other prairie regions include the *steppes* [stĕpz] of eastern Europe, the *savannas* of more tropical regions, the *pampas* [păm′pəz] of Argentina, and the *veld* [vĕlt] of South Africa.

Because they are located on the interiors of the continents, prairies often experience more extreme weather conditions than other areas like the coasts. In the winter, the prairies of the Great Plains are extremely cold and wind-swept, and much snow falls. As the snow melts and the rain begins to fall in the spring, the plains are subject to flooding. Summer days are hot, and *drought* (a time of little or no rain) can be a serious problem. Many droughts have come at the end of summer. At the end of their growing season, certain plants dry up and break off from their roots, becoming **tumbleweeds** that roll across the plains. Fire, which can be started by a bolt of lightning, is a real danger during a drought. The steady winds on the plains can drive the fire across mile after mile of prairie grasses.

Because few trees can grow in the more extreme climate of the prairie, hardy grasses which can stand extremes of climate but not the thick shade of dense forests have a chance to grow and spread. In fact, the prairie has been called a "sea of grass." The grasses provide food for many large and small grazing (grass-eating) animals. The grazing animals are almost always assured a fresh supply of food because grasses grow from a point close to the earth. No matter how much grass most animals cut off with their teeth, new leaves continue to grow upward. Only when very close-cropping grazers like sheep are introduced to the prairies are the grasses actually killed.

A wide variety of brilliant wildflowers add color to the sea of grass, and cattails grow in the marshy areas. Trees grow only near the rivers and lakes. Today, much of the American

64 *New World History & Geography*

tumbleweeds

prairie is planted with fields of corn, wheat, soybeans, and other crops. Through the hard work of American farmers and the invention of new machinery, this vast area has become the "bread basket" of the nation and one of the richest food-producing regions in the world.

Comprehension Check 5A

1. What is a plain or hilly region within the temperate zone that is covered with grasses called?
2. What is the time of little rain or no rain called?
3. What are the dried up plants that break off from their roots and roll across the plains called?
4. Why is this vast area called the "bread basket" of the nation?

The plains have become the "bread basket" of the nation.

5.2 Animals of the Prairies

Because the prairies have few trees for animals to hide under or climb for protection, God provided other means of survival for the animals of the prairies: most of them are either swift runners or tireless diggers. Perhaps the two animals most important to the prairies were the little **prairie dog** and the mighty **bison,** or buffalo. Other mammals include jack rabbits, pronghorn antelopes, coyotes, foxes, skunks, and badgers. Among the birds there are blackbirds, grouse, meadowlarks, quail, sparrows, hawks, burrowing owls, and prairie falcons. Grasshoppers, leafhoppers, and other insects often brought destruction to the prairie grasses.

The American Bison

The most important animal to the Indians of the plains was the buffalo, a kind of wild ox. Although some people call this animal a *buffalo,* naturalists usually use the term *bison* to distinguish it from the water buffalo of India and the cape buffalo of South Africa. Unlike the true buffaloes, the bison has a huge, shaggy head and an

The North American Plains

enormous woolly hump on its shoulders. A long beard hangs from its chin, and two horns curve from the sides of its head.

Bison are hoofed mammals, in the same family as goats, sheep, cattle, and oxen. A bison bull (male bison) may stand over six feet tall at the shoulders and weigh 2,000 pounds or more. It is the largest land animal of the Western Hemisphere. In spite of its immense size, a bison can run up to 35–40 miles per hour. With its great bulk and strength, however, the bison has little need to run from enemies; it simply charges straight at them! The only thing the bison has needed to fear is man.

Until the Europeans brought horses to the plains, the Indians would sometimes cause herds of bison to stampede off cliffs in order to kill them. Once the Indians obtained horses, they were able to chase the bison and get within arrow range. On horseback, they could follow the herds for many miles.

The bison was the Indians' grocery store. They ate its meat and drank its milk. They made shoes, robes, and other clothing from the *hides,* and they also used the hides to cover their houses. They collected the piles of bison *manure* (called chips) and burned them for heating and cooking. The *bones* of the bison were used to make sewing needles, knives, and other utensils. The Indians even used the *sinews* (tendons) to make thread for sewing. The *horns* were used to decorate ceremonial headdresses. Nothing was wasted.

Bison often traveled in large herds that seemed to stretch as far as the eye could see. The trails they beat through the prairie were sometimes used as roads by the pioneers as they traveled westward. Soon after the coming of the white man with his railroads and towns, the bison began to disappear and with them vanished the Plains Indian. The plains were on their way to becoming a huge farm area for feeding much of the world.

Middle United States

66 *New World History & Geography*

Prolonged hunting greatly depleted the bison herds of the American West. In recent years, however, the bison numbers have swelled from under 1,000 in 1895 to well over 200,000 today.

The Prairie Dog

At one time, hundreds of millions of **prairie dogs** lived in vast underground "towns" that stretched endlessly over the prairies. Prairie dogs are not really dogs, but rather ground squirrels, similar to gophers. They are about one foot long. The America pioneers called them "prairie dogs" because their cry sounds something like the bark of a small dog. With their constant activity of plowing up the land, "mowing" the grass to get their food, and fertilizing the earth with their droppings, prairie dogs have done more than any other North American animal except the beaver to shape the surface of the continent. Prairie dogs dig endlessly, even when they are not making homes, just to keep their claws trimmed.

Birds of the Prairie

The **prairie chicken** was a favorite of the Plains Indians both for hunting and eating. In their ceremonial dances, some of the Indians imitated the male prairie chicken's courtship dance, which included puffing up his neck sacks, stomping his feet, and turning around. The prairie falcon, red-tailed hawk, and bald eagle are a few of the many birds of prey that share the seemingly endless sky above the plains. They feed on small rodents and other mammals.

Comprehension Check 5B

1. What was the most important animal to the Indians of the plains?
2. What animal lived in vast underground "towns" that stretched over the prairies?

Think

3. Tell how the Indians used all the parts of the buffalo.

prairie chicken

bison grazing at Wind Cave National Park (South Dakota)

5.3 SPECIAL FEATURES OF THE LAND

Hills above the Plains

Not all of the Central Plains region is flat. The **Ozarks** rise as much as 2,000 feet above the plains just west of the Mississippi River in the states of Missouri and Arkansas. These heavily forested hills are rich in lead, coal, iron, and marble.

In western South Dakota and eastern Wyoming, a range of mountains rise above the plains, averaging 3,000 feet. The Sioux [soo] Indians called them the **Black Hills** because of their dark appearance when seen from a distance. The Black Hills are famous for **Mount Rushmore,** a huge monument with carvings of the faces of Presidents George Washington, Thomas Jefferson, Theodore Roosevelt, and Abraham Lincoln. The carvings are so large that Washington's nose is 20 feet long and one of his eyes is 11 feet across! A few miles east of the Black Hills are the **Badlands,** a region which the Indians called *Mako Sica,* meaning "bad lands." The Badlands of South Dakota are riddled with irregular cliffs and colorful hills striped with gray, white, and red rock.

The **Mesabi** [mə·sä′bē] **Range** in northeast Minnesota contains rich deposits of iron ore. Perhaps because of the contrast between the mountains and the plains surrounding them, the name of this range is an Ojibwa (Chippewa) word meaning "giant."

Mississippi River System

The Indians of the Plains used the Mississippi as their main highway for trade with other tribes. They called it the *Mississippi,* meaning "Big River," and the "Father of Waters."

The Mississippi River and its tributaries drain all or part of thirty-one states—nearly half the area of the United States—including most of the Central Plains. The Mississippi is the chief river of North America and the longest river in the United States.

The **Missouri River,** the chief tributary of the Mississippi, is the second longest river in North America. Because its waters are often cloudy from all the sediment it car-

Mount Rushmore

68 *New World History & Geography*

Badlands

ries, the river has been nicknamed the "Big Muddy." Sometimes the Mississippi and the Missouri are classed together as one river. If they were one river, it would be longer than the Nile River of Africa, the longest river in the world.

The three most important western tributaries of the Mississippi are the Missouri River, the *Arkansas River,* and the *Red River.* Other important rivers, such as the Yellowstone River, the *Platte River,* and the Canadian River, join these rivers as they flow toward the Mississippi. From the east, the **Ohio River** begins in the Allegheny Plateau west of the Appalachian Mountains and winds its way nearly 1,000 miles through some of the richest farmland in the United States. Today, some of the country's busiest industrial regions are located along the Ohio River. As the Ohio flows along, it is joined by several tributaries, the most important of which is the **Tennessee River.**

The Mississippi River itself begins as a small, cold, clear stream flowing from **Lake Itasca** [ī·tăs′kə] in northern Minnesota. At its source, it is about a foot deep and 18 feet wide. As it flows toward the south and is joined by one river after another, it becomes broader and deeper until it is a mile wide in some places and often 200 feet deep at flood time. In all, the Mississippi River system includes about 250 tributaries. It forms <u>one of the greatest inland waterway systems in the world</u>.

The Gulf of Mexico

The Mississippi River empties into the **Gulf of Mexico,** <u>the world's largest gulf</u>. This huge, curved arm of the Atlantic Ocean is almost completely surrounded by Mexico and the southern United States. Two peninsulas guard the entrance to the gulf—**Florida** and the **Yucatán Peninsula** of Mexico. Cuba, the largest island of the West Indies, lies between the peninsulas.

The Gulf of Mexico has several good harbors, and hundreds of lagoons and many salty marshes bordered by sand bars indent its coast. Rivers other than the Mississippi that drain into it include the Rio Grande, the Mobile River, and the Apalachicola [ăp′ə·lăch′ĭ·kō′lə] River. Much of the soil along the gulf is made up of silt deposited by rivers, tides, and currents.

The waters of the Gulf of Mexico are usually warmer than those of the rest of the Atlantic—about 50–75 °F. in January to 80–90 °F. in July. These warm waters are the source of an important Atlantic current, the **Gulf Stream.**

Comprehension Check 5C

1. What 2,000 foot mountains are just west of the Mississippi in the states of Missouri and Arkansas?
2. What is the chief tributary of the Mississippi, and the second longest river in North America?
3. What is the world's largest gulf? What important Atlantic current begins in this gulf?

The North American Plains

5.4 PLAINS INDIANS

Before the white men came to America, the Plains Indians moved from the Eastern Woodlands to the plains. There they lost their skills of farming and pottery-making and became buffalo-hunting wanderers. Many of the ideas that people today have about Indians were true mainly of the Plains Indians.

Sioux Indian in full traditional dress

Wandering Tribes

Blackfoot. One of the oldest Plains tribes was the **Blackfoot** tribe of northern Montana and southern Canada. They were named for the black moccasins they wore. The Blackfoot tribe was caught in the middle of a new era. Tribes who owned horses were invading from the west, and Indians with guns were coming from the north and east. Horses, guns, and Indians all met together on the plains and rapidly changed the Blackfoot way of life.

Dakota. The **Dakota** Indians formerly lived in Minnesota and northern Wisconsin, where they were farmers and hunters. The Ojibwa (Chippewa) Indians drove the Dakota into the plains, where they developed into a nomadic (wandering) tribe. Soon after entering the plains, the Dakota tribes formed a confederacy among themselves and spread all across the northern plains. The Ojibwa called them a name meaning "snakes in the grass." The French changed the word, which was eventually shortened to *Sioux*. Their own name for themselves, *Dakota*, means "friends" or "allies."

Cheyenne. The Ojibwa also drove the **Cheyenne** [shī·ĕn′] Indians out of the Eastern Woodlands and onto the plains, where the Cheyenne gave up farming and hunting for the nomadic life. Over the years, both the Cheyenne and the Sioux lost the skills of pottery-making and cloth weaving. The Cheyenne settled in the area of eastern Wyoming and South Dakota.

Crows and Comanches. The Crow Indians lived in southeastern Montana. They were bitter enemies of the Sioux and Cheyenne, whom they fought frequently. The Comanche [kə·măn′chē] tribe of Texas was originally a branch of the western Shoshone tribe.

Curious Customs

Dreams and visions. The Plains Indians were very emotional. In many tribes, people would cut off a finger to mourn the death of a loved one. Dreams and visions were very important. Warriors supposedly learned how to design their war paint and war bon-

70 New World History & Geography

Most Plains Indians lived in tepees, tentlike homes that they could move easily as they followed the bison herds.

nets through visions, and they also sought knowledge of the future through visions.

Many of the Plains tribes took part in the Sun Dance, which involved fasting and self-torture. During one Sun Dance, **Sitting Bull, a Sioux medicine man and chief**, claimed to have a vision of many white soldiers falling into his camp like grasshoppers from the sky. At this time, the government was trying to move the American Indians onto reservations. On June 25, 1876, a short time after Sitting Bull's dream, the **Battle of Little Bighorn** took place in which **General Custer,** an officer of the United States Army, and over two hundred of his soldiers lost their lives.

Sitting Bull

War. War was a constant threat on the plains. Many of the tribes fought among themselves or banded together to fight the white men.

Homes and belongings. The Plains Indians lived mostly in **tepees,** pole-framed tents covered with skins. Before the horse came, the Indians used dogs as pack animals. Because of their nomadic lifestyle, they did not have many possessions.

Comprehension Check 5D

1. How did the Blackfoot tribe receive its name?
2. What does the term *Dakota* mean?
3. Who drove the Cheyenne Indians onto the central plains?
4. What Sioux medicine man claimed to have a vision of white soldiers falling into his camp? In what battle did the Sioux Indians defeat General Custer and his soldiers?

Sun dance

Chapter 5 Checkup

I. Define these **terms.**

prairie	Mississippi River
tumbleweed	Missouri River
prairie dog	Lake Itasca
buffalo	Gulf of Mexico
prairie chicken	Gulf Stream
Ozarks	Blackfoot
Black Hills	Dakota
Mount Rushmore	Cheyenne
Badlands	Battle of Little Bighorn
Mesabi Range	tepees

II. Tell why these **people** are important.
Sitting Bull
General Custer

III. Identify the locations from **Map Mastery 6.**

The North American Plains 71

Chapter 6
The AMERICAN WEST

The western third of North America is known for having some of the most spectacular scenery on earth. High jagged *mountain ranges;* rugged *plateaus;* deep *canyons;* low-lying *valleys;* hot, dry *deserts;* and the cliff-lined Pacific Coast help make this region world famous for its topography and wildlife.

6.1 THE ROCKY MOUNTAINS

The Cordilleran Chain

The majestic, snowcapped **Rocky Mountains** are part of the **Cordilleras** [kôr′dl·yâr′əz], a system of mountain ranges which reaches from the Arctic Circle to the southern tip of South America. The Cordilleran chain is the longest mountain chain on earth. The Rocky Mountains of Canada and the United States, the Sierra Madre [sĭ·ĕr′ə mäd′rā] of Mexico, and the Andes of South America make up the Cordilleran chain.

Cordilleran chain

The Backbone of North America

The Rockies themselves are made up of more than 60 mountain ranges and extend approximately 3,000 miles. The Rockies are called the "backbone of North America." From their northern peaks in the state of Alaska, they stretch through Canada's Yukon Territory and Northwest Territories, the provinces of British Columbia and Alberta, and the states of Washington, Idaho, Montana, Wyoming, Utah, Colorado, and New Mexico.

The roof of America. The Southern Rockies, in the states of Utah, New Mexico, Colorado, and Wyoming, contain the highest and broadest mountains. Many of the peaks tower more than 8,000 feet above the Great Plains. The upper slopes of the Colorado Rockies are called the "Roof of America." In Colorado alone, there are 55 peaks that rise over 14,000 feet (more than 2½ miles above sea level). **Mt. Elbert** in Colorado is the highest peak in the Rockies (14,433 feet). The *summits* (highest points) of the Rockies rise to the sunny regions above the clouds, and snow stays on some of them year around. The Rockies are much higher than the Appala-

72 *New World History & Geography*

Grand Teton National Park (Wyoming) offers one of the most spectacular views of the Rocky Mountains.

chian Mountains, most of which are about 2,000–4,000 feet above sea level.

Reminders of the Flood. High in the Rockies, fossils of sea creatures can be found. These remains, which are as much as a thousand miles from the nearest ocean today, tell us that the highest mountains of our continent were once covered by ocean waters. Read Genesis 7:17–21 to see how this happened.

Rocky Mountain Flora

Naturalists often use the word *flora* to refer to the plants of a specific region and *fauna* to refer to the animals. The Rocky Mountains are famous for a wide variety of flora and fauna. When a person climbs the mountains, he can see some of the many climate zones in just a few hours. A professional mountain climber could see the same climate zones that could be seen on a trip from the Great Plains to the Arctic Ocean—in one climb up a very high mountain. Close to the level of the Great Plains, **short grasses** grow, and there are few trees except for the pines, willows, and cottonwoods along the streams. Higher up (6,000 to 9,000 feet), **ponderosa pines** are plentiful. These mighty trees can grow straight up for nearly 200 feet, and they are prized for their fine lumber. Above the pines is a region dominated by tall, steeple-shaped spruces. The spruce zone is similar in many ways to the boreal forests of Canada. Open spaces among the forests are blanketed by beautiful wildflowers—columbines, globeflowers, monkshoods [mŭngks′hoŏdz], marsh marigolds, primroses, and many others. Above the tree line is a **tundra** area, where willows grow close to the ground and where beautiful flowers brighten the landscape during the short summer. Above the snow line, little grows except for delicate snow flowers. **Snow** and **ice** cover the ground almost all year long.

The Great Divide

The peaks and ridges of the Rockies form part of North America's *continental divide,* a stretch of high land that divides the river systems of a continent. North America's divide is so massive that it is called the **Great Divide.** If a drop of rain falls even slightly to the east

The American West 73

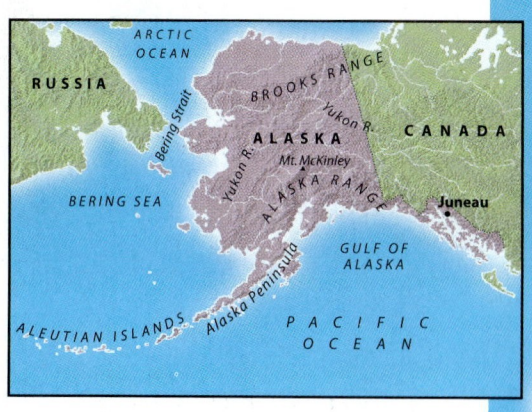

of the divide, it will eventually flow into the Atlantic Ocean or the Arctic Ocean (if it does not evaporate first). A drop of water that falls only a few feet to the west of the Great Divide will eventually flow into the Pacific Ocean.

Rivers beginning in the Colorado Rockies. Four of the great river systems of the United States have their *headwaters* (beginning points) in the Colorado Rockies. Those that flow east across the Great Plains are the Arkansas River, which flows into the Mississippi and then into the Gulf of Mexico; the Platte River, a *tributary* of the Missouri; and the Rio Grande, which forms part of the border between the United States and Mexico and empties into the Gulf of Mexico. Flowing west toward the Pacific Ocean are the **Colorado River** and its tributary, the Green River.

The Colorado River, which drains about one fifteenth of all the land of the continental United States, is the main source of water for the most arid (dry) section of North

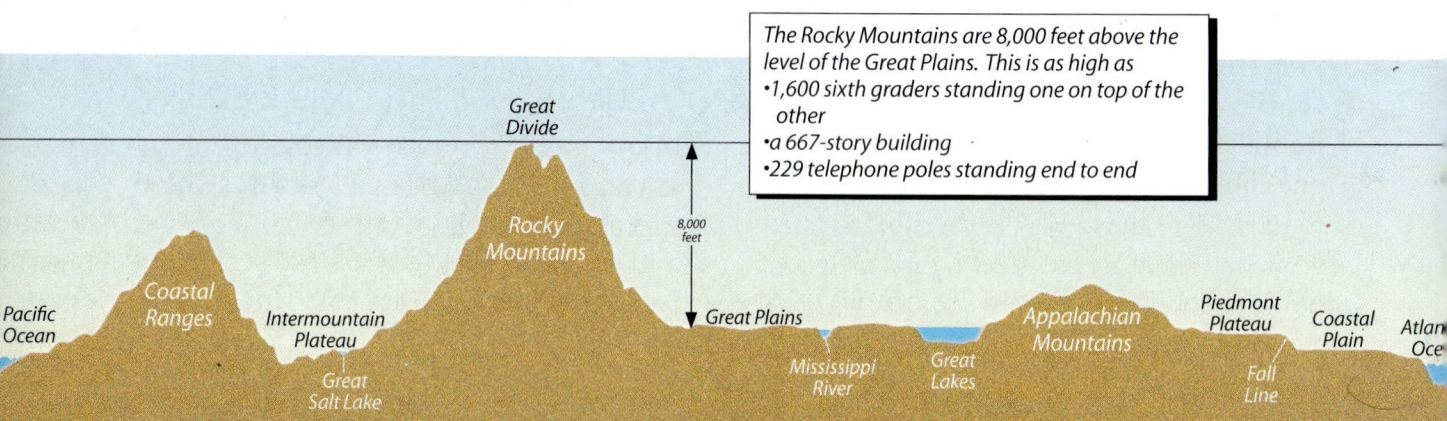

Western United States

The Rocky Mountains are 8,000 feet above the level of the Great Plains. This is as high as
- 1,600 sixth graders standing one on top of the other
- a 667-story building
- 229 telephone poles standing end to end

America—the Southwest. It is noted for the many deep trenches through which it flows and for its foaming white water rapids. It is most famous for being the river that flows through the spectacular **Grand Canyon**.

Rivers beginning in the northern Rockies. Some major rivers that arise in the northern Rockies and flow toward the Pacific Ocean are the Columbia River and its chief tributary the Snake River, and Canada's Fraser River. The **Columbia River** is the largest river flowing into the Pacific Ocean from North America. Flowing eastward from the northern Rockies are the *Missouri River* of the United States and the Saskatchewan River, Athabasca River, and Peace River of Canada. The Mackenzie River, which begins at Great Slave Lake, cannot flow westward across the Great Divide; thus it flows north and empties into the Arctic Ocean. The Mackenzie is the longest river in Canada. Alaska's Yukon River flows west and empties into the Bering Sea. Find these Canadian rivers on the map of Canada in the Atlas, pp. 100–101.

Yellowstone National Park

Many of the natural wonders of the Rocky Mountains can be observed in **Yellowstone National Park,** which lies in the northwestern corner of Wyoming. Yellowstone, established in 1872, is the oldest national park in the world and one of the largest in the United States. Yellowstone is also the largest wildlife preserve in the United States. A wildlife preserve is a place where wild animals are protected from hunters by law.

Yellowstone has more geysers and hot springs than any other area in the world—more than 200 active geysers and thousands of hot springs. A *hot spring* is a spring in which the water is above 98°F. A *geyser* is a hot spring from which columns of boiling water and steam shoot out of the earth into the air.

Old Faithful, the most famous geyser, erupts about every 80 minutes or so, sending 4,000 to 8,500 gallons of steam and boiling water more than 100 feet into the air. This large geyser is named for its reliability; American Indians claim that it has been faithfully erupting for centuries. Old Faithful used to erupt even more frequently before an earthquake changed its pattern in 1998. The world's largest geyser is **Steamboat Geyser,** which once set a world's record by sending its steam more than 400 feet into the air.

Mammoth Hot Springs, the most famous hot springs in the park, has beautiful terraces of limestone that have been deposited as the hot water of the springs has flowed over the ground.

The geysers and hot springs of Yellowstone produce enough heat to melt three tons of ice in one second. Some of the animals in the park make good use of these natural heaters. The bears, for instance, often make their dens near the hot springs where they can enjoy steam heat during the winter months.

Yellowstone Lake is the largest high-altitude lake in North America. It lies 7,731 feet above sea level and is 20 miles long and 14 miles wide.

Old Faithful

Comprehension Check 6A
Identify
1. The term referring to the plants of a specific region. The animals of a region.
2. A stretch of high land that divides the rivers of a continent. Name given to that divide in North America.
3. The backbone of North America.
4. The oldest national park in the world and one of the largest in North America.

The American West

6.2 Animals of the Rockies

A wide variety of animals live among the rugged slopes of the Rocky Mountains. Some are huge and rugged themselves, such as the grizzly bear, the mountain lion, and the mountain goat. Others, like the marmot, pika, and red squirrel, are small, soft, and shy. Few reptiles live in the mountains, but there are many birds and many kinds of rodents.

Bighorn. Bighorn, the wild sheep of North America, are larger and far more intelligent than domestic sheep, and they have a thick coat of hair rather than wool. They live in the highest parts of the mountains, where people can hardly climb at all. The *ewes* (females) teach their little lambs to follow them as they jump from rock to rock in the dangerous heights. The lambs learn to escape from mountain lions and other predators by bounding to safety in the high cliffs.

The *rams* (males) have thick, curling horns that can weigh thirty pounds—as much as all of the bones in their bodies. Two male bighorn sometimes battle for hours during mating time. They back away from each other for a dozen yards, lower their heads, and charge full speed ahead until their horns clash. The resulting crash may be heard a mile away! You might expect them to be hurt, but the animals just shake their heads, back off, and charge again. Their heads are protected by a built-in "football helmet"—a double-layered skull supported with braces of bone.

In the north, bighorn migrate to the mountain tops in summer and down to the valleys in winter to find the best grasses. If they need to, they can eat mosses and leaves, and they can dig down through the snow for food. Eating grass is called *grazing*, and eating leaves, twigs, and young shoots of trees and shrubs is called *browsing*.

Mountain goats. The Rocky Mountain goat, which is somewhat smaller than the bighorn, is one of the most daring climbers in the animal world. It is not really a goat; it is actually more closely related to the antelope family. Mountain goats live all year long on the tops of steep mountains, where few enemies can follow. Their hooves have suction-like cups, allowing the animals to climb almost straight up a cliff without danger and to leap gracefully from cliff to cliff.

The mountain goat is well prepared for the chilly air of the mountain tops. It wears two fur coats in the wintertime—a short, woolly undercoat and a long, shaggy, pure white overcoat. The Indians of British Co-

mountain goats

76 New World History & Geography

lumbia used to gather the fur from the overcoat when it was shed in the summertime and weave it into soft blankets. Food is often scarce on the mountain tops, but the mountain goat is prepared for this, also. It has four stomachs, enabling it to digest almost every portion of the few twigs and shrubs it can find.

Mountain lions. The mountain lion is a cat with many names. It is the most widely distributed carnivorous animal in the New World, ranging from Alaska to the tip of South America. The people of each region have given it a different name. The Inca Indians of Peru called it a *puma,* and the early European settlers called it a *cougar.* In the eastern United States, it is often called a *panther.*

The mountain lion is the second largest cat in the Western Hemisphere (the jaguar of South and Central America is the largest). A full-grown mountain lion can reach a length of six feet, not including the tail, which is two to three feet long. Its little spotted *cubs* weigh only one pound when they are born and are less than a foot long. They are dependent upon their mother for about two years, until they learn to hunt and kill their own food.

Grizzly bears. The ferocious grizzly bear may be the most dangerous animal of North America. Its scientific name, *Ursa horribilis,* means "the horrible bear." Grizzlies are the third largest bears in North America. They can be as much as 8 feet tall when they stand on their hind legs and can weigh up to 900 pounds. Grizzlies will attack humans who enter their territory.

Pikas. The furry, egg-shaped little **American pika** is a member of the same family as hares. It is from 6 to 12 inches long with a tail about 1 inch long. Sometimes it is called a *cony* or a *whistling hare.* Pikas live in large colonies, and they squeak loudly to warn other pikas of danger.

The pika is the fat little farmer of the mountain slopes. Throughout the short summer, it harvests grasses that grow among the rocks on the sides of the mountains. It piles the grass into miniature haystacks to dry, and then stores the hay in protected places. Because it stores food, the pika has no need to hibernate—it eats hay all winter long.

Pikas live in little holes among the rocks on the side of a mountain. They line their rocky homes with dried grasses. When rain floods these homes, the busy little creatures must haul their bedding outside to let it dry again in the sun.

Water ouzel. One of the most contented creatures of the western mountains is the water ouzel [o͞o′zəl], a robin-sized bird that is just as much at home *under* the water as it is flying over it. The water ouzel (also called the *dipper*) usually makes its nest behind a waterfall. It eats mostly water insects. To find them, it wades upstream and turns over small stones with its bill.

The American West 77

water ouzel

If the water is too deep for wading, the water ouzel does not seem to mind a bit. It simply flies down under the water, flapping its wings just as if it were in the air. Then it walks around on the bottom of the stream, turning over stones to find insects. Its large oil glands produce an oily "raincoat" to protect its feathers.

Unlike most birds, the water ouzel stays put when the snows begin to fall and continues to hunt and sing through the winter months. When the streams become covered with ice, it just finds a hole and dives through. A thick layer of fat under its skin insulates it against the icy waters.

The water ouzel sings to the tune of its waterfall. During the autumn months, when the water has died down to a trickle, the water ouzel's song is soft and low. In the spring, when the water flows in torrents, the bird unleashes a flood of melody as sweet and musical as a flute.

Comprehension Check 6B
Identify
1. The animal that is the second largest cat in the Western Hemisphere. Three other common names for this cat.
2. The bear considered to probably be the most dangerous animal in North America.

6.3 THE INTERMOUNTAIN REGION

The Intermountain Region lies between the Rocky Mountains to the east and the Pacific mountain chains to the west. *Intermountain* means "between the mountains." This vast region of low mountains, high plateaus, deep canyons, and dry basins includes the Columbia Plateau and the North American Desert.

The Columbia Plateau

Southeastern Washington, most of eastern Oregon, and part of Idaho are covered by the **Columbia Plateau,** the largest lava plateau in the world. The Columbia Plateau was evidently formed by lava flowing through cracks in the earth. Its elevation varies between 200 and 5,000 feet. Several rivers, including the *Columbia River,* flow at the bottom of deep canyons cut through this plateau. The *Snake River* runs through **Hells Canyon,** the deepest canyon in the United States. Hells Canyon averages one mile in depth and forms part of the border between Oregon and Idaho.

The North American Desert

The **North American Desert** is a vast, arid region that spreads into eleven states and parts of Mexico. It includes small sections of Washington, Oregon, Idaho, Wyoming, and Colorado and larger portions of Nevada, Utah, California, Arizona, New Mexico, and Texas. The desert is divided into five regions, each with distinctive landforms and vegetation. They are the *Great Basin Desert,* the *Colorado Plateau,* the *Mojave* [mō·hä′vē] *Desert,* the *Sonoran* [sə·nō′rən] *Desert,* and the *Chihuahuan* [chə·wä′wän] *Desert.*

The Great Basin Desert

The **Great Basin Desert** is the largest desert area in the United States. Less than 10 inches of rain fall on the Great Basin each

78 New World History & Geography

year. Its most characteristic plant is the **sagebrush,** a bushy plant with a sweet smell and a bitter taste.

The Great Basin **bristlecone pine** lives longer than any other tree in the world. Some bristlecone pines have probably been growing since the time of the Flood. The oldest known living tree is a bristlecone named Methuselah that is said to be over 4,700 years old.

Great Salt Lake. One of the natural wonders of the world is the **Great Salt Lake** in northern Utah. It is the largest saltwater lake in North America and the largest natural lake west of the Mississippi River. It is second only to the Dead Sea in saltiness—over 25 percent pure salts—and is five times saltier than the oceans. Unlike most large lakes, the Great Salt Lake has no outlet. Each year, about two million tons of common salt are removed from the Great Salt Lake. Another kind of salt taken from the lake is used in industries and for medicine. Large flocks of gulls, ducks, geese, and pelicans live on the shores of the Great Salt Lake, but there are no fish in the water—only brine shrimp, brine-fly larvae, and other tiny organisms. Near the Great Salt Lake is the **Great Salt Lake Desert,** which is noted for its extremely level salt beds that are as hard as cement.

The Colorado Plateau

The Colorado Plateau lies in parts of Colorado, New Mexico, Utah, and Arizona. It is noted for its mountains, *mesas* (flat-topped hills), gorges, and deep canyons. Forests grow in some of the mountains, but much of the region is desert.

The Grand Canyon. The **Grand Canyon,** the largest canyon in the world, is a world-famous landmark in this region. It is located in northwest Arizona, and it is one of the Seven Natural Wonders of the World. The Grand Canyon is a *gorge* cut almost straight down through the plateau. It is approximately a mile deep, 217 miles long, and from 4 to 18 miles wide at the top. The Colorado River flows through it. The great canyon was evidently formed by the pressure of moving water, but the river alone cannot account for its creation. The Indians of the area say the canyon was caused by a great Flood which once covered the earth. Christians realize they are referring to the Flood of Noah's day. The first white men to see this canyon were Spaniards exploring with **Coronado** [kôr′ə·nä′dō] and his expedition in 1540. The Spaniards found Pueblo Indians living in the canyon.

Havasupai Indians. Near the bottom of the Grand Canyon live the **Havasupai** [hä′və·soo′pī] **Indians,** whose name means "people of the blue-green water." The Havasupai are one of the most isolated tribes in the United States, and also one of the smallest tribes. Their village, Supai, can be reached only by helicopter, horseback, or foot. The Havasupai grow crops on the canyon floor and get their

Grand Canyon

clothing and other supplies by packtrains sent down from the plateau above them. There is a little mission church in Supai, but few of the people are Christians; most follow the old superstitions and the worship of many gods.

The Painted Desert. Stretching for 200 miles along the Little Colorado River in northeastern Arizona is the magnificent **Painted Desert.** The *buttes, mesas, pinnacles,* and *valleys* of this desert land are made of sandstone colored in beautiful hues of blue, amethyst, yellow, russet, lilac, and red. Sometimes a purple haze or pink mist of dust rises from the desert, causing the air to glow. Navajo [năv′ə·hō] and Hopi [hō′pē] Indians live in the Painted Desert and use the brightly colored sands to make their famous sand paintings.

The Petrified Forest. Within the Painted Desert lies **Petrified Forest National Park.** It consists of huge tree trunks—some up to 125 feet long—whose wood has been replaced by minerals until the trees have become solid stone. There are many petrified forests throughout the world, but the one in Arizona is the largest and most colorful in the world. The logs all lie horizontally on the ground, some broken into many pieces. They appear to have been transported by a huge flood of water from the mountains down to the desert, where they were buried under layers of mud, sand, or volcanic ash. Mineral-containing water then seeped in to fill the empty cells so quickly that the trees had no time to decay. The petrified forests throughout the world are a lasting evidence of the Great Flood that covered the earth during Noah's day.

The Mojave Desert

South of the Great Basin Desert is the **Mojave Desert** (also spelled *Mohave*). This arid section of Nevada and California covers 25,000 square miles. It is made up mostly of dry lake beds (salt flats), but there are also some small mountains and extinct volcanoes.

Death Valley. California's **Death Valley,** the hottest and driest part of North America, lies between the Great Basin and Mojave Deserts. It is about 130 miles long and 6 to 14 miles wide. The lowest point in the Western Hemisphere (282 feet below sea level) is in Death Valley. Just 80 miles from this low point is **Mt. Whitney** (14,494 feet), the highest point in the United States outside Alaska. The average annual rainfall of Death Valley is approximately 2 inches. Temperatures of 125°F are common during the summer. The highest temperature recorded in the United States (134°F) occurred in Death Valley in July 1913. The Indians called Death Valley "Ground Afire."

Sonoran Desert

The **Sonoran Desert** is in western Mexico, southern California, and Arizona. Most of its area is in the Mexican state of Sonora. About one fourth of the Sonoran Desert is below sea level.

The saguaro cactus. The Sonoran Desert is the richest desert in cacti and is the home of the **saguaro** [sə·gwär′ō] **cactus,** the largest cactus in the world. A saguaro can grow over 50 feet tall and live for 150–200 years. It is found nowhere else in the world but in the Sonoran Desert. "Forests" of saguaros can be found in this desert.

The American Indians dried the woody ribs of the cacti's stems for fuel and for house frames. They also ate the fruit and made preserves and syrup from it.

The Chihuahuan Desert

The **Chihuahuan Desert** lies partly in Arizona, New Mexico, and Texas, but mostly

Carlsbad Caverns

in the Mexican state of Chihuahua. It is almost the same size as the Great Basin. Chihuahua is Mexico's largest state. Its capital and chief city, also called Chihuahua, has won fame as the breeding center for the world's smallest breed of dog, the chihuahua.

Carlsbad Caverns. The world's most spectacular limestone caverns lie in part of the Chihuahuan Desert. They are the Carlsbad Caverns of southeastern New Mexico. This chain of huge underground caves covers an area of about 70 square miles and houses the largest underground chamber in North America, the **Big Room.**

White sands. The Chihuahuan Desert has many lava flows, lost rivers, and beaches formed by lakes that have disappeared. It is especially known for its huge dunes of dazzling white sands. These sands are made almost entirely of gypsum, the mineral from which plaster of Paris is made.

Comprehension Check 6C
Identify
1. The five regions that make up the large North American Desert.
2. The largest desert area in the United States. The long-living tree found there.
3. The world's largest canyon.
4. The world's most spectacular limestone caverns.

The North American Desert
Each part of the North American Desert has a distinctive indicator plant.

sagebrush (Great Basin Desert)

petrified log (Colorado Plateau)

Joshua tree (Mojave Desert)

saguaro cactus (Sonoran Desert)

yucca plant (Chihuahuan Desert)

6.4 DESERT FLORA AND FAUNA

The deserts of North America have a greater variety of flora (plant life) and fauna (animal life) than any other deserts in the world. The most famous desert animal, the camel, does not normally live in the New World deserts, but many other creatures designed for arid lands do. Plants and animals of the desert have to cope with two problems—great extremes of temperature (very hot days and very cold nights) and lack of water.

Hardy Plants

The plants of the western deserts are designed to conserve water. Most of them have very tiny leaves or no leaves at all, for large leaves lose large amounts of moisture. Usually, desert plants are covered with thorns or prickles. Their supply of water is held in by a tough, waterproof skin that is often coated with layers of wax. Besides the cacti, the hardy desert plants include *creosote bushes, Joshua trees, sagebrush,* and *yuccas.*

Cacti. Cactus plants are native to the Western Hemisphere. All of the approximately 1,600 species of cacti live in North and South America. Five kinds are also found in the Old World, but naturalists think they were probably carried there by man. Cacti range all over the New World from Canada to the Strait of Magellan at the southern tip of South America. They are found mainly in the deserts, but some are able to grow on trees in the tropical jungles and in Florida's swampy Everglades.

Cacti are "traveling plants." Their hooks and spines catch easily on the fur or skins of animals. The animals unwittingly transport bits of the plant over long distances to a new home, where they very quickly take root and grow. Birds also help by carrying the seeds to new localities.

Cacti come in an overwhelming variety of shapes and sizes, and most kinds are covered with plumes, hooks, spikes, spines, scales, prickles, hairs, or bristles. Once a year, they burst into brilliant bloom. At this time, they rival all other plants in color, variety of bloom, and sweetness of odor. Although one kind of cactus has a flower over a foot in diameter, the largest kinds have small flowers.

Barrel cacti, which can be up to 10 feet tall and 4 feet across, received their name because they are shaped like barrels. They often weigh tons. Many desert travelers have escaped death by drinking the water stored by this plant. Indians used the tough, curved spines of the barrel cactus as fishhooks. The *organ-pipe cactus* has a number of enormous stems and an edible red fruit. The *old man cactus* is named for its shaggy covering of white hair. The **prickly pear,** which is the most widespread cactus, has prickly fruit shaped something like a pear or a fig. Indians ate the fruit of several kinds of cactus, squeezed water from the stems, and ground the seeds into flour for making cakes. Even today cacti fruits are sold or made into candy. The flowers of one kind of cactus are used in salads.

barrel cactus

The horned toad uses camouflaging to hide from predators.

Variety of Animals

Bobcats, jack rabbits, mule deer, cacomistles [kăk′ō·mĭs′′lz], gila [hē′lə] monsters, cactus wrens, bats, sidewinders, rattlesnakes, coyotes, kangaroo rats, pocket mice, and skunks are just a few of the many kinds of animals that are able to live in the harsh desert environment. <u>Most desert animals come out at night</u>. During the day, they burrow underground or find other ways to avoid the extreme heat. Most of them have small bodies and can live without water for several days. Many of them are fast runners.

Reptiles. Because reptiles are dependent upon their environment to heat their bodies, they often thrive in the deserts. They bask in the morning sun and then hide under rocks during the hottest part of the day. At night, they come out looking for the many kinds of insects and small animals that live in the desert. Most of the snakes of the desert are poisonous, and <u>one of only two poisonous lizards</u> in the world, the **gila monster,** is found in the deserts of North America.

Snakes of the American desert include *coral snakes* and *rattlesnakes.* Another desert reptile, the **desert tortoise,** stores water in a sac inside its upper shell. The **chuckwalla,** a harmless lizard that can be up to a foot and a half long, hides in crevices between rocks. If an enemy comes along, the chuckwalla fills its lungs with air and puffs itself up so much that it is difficult for the enemy to pull it out. The **horned toad,** which is really a lizard, has a squat, toadlike body covered with sharp, horny spines. It looks fierce, but it is harmless.

Rodents. Rodents are the most abundant mammals of the desert. The **kangaroo rat,** which is five or more inches long without its long tail, is able to survive on an extremely small amount of water because of its very efficient kidneys and cooling system. It moves about on two legs rather than four, and its strong hind legs can propel it two feet straight up or in any other direction. The **pocket mouse,** a thumb-sized burrower, and the **pack rat,** which collects assorted objects and hides them in its nest, run around on the thorny cacti with no harm.

Jack rabbits. Two kinds of jack rabbits live in the deserts of the southwest—the black-tailed jack rabbit and the antelope jack rabbit. The **antelope jack rabbit** can bound along at 35 miles an hour to escape predators. It uses its huge ears as a cooling system. As blood circulates through the rabbit's thin ears, it is cooled by the air and thus cools the rabbit's body.

The American West

Other mammals. Many other mammals either live in the deserts or spend part of their time there in search of food. The **coyote,** a wild member of the dog family, helps keep down the rodent and rabbit population, which would otherwise destroy all the cacti. Seventeen kinds of **bats** live in caves in or near the deserts. Their droppings, called *guano* [gwä′nō], are mined because they make one of the finest fertilizers known to man. The little **spotted skunk** hunts small *nocturnal* (active at night) desert animals. **Bobcats,** which look like large housecats with stubby tails, live in the mountains and plains as well as in the deserts.

Cacomistles [kăk′ə·mĭs′əlz] are members of the raccoon family; the **ringtail** species can be tamed as pets and mouse catchers. A champion escape artist, the ringtail can wedge itself into tiny crevices to escape predators. The **collared peccary** [pĕk′ə·rē], or javelina [hä′və·lē′nə], is a piglike animal that wanders in bands through the deserts and scrublands looking for cacti and roots to eat. The **kit fox,** which is smaller than most foxes, ranges the desert at night looking for rats, mice, ground squirrels, birds, lizards, snakes, and insects.

California Condor

ringtail

Birds. The **roadrunner** dashes across the desert at speeds up to 15 miles per hour. It stays in the desert all year long, eating insects, mice, snails, lizards, and even rattlesnakes. The **California condor,** a large vulture with a bald, orange head and a reddish neck, is <u>the largest land bird in North America</u> (with a wingspan up to 10 feet). It soars in broad circles looking for *carrion* (the flesh of dead animals) to eat.

Comprehension Check 6D
Identify
1. The most widespread species of cactus.
2. The time most desert animals are more active.
3. The poisonous lizard found in the deserts of North America.
4. The largest land bird in North America.

6.5 THE PACIFIC COAST

West of the Intermountain Region are the mountains, valleys, and plains that border the Pacific Ocean. Most of this region receives much more rain than the Intermountain Region and the Great Plains. It is the home of the tallest trees in North America.

North America's Pacific Shore

Rocky cliffs. Along the shore of the Pacific, great cliffs rise directly from the sea. The water is very deep only a short distance offshore. Huge waves beat endlessly upon the rocky cliffs and the sandy bays that indent the coastline. Driftwood, which may have floated with the currents thousands of miles from Japan, can often be found on the beaches. All along the coast from Alaska to Baja [bä′hä] California, huge beds of kelp (seaweed) grow a short distance from the shore.

Sea mammals. Gray whales, which may be almost 50 feet long, pass through the kelp beds each year. Many seals and **sea lions** can also be found in the region. (Sea lions are a kind of seal.) At one place on the Oregon coast, there is a series of connected caves inhabited by several hundred sea lions. The smaller sea lions, which are known for their intelligence and their loud barking noises, are often trained as comical performing seals for zoos and circuses. A larger kind also lives in these caves. **Seals** live along the coasts of all the continents, and most of them live in the Northern Hemisphere. They usually live in large herds.

Sea birds. The **wandering albatross,** sometimes called the *gooney bird,* has the greatest wingspan of any bird (almost 12 feet). Although it can soar for hours, it is not a fast flier. Two species of albatross are commonly found along North America's Pacific Coast. The **California gull** which is similar to a tern, is another familiar bird along the Pacific shores.

Fish and shellfish. Crabs, clams, and oysters are plentiful in the coastal waters, as are important fish such as cod, flounder, and halibut. At least five kinds of **salmon** live in the North Pacific Ocean. Salmon are hatched during the summer or autumn in

wandering albatross

California coast

85

freshwater streams, sometimes as much as 2,000 miles upstream from the ocean. After a time, they migrate to the ocean. When it is time for the grown salmon to lay their eggs, they make the long trip back up-stream to the very same stream in which they were hatched. Although many of them die along the way, the survivors keep fighting the current and other obstacles until they reach their destination.

Crater Lake

The Pacific Mountains

The Cascade Range. The Cascade Mountain Range, which is located 100 to 150 miles inland from the Pacific Ocean, extends for more than 700 miles through northern California, western Oregon, western Washington, and southern British Columbia. The highest peaks of the Cascades are **Mount Rainier** (14,410 feet) in Washington and **Mount Shasta** (14,162 feet) in northern California.

The Cascade Mountains are composed of *lava* materials, and many of the peaks are *extinct volcanoes*. Lassen Peak of California gives off gassy fumes. Mount St. Helens of Washington erupted on May 18, 1980. This was the first volcanic eruption in the United States (excluding Alaska and Hawaii) since 1917.

Crater Lake of southwestern Oregon fills the hollow (crater) of the top of a dead volcano. It is the deepest lake in the United States. Crater Lake, which has no known outlets or inflows, is about 2,000 feet deep. Its surface lies 6,000 feet above sea level.

The Cascades have numerous lakes, waterfalls, and streams. The largest river passing through the mountains is the **Columbia River.**

Winds blowing in from the Pacific Ocean drop 100 inches or more of precipitation annually on the western slopes of the Cascade Mountains. The high peaks of Mount Rainier can receive over 500 inches of precipitation annually. The rain forests of the Olympic Peninsula, west of Mount Rainier, are among the rainiest places on earth. The moist western slopes have especially thick forests of **Douglas firs** and **hemlocks.** Douglas firs can grow 250 feet tall and 8 feet in diameter. The land to the east of the Cascades is very dry because by the time the clouds get over the mountains they have little moisture remaining.

Coast Ranges. The Coast Ranges are the home of the **California redwood tree.** These giants of the forest thrive in the foggy climate along the western side of the mountains. Redwoods are among the tallest trees in the world. One redwood in northern California is considered to be the world's tallest tree. It is 368 feet high (as high as a 30-story building). Redwoods average about 250 feet in height, and their trunks are often 8 to 12 feet in diameter.

Sierra Nevada. The **Sierra Nevada Range** of California extends from the Cascades in the north to down along the Mojave Desert in the south. The highest peak of the Sierra Nevada Range, **Mount Whitney** (14,494 feet), is also the highest peak in the United States south of Alaska.

Deep canyons lie in the western part of the Sierra Nevada Range. The most outstanding of these is **Yosemite** [yō·sĕm′ĭ·tē] **Valley.** White men first entered Yosemite Valley in 1851 when soldiers captured Tenaya, chief of the Yosemites, to keep the Indians from raiding the settlers who lived in the foothills of the Sierra Nevada. The soldiers eventually let Tenaya return to the valley, which they named for his people. The Yosemite Valley is one of the spectacular sites of **Yosemite National Park.** Another is **Yosemite Falls,** North America's highest waterfall, which leaps from a height of 2,425 feet.

Another outstanding feature of the Sierra Nevada is its vegetation. The **giant sequoia** [sĭ·kwoi′ə], sometimes called the *big tree* or the *Sierra redwood,* grows only on the western slopes of the Sierra Nevada. Some of these gigantic trees have probably been alive since the time that David was king of Israel. The bases of the sequoias' trunks can be up to 100 feet in circumference. Although not the *tallest* tree, the **General Sherman** in Sequoia National Park is considered to be the world's largest tree in volume of wood. It has a circumference of 102 feet. As you already learned, sequoias were named after Sequoya, the inventor of the Cherokee syllabary. **Sequoia National Park,** the second national park (founded in 1890), was also named after him.

The giant sequoia is considered to be the largest species of tree on earth.

Yosemite Falls

Comprehension Check 6E
Identify
1. The fish that is born in freshwater streams, migrates to the ocean, and travels back to its birthplace to lay eggs.
2. Two mountain ranges found in the Pacific Mountains.
3. The large volcano in the Cascades that erupted on May 18, 1980.
4. The lake that fills the top of an extinct volcano and is the deepest lake in the country.
5. North America's highest waterfall.
6. The tree that is considered to be the world's largest in wood volume.

6.6 INDIANS OF THE WEST

You have seen that the western third of North America is a land of great variety. Its mountains, valleys, plateaus, deserts, forests, seashores, rivers, and lakes supported many different kinds of American Indian tribes. The main Indian culture areas of the West are the Northwest Coast, the California Intermountain Region, and the Southwest.

The Northwest Coast

Rich in resources. The Northwest Coastal Region is one of the richest parts of North America in natural resources. Salmon, trout, whales, seals, and shellfish were some of the riches that the Northwest Indians harvested from the sea. They also hunted such inland mammals as deer, elk, bear, caribou, and otters for their skins and meat. The many different trees and other plants yielded a wealth of nuts and berries to supplement their diets. During the spring and summer, the Northwest tribes could easily find enough food to last through the winter.

Several tribes. Some of the Indian tribes of the Northwest included the *Tlingit* [tlĭng′gĭt], *Nootka* [nōōt′kə], *Chinook* [shĭ·nŏŏk′], and *Bella Coola* [bĕl′ə kōō′lə]. Although there were several different tribes, they all had similar customs.

Totem poles reflect the great skill of the Northwestern Indian tribes.

Culture and customs. The Northwest Indians were one of the most advanced Indian cultures of North America, especially after the white man arrived. They did not have farms, but they made good use of the many trees of their region. They made canoes (sometimes 60 feet long), beautiful boxes, wooden houses, and ornately carved totem poles. On their houses and **totem poles** they would carve their family crest or seal. Many relatives would share a house.

The tribes of the Northwest Coast spent their summers gathering food, and the long winter months they spent *weaving, carving,* and *painting*. They also held religious and secret society meetings, many of which were

88 New World History & Geography

very cruel. Sometimes at a gathering called a **Potlatch,** a rich man would kill his most valuable slave just to prove he was rich. He would then throw the slave's scalp at his rival. After the white man came, trading and trapping became very important to the Northwest Indians.

The California-Intermountain Region

The Indians of the California-Intermountain Region lived in the Great Basin and in what is now the state of California. California had one of the largest Indian populations in North America. Indians of this region hunted red squirrels, mule deer, mountain lions, mountain goats, bighorn sheep, and grizzly bears for meat and skins. They also fished the mountain streams and the Pacific for trout, salmon, and other fish and hunted whales, sea lions, and other seals. Some tribes worshiped the California condor. The tribes that lived in the Great Basin had a much more difficult time than those who lived in California. The arid Great Basin could support only a few scattered tribes.

Shoshone. The Shoshone [shō·shō′nē] Indians were named for their curly hair. These people lived in the dry and barren area that is now Nevada, Utah, and Idaho. They ate mostly seeds, roots, fish, birds, and small animals such as rabbits. When food was plentiful and the winter mild, they would live together in villages. But they usually traveled in small family groups of 8 to 10 people, searching for food. Many times when the winter was harsh or the food was scarce, they would leave their sick, elderly, or newborns out to die. It was their custom to name the different family groups after the food they ate; thus some were called the Rabbit Eaters, others the Seed Eaters, and so forth. Every year each family group would return to the same areas to hunt or gather food. Today many Shoshone Indians live in Wyoming, Idaho, and Nevada. They often earn their living as farmers or ranchers.

Sacagawea [săk′ə·gə·wē′ə], also known as *Bird Woman,* was a famous Shoshone. When she was 12 years old, she was captured by enemy Indians and later sold to a French-Canadian trader, who married her. Sacagawea, her husband, and their infant son joined Lewis and Clark, two famous explorers, on their trip across America to the Pacific Ocean. Sacagawea acted as the guide for the group. When the expedition ran into a group of Shoshone Indians led by Sacagawea's brother, Lewis and Clark were pleasantly surprised. Because Sacagawea was with the group, the Shoshones treated the explorers kindly. If it had not been for Sacagawea, Lewis and Clark might not have made it to the Pacific Ocean. A river, a mountain peak, and a mountain pass have been named for this brave Indian woman.

Nez Percé. The Nez Percé [nā′ pĕr′sā′ or nĕz′ pûrs′] were named by a French interpreter. Their name means *pierced nose,* although they rarely pierced their noses.

The Nez Percé lived in Idaho, Washington, and Oregon. They ate berries and roots, and they fished the rivers for salmon. When the horse was introduced to these people, it changed their lives. They began to hunt buffalo. They used the skins for clothes and lived in skin-covered tepees. They became well known for their horsemanship and soon became famous as breeders of the **appaloosa,** a horse with a spotted or splotched coat.

The Nez Percé were always friendly with new settlers and explorers. They were proud, handsome, kindhearted people. Many white settlers would have died if the Nez Percé had not helped them. For over 70 years, they

MISSIONARY HEROES
Marcus and Narcissa Whitman

Trail of many moons. There is an old story that tells how four Indians from tribes of the Northwest journeyed over 3,000 miles from their home to St. Louis, Missouri, in the autumn of 1832. A white man had witnessed to their tribes about a "Book from Heaven" that told of the one true God, and these four men had been sent in search of the Book.

The Indians came to see the famous explorer William Clark of the Lewis and Clark expedition, who was now the Superintendent of Indian Affairs. Clark met with them and showed them many things, but he did not give the Indians what they had come for—a Bible that they could read in their own language and a preacher whom they could take back to their people.

When the time came for the Indians to return home, Clark honored them with an elaborate banquet. It was here that one of the Indians stood and said:

> My people sent me to get the white man's Book from Heaven. You took me where you allow your women to dance, as we do not ours, and the Book was not there. You took me where they worship the Great Spirit with candles, and the Book was not there. You showed me the images of the Great Spirit and pictures of the Good Land beyond, but the Book was not among them to tell me the way.
>
> I am going back the long trail to my people in the dark land. You make my feet heavy with gifts . . . and yet the Book is not among them. When I tell my poor blind people . . . that I do not bring the Book, no word will be spoken . . . . One by one, they will rise up and go out in silence.
>
> My people will die in darkness, and they will go a long path to other hunting grounds. No white man will go with them, and no white man's Book to make the way plain. I have no more words.

God's messengers bring the Book. By 1836, the American Board of Foreign Missions had decided to sponsor **Dr. Marcus Whitman** and **Reverend Henry Spalding** to work among Indians of the Northwest who had requested the gospel. Their wives, **Narcissa Whitman** and Eliza Spalding, became the first white women to journey west of the Rockies. The Whitmans established a mission among the Cayuse Indians in the present state of Washington, and the Spaldings settled in the present state of Idaho and ministered to the Nez Percé.

Martyrs for Christ. The Whitmans provided a good example of Christian living—hard work and service to others backed by prayer and a strong witness for Christ. Then, in 1847, a measles epidemic struck their settlement. Because the Indians lacked a natural immunity to this disease, many fell sick and died. Although the Whitmans exhausted themselves trying to help the Indian children, the Cayuse saw only that most of the white children were recovering while the Indian children perished.

The chief of the Cayuse had lost two children to the epidemic and felt that Dr. Whitman was allowing the Indians to die. On November 29, 1847, as Dr. Whitman sat in his home after returning from doctoring the sick, an Indian brave took a tomahawk and killed him. Indians also killed Mrs. Whitman as she tried to comfort her family.

The Whitman massacre sparked a major conflict between settlers and the Cayuse Indians. To save the rest of their tribe, the Cayuse eventually turned over five of their members accused of the crime to government officials.

Faithful friends. Not all of the Indians were angry with the Whitmans. Many had become Christians. Three of the Whitmans' Indian friends risked their lives to rescue people from the renegade Indians and later helped bury the dead at the mission. As news of the Whitman massacre spread, the Nez Percé protected the Spaldings from also being attacked and killed.

tried to live in peace with the settlers. They eventually moved to Oklahoma and later to a **reservation** (a piece of land set aside by the government as a home for an Indian tribe) in the state of Washington. Their most famous leader was **Chief Joseph.**

Salish. The Salish [sā′lĭsh] Indians, part of a group of tribes known as *Flatheads,* lived in northwest Montana. They were similar to the Plains Indians. After the Salish acquired horses, they would go to the Great Plains each year to hunt buffalo. The Salish often battled with the Indians of the Plains. Most Salish lived in tepees, but some lived in mat-covered A-frame lodges. Fish were an important source of food for the Salish. They used either bark or skin canoes to travel the waters. By 1872, most of the tribe had settled on Flathead Reservation in one of the most beautiful areas of western Montana.

Cayuse. The Cayuse [kī·ūs′] lived in what is now northeast Oregon. Their culture was greatly influenced by the Plains Indians, and they became famous horse breeders and dealers. A kind of small pony that cowboys often used was named the *Cayuse* after this tribe.

Ute. The state of Utah was named after the Ute [ūt] Indians. These people lived in small family groups and roamed the area of Utah and Colorado. By 1870, most of the Ute Indians were on reservations in southwestern Colorado or Utah.

The Southwest

The Southwest is the huge region of hot deserts in present-day Arizona, New Mexico, southern Utah, and northern Mexico. The Indians of the deserts developed cultures quite different from those of other Indians. Many of them retain much of their traditional culture today.

Pueblos. Some of the first Southwestern Indians known to white men were the Pueblos [pwĕb′lōz]. They were the descendants of an earlier civilization called the Anasazi [ä·nə·sä′zē], who were excellent basket weavers. Down through the years, the Pueblos lost their skills in this craft. The Spanish discovered the Pueblo Indians during the Age of Exploration when they were exploring the Southwest in search of cities of gold. They found these tribes living in villages. The word *pueblo* is Spanish for "village." Early Pueblo people cut their multi-room houses into solid rock; some were tall with many rooms like an apartment building. The doorways were usually in the roof, and ladders were needed to reach them.

Chief Joseph of the Nez Percé

The American West 91

ancient cliff dwellings at Mesa Verde National Park

When the Pueblo Indians were under attack, they would pull their ladders up so the enemy could not get in.

The Pueblo Indians are really a group of several tribes whose ancestors lived in similar kinds of houses. Some of the tribes referred to as Pueblo Indians are the **Hopi** [hō′pē: *the peaceful ones*]; the Zuñi [zoō′nyē: unknown]; the Keres [kā′rĕs: *drinkers of the dew*]; and the Tewas [tā′wəs: *moccasins*].

The Pueblos were a peaceful and friendly people. Most of them were farmers; corn, beans, and squash were their most important crops. The Pueblos not only raised corn to eat, but they also worshiped it. These Indians were excellent craftsmen, producing beautiful weavings, pottery, and jewelry.

The rule for all Pueblo people was *everything in moderation, no excess, no waste.* They did not drink, and even though they used over 70 different types of medicinal plants, they never abused any of them.

Mojave. The Mojave [mō·hä′vē] Indians of northwest Arizona were primarily farmers. They would plant their spring crop as soon as the Colorado River floodwaters receded. They did not live in villages, but rather in scattered groups wherever good farmland was found. Because they were scattered, they did not have any formal government other than a hereditary tribal chief who acted as an adviser. The Mojave warriors were divided into groups such as clubbers, stick men, or archers. The warriors earned fame for their success or bravery in battle.

Navajo. The Navajo (sometimes spelled *Navaho*) tribe is the largest Indian tribe in the United States today. They have lived for centuries in their ancestral homeland of Arizona and New Mexico. They often live in mud-covered hogans which they build to face the east. Even a family who lives in a newer home most of the time will also have a hogan for ceremonies. The Navajo are famous for their beautiful woven rugs and silver jewelry. Today, tens of thousand of Navajo live on a reservation in Arizona, New Mexico, and Utah that is 25,000 square miles, about the size of West Virginia.

Apache. The Apache [ə·păch′ē] Indians were related to the Navajo. Both tribes migrated down to the United States from Canada. While the Navajo and most of the Apache settled in the southwest, some Apache Indians drifted into the area that is now Kansas. The Apache lived in tepees or wickiups [wĭk′ē·ŭps: wood-frame huts covered with grass or brush] and wore animal skins for clothing. They were some of the last Indians of the Southwest to resist settlement by the white man.

92 *New World History & Geography*

Geronimo [jə·rŏn′ə·mō′: 1829–1909], an Apache leader, led his people in resisting the Southwestern settlements of the Spaniards and Americans. He was well known and feared for his "hit and run" raids on settlements. On September 3, 1886, Geronimo surrendered and was then placed in exile at Fort Pickens in Pensacola, Florida, with other members of his tribe. After being transferred to Fort Sill, Oklahoma, he accepted Christianity and joined the Dutch Reformed Church.

Comprehension Check 6F

Identify

1. The famous Shoshone woman who traveled across America with Lewis and Clark.
2. The first white women to journey west of the Rockies.
3. The term that is used for a piece of land set aside by the government as a home for an Indian tribe.
4. The largest tribe in the United States today.

Chapter 6 Checkup

I. Define these **terms.**
   flora   fauna

II. Identify these **plants.**
   sagebrush   bristlecone pine tree   cacti (saguaro, barrel cactus, prickly pear)
   giant sequoia tree   California redwood tree   General Sherman

III. Give a noted fact about these **animals.**
   bighorn sheep   grizzly bears   gila monsters   California condors
   mountain goats   pikas   kangaroo rats   wandering albatross
   mountain lions   water ouzels   antelope jack rabbits   salmon

IV. Identify these **landmarks.**
   The Great Divide   Yellowstone Lake   Carlsbad Caverns   Columbia River
   Yellowstone National Park   Hells Canyon   Crater Lake
   Old Faithful   Great Salt Lake   Yosemite Falls
   Mammoth Hot Springs   The Grand Canyon   Death Valley

V. Identify these **mountains** or **mountain ranges.**
   Cordilleran chain   The Cascade Mountain Range   Mount St. Helens   Mt. Elbert
   Backbone of America   The Sierra Nevada   Mt. Whitney

VI. Identify these **deserts.**
   North American Desert   Colorado Plateau   Sonoran Desert
   Great Basin Desert   Mojave Desert   Chihauhaun Desert

VII. Give a noted fact about these **Indian tribes.**
   Havasupai   Salish   Pueblos
   Shoshone   Cayuse   Navajo
   Nez Percé   Mojave   Apache

VIII. Tell why these **people** are important.
   Sacagawea   Geronimo   Chief Joseph   Marcus Whitman

IX. Identify the locations from **Map Masteries 7–9.**

The American West 93

Western Hemisphere

Legend:
- North America
- South America
- Europe
- Africa
- Asia
- Australia
- Antarctica

A1 World Political

Eastern Hemisphere

ARCTIC OCEAN

- NORWAY
- SWEDEN
- FINLAND
- RUSSIA
- KAZAKHSTAN
- MONGOLIA
- UZBEKISTAN
- KYRGYZSTAN
- TURKMENISTAN
- TAJIKISTAN
- NORTH KOREA
- SOUTH KOREA
- JAPAN
- IRAN
- AFGHANISTAN
- CHINA
- PAKISTAN
- BHUTAN
- NEPAL
- BAHRAIN
- QATAR
- UNITED ARAB EMIRATES
- LIBYA
- EGYPT
- SAUDI ARABIA
- OMAN
- BANGLADESH
- INDIA
- MYANMAR
- LAOS
- TAIWAN
- NIGER
- CHAD
- SUDAN
- ERITREA
- YEMEN
- THAILAND
- VIETNAM
- NORTHERN MARIANAS (U.S.)
- NIGERIA
- DJIBOUTI
- CAMBODIA
- GUAM (U.S.)
- CAMEROON
- CENTRAL AFRICAN REPUBLIC
- ETHIOPIA
- SRI LANKA
- PHILIPPINES
- EQUATORIAL GUINEA
- UGANDA
- SOMALIA
- BRUNEI
- FEDERATED STATES OF MICRONESIA
- GABON
- KENYA
- MALAYSIA
- CONGO
- DEMOCRATIC REPUBLIC OF CONGO
- RWANDA
- BURUNDI
- SINGAPORE
- INDONESIA
- PAPUA NEW GUINEA
- TANZANIA
- MALAWI
- AMERICAN SAMOA
- ANGOLA
- ZAMBIA
- MOZAMBIQUE
- MADAGASCAR
- FIJI
- NAMIBIA
- ZIMBABWE
- BOTSWANA
- AUSTRALIA
- LESOTHO
- SWAZILAND
- SOUTH AFRICA
- NEW ZEALAND

PACIFIC OCEAN

INDIAN OCEAN

ANTARCTICA

Arctic Circle (66°)
Tropic of Cancer (23°)
Equator 0°
Tropic of Capricorn (23°)
Antarctic Circle (66°)

NORTHERN HEMISPHERE / SOUTHERN HEMISPHERE

International Date Line

Europe inset

- NORWAY
- SWEDEN
- ESTONIA
- DENMARK
- LATVIA
- LITHUANIA
- RUSSIA
- UNITED KINGDOM
- NETHERLANDS
- BELARUS
- IRELAND
- BELGIUM
- GERMANY
- POLAND
- LUXEMBOURG
- CZECH REP.
- SLOVAKIA
- UKRAINE
- FRANCE
- AUSTRIA
- HUNGARY
- MOLDOVA
- SWITZERLAND
- SLOVENIA
- ROMANIA
- LIECHTENSTEIN
- CROATIA
- BOSNIA AND HERZEGOVINA
- ANDORRA
- SAN MARINO
- YUGOSLAVIA
- BULGARIA
- GEORGIA
- PORTUGAL
- VATICAN CITY
- ITALY
- MACEDONIA
- ARMENIA
- SPAIN
- ALBANIA
- TURKEY
- AZERBAIJAN
- GREECE
- CYPRUS
- SYRIA
- MOROCCO
- TUNISIA
- LEBANON
- IRAQ
- ISRAEL
- ALGERIA
- LIBYA
- EGYPT
- JORDAN
- KUWAIT

95

North America

Arctic Ocean

- 80°
- Greenland
- Arctic Circle (66°)
- Baffin Bay
- Ellesmere Island
- Davis Strait
- Labrador Sea
- Baffin Island
- Queen Elizabeth Islands
- Hudson Strait
- Ungava Peninsula
- Labrador Peninsula
- Island of Newfoundland
- Gulf of St. Lawrence
- Hudson Bay
- St. Lawrence River
- Banks Island
- Victoria Island
- Great Bear Lake
- Great Slave Lake
- Lake Winnipeg
- Great Lakes
- Niagara Falls
- Ohio River
- Appalachian Mountains
- Mt. Mitchell
- Florida Peninsula

Atlantic Ocean

- Tropic of Cancer (23°)
- Pico Duarte
- Lesser Antilles
- West Indies
- Cuba
- Greater Antilles
- Hispaniola
- Caribbean Sea
- Lake Maracaibo
- Orinoco River
- Angel Falls
- Gulf of Mexico
- Bay of Campeche
- Yucatán Peninsula
- Gulf of Honduras
- Panama Isthmus of Panama
- Panama Canal
- Gulf of Tehuantepec
- Sierra Madre Oriental
- Sierra Madre Occidental
- Chihuahuan Desert
- Rio Grande
- Arkansas River
- Great Plains
- Missouri River
- Mississippi River
- Mt. Elbert
- Great Salt Lake
- Snake River
- Columbia River
- Mt. Rainier
- Mt. St. Helens
- Vancouver Island
- Mt. Logan
- Rocky Mountains
- Great Basin
- Yosemite Falls
- Mt. Whitney
- Colorado River
- Mojave Desert
- Sonoran Desert
- Baja California
- Gulf of California
- Mackenzie River
- Beaufort Sea
- Mt. McKinley
- Alaska Peninsula
- Gulf of Alaska
- Yukon River
- Bering Strait
- Bering Sea
- Mauna Kea
- Hawaiian Islands
- Tropic of Cancer (23°)

96

A2 Western Hemisphere
Physical

SOUTH AMERICA

- Equator 0°
- 10°
- 20°
- Tropic of Capricorn (23°)
- 30°
- 40°
- 50°
- 60°
- 70°

Guiana Highlands
Amazon River
Madeira River
Lake Titicaca
Brazilian Highlands
Paraná River
Río de la Plata
Atacama Desert
Mt. Aconcagua
Andes Mountains
Pampas
Patagonia
Galápagos Islands
Easter Island
South Georgia Island
Falkland Islands
Tierra del Fuego
Cape Horn
Strait of Magellan

PACIFIC OCEAN

Antarctica

- 40°
- 50°
- 60°
- 70°
- 80°
- 90°
- 100°
- 110°
- 120°
- 130°
- 140°
- 150°
- 160°

Tropic of Capricorn (23°)
Antarctic Circle (66°)
Equator

97

Map of the Western United States

Countries & Regions: CANADA, MEXICO, RUSSIA

States (Western US):
- WASHINGTON — Olympia, Seattle, Spokane
- OREGON — Salem, Portland
- CALIFORNIA — Sacramento, San Francisco, San José, Los Angeles, San Diego
- NEVADA — Carson City, Reno, Las Vegas
- IDAHO — Boise
- MONTANA — Helena
- WYOMING — Cheyenne
- UTAH — Salt Lake City
- ARIZONA — Phoenix, Tucson
- COLORADO — Denver, Boulder, Colorado Springs, Pueblo
- NEW MEXICO — Santa Fe, Albuquerque
- NORTH DAKOTA — Bismarck, Fargo
- SOUTH DAKOTA — Pierre, Sioux Falls
- NEBRASKA — Lincoln, Omaha, Sioux City
- KANSAS — Topeka, Wichita
- OKLAHOMA — Oklahoma City, Tulsa
- TEXAS — Austin, Dallas, Houston, San Antonio, El Paso
- MINN(ESOTA)
- ALASKA — Fairbanks, Anchorage, Juneau
- HAWAII — Honolulu

Physical Features:
- Vancouver Island, Juan de Fuca Strait, Puget Sound
- Cascade Range, Coast Ranges, Sierra Nevada, Rocky Mountains
- Mt. Rainier, Mt. St. Helens, Mt. Shasta, Mt. Whitney, Mt. Elbert, Mt. McKinley, Mt. Logan, Mauna Kea
- Columbia R., Snake R., Missouri R., James R., Red R., S. Platte R., Arkansas R., Canadian R., Red River, Pecos R., Rio Grande, Colorado R., Yukon
- Yellowstone National Park, Black Hills, Great Salt Lake, Lake Itasca
- Yosemite Falls, Grand Canyon, Colorado Plateau, Great Basin Desert, Mojave Desert, Sonoran Desert, Chihuahuan Desert, Great Plains
- Gulf of California, Bering Sea, Arctic Circle, Arctic Ocean, Pacific Ocean

98

A3 United States
Political/Physical

ARCTIC OCEAN
Beaufort Sea
Banks Island
Amundsen Gulf
Victoria Island
Ellesmere Island
Devon Island
Arctic Circle
Yukon R.
Mackenzie R.
YUKON TERRITORY
Mt. Logan
Whitehorse
NORTHWEST TERRITORIES
Great Bear Lake
Yellowknife
Great Slave Lake
NUNAVUT
COAST MOUNTAINS
ROCKY MOUNTAINS
BRITISH COLUMBIA
CANADA
ALBERTA
SASKATCHEWAN
MANITOBA
Lake Athabasca
Queen Charlotte Islands
Edmonton
Calgary
Regina
Winnipeg
Lake Winnipeg
Vancouver Island
Vancouver
Victoria
PACIFIC OCEAN
UNITED STATES OF AMERICA
80°
180°
70°
170°
160°
150°
60°
140°
50°
40°
120°
110°
100°

A4 Canada
Political/Physical

- GREENLAND
- Baffin Bay
- Davis Strait
- Baffin Island
- Iqaluit
- Southampton Island
- Hudson Strait
- Labrador Sea
- ATLANTIC OCEAN
- Hudson Bay
- NEWFOUNDLAND
- Island of Newfoundland
- St. John's
- James Bay
- QUÉBEC
- Gulf of St. Lawrence
- PRINCE EDWARD ISLAND
- Charlottetown
- ONTARIO
- NEW BRUNSWICK
- Quebec City
- Fredericton
- Halifax
- NOVA SCOTIA
- Montreal
- St. Lawrence R.
- Ottawa
- Lake Superior
- Lake Michigan
- Lake Huron
- Toronto
- Lake Ontario
- Lake Erie
- APPALACHIAN MOUNTAINS

101

110°
100°
90°
California
UNITED STATES OF AMERICA
Arizona
New Mexico
Texas
Alabama
Mississippi
Louisiana
New Orleans
Tijuana
El Paso
Ciudad Juárez
30°
Sonoran Desert
Baja California
Gulf of California
SIERRA MADRE OCCIDENTAL
SIERRA MADRE ORIENTAL
Rio Grande
San Antonio
Chihuahua
Chihuahuan Desert
MEXICO
Mexican Plateau
Monterrey
Gulf of M
Tropic of Cancer
Durango
Mazatlán
Tampico
Bay of Campeche
Mérida
20°
Guadalajara
Yucatán Peninsula
Mexico City
Veracruz
Puebla
Belmopan
BELIZE
Isthmus of Tehuantepec
Acapulco
Oaxaca
Gulf of Tehuantepec
GUATEMALA
Guatemala
San Salvador
EL SALVADOR
Panama Canal
Caribbean Sea
Colón
Gatum Locks
Panamá City
Pedro Miguel Locks
PACIFIC OCEAN
PACIFIC OCEAN
10°

A5 Middle America
Political/Physical

ATLANTIC OCEAN

Georgia

Tropic of Cancer

Florida
- Tampa
- Miami

Nassau
BAHAMAS

TURKS & CAICOS

Havana
CUBA
- Camagüey

HAITI
Port-au-Prince
DOMINICAN REPUBLIC
Santo Domingo
HISPANIOLA

San Juan
Puerto Rico

Virgin Islands
Leeward Islands
St. Kitts & Nevis
Guadeloupe
Martinique

JAMAICA
Kingston

GREATER ANTILLES

LESSER ANTILLES
Windward Islands

BARBADOS
GRENADA
TRINIDAD AND TOBAGO

Netherlands Antilles

Caribbean Sea

Gulf of Honduras

CENTRAL AMERICA

HONDURAS
Tegucigalpa

NICARAGUA
Managua

COSTA RICA
San José

Isthmus of Panama
Panama Canal
PANAMA
Panamá City
Gulf of Panamá

VENEZUELA

COLOMBIA

103

Caribbean Sea
PANAMA
Gulf of Venezuela
Lake Maracaibo
Caracas
Delta del Orinoco
Orinoco R.
Llanos
VENEZUELA
GUIANA HIGHLANDS
Orinoco R.
Bogotá
COLOMBIA
GUYANA
Georgetown
SURINAME
Paramaribo
FRENCH GUIANA
Cayenne
ATLANTIC OCEAN
Equator
Quito
ECUADOR
Manaus
Amazon River
Amazon River
Selvas
Madeira R.
Maranón R.
MONTANA
PERU
ANDES MOUNTAINS
Lima
Lake Titicaca
La Paz
BOLIVIA
Sucre
Altiplano
BRAZIL
São Francisco R.
Brasílla
BRAZILIAN HIGHLANDS
Paraná R.
Belo Horizonte
80°
70°
60°
50°
40°
10°
0°
10°

A6 South America
Political/Physical

- Rio de Janeiro
- São Paulo
- Tropic of Capricorn (23°)

PARAGUAY — Asunción

URUGUAY — Montevideo

ARGENTINA — Córdoba, Buenos Aires
- Río de la Plata
- Paraná R.
- Gran Chaco
- Pampas
- Patagonia

CHILE — Santiago
- Mt. Aconcagua (22,831 ft.)
- ANDES MOUNTAINS
- Atacama Desert
- Tierra del Fuego
- Strait of Magellan
- Cape Horn
- Drake Passage

Falkland Islands (U.K.)

South Georgia Island

ATLANTIC OCEAN

PACIFIC OCEAN

Inset: Galápagos Islands (EC.) — Equator 0°, PACIFIC OCEAN

105

chapter 7
United States History:
The COLONIAL HERITAGE

THE ENGLISH COLONIZE AMERICA

Spain and France in the New World

Shortly after Columbus discovered the New World in **1492,** Spain sent settlers to Puerto Rico and other islands in the West Indies. In 1513, **Juan Ponce de Leon** of Spain discovered Florida while searching for the imaginary Fountain of Youth. As far as we know, he was the first European to reach what is now the mainland of the United States. The Spaniards planted the first permanent European settlement, **St. Augustine,** in Florida in 1565. About the same time, the French began to settle what is now Canada and the United States. Although the French established settlements as far south as South Carolina and Florida, they soon abandoned their southern sites and concentrated on settling Canada. Thus, Spanish settlers lived in the southern part of what is now the United States, and French settlers lived farther north when the English began settling the New World.

England and the Bible

John Cabot claimed part of North America for England in **1497,** but not until the late 1500s did the English begin the difficult task of planting a colony in the wilderness of America. The settlement of the English colonies happened in God's perfect timing, for by 1585 England had become a Protestant country. This exciting change

---

1500 — 1550 — 1600 — 1650 — 1700 — 1750

- **1492** Columbus discovered the New World
- **1497** Cabot claims part of North America for England
- **1513** Ponce de Leon discovers Florida
- **1587** England founds Roanoke Colony
- **1607** English settlers found Jamestown, Virginia
- **1609** Champlain claims part of New York for the French
- **1609** Hudson claims part of New York for the Dutch
- **1619** First blacks arrive in English colonies
- **1620** Pilgrims found Plymouth, Massachusetts
- **1630** Puritans found Massachusetts Bay Colony
- **1634** St. Mary's City, Maryland, founded as a haven for Catholics
- **1636** Roger Williams founds Providence, Rhode Island
- **1647** Ole' Deluder Satan Act passed
- **1682** William Penn and Quakers settle in Pennsylvania
- **1730–1760** Great Awakening
- **1733** Oglethorpe founds Savannah, Georgia

The promise of true freedom drew many Europeans to America's shores.

meant that people were free to read the Bible for themselves. **Queen Elizabeth I** had called for a Bible to be placed in every church. People thronged to the churches to read the Bible, for most of them did not yet own one. English people who could not read listened carefully as a man with a strong voice read the Word of God aloud. Bible reading had an important effect on the kind of people who would come to America and the kind of government they would establish. If the French or the Spanish had remained the dominant settlers in North America, the history of our country would have been very different because the people of France and Spain did not have the Bible freely available to them. The Bible provided the ideas about morality (right and wrong), freedom, and individual responsibility that have made our country great.

Roanoke: The Lost Colony

The "Virgin Queen." Queen Elizabeth I gave permission to her good friend Walter Raleigh [rô′lē] to begin a colony in America, with the condition that Raleigh himself would not go. If a war broke out with Spain, the queen wanted him nearby to help England. Raleigh sent two sea captains to search out the land for him. When they returned, they reported finding an island called **Roanoke** [rō′ə·nōk], a fine place to begin a colony. Both Queen Elizabeth and Raleigh were delighted with the discovery. For his excellent plans, the queen knighted Raleigh, and he was then known as **Sir Walter Raleigh.** The part of the New World that the sea captains had explored was called **Virginia,** after Elizabeth, who was known as the "Virgin Queen."

Roanoke Colony. Sir Walter Raleigh first sent about one hundred men and five ships to begin a colony on Roanoke Island. These men were more interested in becoming rich than in colonizing the New World, however, and they soon ran out of food. After just over a year, the settlers returned to England.

In 1587, Raleigh tried again, this time sending a group of brave men, women, and children to Roanoke Island. Raleigh reasoned that families would be more interested than single men in building houses, planting gar-

The Colonial Heritage 107

dens, and settling down. The colonists arrived safely at Roanoke and began repairing houses that the first colonists had left. Shortly after their arrival, the colonists welcomed <u>the first English child to be born in America</u>, **Virginia Dare.**

When **John White,** the governor of the colony, had to return to England for badly needed supplies, he told the colonists that, if they had to leave the island, they should carve a message on a tree explaining where they had gone. If they were in trouble, they were to carve a cross above the message.

War with Spain. Upon arriving in England, White found the nation ready to go to war. King Philip of Spain had assembled a huge fleet of ships and thousands of men to invade England. Queen Elizabeth gave orders that every English ship be used in the effort to defeat the country's rival. Not even Sir Walter Raleigh could get a ship for John White when he was ready to return to Roanoke. <u>In 1588,</u>

Concepts to Consider
Using Dates and Time Lines

Our dating system is centered on the most important event in history—the coming of Jesus Christ to earth. Each event in history is dated according to how many years before or after the time of Christ it occurred. <u>The letters B.C. stand for "before Christ."</u> Therefore the date 3000 B.C. means "three thousand years before Christ." Those events that have happened since the time of Christ are marked <u>A.D., which stands for the Latin term "anno Domini," meaning "in the year of our Lord."</u> Thus the date A.D. 2000 means "in the two thousandth year of our Lord," or two thousand years after the birth of Christ. We often leave off the A.D. when referring to dates that have been since Christ. Therefore, if you see the date 1860, you know that it is A.D. 1860, not 1860 B.C.

A **time line** is a graph that is used to show events in their correct order. Time lines can be either horizontal (left to right) or vertical (up and down). The time line below begins at 2000 B.C., which is around the time Abraham, the father of the Jewish people, was born. It ends with A.D. 2000, after the time of Christ. Notice that the dates go backward (become smaller) until the time of Christ. Then they move forward and get larger. Can you see why 2000 B.C. happened **before** 500 B.C., while A.D. 2000 happened *after* A.D. 500?

Important events that took place before the time of Abraham were the Creation, the fall of Adam and Eve, Noah's flood, the dispersion of the races of mankind from the Tower of Babel, and the beginnings of great nations in Egypt and Mesopotamia. Between Abraham and Christ, great kingdoms and empires rose and fell in the Old World. Egypt, Assyria, the Babylonian Empire, the Persian Empire, and the Greek Empire each had its time of splendor and dominance.

During the time of Christ, the Roman Empire was supreme. The empire continued for about 480 years after the birth of Christ, and then it fell, ushering in a thousand-year period called the "Middle Ages," or the "Dark Ages" (A.D. 500–1500), during which time the Roman church ruled.

In 1517, Martin Luther began the Protestant Reformation, and the Dark Ages were over. The European explorations of America began just before this time, with Columbus's discovery in 1492. Until then, only the American Indians were familiar with the continents of the Western Hemisphere. Unfortunately, we know little about the history of the Americas before the Europeans discovered them; the Native Americans left few written historical records. In the short period of time since 1492, most of the known history of the New World has taken place.

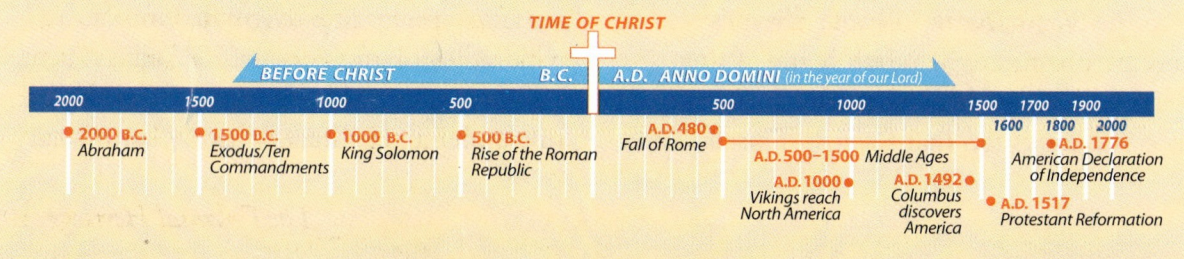

TIME OF CHRIST

BEFORE CHRIST | B.C. | A.D. ANNO DOMINI (in the year of our Lord)

2000 | 1500 | 1000 | 500 | 500 | 1000 | 1500 | 1600 | 1700 | 1800 | 1900 | 2000

- 2000 B.C. Abraham
- 1500 B.C. Exodus/Ten Commandments
- 1000 B.C. King Solomon
- 500 B.C. Rise of the Roman Republic
- A.D. 480 Fall of Rome
- A.D. 500–1500 Middle Ages
- A.D. 1000 Vikings reach North America
- A.D. 1492 Columbus discovers America
- A.D. 1517 Protestant Reformation
- A.D. 1776 American Declaration of Independence

John White finds a message near the deserted colony of Roanoke.

England won the war with Catholic Spain and defeated the powerful fleet called the **Spanish Armada.** Bible-loving England was becoming the most powerful country in the world.

Without a trace. When John White was finally able to return to Roanoke after three years, no one came to greet him. Carved on a tree in the empty settlement was the word *Croatoan,* the name of another island where friendly Indians lived. Although there was no cross over the message and Sir Walter Raleigh sent several search parties, the missing settlers were never found. Today, Roanoke is still known as "The Lost Colony." It has become a great mystery to all who study history, and it shows us what a dangerous task the English had ahead of them in settling the New World.

Jamestown: The First Permanent English Colony

When Queen Elizabeth I died in 1603, **King James I** came to the throne of England. Like Elizabeth, he hoped to plant a successful English colony in the New World. He had several goals: to find a sea passage through America to the riches of the Indies; to find gold, silver, and other valuable minerals; to find the people of the Lost Colony of Roanoke; and to teach the American Indians about Christianity.

The London Company. A group of English merchants formed the **London Company** and obtained a charter from King James to start settlements in America. Each businessman would pay part of the cost of sending the colonists, and the colonists would repay the merchants by sending them furs, lumber, and perhaps gold and silver from the New World. And, of course, if one of the colonists happened to find a sea passage to the Indies, the merchants would have access to the great wealth of the Orient. The charter set up a "common-store system" under which each colonist was supposed to work for the common good of the colony and, in return, would receive his food and supplies from a public storehouse. After seven years, the colonists would be free to pursue their own interests for personal profit.

Choosing the first colonists. A new colony in the wilderness of North America would need hard-working men of good character, but unfortunately these were not the kind of men the London Company chose. Many of the approximately 100 men they sent were wealthy gentlemen, unaccustomed to manual labor. Wealthy men are often hard workers, but not *these* wealthy men. They were drawn to the New World mainly by stories that nuggets of gold lay on the beaches of Virginia just waiting to be picked up. They had no thoughts of building a colony, only of becoming even richer and then returning to England.

The founding of Jamestown. In April of 1607, three small ships, the ***Susan Constant,*** the ***Godspeed,*** and the ***Discovery,*** sailed into the Chesapeake Bay. From the mouth of the Chesapeake Bay, they sailed into a river which the colonists named the **James River,** in honor of their king. Instead of taking time to search out suitable land and plan wisely for

The Colonial Heritage 109

the future, the men hastily chose a swampy peninsula. The new settlement, named **Jamestown,** became the first permanent English settlement.

Before long, the summer heat dried up their water supply. Mosquitoes swarmed in from the swamps, carrying malaria with them. Before the summer was over, half of the colonists had died. Because few gardens had been planted, there was little food to see the survivors through the coming winter. Although they faced starvation, most of the colonists still did little work. They knew that they could get food from the public storehouse just like everyone else and thus live off the labors of their fellow men. By the time ships arrived in 1608 with more settlers and supplies, only a third of the original colonists were still alive.

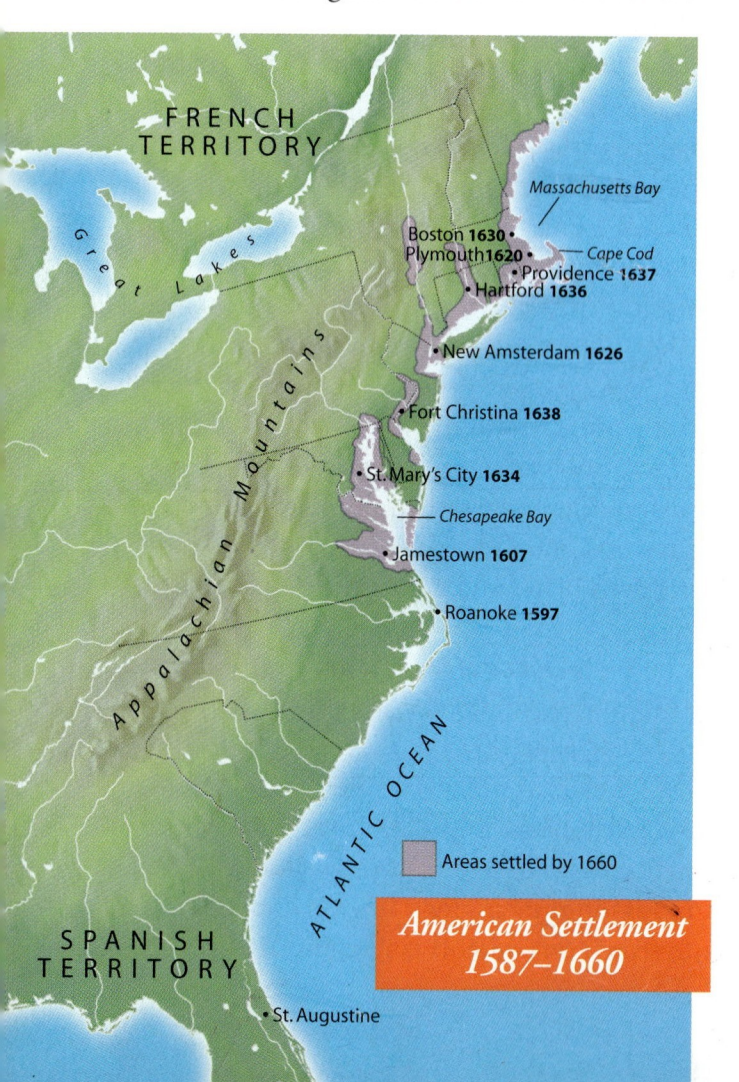

Captain John Smith. Later that year, one of the colonists, **Captain John Smith,** took control of Jamestown. Smith had already supervised the building of huts for housing, and he had purchased corn from the Native Americans to provide food through the winter. Knowing that they would starve again that winter unless everyone, including the wealthy gentlemen, worked hard, he wisely made a new rule: "He that will not work shall not eat." Though at first the gentlemen did not believe Captain Smith, they soon learned that he meant business. Grumbling, they picked up their tools and began working. Life still would not be easy, however, that second winter in Jamestown. The London Company had sent several hundred new colonists but very little food to feed them.

John Smith

The starving time. In the fall of 1609, Captain Smith had to return to England for medical attention. With their leader gone, the gentlemen again refused to work. The winter of 1609–1610 was so difficult that the colonists called it **"the starving time."** By spring, only about sixty out of five hundred colonists remained alive, and they were weak from hunger and sickness.

When a small group of new colonists arrived at Jamestown from Bermuda (where they had been stranded for several months) and saw the failing colony, they welcomed the Jamestown survivors aboard their ships and set sail for England. Soon, they sighted another ship in the distance. The ship was one of several carrying more colonists, supplies, food, and the colony's first governor, **Lord De La Warr** [dĕl'ə·wĕr]. The weary colonists, who probably dreaded the long, difficult voyage

American Settlement 1587–1660

home, turned their ship around and sailed back to Jamestown.

The "common-store system" fails. Like John Smith, De La Warr brought law and order to Jamestown and enforced the common-store system instituted by the London Company charter. Where Smith had used the powerful persuasion of starvation, however, De La Warr used the threat of severe punishment. This communal system would have brought the colony to ruin had it not been for the wisdom of Governor Dale, one of De La Warr's successors. Realizing that the colonists needed personal incentives to work, Dale instituted a *free enterprise system.* The new system allowed the men to have land of their own and to raise crops for personal profit. The incentive to survive and prosper drove the colonists to cultivate the land and begin producing crops for their own use and for trade.

Successful at last. Slowly and painfully, Jamestown became the first successful English colony in America. When the colonists turned from prospecting for gold to farming and other trades, they began to prosper. Hard work, as always, brought success. However, there were still few families in Jamestown; most of the colonists were men.

In 1619, the London Company sent ninety women to become wives for some of the men at Jamestown. With families to take care of, the colonists became eager to build stronger houses and to earn a living to provide for the needs of their families. As these and other men soon learned, the greatest wealth of America was not gold or silver but the happiness found in the freedom of building their own homes and working in a wonderful new land.

That same year, 1619, a Dutch ship brought the first blacks to Virginia. The Dutch traded some of the twenty Africans as slaves and others as indentured servants—people who worked several years for a landowner or craftsman and then became free colonists, sometimes even owning land. (Many of the European immigrants came to the New World as indentured servants.)

Comprehension Check 7A
Identify
1. The first European to reach the mainland of what is now the United States.
2. The British explorer who sent colonists to Virginia.
3. The person for whom Virginia was named.
4. The name of what is now known as the "Lost Colony."
5. The year Jamestown was established.

Think
6. Why couldn't John White return to Roanoke Colony as soon as he had planned? What was the name of the powerful Spanish fleet the British defeated during this time?

Historic Jamestown recreates the way of life from the first settlement in Virginia.

The Colonial Heritage

7.2 THE PILGRIMS: LOVERS OF RELIGIOUS FREEDOM

Desire for religious freedom. Even though the English were a Bible-loving people, they lacked religious freedom. James I, the king of England, claimed to be the head of the church as well as the head of the government. Though many people disagreed with the **Church of England,** the king forced everyone to attend his church. This government interference in religious affairs distressed one group of believers, the **Separatists,** because they thought that the Church of England was not being true to the Bible. The *Separatists* wanted to *separate* from the Church of England. These brave people, desiring to preach and do what the Bible teaches, held secret meetings to study the Bible. The king often sent spies to these meetings and had many Separatists jailed for their beliefs.

The move to Holland. The Separatists loved England, but they loved God and religious freedom more. When they heard that they could have religious freedom in the country of Holland, the Separatists gave up their homes in England and moved their families to Holland. They felt like strangers in Holland, however, and soon longed for a homeland of their own. When they learned of the settlement in Jamestown, the Separatists asked permission from King James to found a colony in America. There, they could remain loyal subjects of the king but still worship God in their own churches. King James gave them permission to go to America.

Aboard the Mayflower. Thus, in September of **1620,** a small ship called the *Mayflower* embarked from England on a sixty-five day voyage westward across the storm-tossed Atlantic Ocean. Of the 102 passengers on board, not including the crew, 35 were Separatists. As strangers bound for a strange land, these passengers of the *Mayflower* would become known as the **Pilgrims,** the name by which we remember them today. When the weary travelers finally sighted land, the *Mayflower*'s captain, Christopher Jones, had some surprising news for them. Although they had planned to land in "Northern Virginia" (actually New York), storms had blown the *Mayflower* off course and had driven it northward. The Pilgrims were looking at the shores of Cape Cod, Massachusetts.

The Mayflower Compact. In order to protect themselves and their right to worship God in the manner they felt was best, the Pilgrims knew that they must set up a government. Therefore, leaders onboard the ship wrote the **Mayflower Compact,** the first written agreement for self-government in America.

The colonists of Jamestown had not chosen their own government; instead, England had appointed a governor for them. The Pilgrims enjoyed **self-government;** they chose their own governor, **John Carver,** and planned their own government. It takes a spe-

The Pilgrims prepare to leave Holland.

112 New World History & Geography

replica of the Mayflower

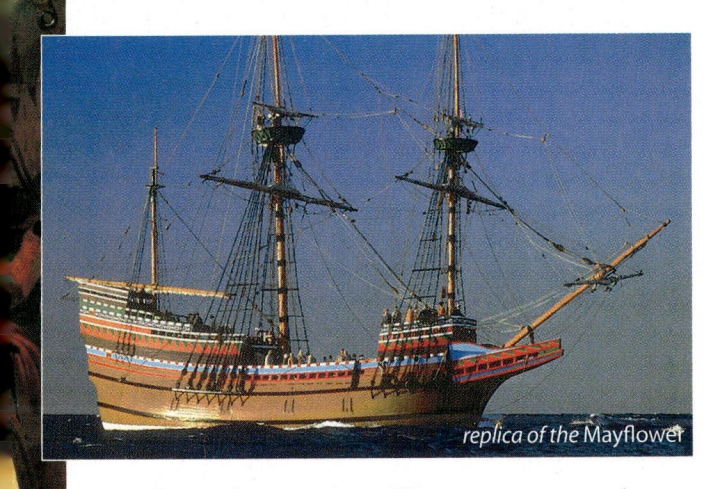

cial people to make self-government work—people who are in subjection to God and able to control their own selfish desires.

In the Mayflower Compact, the Pilgrims promised to make just laws. Here is what they wrote:

> In the name of God, Amen. We whose names are underwritten, the loyal subjects of our dread sovereign Lord, King James, by the grace of God, of Great Britain, France, and Ireland king, defender of the faith, etc. Having undertaken for the glory of God, and advancement of the Christian faith, and honour of our king and country, a voyage to plant the first colony in the Northern parts of Virginia, do by these presents solemnly and mutually in the presence of God, and one of another, covenant and combine ourselves together into a civil body politic, for our better ordering and preservation and furtherance of the ends aforesaid; and by virtue hereof to enact, constitute, and frame such just and equal laws, ordinances, acts, constitutions, and offices, from time to time, as shall be thought most meet and convenient for the general good of the Colony, unto which we promise all due submission and obedience.

About forty men signed the Mayflower Compact on Saturday, November 21, 1620, and then the Pilgrims spent the next day, Sunday, as they always did—praying and listening to the preaching of their minister, **Elder Brewster**. On Monday, the men began looking for a good place for the group to settle. Every day, they asked God for guidance.

Settling in Plymouth. The Pilgrims knew that they must find a place with a good supply of drinking water, a good harbor, and security from hostile Indians. Before leaving England, they had hired **Captain Miles Standish** to help them deal with the Indians and build a settlement. Although Captain Standish was not a Separatist himself, he did much to protect these people.

After a few weeks of exploration, Captain Standish and the Pilgrims found an area that suited their needs. The men sailed the *Mayflower* into a bay and began to clear land for the settlement, which they called **Plymouth.** It was now December and snow covered the ground. After Christmas, the men began chopping down trees to build a **Common House** that would serve as a home, fort, and church for the people that winter. Their food supply was limited, but they could not plant crops until spring. The Pilgrims grew very weak from hunger, and many became sick from the cold. At one time, only seven were strong enough to care for the others. Though by spring half of the settlers had died, the Pilgrims remained confident that God would help them.

signing the Mayflower Compact

The Colonial Heritage

Making friends with the American Indians. Imagine the Pilgrims' surprise when an Indian named **Samoset** walked into their settlement one day and said, "Much welcome, Englishmen!" Samoset introduced the Pilgrims to **Squanto** [skwŏn′tō], who had been to England and who spoke English well. Samoset also presented **Massasoit** [măs′ə·soit′], chief of the Wampanoag tribe, to them. Chief Massasoit and the Pilgrims made a treaty, promising never to fight one another. The promises they made were kept as long as Chief Massasoit lived.

After the other Native Americans who had come with Samoset returned to their homes, Squanto chose to stay with the Pilgrims. They soon realized that he was a blessing sent by God. Without Squanto's help, the Pilgrims might not have survived. Squanto taught the boys and men how to trap game and told the settlers to plant their corn as soon as the leaves of the white oak were as large as a mouse's ear. He also taught them to fertilize their growing grain with fish, because the sandy ground lacked the minerals necessary for healthy plant growth.

A new governor. In April 1621, the *Mayflower* sailed back to England. Although it must have been tempting, not one of the Pilgrims asked to return to England. Shortly after the *Mayflower* sailed away, Governor Carver became ill and died, and the Pilgrims elected **William Bradford** to become the new governor. Governor Bradford made such a good leader that the people elected him again and again. He governed the colony during most of the next 36 years. His book, ***Of Plymouth Plantation,*** tells us much of what we know about the Pilgrims.

The first Thanksgiving. Once they had planted crops, the Pilgrims built homes, became better acquainted with the Indians, and traded with them for furs. When harvest time arrived, most of the Pilgrims' English crops of wheat and peas had died, but the Indian corn had thrived, providing plenty to eat. They lacked the variety of foods and other comforts they enjoyed in England and Holland, but rather than complain about what they did not have, the Pilgrims thanked God for what they did have. They also thanked God for His mercy: He had brought them safely out of a winter of

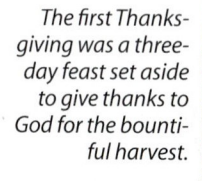

The first Thanksgiving was a three-day feast set aside to give thanks to God for the bountiful harvest.

cold and sickness, given them the strength to plant, and provided a much-needed harvest.

After the harvest of 1621, <u>the grateful Pilgrims set aside a day of thanksgiving to God</u>. Men went out to hunt deer and turkeys and to fish for cod and bass; women cooked pumpkin, corn, and beans; children gathered nuts and berries from the woods. In a letter to a friend in England, Edward Winslow, one of the Pilgrims, described the first Thanksgiving:

> Our corn did prove well, and, GOD be praised, we had a good increase of Indian corn.... Our harvest being gotten in, our governor sent four men on fowling, that so we might after a more special manner rejoice together after we had gathered the fruit of our labours.... And although it be not always so plentiful as it was at this time with us, yet, by the goodness of GOD, we are so far from want that we often wish you partakers of our plenty.

Ninety Indians came with Chief Massasoit to join the three-day feast. They listened as the Pilgrims read the Bible and raised special prayers of thanksgiving to God. The Indians ran races with the Pilgrims, and Captain Standish showed how his men could march. Then everyone feasted together. With happy hearts and full stomachs, the Pilgrims and the Indians finally returned to their homes.

Plymouth grows. Soon after the first Thanksgiving, a ship arrived from England, bringing new settlers. The Pilgrims were glad to see old friends and hear news from England, but they were disappointed to learn that the ship brought little food for the winter. Of course, the Pilgrims would share their homes and their food with the new settlers. There would be less food than they had expected, but there would be enough for all of the colonists during their second cold New England winter.

The Thanksgiving of 1623. Although the previous winter had been damp, the summer of 1623 was so dry that it soon seemed as if the Pilgrims' crops would perish for lack of rain. The Pilgrims set aside a special day for prayer and fasting, and for nine hours they prayed to God for help. Some Indians, hearing that the Pilgrims were going to pray for rain, watched the sky to see what would happen. When the sky finally clouded over and a gentle rain began to fall, the Indians remarked in awe-stricken tones that the God of the white man had heard the white man's prayers.

Ten days of rain followed this day of prayer, and the crops were saved. The Pilgrims were so grateful for God's mercy that they again set aside a special time of thanksgiving. This was not to be the last time the Pilgrims offered thanksgiving to God, for they believed that "In every thing give thanks: for this is the will of God in Christ Jesus." (1 Thess. 5:18). They would thank God many times in the years to come as He delivered them from trials and brought prosperity to the colony.

These brave Pilgrims were true heroes of our country's beginnings. <u>We remember them for their courage and perseverance, for their love of religious freedom, for their establishment of self-government, and for their faith in God and thankfulness to Him.</u>

Comprehension Check 7B

Identify
1. The year the *Mayflower* first came to Massachusetts.
2. The name of the Pilgrims' colony.
3. The American Indian who lived with the Pilgrims and helped them.

Think
4. What was the Mayflower Compact and why was it important?

The Colonial Heritage

7.3 THE NEW ENGLAND COLONIES

The Thirteen Original Colonies

As time passed, more people from England and other countries in Europe journeyed to America, hoping to find a better life. You have learned of Jamestown, the first lasting settlement in Virginia, started in 1607. You have also learned of Plymouth, the colony the Pilgrims founded in 1620. By 1735, many more colonies had joined Massachusetts and Virginia.

The **thirteen original colonies** that eventually became the United States were Virginia, Massachusetts, Rhode Island, New Hampshire, New York, Connecticut, Maryland, Delaware, New Jersey, Pennsylvania, North Carolina, South Carolina, and Georgia. The northernmost of these colonies—Massachusetts, New Hampshire, Connecticut, and Rhode Island—were known as the **New England Colonies.**

Massachusetts and the Puritans

Persecution in England. The **Puritans** were a group of Christians in England who, like the Separatists, disagreed with the Church of England. The Puritans did not want to separate from the Church of England, but they wanted to "purify" it from un-Scriptural teaching and practice. Of course, the king of England would not permit this, because he wanted everyone to believe and worship as he did. He had those who disobeyed thrown into jail. The persecution of dissenters (those who disagreed with the Church of England) grew increasingly worse in the 1620s. Encouraged by the Separatists' success in the New World, the Puritans began to look toward America with hopes of religious freedom. Only one obstacle hindered their departure—no one could start a colony in America without a charter from the king of England.

Obtaining a charter. In 1629, a group of Puritan businessmen formed the **Massachusetts Bay Company** and requested a charter for land in America. Unaware of their religious motives, **King Charles I** granted these businessmen a large tract of land in the New England area. Unlike most charters, however, the charter for the Massachusetts Bay Company failed to specify that the company headquarters must remain in England. Thus, the Puritans could take the charter, and therefore control of the company, to New England with them, establishing a virtually self-governing commonwealth.

Sailing to America. In the spring of 1630, eleven ships carried nearly 1,000 men, women, and children to New England. Later that same year, more ships followed them until 2,000 Puritans had settled in the New World. They called their colony the **Massachusetts Bay Colony** and named the biggest town in the colony **Boston.** Because many of the Puritans were wealthier than their neighbors in Plymouth, they had more money to invest in their colony. The Massachusetts Bay Colony quickly became a prosperous center of trade and commerce, and Boston grew to be one of the most important cities in America. Later, Plymouth would become a part of the colony, and the colony would be called simply **Massachusetts.**

Governor Winthrop. Like the Plymouth colonists, the Puritans were threatened with starvation long before ships could return from England with provisions. The Puritans' leader, **Governor John Winthrop,** generously gave people food from his own storehouse; in fact, he gave the last bit of flour he had to a poor man who came to beg. But the good governor did not suffer for his generosity, because that very day the returning ships sailed into port, bringing provisions for all. Winthrop, a strong and godly leader, served as governor twelve times. The American Indians called him "Single Tongue" because he was a truthful man.

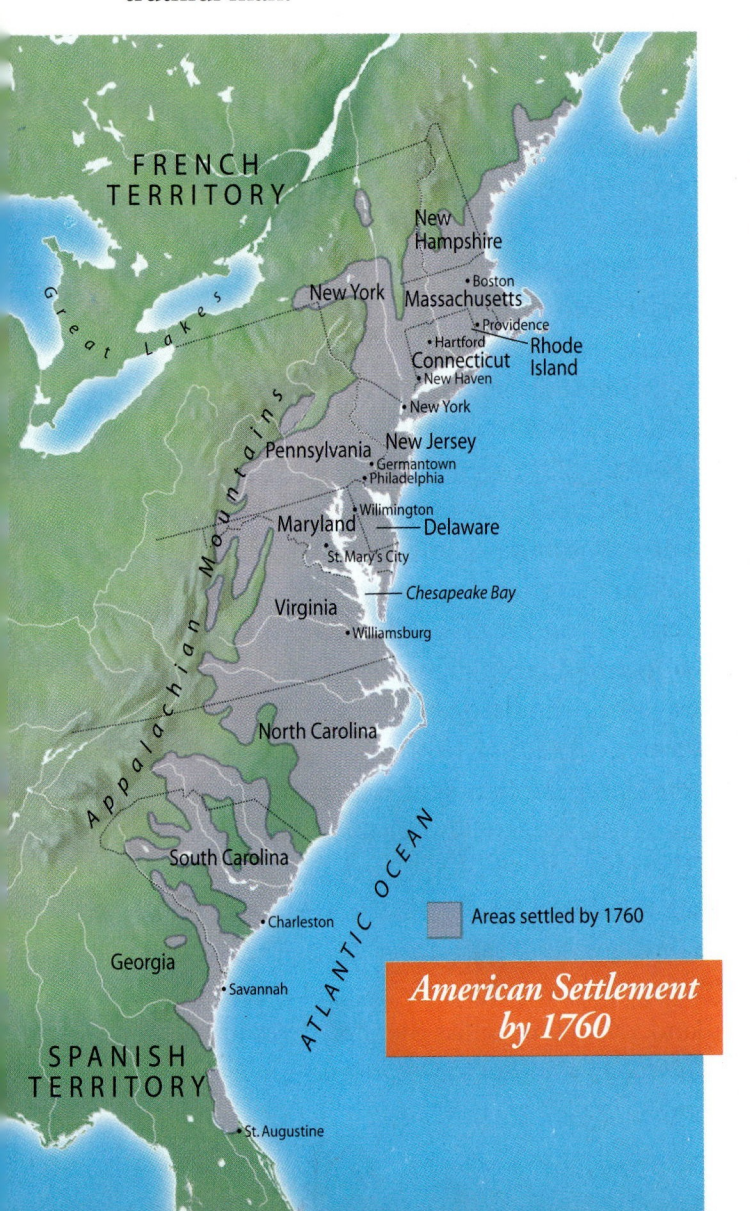

John Winthrop

Massachusetts grows. From 1630 to 1640, more than 20,000 Puritans came to New England in what became known as the "Great Migration." In time, they formed fifty villages, connected by roads and bridges. Each town had its own local government and sent representatives to the General Court, or Assembly, where public matters were discussed and laws were made for the good of the whole colony.

"A city upon a hill." The Puritans are remembered today for their trust in God, their willingness to work hard, their high standards, their strict discipline, and their belief that everyone should have a good education. Governor John Winthrop described their colony as "a city upon a hill," an example of Christian society to the rest of the world. As you have already learned, one Puritan minister from Massachusetts, **John Eliot,** gave the world a fine example of Christian evangelism in his ministry to the Indians of New England.

Education for Christian living. As early as 1642, Massachusetts passed a law requiring all parents to see that their children learn to read. In 1647, Massachusetts passed a law remembered as the **Ole' Deluder Satan Act,** which directed all towns of at least 50 households to hire a teacher to teach their children to read and write. It also provided that towns of at least 100 households establish a school to educate and prepare future ministers for further training at college. Named for its purpose, this act was to defeat "the old deluder, Satan" in his attempt "to keep men from the knowledge of the Scriptures." The act established the first public school system in America, a system which recognized the importance of the Bible in a civilized society. Soon, schools would open their doors to eager children throughout New England.

American Settlement by 1760

The Colonial Heritage

hornbook

Most schoolchildren in Massachusetts and throughout New England used a **hornbook** to learn their alphabet. This paddle-shaped board had a sheet of paper attached to it containing the alphabet and the Lord's Prayer. A thin sheet of transparent film from a cow's horn was nailed over the paper to protect it. After a child memorized the hornbook, he could begin reading from the ***New England Primer*** [prĭm′ər]. This book had lists of words, prayers, poems about Bible stories, and short stories about honesty, obedience, and diligence for the students to practice reading. For over 150 years, millions of American children learned to read from the *New England Primer.* After mastering the primer, they would read the Bible and *Pilgrim's Progress*.

In 1636, the Puritans founded the first college in the colonies—**Harvard College**—to train ministers to preach the gospel. When Harvard College was started, its leaders said,

> Let every student be plainly instructed, and earnestly pressed to consider well, the main end of his life and studies is, to know God and Jesus Christ which is eternal life (John 17:3) and therefore lay Christ in the bottom, as the only foundation of all sound knowledge and learning.

Roger Williams and Rhode Island

Problems in Massachusetts. **Roger Williams,** a missionary to the American Indians and a Puritan preacher in Massachusetts, did much to bring about religious freedom in America. In his day, Christians in Massachusetts were not allowed to attend any church other than the Puritan, or Congregational, church. Like King James, the Puritan leaders insisted that all colonists attend, support, and obey their church. Colonists could not even vote unless they were members of the Puritan church. The Puritans seemed to think that by forcing people to go to their church, they could make everyone become Christians.

Roger Williams upset the Puritan leaders of Massachusetts for several reasons. He believed in salvation by faith alone; he knew that punishment can never make a person believe on Jesus in his heart. Williams also believed that the Indians should be treated fairly. After trading with these people, he would tell them about God. Other Massachusetts settlers would often cheat them, but Roger Williams said that the Indians should be paid for their land and treated fairly and kindly.

Escape into the wilderness. The Puritan leaders told Williams that he must either change his ways or leave Massachusetts. When he continued to oppose them, they ordered a ship to take him back to England. Learning of their plans, Williams escaped into the wilderness in the winter of 1636. There, without proper food and shelter, he succumbed to the weather and became very sick. Fortunately, God's hand was upon Williams: kind Indians found the sick missionary and took care of him until spring, when he could travel again. Southwest of Massachusetts Bay, Williams found suitable land for a settlement near the mouth of the Blackstone River in Narragansett Bay. He offered the Indians money for the land. They were so fond of him, however, that they would accept payment for only a small section of the land. Williams called the place **Providence,** in recognition of God's care and provision.

118 New World History & Geography

Rhode Island becomes a colony. Soon other colonists who had been persecuted for their beliefs began to join Williams. They came to his colony because it offered something special—complete religious freedom. The people of Providence could worship as they chose. Free at last from the opposition of the Puritans, Roger Williams helped found America's first Baptist church in Providence in 1639.

As the colony grew larger, Roger Williams decided that it should set up a government and become an official British colony. Thus he traveled to England and in 1644 obtained a charter creating the colony of Rhode Island and Providence Plantations.

Freedom for all. Thanks to Roger Williams and a small group of brave men, Rhode Island became the first colony to offer complete religious freedom. When Roger Williams began his colony, he could have forced everyone to do what he wanted. But he wanted everyone to be free to make a personal decision to accept Christ by faith alone. He knew that God's truth about spiritual matters can stand alone without being forced upon people by a government. The little colony of Rhode Island offered religious freedom and political freedom—the two important freedoms that all Americans would someday know. George Washington, our first President, said of Rhode Island,

> While the Baptists have always defended the principles of religious liberty, they have never violated them. They have had but one opportunity of forming a system of civil government, and they so formed it as to create an era in the history of civilization. In the Little Baptist State of Rhode Island was the experiment first attempted of leaving religion wholly to herself, unprotected and unsustained by the civil arm. The principles which were here first planted have taken root in other lands, and have born abundant fruit.

New Hampshire: Land of Fish and Lumber

The first English settlers to arrive in New Hampshire came in the early 1620s. By 1623, English fishermen and loggers had established a small settlement on the Atlantic Coast. Several other small settlements were soon established farther inland. The land became known as **New Hampshire** in 1629 when England granted a portion of it to **John Mason,** an early English explorer of New England. He named the land after Hampshire County, where he had lived in England. Although the Puritans made New Hampshire a part of Massachusetts in the 1640s, the king of England made New Hampshire a separate colony in 1679.

Connecticut: "Place of the Long River"

In the early 1630s, English colonists began to settle west of Rhode Island along a river which the American Indians called *Quinnehtukqut* ("place of the long river"). The fertile land soon attracted other settlers to **Connecticut,** the settlers' name for the area.

Roger Williams was found and cared for by kind Indians.

The Colonial Heritage

In 1636, **Thomas Hooker,** a Puritan preacher from the Massachusetts Bay Colony, led his congregation to Connecticut, where they established **Hartford,** the first major settlement in Connecticut. Among the original Puritan settlers of Connecticut were John and Sara Moody, ancestors of the great evangelist D. L. Moody. Hooker led the people of Connecticut to establish their own government, independent of Massachusetts. Under Hooker's leadership, representatives of the towns in Connecticut met at Hartford in 1639 and adopted the **Fundamental Orders of Connecticut,** usually considered to be the first written constitution in America. King Charles II later issued a charter which incorporated these communities into the colony of Connecticut.

New England: A Land of Churches

Many settlers came to America so that they could worship God freely. In most of the English colonies, people could worship openly without fear of persecution. Often, colonial families worshiped together daily, and large churches were built throughout the colonies. These early church buildings were also used for town meetings, where matters of government were discussed. Thus the ideas of political freedom and religious freedom took root in America's church buildings.

New England was a land filled with churches. In the early colonial years, most of them were **Puritan** churches, later called **Congregational** churches. As more and more people came to New England, changes took place. Larger and more decorative Congregational churches were built, and other religious groups began to build their own churches as well. Baptists, Methodists, Quakers, Jews, and others built meeting houses in New England. By the end of the Colonial Period (1776), New England had become a place where people of many faiths lived and worshiped.

Comprehension Check 7C
Identify
1. The thirteen colonies.
2. The company formed by a group of Puritan businessmen and the king, who granted the group a charter for land in America.
3. The famous governor of the Massachusetts Bay Colony who the American Indians called "Single Tongue." The phrase that governor used to describe the Puritans' colony.
4. The colony that Roger Williams founded and the freedom that colony offered before any other colony.

Think
5. What law established the first town education system in America? How did it get its name?
6. Why are the Fundamental Orders of Connecticut important to American history?

This meeting house on Cape Cod, built in 1684, was used for evangelizing Wampanoag Indians.

7.4 THE MIDDLE COLONIES

A wide variety of people came to the **Middle Colonies**—New York, Delaware, New Jersey, and Pennsylvania. Each of these colonies has an interesting early history.

New York: Settled by the Dutch

Exploration. In 1609, English explorer **Henry Hudson** set sail in his ship the *Half Moon* to find a shortcut to Asia for the Dutch trading company who had hired him. (As you remember, Hudson also did some exploring for the British.) Sailing along the North American coast, Hudson searched in vain for a water route to the Far East. What he found instead was a land occupied by friendly Indians and plenty of beaver. Because beaver skin hats and coats were quite popular in Europe at the time, the Dutch were eager to claim the area (which included southern New York) that Hudson explored.

During the same year, **Samuel de Champlain,** a Frenchman, sailed down from Quebec and explored what is now northern New York. Thus, **France** became the second country to claim New York. You will remember that in 1497 John Cabot explored a portion of North America and claimed it for England. Since New York is a part of North America, **England** also claimed New York.

Although three countries claimed New York, only one began to settle the land. The Dutch built a small village, which they called Fort Orange, on the Hudson River. To encourage people to come to the New World, the Dutch government established the West India Company, a group which would handle settlement and travel to the colony. In 1626, the Dutch bought Manhattan Island from the Indians for about $24-worth of goods and built a village there. They named this settlement **New Amsterdam,** after the capital of the Netherlands, and they called their colony **New Netherland.**

Settlement of New Netherland. At this time, Holland was known for its freedom of religion. Religious groups from all over Europe had, like the Pilgrims, taken refuge in Holland. Some of these refugees migrated to New Netherland, hoping to enjoy the same freedoms that they had in Holland. By the 1640s, as many as 18 different languages were spoken in New Amsterdam! Unfortunately, New Netherland did not offer the freedom available in Holland, because the West India Company had established a **patroon system.** Under this system, the company granted land along a navigable river to wealthy men called *patroons* (patrons), who came to New Netherland and established large estates. In return, each patroon was to transport 50 people to the New World to settle on his land. These patroons had great power over their land and the settlers who farmed it, permitting little freedom. Thus, in spite of the wide variety within its population, New Netherland did not grow as rapidly as the English colonies.

Surrender to England. In 1664, the English sailed into the harbor and announced that England was taking over New Netherland. At first, the determined governor of the colony, **Peter Stuyvesant** [stī′vĭ·sənt], refused to surrender. The colonists knew they did not have the military strength to fight the British, however, and refused to fight. Thus, Stuyvesant was forced to surrender, without firing a single shot, and the British gained control of New Netherland.

The Colonial Heritage 121

Peter Stuyvesant surrendered New Netherland to the British without firing a shot.

Britain permitted the New Netherland colonists to continue living there relatively undisturbed. The British did change some names of places—for example, New Amsterdam became **New York City,** and New Netherland became **New York,** after the Duke of York. The British now governed another colony in America. Eventually, England would control all thirteen American colonies.

Delaware: New Sweden

Settlers arrive. While exploring for the Dutch along the coastline south of New York, Henry Hudson discovered a fine bay in what is now the state of Delaware. A year later, in 1610, a ship from Virginia sailed into the same bay. The English captain named the bay after the governor of Virginia, Lord De La Warr. In 1631, the **Dutch** began the first European settlement on Delaware soil, but they had trouble with the Indians and the settlement failed.

Several years later, in 1638, settlers from **Sweden** arrived and built a fort beside the Delaware River. (Today, the city of Wilmington, Delaware, stands near this historic site.) They named the site **Fort Christina** in honor of Sweden's twelve-year-old queen. The Swedes established the first successful European settlement in what is now Delaware, calling the surrounding area **New Sweden.**

The Swedes were peaceful farmers and hard workers who got along well with the Indians living around them. Swedish settlers built the first **log cabins** in America—sturdy buildings they had developed in the forests of their Scandinavian homeland. The log cabin became a symbol of the American frontier.

colonial log cabin at Fort Christina

122 New World History & Geography

Changes for the small colony. New settlers arrived in New Sweden over the next several years, but New Sweden never grew large. In 1655, the Dutch took control of the colony, and about 10 years later the English claimed it.

Pennsylvania: Quaker State

Discovery by the Dutch. Dutch explorers discovered what would become the colony of Pennsylvania when they sailed up the Delaware River in 1615, six years after Henry Hudson discovered the mouth of the river. Although Swedish settlers had established the first European settlements in the region, the Dutch took control in 1655 when they captured New Sweden (which included part of Delaware). The Dutch, in turn, surrendered the land to the British in 1664, when England took over the Dutch colonies.

William Penn. About the time that Britain took over Holland's colonies, a young Englishman named William Penn learned about religious freedom and came to believe that people should be able to worship as they choose. His beliefs greatly troubled his father, a prestigious British admiral and a good friend of the king of England. Hoping to change the boy's religious ways, the admiral sent him across the English Channel to study in Europe. When William returned after two years, he seemed to have settled down, much to his father's relief. Then, in 1667, Penn met a Quaker preacher and soon converted to the Quaker religion. Although the religious group called itself the **Society of Friends,** most people called the members **"Quakers,"** a term of derision.

The Quakers believed that all people are equal and refused to show more respect for one person than another. They would not even bow before the king of England. Also, because the Quakers were pacifists (people who do not believe in any kind of fighting), they would not fight to protect themselves or their country in times of war. They had no ministers, followed no organized system of worship, and gathered together in meeting houses rather than in formal churches. Although they were a peaceful group, the Quakers' strange beliefs made them outcasts. In England, they were often arrested. Those Quakers who did go to the colonies were often treated worse there than they had been in England.

"Penn's Woods." After his father died, William Penn convinced the king to repay a debt he still owed to Penn's father with a grant of land in America. Penn hoped to start a colony for the Quakers. The king granted his wish, partly because he could easily repay the debt with land in distant America, and partly because he could also rid England of the troublesome Quakers. The king named the new colony **Pennsylvania,** meaning "Penn's

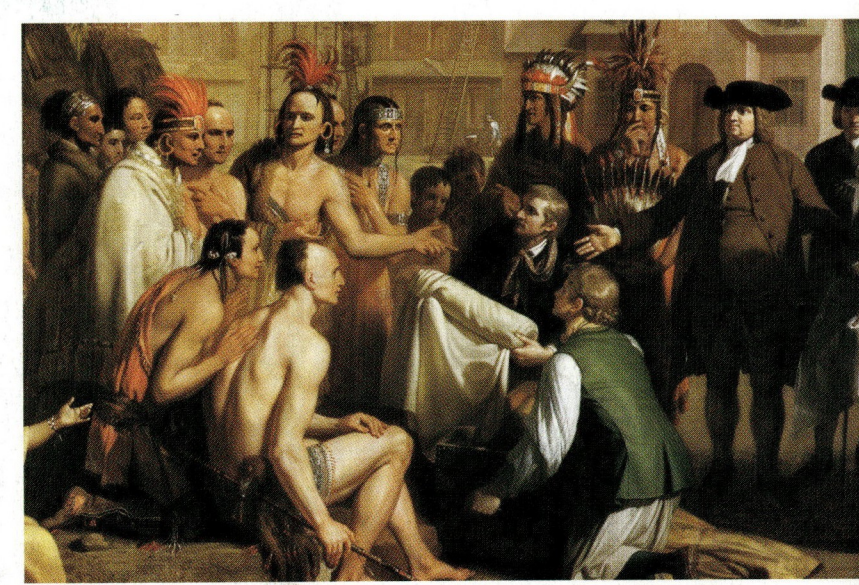

William Penn made a peace treaty with the Indians to establish a colony in Pennsylvania.

The Colonial Heritage 123

Woods," in honor of William's father. In 1682, William Penn brought a group of colonists to Pennsylvania.

The "City of Brotherly Love." As governor of Pennsylvania, William Penn established a peace treaty with the local Indians and purchased land from them to build a settlement. Penn chose to name the city **Philadelphia,** which means "The City of Brotherly Love." Philadelphia quickly became an important trading center and one of the largest cities in the colonies.

Freedom, peace, and opportunity. Pennsylvania had much to offer new colonists. Although Penn's main purpose was to create a haven for Quakers, he offered religious freedom to all people who professed belief in "one almighty and eternal God." He sold land at a reasonable price and even rented to those who could not afford to buy. He drafted a constitution for the colony which provided for a system of self-government, and he maintained peaceful relations with the Indians.

Settlers came from many different European countries seeking the peace and freedoms that Pennsylvania had to offer. Among them were many *Germans,* who called themselves "Deutsch" [doich]. People misunderstood the word and mistakenly called them the **"Pennsylvania Dutch."** One notable group of Germans, the **Moravians,** came to Pennsylvania in 1740. The Moravians followed the teachings of Reformation leader **John Huss** of Bohemia (a historical region of central Europe) and were very active in missionary work. These people were very gifted musically, writing some of the first sacred classical music composed in the Colonies. Many of their songs were sung in colonial churches. Moravians also settled in North Carolina. The great leader of the Moravians, **Count von Zinzendorf,** spent fourteen weeks in America himself and founded a Moravian settlement in Bethlehem, Pennsylvania.

New Jersey: Haven of Religious Freedom

The Dutch and Swedes began the first permanent settlements in **New Jersey.** But when English warships took over New Amsterdam in 1664, they also took control of New Jersey. The king of England gave New Netherland and New Jersey to his brother, the Duke of York, who inherited the throne. He in turn split New Jersey into two parts, giving a part to each of his friends, **Sir George Carteret** and **Lord John Berkeley.** King James named the colony New Jersey in honor of Carteret who had served as governor of the island of Jersey in the English Channel. Carteret and Berkeley offered to sell land at low prices to colonists, granting freedom of re-

the marriage of John Rolfe and Pocahontas

124 *New World History & Geography*

ligion as well. These offers brought many colonists to New Jersey, including Baptists, Quakers, and Covenanters (Scottish Protestants who had bound themselves to remain true to the Presbyterian doctrines).

Churches and Schools in the Middle Colonies

The settlers who built their homes in the Middle Colonies represented many different religions, and the Middle Colonies soon became known as a land of religious freedom. Many Quakers came to the Middle Colonies to escape the persecution they had faced in England. Other groups who came included Mennonites, Presbyterians, Baptists, Moravians, Anglicans, and Dutch Reformed. In the Middle Colonies, these groups were free to worship God in the way they believed was right.

The Middle Colonies had fewer schools than New England, mainly because the farms in this fertile area were larger and the people lived farther apart than the people of New England. Children sometimes had to walk as far as two to four miles one way to reach the one-room schoolhouse. Those who lived farther away were either taught by their parents or not taught at all. Sometimes the minister of a church would teach the children, holding his school in the church building.

Comprehension Check 7D

Identify
1. The Dutch governor who surrendered his colony to the English in 1664.
2. The Englishman responsible for establishing Pennsylvania and the religious group to which he belonged.
3. The two men to whom the King of England gave New Jersey.

Think
4. Why were there fewer schools in the Middle Colonies than there were in the New England Colonies?

7.5 The Southern Colonies

The first colony to be settled—Virginia—and the last colony—Georgia—were both **Southern Colonies.** The other Southern Colonies were Maryland, North Carolina, and South Carolina.

Virginia: The Oldest Colony

As you have already learned, in 1587 the first English settlers in Virginia established the colony at Roanoke, an island off the coast of present-day North Carolina. The mysterious disappearance of the Roanoke settlers discouraged further settlement of Virginia for several years. Finally, the London Company established Jamestown in 1607. Although the Jamestown colony struggled the first few years, its determined settlers finally conquered the land and began to prosper. In 1624, Virginia became a **royal colony,** a colony owned by the king of England.

Tobacco brings wealth. Virginia's economic success was largely due to the cultivation of a common New World crop, **tobacco.** The colonists did not care for the kind of tobacco the American Indians planted. Then, **John Rolfe,** an Englishman, came to Jamestown in 1610. On his way to Jamestown, Rolfe had been shipwrecked in the West Indies, where he saw prosperous tobacco plantations. Soon after he arrived in Jamestown, Rolfe married **Pocahontas,** an Indian princess. In his contact with the Native Americans, Rolfe learned more about the raising and curing of tobacco. Realizing the profit that tobacco could bring to the struggling colony, he obtained seeds for the more popular Carribbean tobacco and

The Colonial Heritage

introduced the crop to the colonists. Before long, tobacco became one of Virginia's chief exports. Although King James I opposed the industry and described tobacco smoking as "a custom loathsome to the eye, hateful to the nose, harmful to the brain, [and] dangerous to the lungs," tobacco was popular in Europe and made Virginia a prosperous colony.

Representative government. In 1619, Virginia set an important precedent, or example to be followed in the future, when the colonists elected delegates, or *burgesses,* to represent them at an assembly in Jamestown. The delegates met for the first time in the choir loft of the Jamestown church on July 30, 1619. This elected body, called the **House of Burgesses,** represented the colonists by advising the governor of the colony on taxes, laws, and other civil issues. The House of Burgesses set an important example for *representative government* in America. Representative government allows citizens to choose people to represent them in an assembly like the House of Burgesses or our nation's Congress. After Jamestown burned to the ground in 1698, the people of Virginia decided to move their capital to **Williamsburg** in 1699.

Maryland: Freedom for Catholics

In England, the Separatists were not the only ones who could not worship as they pleased. Catholics were also forced to attend the Church of England. **George Calvert** (whose title was **Lord Baltimore**), a Catholic man who worked as a secretary to the king, proved himself a good worker and became the king's friend. He asked the king for land in America where he could begin a colony, a haven for English Catholics.

The king granted him his wish. While plans were still being made for the new colony, Lord Baltimore died. His son, Cecilius Calvert, the second Lord Baltimore, continued his father's plans for Maryland. Because he had much work to do in England, Cecilius Calvert could not go to Maryland. Instead, he sent his brother, Leonard Calvert, who was to become the first governor of Maryland.

Two small ships named the *Ark* and the *Dove* set sail from England with about two hundred passengers who were coming to the New World for religious freedom. In 1634, the ships sailed up the Chesapeake Bay. The colonists bought land from friendly Indians, who were planning to move anyway, and built their first settlement, **St. Mary's City.**

Maryland Dove, *a replica of the* Dove, *in St. Mary's City harbor*

The colonists had much for which to be thankful. They had arrived in early spring, and they busied themselves with planting gardens. Helpful Indians taught them how to plant corn. The rivers teemed with crabs, oysters, and fish, and the forests had plenty of deer and other animals. The Indians from whom they had bought their land left their huts for the colonists to live in until they had time to build their own houses.

The founding of Maryland is important because it showed that in America, Catholics would be able to worship freely. Although Maryland was founded as a haven for Catholics, in 1649 the colony passed an act providing that anyone who believed in God would enjoy freedom of worship there as well.

The Carolinas: The "Southern Plantation"

By 1650, some of the Virginia colonists had moved south into what is now North Carolina. To distinguish the area from Virginia, the colonists began calling it "Southern Plantation." Thus, the first settlers of what would become the Carolinas did not come from across the ocean—they came from Virginia. Other settlers soon came from England, Ireland, Germany, and the British West Indies. Some also migrated to the south from the New England Colonies. French Huguenots (Protestants who had been driven from France for their faith) settled there as well.

In 1663, eight English noblemen asked King Charles II of England for land to begin a colony in America. To reward them for their support of his reign, King Charles gave them the tract of land south of Virginia known as the Southern Plantation. The noblemen renamed the land **Carolina,** in honor of the king (*Carolus* is Latin for *Charles*). At the new colony's founding, its owners determined that the boundaries of Carolina stretched from the Atlantic Ocean westward all the way to the South Pacific! They did not know how far Carolina was from the West Coast. The great size of our land would not be discovered until explorers and pioneers ventured farther west in the years ahead.

As the owners of Carolina, these eight noblemen could make their own laws for the settlers to obey. Their main goal was to make money from the new colony. In 1670, they ordered the little village of Charles Town be built. (Charles Town later became the city of **Charleston,** South Carolina.) They eventually moved Charles Town to a better location with a good harbor, where ships could bring settlers from Europe and goods for the settlers to buy. As a result, Charles Town, South Carolina's first permanent settlement, grew rapidly.

The noblemen failed to set up a good government for the settlers of Carolina. They passed unjust laws for the colonists to obey and took land unfairly from the Native Americans. Angered, the Indians fought the settlers. After many years, the noblemen sold their land back to the king of England.

The Carolinas. The king divided the land into two colonies, North Carolina and South Carolina, and appointed a governor for each colony. Although once joined, the two colonies soon developed distinctive characteristics, making each one different from the other.

South Carolina grew quickly. The colonists found that **rice, cotton,** and **indigo** (a plant native to India from which a blue dye is made) grew very well there, although all three crops required much work to grow and harvest. Wealthier settlers soon built large **plantations** to grow these valuable crops. Because there were not enough white settlers

The Colonial Heritage

The Drayton Hall Plantation was completed in 1742.

to work in the fields, the plantation owners began to buy slaves from Africa to do the work.

North Carolina did not grow as quickly as South Carolina. Most of the people who settled North Carolina were poor, simple, and hard working. Many built log cabins on smaller farms. Because most landowners planted and worked their own fields, there were fewer slaves in North Carolina.

Georgia: Last of the Thirteen Colonies

England, 1732. Over a hundred years had passed since England had begun its first successful colony in the New World. As you have learned, twelve English colonies struggled to success during those years. Now, England planned to establish its thirteenth colony—a colony for the poor and unemployed.

Many of the poor people in England were willing to work, but they could not find jobs. At that time, if a person could not pay his bills, he was thrown into prison. Of course, he could do nothing to pay his debts while in jail. Unless he knew someone who would pay his debts for him, he would spend the rest of his life in prison.

In the 1700s, England's prisons were crowded with poor people. Prisons in those days were dirty, cold, and wet. Diseases spread quickly. The jailers were cruel, often beating their prisoners and taking away their food. Many prisoners died of starvation or disease.

James Oglethorpe. James Oglethorpe, a member of the English Parliament, studied these problems of the poor. "If only the poor could go to America! Then, they would have a chance to prosper," he thought. But how could they pay their way across the Atlantic?

King George II considered Oglethorpe's idea and decided that he liked it. A colony south of the Carolinas would provide a buffer between the Spanish colony in Florida and the English colonies farther north. He reasoned that if England did not colonize the region, Spain probably would before long. Thus, <u>the king appointed a group of men called *Trustees* to choose settlers for the new colony, write laws for the colonists to follow, and govern</u>

128 *New World History & Geography*

the new colony. Parliament gave these men the money needed to transport the colonists to the New World, and many churches and wealthy families donated food and supplies for the expedition. When the people of England heard of the opportunity to go to the new colony, so many responded that Oglethorpe had to turn some away. In fact, no debtors were able to join the first voyage.

A new colony. The new colony would be named Georgia, in honor of King George II. James Oglethorpe traveled with over 100 colonists who were chosen to go on the first ship sent to Georgia. He was a compassionate man—onboard the ship, he visited the sick and helped the colonists in whatever way he could. As they began settling the new colony, Oglethorpe often used his own money to meet the needs of the colonists.

In February 1733, the colonists arrived in Georgia. James Oglethorpe acted as their first governor, and in many ways, proved to be a wise, brave, and kind leader. He made lasting friendships with the Indians from whom he bought the land. They presented him with a buffalo robe lined with eagle feathers, saying: "The eagle's feathers are soft and signify love; the buffalo's skin is warm and means protection: therefore, love and protect our families." Presenting them with gifts of his own, Oglethorpe promised to protect them and to ensure fair trade among Indians and colonists. He kept his promises.

Not long after arriving in the new colony, James Oglethorpe planned and directed the building of the first Georgian settlement, **Savannah.** When war broke out between Spain and England, Spain tried to destroy the English settlement of Georgia, but Oglethorpe successfully defended the colony. Without his aid, Georgia may not have remained a British colony.

Growth in Georgia. Following the king's wishes, the colonists tried to grow olive trees and breed silkworms, but they were not successful. Soon rice became an important crop in the colony, and the first fine cotton was raised there with seed brought from India.

A variety of people settled in Georgia; some sought religious freedom and others sought economic opportunity. Among the early settlers were Englishmen, German Lutherans and Moravians, Swiss Calvinists, and Scottish Covenanters. Oglethorpe, wanting to give his colony a good start, prohibited rum and slaves. Both he and **John Wesley,** who was in Georgia at that time, tried to persuade the colonists that they would be far better off if they did their own work and stayed sober. The people listened for a while, but they later decided that they wanted both rum and slavery in their colony.

James Oglethorpe formed lasting friendships with the Indians that he purchased land from.

The Colonial Heritage 129

George Whitefield, the great preacher of colonial America, visited Georgia several times and established the first orphanage in the English colonies in 1740.

After more success against the Spanish, Oglethorpe was promoted to General in the British army, and, in 1743, he returned home to England. Because the colony did not prosper under the Trustees' government, the Trustees surrendered their rule to the British crown in 1752. Georgia then became a royal colony, like Virginia. Back in England, Oglethorpe remained interested in the colony he founded and lived to see it join the other colonies in 1776 as part of the United States of America.

Churches and Schools in the Southern Colonies

The Southern Colonies had fewer churches than the other colonies. The Southern colonists planted large farms that separated the families from each other. Rather than traveling many miles each Sunday to meet in churches, the colonists would wait for traveling preachers to come preach to them. Sometimes an Anglican (Church of England) priest would travel around to the farms and perform Anglican services for the many Southerners who belonged to the Church of England.

For a long time, there were few schools in the South. The wealthy planters paid tutors to come to their homes and teach their children privately, but the people of smaller farms could not afford these tutors. Eventually, parents in some areas of the South started to get together to hire teachers for their children. Sometimes, a teacher and students would meet in a shabby building in an old field, in what was called an **old-field school.** This is the kind of school that young George Washington attended. One year, he had to ride ten miles on horseback every day to attend his old-field school. Another year, he rowed a boat across the river every day, even when it was storming, to get to school.

old-field school

Comprehension Check 7E

Identify

1. The Catholic man who asked the king of England for land in America for a colony where Catholics and others would be free to worship.
2. South Carolina's first permanent settlement.
3. The brave and kind leader of English settlers in Georgia and the name of the first settlement of Georgia which this man planned.
4. The name of the founder of the first orphanage in the English colonies and the location of that orphanage.

Think

5. Why is the House of Burgesses an important part of our nation's history?
6. Compare schools and churches in the New England Colonies with schools and churches in the Southern Colonies. List the main differences.

7.6 THE GREAT AWAKENING

Colonial America experienced amazing spiritual revival from about 1730 to 1760 in what became known as the **Great Awakening**. The leaders of the Great Awakening have been called the spiritual Founding Fathers of America, for their teaching did much to shape the spiritual heritage of the country.

In the 1700s, many of the colonists had never made a personal decision to accept Christ as their Savior, though they went to church and tried to live good lives. Many were depending on their good works to get them to Heaven. In most of the colonies, only church members could vote, which encouraged unsaved people to become members. Nine of the colonies had official churches, and the people had to pay taxes to support those churches. Often, people joined churches to gain favor with government officials. This kind of religion pleased the church leaders who wanted many members, but it did nothing for the people, because it did not help them to personally accept Christ.

Jonathan Edwards: A Great Puritan Preacher

Jonathan Edwards, one of the first leaders in the Great Awakening, was born in Connecticut in 1703, the only boy in a family of eleven children. He began to read almost as soon as he could speak. When he was just seven years old, he could read books in English and Latin, and he also knew some Greek and Hebrew. Jonathan excelled in arithmetic and science, too. At the age of twelve, he studied spiders and wrote an amazing paper about them. When he was thirteen, he went to Yale College, where he was an outstanding student.

As a boy, Jonathan tried hard to be right with God. He made up a list of good resolutions to follow, and for a while he prayed five times a day. But none of these good works gave him peace with God. Finally, at the age of eighteen, he stopped trusting his good works and accepted Christ as his personal Savior. Now he had peace with God.

In 1734, Jonathan Edwards preached a series of sermons about salvation in his Congregational church in Northampton, Massachusetts, and a wonderful thing happened. The Spirit of God moved over the congregation, convicting the people of their sins and their need for Christ. "There was scarcely a single person in the town, old or young," Edwards wrote, "left unconcerned about the great things of the eternal world . . . souls did as it were come by flocks to Jesus Christ."

What a change this revival brought to the town of Northampton! Jonathan Edwards wrote this about it:

> This work of God, as it was carried on, and the number of true saints multiplied, soon made a glorious alteration in the town; so that in the spring and summer following . . . the town seemed to be full of the presence of God. . . .

There was a change in the homes of the town, too:

> There were remarkable tokens of God's presence in almost every house. It was a time of joy in families on account of salvation being brought unto them; parents rejoicing over their children as new born, and husbands over their wives, and wives over their husbands.

This great moving of the Spirit of God upon individuals, households, and whole communities spread throughout New England and eventually to most of the colonies. But opposition soon arose. The Congregational church leaders, who disagreed with Edwards' beliefs, ordered him to stop preaching in Northampton.

The Colonial Heritage

George Whitefield, a popular preacher during the Great Awakening, usually preached outdoors, in open fields.

This did not keep Edwards from serving the Lord. In 1750, he moved to the little frontier town of Stockbridge, Massachusetts, where he served as church pastor to a small congregation of white settlers and as missionary to the nearby Indians. The lower income made it more difficult for him to provide for his wife and the eight children who were still at home, but he remained faithful in his ministry. Because he had more time there, he was able to write some important books about the Bible. His preaching and writing did much to turn the people of America back to the Biblical truths, and it is the Bible, above all, that has made America a great nation.

Jonathan Edwards was one of the most intelligent men in colonial America as well as one of the best educated. (For a time, he served as president of the Presbyterian college which became Princeton University.) But it was his faithful preaching of God's Word that made him great and that blessed America.

George Whitefield: The Great Evangelist to America

Perhaps the most popular man in the colonies in the early 1700s was **George Whitefield** [hwĭt′fēld/], a great preacher from England. When Whitefield first came to America in 1738, he preached in many different kinds of churches. After hearing the great evangelist, many preachers started telling their own people how to get right with God, a thing they had sadly neglected to do.

In Georgia, Whitefield preached the gospel and started the first orphanage in the British colonies in 1738. He returned to England the next year, sometimes preaching to crowds of 20,000 people at once. He traveled thousands of miles to carry the gospel to the people of England, Scotland, and Wales.

In 1739, Whitefield sailed to Philadelphia to begin the second of his seven tours of America. During these tours, he preached from Georgia to New England, spreading the

132 New World History & Geography

gospel and collecting offerings for his orphanage. Whitefield usually preached outdoors in open fields, a practice he had begun in England, in order to accommodate the great crowds that gathered to hear him.

One good friend of George Whitefield was the great American inventor and statesman **Benjamin Franklin.** When Whitefield preached in Philadelphia, Franklin was so impressed by the change that took place in the people that he wrote in his *Autobiography:*

It was wonderful to see the change soon made in the manners of our inhabitants. From being thoughtless or indifferent about religion, it seemed as if all the world were growing religious, so that one could not walk through the town in an evening without hearing psalms sung in different families of every street.

Because George Whitefield believed that the gospel is for all people, he wanted to help everyone—children, adults, American Indians, slaves, poor people, rich people, orphans, people with no education, and people with

People in History
Phillis Wheatley: Child of the Great Awakening

Around the year 1760, an eight-year-old girl ran through the jungles of western Africa, terror gripping her heart. Men from another tribe were chasing her, intent on selling her and other members of her village to slave traders. The men soon caught the girl and loaded her onto a crowded ship bound for America.

The ship carried the terrified child to Boston, where John Wheatley, a tailor, bought her as a servant for his wife. The Wheatleys treated the girl like a second daughter, and they named her *Phillis*—Phillis Wheatley.

The Wheatley family soon realized that Phillis was extremely intelligent. She learned the English language in only sixteen months, and the Wheatleys taught her to read and write. They also taught her about Christ and the way of salvation. Phillis was an eager learner, and they let her spend much of her time learning geography, history, Latin, Greek, and the Bible. At the age of thirteen, she wrote her first poem, in honor of George Whitefield.

Phillis did not feel bitter that she was a slave but thankful, because her slavery had given her a chance to hear about Christ and accept Him as her Savior. She wrote about God's mercy in one of her most famous poems (to the right).

Phillis was sickly most of her life, and in 1773, the Wheatleys took her to England for medical care. While there, she was often invited to the homes of many English lords and ladies, who enjoyed her company. It was also in England where her book of poetry was published. Phillis sent this book to George Washington, who was so delighted with her work that he invited her to visit him.

Phillis Wheatley died in 1784 at around age thirty. Though her life was brief, she used her wonderful talents to benefit other people. She is remembered in history as the first black woman writer in America to have a book published, and she was also one of our country's earliest popular poets. Her life was one of hard work, study, cheerfulness, and thankfulness to God for her salvation.

On Being Brought from Africa to America

'Twas mercy brought me from
   my pagan land,
Taught my benighted soul to
   understand
That there's a God,
   that there's a Saviour too:
Once I redemption neither
   sought nor knew.
Some view our sable race with
   scornful eye,
"Their color is a diabolic die."
Remember Christians,
   Negroes, black as Cain,
May be refin'd, and join
   th' angelic train.

The Colonial Heritage

much education. Whitefield became very concerned about the slaves in America. He had Benjamin Franklin print a letter from him urging the colonists to treat the slaves with more kindness. This letter was printed in newspapers all over the colonies. Many times, Whitefield preached directly to the slaves. He also wrote a gospel tract for Indians.

George Whitefield preached over 18,000 sermons between 1736 and 1770 to over ten million people! His preaching of the gospel—that each person needs to be saved—affected all areas of American life. Whitefield's care for orphans provided an example for others to help and educate young children. His interest in the slaves and his efforts to preach to them encouraged others to treat them kindly. His interest in the Indians inspired many people to become missionaries. Because he saw the importance of education, he influenced the founding of about fifty colleges in America.

How the Great Awakening Shaped America

Because of the Great Awakening, many Americans became missionaries. The first American missionaries went to settlers on the frontiers of America and to the Indians. Partly because of the Great Awakening, America would later become known as a great missionary nation, and Americans would go to all corners of the earth to preach the gospel. Even today, America has more Christian missionaries around the world than any other country. This missionary spirit is probably one of the reasons God has blessed the nation so richly.

David Brainerd, a native of Connecticut, was one of the first missionaries spurred by the Great Awakening to do great things for God. After his death, other great missionaries followed his example. At first, they worked among the Indians and the settlers on the frontier; later, they began going to Canada and then overseas. In 1812, America's first overseas missionary, Adoniram Judson, would go to Burma (now called Myanmar).

The preaching of George Whitefield, Jonathan Edwards, and the other leaders of the Great Awakening helped the colonists to see more than ever that all men are equal before God. The Great Awakening did more than perhaps anything else to draw the colonists together so that our country would truly become one nation under God.

The colonists saw that since all men are equal in the eyes of God, no man is better than any other man. Therefore, all men should be equal in the sight of the law. All deserve equal justice, no matter who they are and no matter what their religious beliefs may be. This truth paved the way for the colonists to write just a few years later:

> We hold these truths to be self-evident:—That all men are created equal; that they are endowed by their Creator with certain unalienable rights; that among these are life, liberty, and the pursuit of happiness. (from the Declaration of Independence)

Christian thought and Biblical principles influenced many other areas of American life such as architecture, music, philosophy, poetry, and history. In addition to promoting moral living, Christianity gave people a sense of the nobility of hard work. The Scriptures played a major role in early American history and are still helping to shape our nation today.

Comprehension Check 7F

Identify

1. The spiritual revival that took place in the colonies from the 1730s to the 1760s.
2. The great Congregational preacher who led many to Christ during this spiritual revival.
3. The English evangelist who was famous for traveling through the colonies, preaching at large open-air meetings during the 1700s.
4. The first black woman writer in America to publish a book.

Think

5. Describe the effect(s) the Great Awakening had on the American colonies.

Chapter 7 Checkup

I. Tell why these **people** are important.

Explorers
Ponce de Leon
John Cabot
Henry Hudson
Samuel de Champlain

Governors
John White
Lord De La Warr
John Carver
William Bradford
John Winthrop
Peter Stuyvesant

Colony Founders
Sir Walter Raleigh
Roger Williams
John Mason
Thomas Hooker
William Penn
Sir George Carteret
Lord John Berkeley
George Calvert
James Oglethorpe

Rulers
Queen Elizabeth I
King James I
King Charles I

Noted Individuals
Captain John Smith
Virginia Dare
Captain Miles Standish
Samoset
Squanto
Chief Massasoit
John Rolfe
Phillis Wheatley

Religious Groups/Leaders
Separatists
Elder Brewster
Puritans
John Eliot
Quakers
Count von Zinzendorf
Moravians
Jonathan Edwards
George Whitefield
David Brainerd

II. Tell why these **settlements** or **cities** are important.

Settlements
St. Augustine
Roanoke
Jamestown

New England Colonies
Massachusetts Bay
Plymouth
Hartford

Middle Colonies
New Netherlands
New Amsterdam
Philadelphia
Fort Christina

Southern Colonies
Williamsburg
St. Mary's City
Charleston
Savannah

III. Identify the following.

Pilgrims
B.C.
A.D.
time line
Spanish Armada
London Company
Susan Constant, Godspeed, Discovery
Mayflower Compact
Massachusetts Bay Company
Ole' Deluder Satan Act
hornbook
New England Primer
Harvard College
Half Moon
Fundamental Orders of Connecticut
log cabin
royal colony
tobacco
House of Burgesses
Ark and *Dove*
old-field school
Great Awakening

IV. Give the noted event for these **dates**.
1492
1607
1620
1630
1647
1730–1760

V. Identify the locations from **Map Mastery 10**.

The Colonial Heritage 135

Chapter 8

United States History:
GEORGE WASHINGTON and the NEW WORLD'S FIRST REPUBLIC

8.1 YOUNG HERO OF THE FRENCH AND INDIAN WAR

The French Settle New France

While the English were building their first successful settlement at Jamestown (1607), the French were building Quebec, their first permanent settlement in New France, the French territory in the New World. Before long, both countries had claimed the land along the **Ohio River** between the Appalachian Mountains and the Mississippi River. To strengthen her claim, France built forts along the Ohio River.

As the English colonists began to move west of the Appalachians, they entered land that both the French and the English claimed as their own. When the English began to clear the land and build homes, the French fur traders became concerned that the fur-bearing animals would become scarce. The French reacted by strengthening their forts and stirring up the American Indians. They told the Indians that the English settlers were enemies who would destroy the hunting grounds and take over the land. Before long, the French had persuaded the Indians to join them in a fight against the English.

Bands of Indians, often accompanied by the French, began raiding English frontier settlements in the early 1700s. Without warning, these groups would attack the settlers and burn their cabins. Men, women, and children were often killed, but sometimes they were taken captive by the Indians. The Indians

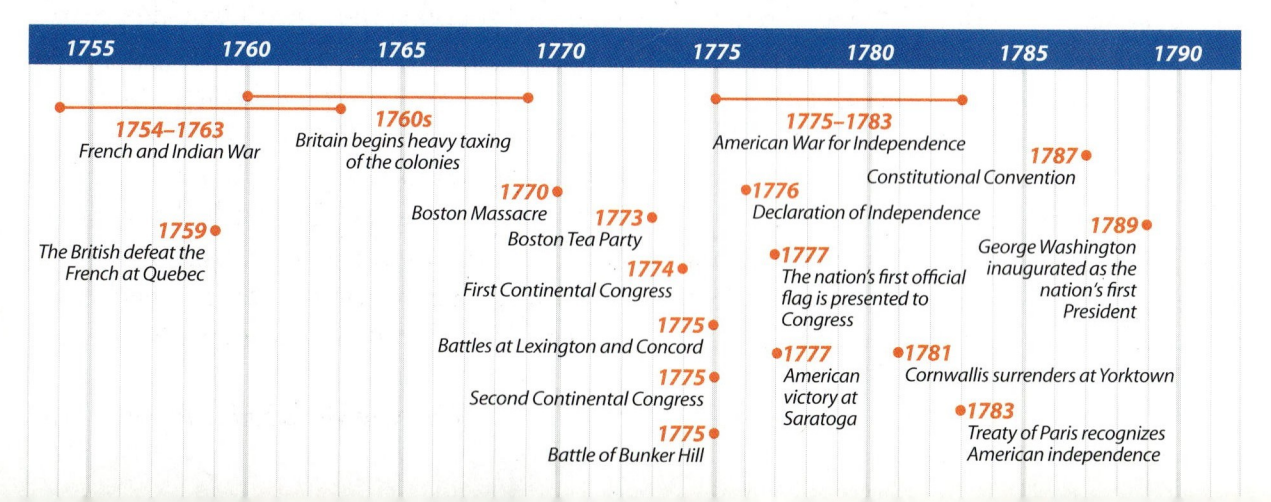

Timeline: 1755 – 1790

- **1754–1763** French and Indian War
- **1759** The British defeat the French at Quebec
- **1760s** Britain begins heavy taxing of the colonies
- **1770** Boston Massacre
- **1773** Boston Tea Party
- **1774** First Continental Congress
- **1775** Battles at Lexington and Concord
- **1775** Second Continental Congress
- **1775** Battle of Bunker Hill
- **1775–1783** American War for Independence
- **1776** Declaration of Independence
- **1777** The nation's first official flag is presented to Congress
- **1777** American victory at Saratoga
- **1781** Cornwallis surrenders at Yorktown
- **1783** Treaty of Paris recognizes American independence
- **1787** Constitutional Convention
- **1789** George Washington inaugurated as the nation's first President

George Washington's wisdom and strong character made him a great leader during the War for Independence.

would either sell their captives as servants to the French colonists or keep them as slaves. Many times, English children were adopted by the Indian tribes and reared as Indian children. These attacks increased the tensions between the English and the French.

The French and Indian War

Between 1689 and 1763, France and England fought four wars, the last of which had a great effect on the history of our country. Unlike the three previous wars, this last war began in America and spread to Europe. Because the French and Indians allied themselves against the British, this war is known as the **French and Indian War** in America, where it lasted from 1754 to 1763. In Europe, where the war lasted from 1756 to 1763, it was called the Seven Years' War.

George Washington delivers a message. In 1753, Governor Dinwiddie of Virginia, determined to defend England's claim to the Ohio Country, decided to send a messenger to the French officer at distant **Fort le Boeuf** [lə bŭf] and ask the French to leave. The messenger would have to travel hundreds of miles through the wilderness to reach the French fort. The governor decided that **George Washington,** a twenty-one-year-old Virginian with a reputation for being both brave and wise, was just the one to deliver the message.

Accompanied by an interpreter and a guide, Washington left on a chilly October day. As he and his men crossed the mountains, they watched for the danger of Indian attack. After weeks of traveling through the wilderness, they reached Fort le Boeuf. The French officer read the message from the governor of Virginia that young Washington handed him and then politely explained that the French did not intend to give up the land. Noting the preparations the French had already made to fortify the region, Washington could see that the English would have to fight for their claim.

The French officer quickly wrote a firm response to the English governor and sent the messengers on their way. Winter had set in, and the men had to battle heavy snowstorms. Once, George Washington nearly drowned when he fell into the icy Allegheny River. After several difficult weeks, Washing-

The New World's First Republic 137

ton delivered the French officer's response to the governor of Virginia.

The governor decided to raise a small army of colonists and drive the French out of the Ohio Valley. By 1754, George Washington's courageous journey through the wilderness to Fort le Boeuf had made him a hero among the Virginians. The governor promoted Washington to a lieutenant colonel in the colonial militia. Although Washington and his men fought bravely, they were greatly outnumbered and were forced to surrender. George Washington had led the first battle of the French and Indian War.

British soldiers join the colonists. Seeing that the colonists could not defeat the French by themselves, the king of England made **General Edward Braddock** the commander of all British forces in the North American colonies and sent him with an army of trained soldiers to America. Many colonists volunteered to help the British soldiers drive the French out of the land. When General Braddock heard about George Washington's brave feats, he asked him to serve on his staff as an aide. Washington, who loved his country and would fight for it, gladly accepted the invitation.

The British troops looked impressive in their red uniforms. They could march together in perfect step and knew all of the rules of war in Europe. They would not think of hiding behind a tree or rock to shoot. To them, such maneuvers would be cowardly. According to the rules of European warfare, they must fight out in the open. But in America, the Indians had their own rules for war. Unlike the British, the colonial soldiers wore clothes made out of homespun material and buckskin. They could not march in perfect step, nor did they know the rules for fighting in Europe. But they knew better than the British the rules for fighting in America.

The British are defeated. In July of 1755, Braddock gathered his British soldiers along with colonial militia (volunteer soldiers) and a few American Indians in a march to take **Fort Duquesne** [doo̅/kān/], a French frontier stronghold. Washington, as well as other colonists, warned General Braddock that the French and their Indian allies hid behind trees and bushes while they shot. The British would make easy targets in their red uniforms. But General Braddock ignored their cautions and insisted that his men would not fight like "cowards." With drums beating, General Braddock led his army through the forest. The British had to widen the narrow trail to accommodate their wagons of food and supplies, greatly slowing their progress. A long line of unprotected soldiers and wagons stretched out for miles.

As the group marched toward Fort Duquesne, shots suddenly rang out. The woods were full of French soldiers and Indians hiding behind trees, rocks, and bushes. The colonists jumped behind

French and Indian War

138 *New World History & Geography*

General Braddock suffered a defeat at Fort Duquesne.

trees and fought back, but the British soldiers fought where they stood. Because they could not see their enemy, they did not know where to aim their guns. In their famous red coats, the British made easy targets for their well-hidden opponents, and more than half of the men were killed. When a bullet hit General Braddock, the British soldiers lost courage and ran. As the battle continued over several hours, George Washington again proved himself a leader, encouraging his fellow soldiers in the effort. When the enemy shot his horse out from under him, Washington quickly mounted another, and when they shot that horse, too, he bravely mounted a third horse and kept fighting. Though pieces of his coat were torn by bullets, Washington was not hurt. He later wrote the following in a letter to his brother:

> By the all-powerful dispensations of Providence, I have been protected beyond all human probability or expectation; for I had four bullets through my coat, and two horses shot under me, yet escaped unhurt, although death was leveling my companions on every side of me!

The British lost this battle, but God had spared twenty-three-year-old George Washington for a greater purpose.

Victories come at last. General Braddock died shortly after the battle, leaving the British without a general to lead their army. The war continued for several years, and the British lost many battles. The strong French army, with the help of many Indians, gradually gained control of the vast frontier. While the British army could not be everywhere at once, Indian tribes all along the frontier destroyed homes and killed and captured the settlers who were too spread out to fight together.

Finally, in 1758, the king of Great Britain sent the much-needed relief of another army, under more capable leadership, to the colonies. Soon the British began to take the French forts in the Ohio Valley. <u>With the help of George Washington and the Virginia militia, the English drove the French completely out of the Ohio Valley</u>.

<u>The French still controlled most of what is now Canada, however.</u> If they were allowed to stay there, they could rebuild their strength

The New World's First Republic 139

and threaten the English colonies again. The British decided that Quebec, the most important settlement in New France, must be captured. As long as the French army occupied part of North America, the war would not be over.

Victory at Quebec. Attacking Quebec would not be easy. The settlement stood high on a cliff beside the St. Lawrence River. Because the French thought it would be impossible for the English to climb such a steep rock without being seen, they left the cliff unguarded.

Late one night in 1759, British soldiers quietly climbed the steep rock. Imagine the surprise of the French the next morning when more than 4,000 British soldiers stood outside their city, ready to attack. After a bitter fight, the French had to surrender. The British flag soon flew over Quebec. The war continued after the capture of Quebec, but the French had lost their advantage and gradually lost the war due to defeats not only in North America but also abroad.

Thus, with the victory of the French and Indian War, Britain gained control of North America east of the Mississippi River. The American colonists were now free to settle west of the Appalachians, and they would soon discover how much they valued the freedoms they enjoyed.

Comprehension Check 8A

Identify
1. The river along which both France and Britain had claimed lands.
2. The war France and Britain fought in the New World between 1754 and 1763.
3. The young Virginian that Governor Dinwiddie sent to the Ohio Country with a message for the French.

Think
4. Why did the Indians side with the French during the French and Indian War?

8.2 THREATS TO AMERICAN FREEDOMS

A New King

Before the French and Indian War was over, Britain had a new king, **George III.** When the war ended in 1763, Great Britain was the most powerful kingdom in the world, and King George wanted even more power for himself. To show his might, he decided to bring the American colonies under greater British control. Because 3,000 miles of ocean separated England from the New World, the British government did not govern the colonies directly. Instead, nearly all of the thirteen colonies were under a system of self-government. By the mid-1700s, many colonists had been born in America and had never seen British soil. While some colonists felt great loyalty to their mother country, others began to view themselves more as American colonists and less as British citizens. When King George started tightening control, opposition arose in the colonies.

George III

The Stamp Act

King George and Parliament decided that the colonists should pay for the protection that the British army had given them during the French and Indian War, even though the colonists had actually done much of the fighting. One of the laws passed in 1765 to control the colonies and pay for war expenses, the **Stamp Act,** required that newspapers, almanacs, marriage certificates, and other documents purchased by the colonists have special stamps or seals affixed to them proving that the purchasers had paid a special tax for the documents. (A **tax** is money that people pay to their government for use in helping to run the government.)

Unlike the people of England, the colonists could not send a representative to Parliament to represent them and protect their rights. Because they had no say in the taxes they had to pay, the colonists felt that the taxes were unjust. To show their disapproval of the Stamp Act, the colonists refused to buy the stamps and British goods. Men from nine colonies decided at a meeting in New York, the Stamp Act Congress, that the colonists should complain to the king. <u>In 1766, the British government felt forced to drop the Stamp Act</u>.

the Boston Massacre depicted in a political cartoon by Paul Revere

The Boston Massacre

Taxes, however, did not stop with the repeal of the Stamp Act. Next, the British government proposed a new tax on glass, paint, paper, and tea sold in the American colonies. Many colonists refused to buy the imported goods that carried the tax, still insisting that the taxes were unjust. Others, however, began to desire more than just representation in Parliament—they began to long for freedom. <u>Those who wanted America to be free from Britain's heavy control</u> soon became known as **patriots.**

When the people of Boston grew restless over the new taxes, England sent soldiers to keep the peace and force the colonists to obey. On a cold, snowy evening in March 1770, a small mob of ruffians began throwing snowballs at a British soldier. Some of the mob began throwing stones as well. British soldiers came running to stop the fight. Suddenly, an unknown person shouted the order to fire. In the confusion, the soldiers fired their guns, and five colonists were killed. Crispus Attucks, a black merchant seaman, was the first to fall and therefore one of the first to die in the American colonies' struggle for freedom.

The people of Boston angrily called this incident the **"Boston Massacre."**

Realizing that the tax on glass, paint, paper, and tea was causing more trouble than it was worth, England dropped all of the taxes but one. To show the colonists that the British government still had the right to tax them, <u>Britain kept a small tax on tea</u>. Of course, many colonists refused to buy tea from England.

The Boston Tea Party

After three years passed and many colonists still refused to buy tea from England, the British government decided to entice them to buy tea by making it available at a lower price. Three ships loaded with bargain-priced tea sailed into Boston Harbor. On a chilly December night in 1773, about 50 colonists dressed like Mohawk Indians boarded the ships, smashed open over 300 chests of tea with their tomahawks, and dumped the tea into the water. Then they quietly went back to

The New World's First Republic

their homes. This event became known as the **Boston Tea Party.**

News of the Boston Tea Party spread quickly to the other colonies. Many colonists cheered the people of Boston for their courage. Others said that the men had wrongfully destroyed the property of others. Everyone wondered what England would do next. To discipline the colonies, England closed Boston Harbor. Because no ships could sail in or out, the people of Boston had no way of buying supplies or food. The British government announced that the port would stay closed until the citizens paid for the tea they destroyed. If the harbor remained closed, the people of Boston could starve to death.

When the other colonies heard of the laws forced upon the people of Boston, they sent gifts. South Carolina sent food, Virginia sent grain, and Connecticut and New York sent herds of sheep and cattle. A feeling of kinship spread through the colonies as they rushed to aid a city in need. The English were able to keep ships from sailing into Boston's port, but they could not keep other colonists from traveling over the New England paths and hills to bring food and supplies to the people of Boston.

The Quebec Act

Another act of Parliament that horrified the colonists was the **Quebec Act.** This law extended the boundaries of Quebec as far west as the Mississippi River and as far south as the Ohio River. Thus the frontier land in the Ohio Valley for which the colonists had fought so valiantly in the French and Indian War was now closed to them. Worse yet,

the Boston Tea Party

Parliament had made Catholicism the main religion of Quebec, thereby raising fears that this vast territory would be closed to Bible reading, evangelism, and free churches.

The First Continental Congress

In September of 1774, about fifty men from the colonies met in Philadelphia. They put into writing a request that their rights as Englishmen be respected, and they agreed not to buy goods made in Great Britain. This meeting was called the **First Continental Congress.** Determined to force the colonists to obey, King George III responded by sending warships and more soldiers to the colonies.

The Colonists Prepare to Fight

After the British warships and soldiers arrived in the colonies, the colonists began to train as soldiers and to hide gunpowder and ammunition. Many Massachusetts men called themselves **minutemen** because they said they could be ready to fight at a minute's notice. A fight seemed certain when England would not compromise, and, as a result of the Boston Tea Party, Boston was ruled by the British military. Many colonists volunteered to join the militia and fight for the freedoms they valued. These patriot soldiers came from all walks of life: many were farmers, and some were little more than boys. One black minuteman, **Lemuel Haynes,** interrupted his studies for the ministry to join the militia. God protected him through the war, including the important battle at Fort Ticonderoga, and he went on to become a great Congregational preacher in New England.

Many colonists hoped that once King George realized they meant business, he would give them their rights again. Some did not want to fight Britain at all. Understanding what great freedoms were at stake, a young Virginian named **Patrick Henry** gave a stirring speech to the House of Burgesses. In his argument for fighting for independence, Patrick Henry cried:

> Is life so dear, or peace so sweet, as to be purchased at the price of chains and slavery? Forbid it, Almighty God! I know not what course others may take; but as for me, **give me liberty, or give me death!**

Around the time Patrick Henry made his speech in the spring of 1775, the British learned that the patriots were storing guns and ammunition in the town of Concord, Massachusetts, and that two patriot leaders, John Hancock and Samuel Adams, were staying in the town of Lexington. Both Concord and Lexington were close to Boston. <u>Hoping to capture the patriot leaders and their supply of guns and ammunition, the British made plans to march to Lexington and Concord.</u>

The Midnight Ride of Paul Revere

Fortunately, a group of Boston patriots discovered Britain's plans and warned their fellow patriots across the Charles River, near Lexington and Concord, by flashing two lanterns in the belfry of the Old North Church. If the minutemen were warned, perhaps they could stop the British. **Paul Revere,** a well-known Boston patriot, saw the flashing lights and jumped on his horse. William Dawes, another patriot, joined Revere in his ride through the nighttime countryside. After learning of the British plot, Dr. Samuel Prescott became the third member of their party. To wake and warn the colonists, they shouted, "The British are coming!" The minutemen jumped out of their beds and prepared to fight.

Paul Revere rode through the night to warn the minutemen that the British were coming.

the Battle at Lexington

The Shot Heard 'round the World

When the British soldiers reached Lexington, a group of minutemen was waiting for them on the town green. Suddenly, the sound of a gunshot shattered the silence at Lexington. No one knows who fired the first shot, but it started the **American War for Independence** and signaled the birth of American freedom. From this shot would come a struggle for liberty that the whole world would watch with interest as a new country would be born. Because that one shot changed history, it has come to be called the "shot heard 'round the world."

After that first battle at **Lexington,** the British marched to **Concord,** where they found minutemen ready for battle. When the struggle had ended, the patriots had forced the British to retreat with severe losses. They could not even take the colonists' stores of ammunition because the minutemen had removed most of the supply already. With the battles of Lexington and Concord, the war had begun, but the purpose of the war was still unclear. Were the colonists going to fight for their rights as British subjects, or were they going to fight for their independence?

Comprehension Check 8B
Identify
1. The law requiring most printed materials to have a stamp or seal affixed to them proving that the purchasers had paid a special tax for the documents.
2. The skirmish between a group of Bostonians and some British soldiers which resulted in the deaths of five of the colonists.
3. The incident in which a band of colonists dressed like Mohawk Indians dumped tea into Boston Harbor in protest to Britain's tax on tea.
4. The meeting of colonists in Philadelphia to request that Britain respect their rights as Englishmen.
5. The battle location where the first shot in the American War for Independence was fired.

Think
6. Why did the colonists feel that the taxes imposed by Great Britain were unjust?

144 New World History & Geography

8.3 THE FIGHT FOR INDEPENDENCE

The Second Continental Congress

Because the king of England refused to listen to the colonists' list of complaints, representatives went to Philadelphia in May of 1775 for another meeting—the **Second Continental Congress.** Many important decisions were made at this meeting. Two of the most important were that (1) America must have an organized Continental Army, and (2) George Washington would command the new army. The Second Continental Congress would serve as the representative government for the American people over the next several years.

Ethan Allen and the Green Mountain Boys

On the very day that the Second Continental Congress convened in 1775, patriots in New England fought an important battle. **Ethan Allen** and a group of about 100 patriots who called themselves the **"Green Mountain Boys,"** decided to attack and take Fort Ticonderoga from the British. Located on the eastern shore of Lake Champlain, this fort guarded the main road between Canada and New York. In the early morning hours while the unsuspecting British slept, the Green Mountain Boys easily entered Fort Ticonderoga. Storming the fort, Ethan Allen then demanded that the British commander surrender. When the stunned commander saw that the fort was already captured, he knew he had no choice but to surrender.

The supplies inside the fort were most valuable to the Continental Army, for the colonists had few guns and little gunpowder to fight a war with the British. The patriots later used the cannons taken from Fort Ticonderoga to drive the British army out of Boston.

The Battle of Bunker Hill

A month later, British and American forces met again near Boston. In the darkness of night while the British soldiers were sleeping, more than a thousand colonists climbed Bunker Hill and Breed's Hill, which overlook Boston. All through the night, they dug *trenches* to protect themselves and to surround the city. When morning came, they surprised the British. On June 17, 1775, the **Battle of Bunker Hill** was fought. Many people who lived in Boston climbed on their roofs to watch the battle. Twice the British tried to climb the hill, but the colonists beat them back. When the British tried a third time, the colonists ran out of gunpowder and had to retreat. As a result, the British secured the first victory in a major battle of the War for Independence. Nevertheless, the Americans had shown the British that they could fight with determination even though they were not trained soldiers.

the Battle of Bunker Hill

King George Hires German Soldiers

Meanwhile, the Second Continental Congress continued meeting in Philadelphia. Many of the representatives still hoped that King George III would change his mind and that the Americans could become peaceful colonists of England once again. These hopes were soon crushed when the colonists learned that King George had hired German soldiers called **Hessians** [hĕsh′ənz] to help fight against the Americans. The colonial army had outnumbered the British, but the Hessian soldiers would take away the colonists' advantage. News of the hired soldiers destroyed most of the colonists' remaining loyalty to England. They realized that they must fight for independence from England. In 1776, the representatives of the Second Continental Congress asked that a declaration be written to state the reasons why the colonists wanted their independence.

The Declaration of Independence

The Second Continental Congress asked a committee of five men to work together to write the **Declaration of Independence**—Thomas Jefferson, John Adams, Benjamin Franklin, Roger Sherman, and Robert Livingston. Thomas Jefferson did the actual writing of the great document.

On July 2, 1776, the delegates agreed that the thirteen colonies should be free and independent states. The members of Congress then discussed the Declaration and made a few more changes to it. On July 4 (the day which we know as Independence Day, or the Fourth of July), the Declaration of Independence was officially adopted by twelve of the thirteen colonies. (New York, the last colony to vote, adopted the Declaration a few days later.)

The document was then copied by hand onto parchment paper and signed by the

signing the Declaration of Independence

146 *New World History & Geography*

congressional delegates. **John Hancock,** the President of the Congress, signed first. As Hancock wrote his name in large, clear letters, he said, "There, John Bull [meaning England] can read that without spectacles, and now may double his reward of five hundred pounds for my head." He knew what great danger he had put himself in by signing the Declaration of Independence. The English would know who he was, and they might want to hunt him down for signing his name to this document. Benjamin Franklin also realized the risk of signing the document; he warned the other delegates: "We must all hang together, or assuredly we shall all hang separately."

The People Hear the News

Copies of the Declaration were promptly made and distributed to each colony. In Philadelphia, the ringing of the **Liberty Bell** called the people of the town together. On this bell are written these words from the Bible: *"Proclaim liberty throughout all the land unto all the inhabitants thereof"* (Lev. 25:10). The people of Philadelphia gathered to hear the words of the Declaration of Independence.

Of course, there were no telephones, televisions, or radios to speed the news to the other colonies. Riders packed copies of the Declaration in their saddle bags and jumped on their horses. Over dusty roads, through shallow streams, and across creaking bridges they rode as fast as possible to carry the news. Even so, it took months for the people in some settlements to hear the news. Thus, our country's first Independence Day was celebrated on many different days, as each town or settlement heard the news. When the news came to a town, church bells rang, and guns and cannons were fired to salute the new nation.

General George Washington: Commander in Chief

The Declaration of Independence did not end the war, however, nor did it give the colonists their freedom. The Americans now had to prove that they meant what they said. They must win the war. No longer were they fighting for their rights as British colonists. They were fighting to become free and independent from England. All the world watched to see what would happen.

When the Second Continental Congress made **George Washington** commander in chief of the Continental Army in 1775, he accepted the honor with a sense of grave responsibility. Washington worked without pay to lead the Americans and even gave some of his own money to buy supplies for the army. Because he did perhaps more than any other man to help the United States gain independence, George Washington is often called the Father of His Country.

You will remember that the first fighting began around Boston. Now the British made plans to capture **New York City.** If the British controlled this city's excellent harbor, ships from England could easily bring the British army fresh food and supplies. General Washington moved his army to New York, where his men fought bravely but could not stop the British. The British army had gained control of New York City. General Washington then moved his army to New Jersey.

The New World's First Republic

George Washington's men rowed across the Delaware River on Christmas night to deliver a surprise attack on the Hessians at Trenton, New Jersey.

Patriots risk their lives. Despite the discouraging defeat at New York, the Americans kept on fighting for their freedom. **James Armistead,** a black slave, served the colonial army as a spy, risking his life to obtain important information from the British. Armistead, like many other slaves who fought for the colonies, was granted his freedom after the war for his courageous military service.

Another patriot, **Nathan Hale,** a young schoolteacher from Connecticut, volunteered to sneak behind enemy lines to find out what the British army was planning. He knew that if he were captured, he would be executed as a spy, but he did not worry about his own life; he wanted to serve his country no matter what the cost. The British did capture Nathan Hale and condemn him to death. The last words he spoke before he was hanged were, "I only regret that I have but one life to lose for my country."

Even the British were impressed with the bravery and patriotism of these great heroes. American soldiers everywhere were stirred and reminded that they, too, should be willing to give their lives to make America a free land.

Washington Crosses the Delaware

As Christmas approached, General Washington's men became discouraged. They had won few battles, their clothes were ragged, and their food and supplies were almost gone. Some soldiers gave up and went back to their homes. Though Washington was discouraged, too, he would not give up hope. He knew that over a thousand Hessians were staying in **Trenton,** New Jersey.

Defying the bitter cold and dodging the large chunks of ice that floated down the Delaware River, Washington's men rowed all that Christmas night until every one of his 2,000 soldiers had safely crossed the dangerous, icy Delaware River in small boats. Early in the morning, his soldiers surrounded Trenton and took the Germans by surprise.

While Washington's men were crossing the Delaware, the German soldiers had been celebrating Christmas. Now they were fast asleep. Imagine their surprise when they awoke to find themselves surrounded by the American army! After a battle, the Hessians surrendered and became Washington's prisoners. Hope began to return to the American army.

148 New World History & Geography

A Flag for Our Country

Americans had wanted a national flag for a long time. Many people had made their own flags with their own designs. Now the Second Continental Congress made this decision:

> Resolved, that the Flag of the United States be thirteen stripes, alternate red and white, that the "Union" be thirteen stars, white in a blue field. . . .

The thirteen stripes and thirteen stars stood for the thirteen colonies. Later, a new star would be added for each new state that became a part of the United States of America. According to an old story, **Betsy Ross** stitched together the first official American flag. On June 14, 1777, George Washington presented the new flag to Congress. June 14 has become known as **Flag Day.**

Comprehension Check 8C

Identify

1. The meeting held in Philadelphia in May 1775 and the two important decisions that were made.
2. The leader of the Green Mountain Boys and the British fort he captured.
3. The battle that took place on June 17, 1775, near Boston and proved Americans could fight with determination.
4. The date on which most of the delegates to the Second Continental Congress adopted the Declaration of Independence.

Think

5. What were some ways that colonists first celebrated our nation's independence from Great Britain?

8.4 INDEPENDENCE FOR AMERICA

The Battle of Saratoga

Having already captured New York City, the British now made plans to capture all of New York because it was the colony that separated the New England colonies from the other colonies. If the British controlled New York, the northern colonies would have no way of communicating with those in the South.

Fortunately, the American army was able to stop the British from capturing New York in the **Battle of Saratoga.** The Battle of Saratoga is often called the turning point of the American War for Independence, for, although this battle did not end the war, it did prove to the world that America had a chance of winning. France had been watching, and the Battle of Saratoga persuaded the king of France to help the Americans. Because news traveled slowly in those days, however, it would be a while before the French arrived to help.

The Winter at Valley Forge

More trouble lay ahead for the colonists. The British had captured Philadelphia and now planned to spend the winter in the warm homes of the colonists there. Washington's men were not so fortunate. Even the victory of Saratoga cheered them only for a time, because they had no warm place to spend the winter. When they failed to drive the British out of Philadelphia, Washington's army marched to nearby **Valley Forge,** where they would spend a dreadful winter, battling their worst enemies yet—hunger and cold.

The drafty log huts in which they stayed gave them little protection against the cruel winter storms. Washington had no money to buy badly needed food, clothes, blankets, or

The New World's First Republic 149

supplies for the men, who wore thin, ragged clothing and often did not even have shoes for their cold, sore feet. As they walked, they left bloody footprints in the snow. For the sick, there was very little medicine.

Although some of Washington's men gave up and went home, most braved the winter and waited for springtime, when they could begin fighting again. If these men had not been brave enough to stay, there might never have been a United States of America. The thought of a free country—their own country—gave them the strength to continue. The strength of their brave leader gave them courage, too. Someone has painted a picture of George Washington praying in the snow at Valley Forge. From what we know about Washington's character, this is probably exactly what he did, and he probably did it more than once.

Trouble on the Frontier

Some colonists had moved into the western frontier, which at that time included Vermont, the western parts of New York, Pennsylvania, Virginia, and the Carolinas, and the land as far west as the Mississippi River. Although the frontier had only a few small settlements, the British decided to stir up trouble there, too, by persuading some of the Indian tribes to fight against the colonists. While some tribes decided to help the Americans, others made war on the frontier settlements, killing and burning as they went.

A bold young man named **George Rogers Clark** led a group of men from Virginia down the Ohio River, through swamps and forests, to help the colonists. In the summer of 1778, Clark and his men captured two British posts (military stations) along the Mississippi River. Later, they captured an important fort in present-day Indiana. Because of Clark's successes, the Americans were able to control the northwest frontier.

Washington praying at Valley Forge

A New Navy

Before the War for Independence, the American colonists had relied on the British navy to protect them. Now the Americans needed a navy of their own. Of course, our new country could not afford to build a large, powerful navy. It would have to be a small one organized and commanded by determined men.

John Paul Jones, an American seaman from Scotland, became one of the first officers of our navy. His courage and determination helped our first navy to be successful. The most famous of his sea battles was a fight between the American ship the ***Bonhomme Richard*** (named after Benjamin Franklin's *Poor Richard's Almanack*) and the British ship the ***Serapis.*** The *Serapis* was a better equipped vessel, but Jones bravely engaged his smaller ship in a fight off the coast of Scotland. In the midst of the battle, John Paul Jones brought the *Bonhomme Richard* so close to the *Serapis* that the cannons of the two vessels almost touched.

The British officer onboard the *Serapis* demanded that the patriots surrender. With a clear, determined voice, John Paul Jones answered back, "I have not yet begun to fight!"

The guns of both ships boomed as they resumed firing. Many on both sides were killed. At last, the British officer surrendered his ship. As the victorious but badly damaged *Bonhomme Richard* sank, the Americans were able to board the *Serapis*. John Paul Jones took command of the British ship, eventually returning to America where he would be honored as one of our country's first naval heroes.

The War in the South

In 1778, the British decided to move their fighting to the southern colonies. From this time until the end of the war, most of the remaining battles of the War for Independence took place in the southern part of America. Under General **Lord Cornwallis,** the British captured Georgia and then almost all of South Carolina. General Washington sent one of his trusted generals, **Nathanael Greene,** to fight in the South. With Greene's help, the Americans reclaimed most of South Carolina and Georgia.

Victory at Yorktown. At last, the French navy arrived to help the Americans. When English General Cornwallis moved into **Yorktown,** Virginia, he expected help from the British navy. But before the British navy could reach Yorktown, the French navy sailed into the Chesapeake Bay. With the powerful French navy blocking the bay, Cornwallis was trapped. He could not sail out to escape, and no British ship could sail in to help him.

Meanwhile, General Washington had begun marching his army to Yorktown. Thousands of French soldiers joined him, until General Cornwallis's army was surrounded both at sea and on land. Although he knew it was hopeless, Cornwallis fought bravely. At last, on October 19, 1781, Cornwallis surrendered his army. Scattered fighting continued mainly on the high seas, but for most Americans, the war was over. America had won its independence.

The Americans realized that God had been with them in their struggle for freedom. Now, as General Washington himself recommended, prayers of thanksgiving were raised in the American army, in churches across this new nation, and in the homes and hearts of thankful Americans.

The Treaty of Paris

Although Cornwallis surrendered in 1781, almost two more years passed before England signed the **Treaty of Paris** in **1783.** (A treaty is an agreement or understanding between two or more countries.) Under this treaty, England gave up her American colonies and any claims to land east of the Mississippi. The colonies were now free and independent states.

battle between the Bonhomme Richard *and the* Serapis

151

North America—1783

The Treaty of Paris gave the Americans the land from Florida to Canada, and from the Atlantic Ocean to the Mississippi River. Part of the new land west of the thirteen colonies became known as the **Northwest Territory.** You will remember that George Rogers Clark battled his way through this wilderness to defeat the British on the frontier. His triumph in winning two posts and a fort was of great importance to our country. If Clark had not persevered and won, it is possible that our land would have gone only as far as the Ohio River.

Comprehension Check 8D

Identify

1. The battle that is often called the turning point of the American War for Independence.
2. The naval hero who said, "I have not yet begun to fight" and the circumstances under which he said this.
3. The leader of British forces when England captured Georgia and most of South Carolina, and the place where that leader surrendered his army.

Think

4. What character qualities did George Washington and his men show at Valley Forge?
5. What were the terms of the Treaty of Paris signed after the War for Independence?

8.5 Building a New Nation

Once the Americans had won the War for Independence, they busied themselves with the important task of building a new nation. The first challenge for the thirteen states was to achieve unity. Instead of acting as one big country, the thirteen states were acting as if they were thirteen small countries, each ruling itself. Many people were afraid of one strong government because it reminded them too much of the powerful British government from which they had just won their freedom.

The Articles of Confederation

The first plan of government that the states agreed upon was called the **Articles of Confederation.** This plan was adopted before American independence had been won. Under this plan, the government could not be strong. It had no power to tax. Though requests went out to the states for money, very little came in because the states knew that the government could not force them to give. Thus the new government had little money for anything. It also had no power to settle quarrels that might arise between two states. The states could refuse to do anything that the government asked them to do. In order for this government to work properly, all of the states would have to agree all the time. You can imagine the problems that would arise. This government was too weak to work.

The Constitution of the United States

Finally, in the summer of 1787, a meeting was held in **Philadelphia** to discuss what could be done to make our government stronger. This meeting, called the **Constitutional Convention,** was held in Independence Hall, where the Declaration of Independence had been signed eleven years earlier. Many wise and important delegates

152 New World History & Geography

gathered for this meeting. They chose George Washington to preside. Benjamin Franklin, now 81 years old, also attended. The man who did the most important work at this convention was **James Madison,** who would later become the fourth President of the United States.

The men at the convention quickly decided that America needed a brand new government. The plan for that new government, which our country still follows today, is the **Constitution of the United States.**

The political wisdom that our Founding Fathers showed at that convention has never been equaled. The Constitution of the United States has contributed to the happiness and progress of much of mankind. Although this document was written for America, the whole world has learned a lesson from it—

CONCEPTS TO CONSIDER
Civil Government

God established government after the Flood of Noah's day, when He said that if anyone killed another person, the murderer must be punished by death. This was God's command regarding capital punishment. ("Whoso sheddeth man's blood, by man shall his blood be shed: for in the image of God made he man." Gen. 9:6) Thus God ordained government to limit violence and bloodshed.

Civil government is a body or organization set up to rule the people of a certain area. Since the time of Noah, men have established many different forms of government, some of which were good and others which were bad. Throughout history, many people have lived under a **monarchy,** a government ruled by a king or queen. Monarchs usually inherit their authority from their family, and they usually rule until they die. Other titles given to monarchs include *sultan, czar* [zär], and *shah*. In an **absolute monarchy,** the ruler possesses absolute, or complete, power over his people. Everyone must do exactly as he says or be punished. In a **constitutional monarchy,** the ruler's power is limited by a constitution, and power is usually shared with an assembly that represents the people. Most nations that have kings or queens today are constitutional monarchies rather than absolute monarchies.

A **dictatorship** is a form of government ruled by a person who has absolute authority and who has come to power by the aid of friends or force rather than by inheritance. Like an absolute monarch, a dictator has total control over the people of his country. Many countries, such as Cuba, that have called themselves republics are actually dictatorships. In some cases, such as Communist China, a few top members of a political party will work together to dictate the rules. The result is basically the same as a dictatorship.

A government in which the people elect officials to represent them is called a **republic.** A republic's highest leader, who is often an elected president, shares the responsibility of running the government with many other elected officials. Citizens in a republic can choose to become actively involved in the process of government, voting which officials to elect or even becoming part of the government themselves. The Founding Fathers of the United States gave their country a republican form of government.

A **democracy** is a government in which the people hold the ruling power. The ancient Greeks were the first to develop the idea of citizens taking an active part in the government of their country. The word "democracy" comes from two Greek words that mean *people* and *rule*. It meant rule by laws that the people had made. A republic is a form of ***representative democracy.***

No matter what kind of government a country has, the Bible says that a Christian should respect his government's officials, obey their civil authority, and pray for them (Rom. 13:1–7; Prov. 24:21; 1 Pet. 2:13–16; 1 Tim. 2:1–2).

The New World's First Republic

what it means to be a free people. Everyone was convinced that the hand of God was at work in the convention. They also knew that no country can be strong without God's continuing help. At one point during the convention, it seemed that the states would never be able to reach an agreement. Benjamin Franklin finally stood and said:

> I have lived, Sir, a long time, and the longer I live, the more convincing proofs I see of this truth, that *God governs in the affairs of men.* And if a sparrow cannot fall to the ground without His notice, is it probable that an empire can rise without His aid?

Franklin proceeded to suggest that the Constitutional Convention begin each morning with prayer, asking for God's guidance and wisdom. Although this proposal was never formally approved, delegates met for a special church service on July 4, the anniversary of America's birthday. From this time on, the convention proceeded more smoothly as the delegates began to cooperate with one another. They realized that no one person or one state could have its own way completely. Each side had to give a little. In this way, they began to work together through the long, hot summer months to answer some important questions.

Most delegates agreed on the purpose of the new government. The government would protect the freedoms discussed in the Declaration of Independence and defended in the War for Independence. Although almost everyone agreed on the purpose, many disagreed on the kind of government that could best protect our freedoms. <u>The government would have to be powerful but not too powerful. It would have to be strong enough to protect people from criminals and yet not so strong that it could take away the freedoms of people who obey the laws.</u>

Here are some of the questions that were discussed:

- What powers should the federal (national) government have? How much power should be left with the states?
- How should the federal government be set up so that it could protect the country from foreign enemies but not become the enemy of the country it was supposed to protect?
- Should there be limits on what the state governments could do?
- What could be done to keep bad men from using government for selfish purposes?

When the Founders of the United States signed the Constitution, they established a form of government that would become a model for free countries.

The New Republic

America's Founding Fathers wisely gave the country a **constitutional republic,** a form of government in which the people and their elected representatives are limited by a constitution. Never before in history had any country as large as ours tried to have self-government. The head of our new government would be a **President,** who would have **executive** power, the power to see that the laws were obeyed. A **Congress** made up of two groups called houses would have **legislative power,** the power to make our country's national laws. One house, the **Senate,** would include two senators from each state. The other house, the **House of Representatives,** would also include representatives from each state. The number of representatives would depend on the population of the state. A large state like Virginia could send more representatives than a small state like New Jersey.

The idea of a Senate pleased the small states, because in the Senate every state, no matter what its size, would have the same power. The House of Representatives pleased the larger states, because in it they would have more power. Yet neither house would be more important than the other. The Senate and the House of Representatives would both have to agree on a bill before it became a law.

Since the new government would need to make and enforce many new laws, it would need a system of courts and judges. To meet this need, the Founding Fathers established

The Three Branches of Government in the United States

Branch	Duties	Structure
1. LEGISLATIVE (Congress)	• **Makes laws** • Appropriates money (sets it aside for a specific use) • Imposes taxes • Approves treaties and candidates for appointment to government positions	A Congress of two houses: • **Senate**—two members from each state. (There are 100 senators today, because there are 50 states.) • **House of Representatives**—number based on state population.
2. EXECUTIVE (President)	• **Enforces laws** • Appoints people to government positions • Commands the armed forces • Has veto power	• A **President** who serves as chief executive. • A **Vice President** who serves as Senate president and becomes President of the country in the event that the President is unable to finish his term. • **Executive Assistants** appointed by the President. The heads of the executive departments serve as the President's advisory board, or **Cabinet.**
3. JUDICIAL (Supreme Court)	• **Interprets laws** • Tries cases involving federal law	• The **Supreme Court**—made up of nine justices, one of whom serves as the **Chief Justice.** The justices are appointed by the President and approved by the Senate. • **Lower federal courts**—eleven **Circuit Courts of Appeals,** 90 **District Courts,** and several special courts.

the **Supreme Court,** the highest court in the land, which would have **judicial power,** the power to interpret the Constitution and apply it to cases of national importance.

To keep the federal government from having all the power, the Founders limited its authority and gave certain powers to the state governments. They knew that the people of the various states would have different needs and concerns; therefore, they should be able to decide some of their own laws. Once the Constitution was complete, the individual states needed to approve it. By signing the Constitution, each state yielded some of its rights, putting its trust in a brand new government, a government of the people, by the people, and for the people. It has been said that as Benjamin Franklin left the Constitutional Convention, a woman asked him, "What kind of government has been formed?" His thoughtful answer was, "A republic, if you can keep it!"

Comprehension Check 8E

Identify
1. The definition of civil government.
2. The document written in Philadelphia to establish a new government.
3. The three branches of government.

Think
4. Why weren't the Articles of Confederation a successful plan of government?

The Bill of Rights

The people of the United States knew from the very beginning that it was important to make sure that freedom of religion and other important freedoms were protected by law. To protect the freedoms of individuals and groups, they added a **Bill of Rights** to the Constitution. The Bill of Rights is a list of the rights or freedoms that the Constitution gives to Americans. The Bill of Rights forbids the federal government from taking these freedoms from us as long as we do not threaten the property or lives of other law-abiding citizens.

The Bill of Rights includes the right to print and read what we want, within certain

Rights and Responsibilities of Americans

The rights given to us by our constitution carry with them important responsibilities.

Right	Responsibility
freedom of worship	honor God with our worship and our lives
freedom of speech	speak honestly and purely; respect the opinions of others
freedom of press	keep informed and analyze what we read; do not print things that would harm others
freedom to keep and bear arms	use firearms safely and properly, without endangering the lives of law-abiding citizens
freedom to vote	vote faithfully and wisely for what is best for the country
freedom to own property	be good stewards of our possessions; respect the property of others
freedom to earn a living in one's chosen vocation	take advantage of educational opportunities; develop good work habits; be responsible employees
freedom of assembly	meet with others to share ideas; recognize un-American and anti-Christian activities and emotions and avoid them

limits. It also includes the right for someone accused of a crime to be tried by a jury in a court of law. The new government could not interfere in these areas. The Bill of Rights also protected the states and their powers from being taken over by the new government. The delegates at the Constitutional Convention believed it was wise to avoid giving too much power to any one person or group, or even to the government.

The Bill of Rights is written in the form of ten amendments, or changes, to the Constitution. The First Amendment is especially important because it gives us freedom of religion, freedom of speech, freedom of the press, and freedom of assembly. This is what this amendment says:

> Congress shall make no law respecting an establishment of religion, or prohibiting the free exercise thereof; or abridging the freedom of speech, or of the press; or the right of the people peaceably to assemble, and to petition the government for a redress of grievances.

The United States was one of the first nations in the history of the world in which people were free to preach and practice any form of religion that did not interfere with the morals or welfare of the community. The First Amendment declares that the government cannot control the churches.

Our First President

Now there was another decision to be made. Who would be the first President of the United States? This was not a hard decision. The man who had led our country through the War for Independence was already loved and trusted. **George Washington** (1732–1799) became our first President, and **John Adams** (1735–1826) our first Vice President.

After being elected, Washington traveled in a horse-drawn coach to our nation's first capital—**New York City.** People crowded the roads that the coach traveled. All along the way, he was met by cheering crowds. Little girls threw flowers in his path, and guns were fired to salute the President of the United States. On **Inauguration Day,** April 30, 1789, Washington took the oath of office, with his hand resting on the Word of God.

the inauguration of George Washington

The New World's First Republic 157

PEOPLE IN HISTORY
Benjamin Banneker: SCIENTIST, ARCHITECT, PATRIOT

Benjamin Banneker (1731–1806), one of the men who helped to plan Washington, D.C., was also the first black American to write a scientific book.

Banneker was born in Maryland, the son of a freed slave. After his grandmother taught him how to read from her Bible, Banneker attended a Quaker school. There he developed a keen interest in science and mathematics.

In 1763, Banneker built one of the first clocks assembled in the United States. It was carved entirely of wood and kept almost perfect time for over fifty years. It was a remarkable work of engineering and craftsmanship.

In 1791, President Washington appointed Banneker as assistant to surveyor Andrew Ellicott and French architect Pierre L'Enfant, who were designing and laying out our nation's capital. When L'Enfant was dismissed from the job, he returned to France, taking his plans with him. Benjamin Banneker is said to have reproduced the complicated plans from memory.

From 1791 to 1802, Benjamin Banneker published a yearly almanac, which contained his carefully made calculations of astronomy, tides, and weather. The almanac became an immediate success.

These many accomplishments made Benjamin Banneker one of the most famous black persons in America at the time of our nation's founding.

All of our Presidents since then have been sworn in on a Bible. A few years later, as President, George Washington would state that "It is impossible to rightly govern the world without God and the Bible."

Striving to set a good example for those Presidents who would follow him, George Washington made sure that his official actions were done carefully, cautiously, and thoughtfully. Because he set such a high example, Washington is regarded by historians as one of the greatest of all the Presidents. He served his first term of four years so well that the people elected him to a second term. When it came time for the third election, the people wanted to elect him again—but this time he refused.

In Washington's **Farewell Address,** he thanked the people of America for allowing him to serve his country as President for eight years. He then warned the people that unless they acted like responsible citizens, the freedom for which they had fought might disappear. As a man faithful to God and country, Washington emphasized respect for and obedience to the nation's laws. He warned Americans that loyalty to their country should never be replaced by loyalty to a political party, urging people from the north, south, east, and west to think not only about what would be good for their part of the country, but what would be good for the country as a whole. Above all, he stressed that a republic could work only if the people continued to do right according to God's laws. He said that people would be moral only if the churches remained strong and the people continued to love and obey God.

A short time after writing this address, Washington and his wife Martha retired to Mount Vernon, their beautiful plantation in Virginia. Honest, hard working John Adams took his place and became the second President of the United States in 1797.

158 New World History & Geography

A New Capital

You will remember that our nation's first capital was New York. For a time, the capital was changed to Philadelphia, but soon plans were made to move it to a new location. Both Virginia and Maryland gave land to build the city on the banks of the **Potomac River.** George Washington chose the site and hired the surveyors and architects while he was still President. Although he never lived there, the city was named Washington in his honor. The land that the city was built on was called the **District of Columbia.** Thus, we get the name **Washington, D.C.**

Comprehension Check 8F

Identify
1. The list of freedoms that the Constitution gives to all Americans.
2. Our nation's first capital.
3. The first black American to write a scientific book.

Think

4. List three of the freedoms provided in the Bill of Rights and the responsibility that comes with each.

Chapter 8 Checkup

I. Define these **terms.**
- tax
- patriot
- minutemen
- First Continental Congress
- 3 branches of government
- Second Continental Congress
- "Shot Heard 'round the World"
- Liberty Bell
- Hessians
- *Bonhomme Richard*
- *Serapis*
- civil government
- Constitutional Convention
- constitutional republic
- Supreme Court

II. Know these **documents** or **acts.**
- Stamp Act
- Quebec Act
- Declaration of Independence
- Treaty of Paris
- Articles of Confederation
- Constitution of the United States
- Bill of Rights
- First Amendment

III. Tell why these **people** are important.
- George Washington
- General Edward Braddock
- King George III
- Lemuel Haynes
- Patrick Henry
- Paul Revere
- Ethan Allen and the Green Mountain Boys
- Thomas Jefferson
- John Hancock
- James Armistead
- Nathan Hale
- Betsy Ross
- George Rogers Clark
- John Paul Jones
- General Lord Cornwallis
- Nathanael Greene
- James Madison
- John Adams
- Benjamin Banneker

IV. Give the noted event for these **dates.**
- 1754–1763
- September 1774
- July 4, 1776
- June 14, 1777

V. Identify these **events, places,** or **battles.**
- French and Indian War
- Fort le Boeuf
- Fort Duquesne
- Boston Massacre
- Boston Tea Party
- Battle of Bunker Hill
- Battle of Saratoga
- Valley Forge
- Yorktown
- New York City
- Washington, D.C.
- Inauguration Day
- farewell address

VI. Identify the locations from **Map Mastery 11.**

The New World's First Republic

chapter 9
United States History:
EXPANSION and EVANGELISM

9.1 PIONEERS PUSH FARTHER WEST

The first thirteen states of the United States were in the East, all near the Atlantic Ocean. As the years passed, the borders of our country moved farther and farther west. Although today we think of the "West" as California, Oregon, Washington, Alaska, and so forth, in the early 1800s, the "West" meant any land that was still frontier land. The "West" kept moving farther west as America continued to grow.

Daniel Boone and the Wilderness Road

Farm boy and frontiersman. A **pioneer** is a person who does something first, preparing the way for others. Even before the American War for Independence, pioneers had started moving westward. The most famous pioneer of colonial times was **Daniel Boone** (1734–1820). Daniel was born into a Quaker family in Pennsylvania, and when he was ten, he began working for his father on a farm some distance from home. Friendly Indians taught the boy how to survive in the woods. Daniel's father gave him a rifle when he was twelve, and Daniel soon learned to be an excellent hunter. In 1750, Daniel's father moved the family to the wild frontiers of North Carolina. While his father and brothers farmed, Daniel kept the family supplied with deer meat and other game. He also traded the animal skins for family supplies.

Exploring Kentucky. At the age of 20, Daniel Boone joined the colonial army to fight in the French and Indian War. During the war, he heard tall tales about the wilderness

Timeline: 1765 — 1785 — 1805 — 1825 — 1845 — 1865

- **1775** Daniel Boone blazes the Wilderness Road
- **1787** Northwest Ordinance
- **1790** Second Great Awakening begins
- **1803** Louisiana Purchase
- **1803** Peter Cartwright begins his circuit-riding ministry
- **1810** Judson and Mills help found America's first foreign missionary society
- **1812–1814** War of 1812
- **1814** British burn Washington, D.C.
- **1814** Treaty of Ghent ends the war
- **1835–1836** Texas War for Independence
- **1836** Battle of the Alamo
- **1836** Battle of San Jacinto
- **1846–1848** Mexican War
- **1848** Treaty ends the war
- **1848** Mexican Cession
- **1849** California Gold Rush
- **1853** Gadsden Purchase
- **1858** Townsend Harris Treaty opens Japan to missionaries

Daniel Boone leading a group over the Wilderness Road.

of **Kentucky** that made him long to see that land. The next year, he married Rebecca, who became a courageous and uncomplaining pioneer wife. Daniel had not lost his longing to see Kentucky, however. In 1769, Daniel and some friends finally explored the area he had dreamed of visiting. When he returned home after two years, Daniel had many exciting stories to tell his wife and children. He hoped that one day he could move his family to Kentucky.

The Wilderness Road. By 1775, Daniel Boone was asked to return to Kentucky to blaze a trail so that other pioneers could follow. Together with about thirty strong men, Daniel cleared a narrow path, the **Wilderness Road,** through the thick forests and over the mountains through the **Cumberland Gap.** At first, the path was too narrow for wagons, so the pioneers had to walk or ride horses.

Around the time that the American War for Independence started (1775), pioneers built a settlement in Kentucky called **Boonesborough** in honor of Daniel Boone. Daniel soon returned home and brought his family back to live in Kentucky. Later, after more and more settlers arrived in Kentucky, Boone and his family pushed farther west into unsettled Missouri.

The Wilderness Road led many of the first pioneers West. For this reason, Daniel Boone has been called "the pioneer of pioneers." With the passing years, pioneers widened the Wilderness Road, and thousands of wagons and families traveled over it.

Settling the Northwest Territory

Northwest Ordinance. After the War for Independence, the United States gained the **Northwest Territory.** Someday this large piece of land would make up the states of **Ohio, Indiana, Illinois, Michigan, Wisconsin,** and part of **Minnesota.** Because our government knew that many settlers would flock to the Northwest Territory, Congress passed laws that would bring order and government to the territory.

One of the most important laws passed, the **Northwest Ordinance of 1787** guaranteed that the freedoms which the states enjoyed would also be present in the territories. It guaranteed freedom of religion, outlawed

Expansion and Evangelism

flatboat

slavery, guaranteed fair treatment of American Indians, and provided for a trial by a jury for all citizens accused of crimes. In addition to the liberties it secured, the Northwest Ordinance also provided for government in the new territory. The ordinance stated that Congress would appoint a governor and judges to bring order to the territory until its population reached 5,000 free men of voting age. At that time, the territory could elect its own legislature and a representative to Congress.

Perhaps the most important part of the Northwest Ordinance was the following promise:

> "Religion, morality, and knowledge being necessary to good government and the happiness of mankind, schools and the means of education shall forever be encouraged."

Finally, the Northwest Ordinance stated that when the population of an area reached 60,000, that area could become a state and enter the Union. The Northwest Ordinance would become the pattern for the orderly settlement of the American West.

Moving to Ohio. Some men moved their families into the Northwest Territory because they felt too crowded where they were; others came for adventure and a new way of living. Together, these families formed one courageous group of pioneers, helping our country to grow. Ohio was the first region to be settled in the Northwest Territory.

To reach Ohio from Pennsylvania, a family would first buy a **covered wagon** and load it with the supplies they knew they could not get in Ohio—seeds for gardens, a plow, tools, nails, guns, an iron kettle, cooking utensils, a spinning wheel, and blankets. They had to pack enough flour, salt, bacon, and other food to last them until they reached Pittsburgh. Because they needed their livestock for eggs, milk, and meat, a family might tie a crate of chickens to one side of the wagon and a crate of piglets to the other side. Behind the wagon would walk a cow. Since they had little room for furniture, the pioneers would have to make their own homemade furniture when they reached Ohio. Most pioneers found room to pack the family Bible, though. With chickens cackling and piglets squealing, the wagon began creaking down the rough road.

162 *New World History & Geography*

In a few days, the family reached the city of Pittsburgh, Pennsylvania. In Pittsburgh, they sold their wagon and bought a **flatboat,** a long boat with a flat bottom, which they loaded with supplies from the wagon. Chickens, piglets, and even horses and cows were loaded onto the boat. The family also bought more food and supplies. On the waters of the Ohio River, the flatboat could be even more dangerous than the covered wagon had been along the bumpy roads and trails. Once the pioneers traveled west of Pittsburgh, they left the protection of forts and soldiers. When the family reached their new home in Ohio, they carefully took apart their flatboat and used the lumber and nails to build a home.

New states. As more Americans moved west, new states were added to the original thirteen states. Vermont, which already had quite a few residents before the War for Independence, became the fourteenth state in 1791. Kentucky (1792) and Tennessee (1796) followed. The population of **Ohio** grew so quickly that she became our seventeenth state in 1803. New pioneers who wished to settle in the frontier of the Northwest Territory kept moving westward into Indiana, Illinois, Michigan, and Wisconsin. As the years passed, more of our frontier became settled, and more states were formed.

The Erie Canal

One way people later journeyed to Ohio and even farther west was by following the **Erie Canal,** the first major man-made canal in the United States. This canal connected Lake Erie with the Hudson River—a distance of 363 miles. The man whose foresight made the Erie Canal possible was Governor DeWitt Clinton of New York, one of the early leaders in the American Bible Society.

Workers finished digging the forty-foot wide, four-foot deep canal in 1825. Although the canal cost the state of New York over seven million dollars, it repaid the state in tolls within a few years and continued to earn more money.

During the early days of operation, a boat would be pulled through the canal by mules. A towline would be fastened to the boat and to a mule walking alongshore. People on the boat used long poles to help push the boat through the canal and to keep it from bumping against the banks.

The Erie Canal proved to be a wise investment. It allowed farmers to ship agricul-

the Erie Canal

Expansion and Evangelism 163

tural products east and manufacturers to ship manufactured goods west in a much easier and faster way than was possible over land.

New Schools and Schoolbooks

As the country grew, more and more schools were opened. Americans believed strongly that each child should learn to read the Bible for himself and should be educated for citizenship in the republic. Before long, children throughout the country were attending school.

The "Blue-Backed Speller." One New England man who helped shape American education was **Noah Webster,** a scholar from Connecticut who wrote the first major American dictionary. Webster became concerned that there were no good American textbooks for students to use. Most schools used books printed in England. To remedy the situation, Webster decided to write textbooks himself. His books not only taught children to read, but they also taught children to do right, to be loyal Americans, and to love God and His Word. Written in 1783, Webster's most famous book was *The American Spelling Book,* nicknamed the "Blue-Backed Speller" because of its blue cover. The "Blue-Backed Speller" has sold an estimated 100 million copies. Noah Webster's books had such a good influence on American children that someone said he "taught thousands to read, but not one to sin."

The McGuffey readers. Between 1836 and 1857, **William H. McGuffey,** a Presbyterian minister from Pennsylvania and Ohio, also wrote a series of textbooks. The McGuffey readers sold over 122 million copies. Some of the stories in these readers contained useful information about geography and science; some taught valuable lessons about honesty, obedience, punctuality, kindness, and love of God and country; and others were simply filled with good fun. But all of them helped children learn.

Webster, McGuffey, and other textbook writers helped make America a great country by teaching children to think of others, to obey authorities, to be good citizens, to fear God, and to serve Him by obeying His

a teacher and her students in front of their one-room schoolhouse

Word. These principles were the foundation of American education.

One-room schoolhouses. Most students in the 1800s attended one-room schoolhouses. They did not have separate classes; all of the boys sat together on one side of the classroom, and all of the girls on the other side of the classroom. The teacher would call the students by groups to the front of the classroom to recite their lessons. First, she might help the fourth graders with their reading; next, she might quiz a sixth grader on his spelling; after that, she might help the first graders with their phonics. The teacher always stayed busy teaching the students and making sure they behaved themselves. Most of the teachers were Christians, and all of them believed in being good examples of righteous living.

Although the schoolhouse was small and simple, the children took pride in it and kept it clean. They helped with chores, such as bringing in wood for the stove and carrying water from the well or stream. The schoolhouse had few maps or globes, and, of course, no video players, computers, or other fancy machines. But still the children learned because they had the right tools for learning—good textbooks and a teacher who loved them and wanted to help them learn.

Comprehension Check 9A

Identify

1. The most famous pioneer of colonial times.
2. The states or parts of states which would be formed from the Northwest Territory.
3. The law Congress passed to provide government for the Northwest Territory.

Think

4. How did a pioneer family prepare to move west? What routes might they take? What types of vehicles might they use for transportation?
5. How did the Erie Canal benefit farmers in the West and manufacturers in the East?

9.2 Revival and Missions
The Second Great Awakening

The beginnings of revival. While Americans enjoyed the peace and prosperity following the War for Independence, their attention to spiritual matters decreased. But in the 1790s, much-needed revivals began quietly where the Great Awakening had started years earlier—in New England. This new revival, called the **Second Great Awakening,** brought renewed spiritual fervor and interest in sharing the gospel.

Circuit-riding preachers. In 1771, a few years before the Second Great Awakening, the great English founder of the Methodist church, **John Wesley,** sent a young Methodist evangelist named **Francis Asbury** to America to establish churches and Bible studies on the frontier. Asbury began training young men to preach, stressing that sermons should use simple illustrations of Biblical truth. The Methodists encouraged participation of the whole congregation, regular Bible study, and complete submission to the will of God.

Asbury's students became known as **circuit-riding preachers,** because they rode regular routes, or circuits, preaching in areas that did not have a pastor and wherever churches were in need of revival. They preached every day of the week, sometimes as many as six sermons a day. You can imagine what a great number of Americans heard the gospel when this method was used!

As more and more people settled the western regions, circuit-riding preachers began to ride around the territories, preaching in each settlement to all who would listen. The preaching of these men started a great revival on the frontier, beginning in Kentucky (the territory which Daniel Boone had opened up to settlers) and spreading to neighboring areas as far as the Northwest Territory. Soon

Expansion and Evangelism

Peter Cartwright

many were being converted under the preaching of Baptist, Methodist, and Presbyterian evangelists. Thus, the Second Great Awakening spread through even the most remote areas of the nation.

One of the best known circuit riders, **Peter Cartwright,** preached the gospel throughout the frontier, particularly in Tennessee and Kentucky, for nearly fifty years. A circuit rider had to be a strong man to face the many difficulties of his job. The West was not a place for cowards or for preachers who wanted to make a lot of money. Peter Cartwright said that in his day the average salary paid to preachers in the West was only thirty to forty dollars *per year.* Why did these circuit riders spend their lives doing such hard work? They preached because they loved God, and they wanted to see the frontier people come to Christ.

The first black denomination. A slave named **Richard Allen** (1760–1831) accepted Christ at the age of seventeen through the preaching of a Methodist circuit rider. After his master saw the wonderful change in Allen's life, he became a Christian himself and gave Allen and his brother the option of working extra hours to purchase their freedom. While young Richard Allen worked, he also served as a traveling Methodist preacher, and his preaching became very popular. In the mid-1780s, Richard Allen settled in Philadelphia, Pennsylvania, eventually founding a black congregation called Bethel Church. Francis Asbury later ordained him as the first black deacon of the Methodist church in 1799. Bethel Church became the core for the first black denomination in the United States, the African Methodist Episcopal Church, which Allen helped found in 1816.

Camp meetings. For many years, the spirit of revival was kept alive in America by **camp meetings.** Each year, preachers held camp meetings in virtually every county of every state. People from all around gathered together for a week to hear gospel preaching. Because people lived so far apart, many of them traveled several miles to the campsite. There they would set up a tent, living and cooking camp style for the week.

The hymns. The Second Great Awakening and the camp meetings that followed inspired a love for hymns. The music of great English writers **Isaac Watts** and **Charles Wesley,** for example, experienced great popularity. During the first half of the 18th century, Watts wrote such classics as "When I Survey the Wondrous Cross" and "Joy to the World." Charles Wesley, brother of John Wesley the founder of the Methodist Church in England, is the author of nearly 6,500 hymns including "O for a Thousand Tongues to Sing" and "Hark! The Herald Angels Sing." Christians in early America soon realized that sacred music is a wonderful way to worship God, whether in church or at home or traveling in a wagon across the frontier.

The Beginnings of American Missions

George Liele: missionary pioneer. One of the reasons God has blessed America is that the people of our land have done much to reach other peoples through missionary activity. America's first missionary to a foreign land was **George Liele** (1752–1825), a black preacher who earned his own support while a missionary in Jamaica. George Liele was born in Virginia and taken to Savannah, Georgia, by his master, Henry Sharp. When an ordained Baptist pastor realized how much Liele loved the Lord and witnessed his wonderful ability to explain the Scriptures, he ordained him to preach, making him one of the first ordained black preachers in America. Henry Sharp learned of Liele's call to preach and decided to free Liele from slavery so he could spend all of his time preaching the gospel. The former slave preached in Georgia throughout the War for Independence, and he and his follower Andrew Bryan founded America's first black Baptist congregation in Savannah. Shortly thereafter, Liele sailed to Jamaica, paying for his passage by going as an indentured servant. He preached in the streets of Kingston, Jamaica, and eventually started Jamaica's first Baptist church, which grew from 4 members to 500 members in 8 years. Liele organized a missionary society in Jamaica that sent 50 Jamaican missionaries to Africa and about 20 to the United States to minister to blacks there. George Liele went to Jamaica fourteen years before William Carey, the Father of Modern Missions, went from England to India, and thirty-three years before Adoniram Judson, the Father of American Missions, went from the United States to Burma (Myanmar).

The haystack prayer meeting. **Samuel J. Mills** (1783–1818) was about fifteen when the Second Great Awakening came to his town in Connecticut. Three years later, as a freshman at Williams College in Massachusetts, Samuel Mills accepted Christ as his personal Savior, and he soon felt called to be a missionary. While at the college, he became a leader of other young men interested in missions. They often met to pray for people across the seas who had never heard the gospel. One day while these young men were meeting at their usual location for prayer, a meadow near the college, it suddenly began to rain. Rather than cancel their prayer time, they ran to a nearby haystack and prayed under the hay. This event has gone down in history as the **"haystack prayer meeting."** Before long, God would answer the prayers of these earnest young men by sending out the Father of American Missions, **Adoniram Judson,** who was a friend of Samuel Mills when both were students at Andover Theological Seminary in Massachusetts.

The first foreign missionary society. Judson, Mills, and others at Andover prayed for world missions and talked to their fellow students as well as their teachers and preachers about the need for missionaries. In 1810, they presented the need to their church council and volunteered to go themselves as missionaries if the churches would sponsor them. As a

camp meeting

Expansion and Evangelism

result of their efforts, America's first foreign missionary society was begun.

Adoniram Judson went to Asia in 1812 with the society's first group of missionaries. He and a missionary on another ship, **Luther Rice** (1783–1836), became Baptists on their voyages after studying the Greek New Testament. Rice and Judson soon encouraged the formation of America's first Baptist mission board.

The work of Samuel J. Mills. Samuel Mills did not work for years in a foreign land, as Adoniram Judson did. His main ministry in life was to help others become missionaries. While studying at Yale College, he met a young Hawaiian boy, **Henry Obookiah**. Mills became very interested in Henry and

---

Missionary Heroes

Adoniram Judson: The Father of American Missions

Adoniram Judson's (1788–1850) goal in life was to be rich and famous. And while he was in college, a man named Jacob Eames convinced Adoniram to become a skeptic (one who foolishly does not believe in God and the Bible).

After graduation, Judson drifted from job to job, finding no satisfaction in life. One night, while staying in a hotel, he heard groans and noises coming from nearby, and he learned that the man in the next room was dying.

The next day, he was surprised to find out that the dying man had been Jacob Eames, his college friend! Remembering the groans, Judson realized that Eames's beliefs had not helped him as he faced death. This incident started Judson thinking about his own spiritual condition, and he soon gave his heart to the Lord. Then he started praying about becoming a missionary.

In 1812, Adoniram Judson and his wife Ann sailed to **Rangoon, Burma** (modern-day Yangon, Myanmar). There, Ann started a school for both women and children, and Adoniram opened a *zayat,* a gathering place for the local people. As the Burmese people came to the zayat to socialize, Adoniram told them of Christ. And by 1819, the Judsons had won eighteen Burmese to the Lord.

The Burmese king encouraged their work, but in 1824, things changed. A war broke out between Burma and England, and all foreigners were treated as spies. Adoniram Judson was taken to prison. Although constantly ill, Ann Judson kept the mission work going as much as she could and prayed daily for Adoniram's release.

The Lord answered her prayer. In late 1825, Adoniram was released. The couple enjoyed several months together, but then Adoniram found out that the British needed him to interpret a treaty. He left home, planning to be gone only a short time, but the trip took longer than he expected. Before he returned, Adoniram received word that his wife had died. He grieved for a long time, but he later remarried and continued his work.

By the time he died in 1850, Judson had completed a translation of the Bible into Burmese and most of a dictionary. Though Judson's dictionary was not finished, it has been used to translate the Bible into other languages similar to Burmese. And because of his hard work, thousands of Burmese have gotten saved.

The man who once longed for worldly fame and fortune gave it all up for Christ. Yet Christians all over the world have heard of his life and been inspired by it to serve God. Judson knew that a man's greatest reward is to hear his Lord say, "Well done, thou good and faithful servant . . . enter thou into the joy of thy Lord" (Matt. 25:21).

The following poem by Adoniram Judson tells of this everlasting reward:

In Spite of Sorrow
In spite of sorrow, loss, and pain,
  Our course be onward still;
We sow on Burma's barren plain,
  We reap on Zion's hill.

provided for his education so that Henry could return to the Hawaiian Islands as a missionary. Henry Obookiah died before he could get back to Hawaii, but his testimony led to the sending of many other missionaries to those Pacific islands.

Samuel Mills made two trips to America's new frontier to help start Bible societies. In 1816, Mills helped form the **American Bible Society.** He also worked among the poor in New York City and gave money to start a college for training freed slaves to spread the gospel to the slaves in the South. He helped other freed slaves go to Africa, where they established the nation of **Liberia** in northwest Africa. Liberia would later become Africa's first black republic. Mills went to Africa himself, arriving in 1818, to help the nation get started, and he died on his way back to America that same year at the age of 35. Although his life was short and his work on a foreign mission field brief, Samuel J. Mills accomplished great things for the beginnings of American missions through his prayers, gifts, labors, and encouragements. His dreams for Africa would be carried forward by a great black American Christian, Lott Carey.

Comprehension Check 9B
Identify
1. The great English founder of the Methodist church.
2. The famous circuit rider who preached the gospel to the frontier people of Tennessee and Kentucky.
3. The founder of the congregation which became the core for the first black denomination in the United States.
4. Two English hymn writers whose songs enjoyed great popularity in America.
5. America's first missionary to a foreign land.
6. The Father of American Missions.

9.3 CHRISTIANITY AMONG BLACK AMERICANS

Many black Americans distinguished themselves as servants of God. Often a plantation owner's wife would teach some of the slave children to read and write, using the Bible as a reading text. Others learned to read and write in their churches and Sunday schools. Some of these young blacks developed great ability to expound the Scriptures, and God called them to preach. The Methodist, Presbyterian, and Baptist churches pioneered church-planting programs among the black communities, as well as the training of black preachers.

Lott Carey: Black Missionary to Africa

In 1807, a young slave named **Lott Carey** (1780–1828) accepted Christ and was baptized at the First Baptist Church in Richmond, Virginia. A white member of the church taught Carey to read from the New Testament, and Carey soon became a licensed Baptist preacher. Through his hard work and the help of merchant friends, Lott Carey bought his freedom in 1813. He also purchased the freedom of his children, but by this time his wife had died. After learning of missionary efforts in West Africa, he founded the **African Baptist Missionary Society of Richmond.**

By 1821, Lott Carey owned a prospering farm, preached to slaves throughout the surrounding countryside, and eventually pastored a predominantly black congregation in Richmond. But Carey felt burdened for Africa. The forerunner of the Southern Baptist Convention decided to sponsor him as a missionary to the newly founded colony of Liberia. Lott Carey's long-time friend and associate preacher, **Collin Teague,** also a black American, volunteered to go with him.

Expansion and Evangelism

In his farewell sermon, Carey preached from Romans 8:32 about God's gift of His Son and our obligation to give of ourselves:

> I am about to leave you, and expect to see your faces no more. I long to preach to the poor Africans the way of life and salvation. I don't know what may befall me, whether I may find a grave in the ocean, or among the savage men or more savage wild beasts of the coasts of Africa; nor am I anxious what may become of me. I feel it my duty to go. . . . The Savior may ask where have you been? What have you been doing? Have you endeavored to the utmost of your ability to fulfill the commands I gave you?

Lott Carey and Collin Teague sailed for Africa on January 23, 1821. After arriving in Liberia, they started a church in **Monrovia,** the capital city (named for American President James Monroe). They preached the gospel and also built schools. Carey later became the governor of Liberia. He managed to fulfill his civic duties in the government but always gave first priority to his preaching. He became known as the Father of Western African Missions. Lott Carey was killed in an accidental explosion in 1828 and buried near the town of Careysburg, Liberia, which was named in his honor. The Foreign Mission Board of the Southern Baptist Convention marked his grave with a marble stone in 1851. Visitors to Liberia can still visit the grave site. Because of Lott Carey's dedication and burden, many missionaries followed in his footsteps to northwest Africa to spread the gospel.

Some Famous Black Preachers

Lemuel Haynes, a patriot and a preacher. You already know of one famous black preacher, **Lemuel Haynes** (1753–1833). As a young man studying for the ministry, Haynes was called upon to serve as a minuteman in the American War for Independence. Like many other Massachusetts citizens, he first took up arms to defend his home, and later, as a soldier in the Continental Army under George Washington, to fight for his country. After the war, he completed his studies and became a well-known pastor and writer in New England. During the Second Great Awakening, Lemuel Haynes held revivals in Vermont and Connecticut.

John Jasper in Richmond. In 1839, a slave by the name of **John Jasper** (1812–1901) came to know Christ as his Savior after hearing the gospel in the Capital Square of Richmond, Virginia. Using an old spelling book, he taught himself to read. Jasper studied the Bible so thoroughly that one minister said of him:

> It did seem to me sometimes that Reverend Jasper came into the world with a Bible in his heart, head, and tongue.

Jasper eventually committed much of the Scriptures to memory.

Jasper, while still a slave, began preaching wherever he could find a congregation, often at funerals where he could minister to sorrowing families. While the Civil War raged, he ministered to wounded soldiers in Confederate hospitals. After the war, he preached in churches throughout Virginia, Maryland, and

John Jasper

PEOPLE IN HISTORY
Catherine Ferguson: SUNDAY SCHOOL TEACHER AND FRIEND OF ORPHANS

Eight-year-old Catherine (Katy) Ferguson (?–1854) said goodbye to her mother, a black slave, for the last time when another family purchased the woman and took her away. But Katy did not allow her loss to make her bitter. From that day forward, she felt compassion for orphans of any race. Although Katy Ferguson did not know it at the time, God intended to use her loss for His glory.

God had placed Katy in the possession of a kind woman who took her to church and encouraged her spiritual development. When Katy was 16 years old, God sent another compassionate woman to purchase the girl's freedom. But Katy's lessons were not over yet. Two years later, Katy married and started a family of her own. Though she had two children, both died as infants. The loss of her children motivated Katy to begin a great work for God.

In 1793, Katy began holding a Sunday school for local children in her home. This is believed to be New York City's first Sunday school program. As the work grew, a local pastor learned that Katy needed more room and offered the use of his church basement. Soon the Murray Street Sabbath School was thriving every Sunday morning, and on Sunday afternoons and on Fridays, Katy taught children at her home.

In addition to her teaching, Katy helped place a total of 48 starving children into good homes that could better meet their needs. The Katy Ferguson Home for unwed mothers was founded in 1920 in honor of this dedicated, compassionate woman.

New Jersey. He once preached before the entire Virginia General Assembly. Multitudes came to hear the fiery black preacher. Many received Christ as their Savior after hearing Jasper's vivid descriptions of hell.

John Chavis and education. John Chavis (176?–1838) was a free black man with great abilities. He was born in Virginia and attended Washington Academy (now Washington and Lee University) in Lexington, Virginia, where he studied to become a Presbyterian minister. In 1801, the Presbyterian Church of the United States appointed Chavis to be a missionary to other blacks. He went on to minister first in Virginia and later in North Carolina, preaching in churches. In North Carolina, he founded a preparatory school for white students and a night school for black children. Among his pupils at the preparatory school were a future United States senator and Charles Manly, a future governor of North Carolina.

America's Own Music: The Spirituals

As the black slaves in the South heard sermons from the Scriptures, they applied to themselves the stories of the Hebrew children enslaved in Egypt. Suffering the hardships of slavery, many turned to the Lord as the source of their strength. In order to help His children endure their bondage, God gave them the gift of the **spirituals,** which are recognized as <u>America's greatest contribution to the field of music</u>. The slaves would sing these melodic, rhythmic songs together as they worked on the plantations.

Some of the best-loved spirituals are "Swing Low, Sweet Chariot," "Deep River," and "Go Down, Moses." The song "Go Down, Moses" is a good example of the comparison between the slavery of the Hebrew children and that of the black people.

Go down, Moses—
'Way down in Egypt land,
Tell ole Pharaoh,
To let my people go!

Expansion and Evangelism 171

Fisk Jubilee Singers

When a spiritual spoke of freedom, it referred to the spiritual freedom of life with the Savior. In fact, the slave who was a Christian had more freedom than any free person who was not saved. By first giving them their spiritual freedom, God was preparing the slaves for their coming physical freedom.

In later years, several talented black Americans put together collections of spirituals, which can be found in the works of James Weldon Johnson (1871–1938), John Wesley Work, Sr. (1873–1925), and Harry T. Burleigh (1866–1949). The **Fisk Jubilee Singers** of Tennessee introduced the spirituals to the northern states and Europe beginning in 1871. Some of America's most beloved musical performers have included spirituals in their musical repertoire, such as the great black American opera stars Marian Anderson (1897–1993) and Mary Leontyne Price (1927–).

Comprehension Check 9C
Identify
1. Former slave who became known as Father of Western African Missions.
2. The black slave who preached in Civil War hospitals.
3. America's greatest contribution to the field of music.
4. The woman said to have founded New York City's first Sunday school.

9.4 FROM THE GULF OF MEXICO TO THE ROCKY MOUNTAINS

The Louisiana Purchase

The city of **New Orleans,** which guards the mouth of the Mississippi River, was a part of the **Louisiana Territory.** This land had belonged to Spain, but Spain turned the land over to France. **Thomas Jefferson** (1743–1826), our third President, offered the French ruler, **Napoleon Bonaparte,** two million dollars for the city of New Orleans. The United States desired this city so American ships could load and trade there freely. To President Jefferson's surprise, Napoleon decided to sell not only New Orleans but also all of the Louisiana Territory for only $15 million—a small price for so much land. Thomas Jefferson accepted Napoleon's offer and bought the Louisiana Territory in 1803. The **Louisiana Purchase** more than doubled the size of the United States. In the years to come, the Louisiana Purchase would provide all or part of the land for 15 new states: Louisiana, Arkansas, Missouri, Iowa, Minnesota, North Dakota, South Dakota, Nebraska, Kansas, Oklahoma, Montana, Wyoming, Colorado, New Mexico, and Texas.

Exploring the Louisiana Territory

Because hardly anything was known about the land that made up the Louisiana Territory, President Jefferson chose Captain **Meriwether Lewis** to explore the region. Lewis then asked **William Clark,** brother of George Rogers Clark who fought on the frontier in the War for Independence, to accompany him. Along the way, Lewis and Clark met Indians, but the explorers had a difficult time understanding the tribes' languages. In what is now North Dakota, they fortunately met a French trapper whose wife, **Sacagawea,** was a Shoshone Indian. Both agreed to go with Lewis and Clark as interpreters and guides. Sacagawea's presence in the group created more peaceful relations when they encountered Indians. Together, they climbed mountains and crossed rivers until at last they came to the Pacific Ocean. Lewis and Clark returned to Washington, D.C., with good reports for President Jefferson. They presented the President with treasures from the expedition including animal skins, insect and plant specimens, and even a live prairie dog (a type of squirrel), according to Lewis's list of the items collected.

When Americans heard about the vast, new territory that Lewis and Clark explored on their exciting trip, many became eager to move away from the crowded East in search of land and prosperity. Soon more pioneers began pushing their way West to make new homes on the frontier.

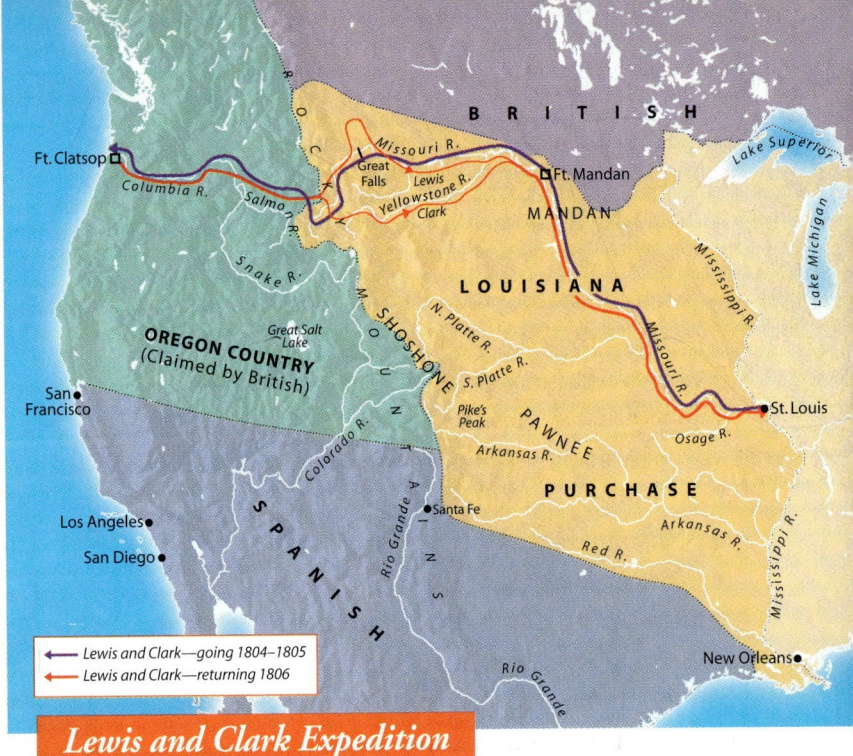

Lewis and Clark Expedition

Sacagawea guiding Lewis and Clark

The War of 1812

France and England at war. Napoleon Bonaparte, the powerful French soldier who ruled France in the early 1800s, aspired to rule all of Europe. He had agreed to sell the Louisiana Territory to the United States partly because he needed money to carry on his wars in Europe.

Problems for American ships. Although America lay across the ocean from Europe, she became involved in a war between France and England when English warships began stopping American ships and abducting American sailors to fight for the British navy. Soon hundreds of American sailors had been kidnapped and forced into the British navy. Neither France nor England respected American ships on the seas. In addition to the problems caused on the seas, Britain also had violated trade rights with America and stirred up Indians on the frontier. <u>The United States declared war on England in 1812.</u> The **War of 1812,** between the Americans and the British, lasted for over two years.

Expansion and Evangelism 173

In 1814, the British marched into Washington, D.C., where they burned the new Capitol building and the White House. **James Madison** (1751–1836), our fourth President, was in office at this time. Before fleeing the White House, First Lady **Dolly Madison,** a favorite of the American people, made certain that important government papers and a portrait of George Washington were saved. Her swift actions kept valuable historic items from being destroyed by the flames.

Our national anthem. The British next planned to capture Baltimore, Maryland. **Francis Scott Key** watched the attack on **Fort McHenry** (which guarded the entrance to Baltimore Harbor) from one of the English warships where he was seeking the release of his friend William Beanes, a prisoner of war. All through the night, the battle raged. When dawn finally came, Key saw that our flag still flew over the fort—the British had failed to capture Baltimore. The sight of our battle-torn flag inspired Francis Scott Key to write the words that became our national anthem, "The Star-Spangled Banner."

The results of the War of 1812. Although the **Treaty of Ghent** [gĕnt] officially ended the war in 1814, the fighting did not cease until 1815. British troops attacked the city of New Orleans in January of 1815 before news of the treaty had reached the United States. The Americans, under the leadership of **General Andrew Jackson,** soundly defeated the British in the **Battle of New Orleans.** After three years of fighting, each side was ready to make peace. England finally respected our ships on the seas, and we also gained the respect of other countries who were watching to see what the outcome would be. The United States proved to herself and others that she could protect herself. The people of the United States became even more thankful to be Americans.

the star-spangled banner

The United States Gains Florida

Although Spain had owned Florida for a long time, it had not ruled the land well. **James Monroe** (1758–1831), the fifth President of the United States, convinced Spain to turn Florida over to the United States. In return, the United States government agreed to pay $5 million in claims which Spain owed U.S. citizens for damage to property. (The Spanish in Florida had attacked settlers in Georgia and Alabama causing damage to homes and farms.) The same treaty, signed in 1819, settled the boundary of the Louisiana Territory between the Spanish and Mexican territories. The United States as we know it today was beginning to come together like a puzzle.

The United States Wins the Southwest from Mexico

In 1821, the country of Mexico fought for and won her independence from Spain. At that time Texas, New Mexico, Arizona, and California were all part of Mexico.

Mexico invites Americans to Texas. In the early 1800s the Mexican government, eager to attract more settlers to Texas, offered land at cheap prices to Americans to establish settlements. Thousands of Americans accepted Mexico's offer. Soon there were more Americans in Texas than there were Mexicans. The Mexican government, fearing that the Americans might try to take over Texas, decided to stop any more U.S. citizens from coming to Texas. Mexican soldiers were sent to guard the border. Then the Mexican government tried to take away the freedoms of the Americans already living in Texas.

In 1833, a dictator named **General Santa Anna** took complete control of Mexico. Two years after coming to power, he led an army north to Texas to bring the American community into subjection to his rule. After several battles with the Mexican army, the Americans in Texas voted for independence in 1836.

Remember the Alamo! The most heroic and best-remembered battle in the Texas struggle for independence took place in San Antonio, Texas, where a group of 187 men gathered inside an old Spanish mission called the **Alamo** and prepared to fight the Mexican army. The men fought so valiantly that for eleven days the army of 3,000 could not get near the Alamo. Finally the Texans ran low on ammunition, and the Mexicans poured into the old mission. The men fought courageously until all 187 of them had been killed. Not one man would give up.

Not all of the men in the Alamo were Texans; some of them, including frontiersman **Davy Crockett** of Tennessee, had come from the United States to help the Texans fight. Aware that he might not return, Crockett wrote a beautiful poem of farewell to his home and his family, ending with "Farewell to ye all! In the land of the stranger I rise or I fall!"

In times of danger, Davy was not afraid. He always said that his life's motto was, "Be always sure you're right—then go ahead!" The night before his death, Crockett made this last entry in his diary:

> March 5. Pop, pop, pop! Bom, bom, bom!—throughout the day. No time for memorandums now. Go ahead! Liberty and independence forever!

It was for liberty and independence that Davy Crockett and the other men in the Alamo gave their lives. After the battle, the cry "Remember the Alamo!" swept through Texas as men prepared to fight Santa Anna. Texans led by **General Sam Houston** took

the battle at the Alamo

Expansion and Evangelism 175

the Mexican army by surprise at the **Battle of San Jacinto** and captured Santa Anna himself along with the Mexican army. Texas now considered herself a free nation. The Texans elected Sam Houston to be their president. Texas remained independent until 1845, when she became the twenty-eighth state to join the Union.

The Mexican War. When Texas became a state, Mexico became bitter toward the United States, and a quarrel arose over the boundary line that separated Texas from Mexico. Texas claimed the **Rio Grande** as her western boundary, while Mexico claimed another boundary that gave Texas less land. United States **President James K. Polk (1795–1849)** sent General Zachary Taylor, who would later become the twelfth President, with an army to guard the Rio Grande. The Mexicans, still claiming this land as theirs, attacked the American army. In the fight, some Americans were killed. The United States then declared war on Mexico.

The war with Mexico began in 1846 and lasted for two years. Traveling into Mexico, American forces captured Mexico City in 1847. By the time the United States secured San Diego that same year, victory was certain. By the treaty of peace, Mexico accepted the Rio Grande as the border between Texas and Mexico and ceded to the United States the large area of land which makes up the present states of **California, Nevada, Utah,** and parts of **Arizona, New Mexico, Wyoming,** and **Colorado.** Americans called this land the **Mexican Cession.** The United States agreed to pay Mexico fifteen million dollars for this piece of land.

The Gadsden Purchase. Five years later, in 1853, the United States bought more land from Mexico. This strip of land, known as the **Gadsden Purchase,** made up the southern parts of what are now New Mexico and Arizona. The purpose of this purchase was to build a railroad through the Southwest.

Comprehension Check 9D
Identify
1. The name of the land purchase between the United States and France which more than doubled the size of the United States.
2. The two explorers President Jefferson sent to explore the Louisiana Territory.
3. The Shoshone Indian guide who helped these explorers.
4. The war fought in the early 1800s between the Americans and the British.
5. The strip of land purchased by the United States from Mexico to be used for a railroad.

Think
6. Who wrote our national anthem and what circumstances inspired him?
7. Who was Davy Crockett? What was his life's motto? In what major battle did he fight and die?

9.5 FROM SEA TO SHINING SEA
The California Gold Rush

In 1848, **James Marshall**, a ranch hand on **John Sutter's** ranch in California, discovered gold. Sutter warned Marshall not to tell anyone, because he knew that greedy prospectors would destroy his land if they knew about the gold. But the news spread, and before long, the whole United States had heard. Many people from both the North and the South left their jobs and homes to go to California. In those days, such a trip was long and dangerous, for there were mountains and deserts to cross as well as warlike Indian tribes to encounter. A new group of people came to America for this gold rush, also—large numbers of Chinese workers.

People became obsessed with gold. So great was their desire for gold that it became known as "gold fever." Although gold had been discovered in 1848, it was 1849 before the great crowd of gold seekers began arriving in California. For this reason, the gold miners became known as **"forty-niners."** The movement of the forty-niners westward was called the **California Gold Rush.**

Most miners did not find enough gold to pay for all of their troubles in reaching California. As John Sutter had feared, thousands of greedy, uninvited gold seekers swarmed over his land. Caring nothing for Sutter's crops or the animals he was raising, they ruined Sutter's farm.

Life in a California gold-mining town. Towns grew rapidly as thousands of gold miners made their way into California. The miners often found life difficult in a gold-mining town. Storekeepers demanded that their goods be paid for in gold dust rather than money. One egg might cost fifty cents or even a dollar, and one pound of flour often cost more than a dollar's worth of gold! With prices like these, the storekeepers often became richer than those who found the gold.

men panning for gold in California during the gold rush of 1849

ghost town

Along with the honest gold miners came dishonest men who would steal or kill for gold. Because California was not yet a state, there was little or no law. The people had to do what they could to protect themselves.

Lumber was so expensive that many men chose to live in tents rather than to build buildings. Some cities were made up almost entirely of tents, but others had rough wooden buildings. As long as the miners found gold, their towns remained prosperous. What happened to those towns whose miners could no longer find gold? Some became **ghost towns**—empty, deserted towns where no one lived. In other towns, some miners finally decided to settle down and build farms or businesses.

California becomes a state. By 1850, only one year after the gold rush, the population of California had grown so much that the people who lived there asked if it could become a state. In that same year, Congress approved the request and California became the thirty-first state to join the Union.

The Oregon Territory

The next piece of land to be added to the United States, the **Oregon Territory,** included the present states of **Oregon, Washington,** and **Idaho** as well as part of **Montana** and **Wyoming.** Before 1846, the territory was a part of the **Oregon Country,** which belonged to both England and the United States. The Oregon Country also included the land which makes up the province of British Columbia.

If you have ever traveled in the northwestern states, you know what beautiful country there is to see. You might then ask, why did it take so long for the Oregon Territory to be added to the United States? Perhaps it was because it involved a long, dangerous journey to get there. The **Oregon Trail** was almost 2,000 miles long, stretching over wild country and hazardous mountains. Before Oregon could be settled, someone had to see it and then travel all the way back East to persuade pioneers to come.

Missionaries to Oregon. Missionaries were among the first to travel to Oregon. They went to teach the Indians. As you have learned, the most famous missionaries to Oregon were **Dr. Marcus Whitman** and his wife **Narcissa.** Narcissa Whitman and another missionary, Eliza Spalding, were the first white women to travel west of the Rockies. Mrs. Whitman had to abandon her precious belongings along the trail, including her wedding chest. The Whitmans worked hard to teach the Indians, and they labored to bring pioneers to Oregon. During one winter, Marcus Whitman made a daring 3,000-mile ride back East to tell the people about Oregon. When he returned, he led the "Great Migration" of nearly 1,000 pioneers safely to Oregon.

Pioneers on the Oregon Trail. Slowly, more people back East heard about Oregon. To make the journey, Oregon-bound pioneers traveled to **Independence, Missouri,** where the Oregon Trail began, and then waited until enough pioneer families came to form a wagon train. The families had to work together to make the 2,000-mile journey a success. The

178 New World History & Geography

men had to keep the wagons repaired and defend the wagon train in an Indian attack. Many of the pioneers would die of sickness or be killed before they reached Oregon.

Oregon becomes a state. By 1845, thousands of pioneers had come to Oregon. It became clear to both Great Britain and the United States that there would have to be a boundary line dividing Oregon into British-owned land and American-owned land. In 1846, the two countries reached an agreement establishing the present border between Canada and the United States. In 1859, **Oregon** became a state. The state of Oregon did not include all of the Oregon Territory, however. Later, **Washington** and **Idaho** also became states. Our country now stretched from "sea to shining sea."

Comprehension Check 9E
Identify
1. Gold seekers who arrived in California in 1849.
2. States or parts of states formed from the Oregon Territory.
3. The most famous missionaries to Oregon.

Think
4. Describe life in a California gold-mining town.

pioneers headed west on the Oregon Trail

9.6 NEW FRIENDS IN JAPAN
Mysterious Land across the Sea

As the United States expanded its territory from the Atlantic to the Pacific, many Americans became interested in learning more about lands across the seas. Japan, the island nation in the Pacific just off the east coast of Asia, fascinated many Americans. The people of Japan were highly cultured, intelligent, and industrious, and their way of life at the time was completely different from the American way of life.

For two hundred years, Japan had been closed to foreigners, ever since Catholic priests from Spain and Portugal had tried to make the people become Catholics. The emperor had issued the following edict against all people who called themselves Christians:

> So long as the sun warms the earth, let no Christian be so bold as to enter into Japan; and let all know that the king of Spain himself, or the Christian's God, or the great God of all, if he violate this command, shall pay for it with his head.

Throughout the United States and England, Christians were praying that the Japanese would come to know the truth about God. If only Japan would allow Christian missionaries to come, the people would have a chance to hear the gospel. The only Japanese Christians were a few shipwrecked sailors who heard the gospel in the United States or at missionary stations in China or Hawaii.

Seven Shipwrecked Sailors

In 1837, two American missionaries and a German missionary living in China attempted to return seven shipwrecked Japanese sailors to their home in Japan. They persuaded a ship captain who wanted to trade with Japan to take them and the shipwrecked sailors to Japan. Their mission of mercy

Expansion and Evangelism 179

was answered with gunfire from the Japanese. The seven Japanese men decided to return to China rather than risk the wrath of their countrymen. Four of them helped the missionaries learn the Japanese language and translate parts of the Bible into Japanese. Christians kept praying that Japan would open its doors to foreigners.

Commodore Perry in Japan

Mission from the President. God answered those prayers through an action of the United States government, which desired to trade with the hard-working Japanese. In 1853, **President Millard Fillmore** (1850–1853) sent a high-ranking United States naval officer, **Commodore Matthew Perry,** to Japan with a fleet of navy ships. Perry's task was to open Japan for trade with the United States.

Perry's Christian testimony. Commodore Perry and his ships arrived in Japan on Thursday, July 8, with a letter from President Fillmore addressed to the Emperor of Japan. After much consultation, the Japanese agreed to deliver the letter. Three days later, Commodore Perry himself conducted the first Protestant worship service in Japan. Because it was Sunday, Perry refused to negotiate with the Japanese officials who had come to see him. The commodore explained to them that Americans do not conduct business on the Sabbath because it is a day set aside to worship God. He had the navy's brass band play hymns on the deck of his flagship while the sailors sang out to the Japanese people:

All people that on earth do dwell,
  Sing to the Lord with cheerful voice,
Him serve with mirth, his praise forthtell,
  Come ye before him and rejoice.

A few days later, after one of Perry's sailors died, the Americans conducted the first Christian burial service the Japanese had ever witnessed. Perry sailed away, but he returned eight months later, in 1854, and convinced the Japanese to sign the trade treaty. This treaty did not permit missionaries to enter Japan, but it did help to unlock the closed door.

Goble's first Japanese convert. Commodore Perry's interpreter in Japan was **Samuel Wells Williams,** one of the three missionaries who had tried to return the seven shipwrecked sailors to their home. A young United States Marine, **Jonathan Goble,** accompanied Perry's fleet. Goble had one overriding purpose for sailing with Perry: he wanted to learn all he could about Japan and return there some day as a missionary. He had tried to get to Japan on his own earlier, but he had always been turned back by armed soldiers guarding the coast. Once he even tried to float in inside a barrel! Goble could not go ashore during Perry's first visit to Japan, but he did meet a young Japanese boy who had stowed away on the ship. Seeing this boy as his chance to learn the Japanese language, Goble took the boy in, and while the boy taught him

Commodore Matthew Perry meeting with the Imperial Commissioners in Japan

Japanese, he taught the boy the Word of God. Soon, Goble had his first Japanese convert. Together, Jonathan Goble and his Japanese friend translated portions of the Bible into Japanese in preparation for a day when Goble could actually get into Japan as a missionary.

Harris opens Japan to the gospel. The first diplomatic representative that the United States sent to Japan was a devout Christian named **Townsend Harris**. He held Bible studies with some of the Japanese, and his deep faith and outstanding testimony impressed the well-mannered Japanese people. In addition to opening Japan for trade, the Harris Treaty, signed in 1858, opened Japan to Christian missionaries.

Missionary to Japan. Two years later, Jonathan Goble became the first Baptist missionary to Japan. Jonathan Goble's wife became very sick in Japan and was left unable to walk. To help her get around, Goble invented the world's first rickshaw. Before long, the rickshaw became a famous Japanese mode of transportation.

Comprehension Check 9F
Identify
1. The man who led the American naval fleet to Japan to open trade relations and conducted the first Protestant worship service in Japan.
2. Diplomatic representative who helped open Japan to American trade as well as Christian missionaries.
3. The first Baptist missionary in Japan.

Chapter 9 Checkup

I. Tell why these **people** are important.

Daniel Boone	Samuel J. Mills	Meriwether Lewis	James K. Polk
Noah Webster	Adoniram Judson	William Clark	John Marshall
William McGuffey	Luther Rice	Sacagawea	John Sutter
John Wesley	Lott Carey	James and Dolly Madison	Dr. Marcus and Narcissa Whitman
Francis Asbury	Collin Teague	Francis Scott Key	Millard Fillmore
Peter Cartwright	Lemuel Haynes	General Andrew Jackson	Commodore Matthew Perry
Richard Allen	John Jasper	James Monroe	
Isaac Watts	John Chavis	General Santa Anna	Samuel Wells Williams
Charles Wesley	Catherine Ferguson	Davy Crockett	Jonathan Goble
George Liele	Thomas Jefferson	General Sam Houston	Townsend Harris

II. Identify the following.

pioneer	circuit-riding preachers	Treaty of Ghent	ghost towns
Wilderness Road	camp meeting	Battle of New Orleans	Oregon Trail
Northwest Ordinance of 1787	American Bible Society	the Alamo	Independence, Missouri
flatboat	spirituals	Battle of San Jacinto	
Erie Canal	Fisk Jubilee Singers	"forty-niners"	
	War of 1812	California Gold Rush	

III. Give the importance of these **territories.**
   Louisiana Purchase   Mexican Cession   Oregon Territory   Gadsden Purchase

IV. Identify the locations from **Map Mastery 12.**

Expansion and Evangelism 181

chapter 10
United States History:
DIVISION and REUNION

10.1 SLAVERY, COMPROMISE, AND STATES' RIGHTS

Slavery Grows in the South

When **Eli Whitney,** a young schoolteacher from Massachusetts, moved to Georgia in 1792, few Southern farmers bothered to plant cotton. It took so long to separate the seeds from the cotton fibers (lint) by hand that cotton cost too much to prepare. Then, in 1793, Whitney invented the **cotton gin,** a machine which removed the seeds quickly and greatly increased the speed of harvesting cotton. Because the cotton gin made cotton cloth cheaper to make, cotton became a valuable crop in the South. Not only the Northern states but also England and France bought cotton from the South. As smoking tobacco became a more popular habit, tobacco continued to be an important crop.

To meet the rising demand for cotton and tobacco, some Southern planters bought additional land to plant more of these crops. Because plantation farming required a large number of workers, some planters unfortunately turned to buying slaves.

Opposition to Slavery Grows

Abolitionists. Until the late 1700s, some slavery existed in every American colony. Then slavery began to disappear from the

---

Timeline (1800–1890):

- **1793** Eli Whitney invents the cotton gin
- **1820** Missouri Compromise
- **1860** Southern states begin to secede
- **1860** Pony Express
- **1861** Southern states form Confederacy
- **1861** Battle at Fort Sumter
- **1861–1865** The Civil War
- **1863** Emancipation Proclamation
- **1863** Battle of Gettysburg
- **1863** Battle of Vicksburg
- **1864** Union troops take Atlanta and Savannah
- **1865** General R. E. Lee surrenders at Appomattox Court House
- **1865** President Lincoln is shot
- **1869** Transcontinental Railroad completed
- **1881** Clara Barton founds American Red Cross
- **1881** Booker T. Washington founds Tuskegee Institute
- **1896** George Washington Carver joins the faculty of Tuskegee Institute

During the Civil War, Abraham Lincoln became one of America's greatest Presidents.

North because the farms there were small and the factories did not need slave labor. **Abolitionists** (people who spent much time trying to outlaw slavery) both in the North and the South began to speak out against slavery. "How can we call this a free country when we allow one man to own another?" they asked the Southern slave owners. One abolitionist, **Sojourner Truth** (1820–1892), a freed black woman from New York, traveled throughout the North, speaking out against slavery. Another abolitionist, **Harriet Beecher Stowe** (1811–1896), an author from Connecticut, wrote a novel called ***Uncle Tom's Cabin,*** in which she portrayed the evils of slavery. Many Northerners who had previously ignored the issue began to side with the abolitionists. But by this time, the South depended on its slaves, even though fewer than five percent of the white Southerners owned slaves, and half of these had no more than five slaves each. If the Southerners freed their slaves, how could they make a living? And how would the freed slaves earn a living? There were no easy solutions to the problem of slavery.

The Underground Railroad. By the mid-1800s, a system of escape routes and hiding places had developed between the Southern states and Canada. This secret network soon became known as the **Underground Railroad.** White abolitionists in both the North and the South, free blacks, and escaped slaves helped runaway slaves as they fled to freedom. Runaway slaves traveled during the night and hid during the day. Along the way, *conductors* (those who helped the slaves) hid them, gave them directions to *stations* (hiding places) farther north, and provided them with food and clothing. Thousands of slaves escaped to the North by means of the Underground Railroad. One of the most famous leaders of the railroad was **Harriet Tubman** (1820–1913), an escaped

Harriet Tubman (far left) with some slaves she helped to freedom.

slave from Maryland. Tubman made 19 dangerous trips to the South and guided as many as 300 slaves to freedom. As more Northerners showed sympathy to the slaves and more slaves escaped to the North, tension between the North and South increased.

The Missouri Compromise

As new states joined the Union, a new question arose. Should these new states be admitted as *free states* (states not allowing people to own slaves) or as *slave states* (states that allowed people to own slaves)? Remember that each state is represented by two senators in the Senate. If the slave states outnumbered the free states, the Senate would favor the slave states. However, if the free states controlled the Senate, the Senate would favor the free states. To keep both the free and the slave states happy, Congress had to maintain an equal number of free and slave states.

In 1818 and 1819, Missouri and Maine asked to join the Union. To maintain a balance in the Senate, Missouri would have to be admitted as a slave state and Maine as a free state. Some of the people in Missouri were against slavery, however. Finally, in 1820, Congress agreed to admit Missouri as a slave state and Maine as a free state, but only after a **compromise** was made. A compromise is a decision that tries to satisfy both sides of an argument. Since Missouri was to become a slave state, no other territories north of an established boundary line could enter the Union as slave states. This decision became known as the **Missouri Compromise**.

Tariffs and States' Rights

Many Southern states believed that each state had the right to make its own decisions and laws. They were especially upset by taxes called **tariffs** which the federal government had placed on goods imported from other countries. These tariffs were intended to aid manufacturers in the North by discouraging foreign competition. But because the South did much of its trading with Great Britain, the tariffs forced Southerners to pay more for their goods and thus they had less money to spend on their families. In their desperation, some Southerners even began to talk about separating from the United States and forming their own nation. Most Southerners, whether they agreed with slavery or not, believed that because their states had joined the United States voluntarily, they had a right to leave the Union just as easily. But the North insisted that no state could leave the Union.

The Man Who Saved the Union

Indiana farmboy. In 1809, a boy named **Abraham Lincoln** (1809–1865) was born in the hills of Kentucky to Thomas and Nancy Lincoln. The family moved to southern Indiana in 1816, where they established a modest farm. Farming kept young Abe so busy that he had little time for formal schooling. Because he didn't want to be ignorant, Abe read any books he could get his hands on. He especially enjoyed reading the Bible, *Pilgrim's Progress,* and a biography of George Washington. As he grew older and continued to read, Abe developed a talent for speaking and telling stories. People loved to swap stories with the friendly farm boy.

Abe once accompanied a load of farm produce down the Mississippi River to New Orleans. Although he enjoyed the trip, he saw something there which deeply disturbed him. He saw men, women, and children being sold like animals at a slave auction. From that day forward, he longed to help those poor people.

Honest Abe. In 1831, Abe moved to the town of New Salem, Illinois. A year later, the

184 *New World History & Geography*

Black Hawk Indians tried to regain their tribal lands in Illinois. When Abe volunteered to serve in the Illinois militia, the men of New Salem chose him to be the captain of their company. He won their respect and admiration for his brave leadership.

After the war, Abe tried his hand at several occupations. For a time, he owned and operated a store in New Salem. The store failed, however, leaving him in debt. Abe also served as county postmaster and surveyor. Serving in these public offices and working at odd jobs, he finally earned enough money to pay off his debts. Lincoln's determination to pay his debts and deal honestly earned him the nickname of "Honest Abe."

Law and politics. In 1834, Abe Lincoln won a seat in the Illinois legislature. On the advice of John T. Stuart, an attorney and member of the legislature, Lincoln began to study for a law career. By 1837, Lincoln had earned his license and joined Stuart's law firm. He served on the state legislature until 1842 and practiced law until he was elected to the United States House of Representatives in 1846.

After a term in Congress, Lincoln returned to his law practice, where he prospered greatly and established a good reputation across the state. <u>Although Lincoln was not an abolitionist, he opposed slavery and hoped to see it die out in time. He knew that sooner or later America would have to decide either to accept slavery or to reject it</u>. **"'A house divided against itself cannot stand,'"** he said. "I believe this government cannot endure permanently half slave and half free. I do not expect the Union to be dissolved—I do not expect the house to fall—but I do expect it will cease to be divided. It will become all one thing, or all the other."

For several years, Lincoln worked tirelessly to oppose Senator **Stephen A. Douglas,** a Democrat who sought to pass a bill which would allow settlers in new states to own slaves. In 1858, Lincoln ran against Douglas for senator. Though he lost the election, Lincoln gained the attention of the nation with his powerful campaign speeches.

Lincoln becomes President. When the time came for a new President to be elected in 1860, many Americans looked to Lincoln with great expectations. Lincoln wanted to preserve the Union. He did not want to see

young Abraham Lincoln reading by the light of the fire

our country divided. Although Lincoln cared about the South's problems, the South said they could not trust him as their President because he opposed slavery. They threatened to leave the Union if Lincoln became President. Nevertheless, <u>Abraham Lincoln was elected the 16th President in 1860</u>.

The South Leaves the Union

South Carolina left the Union shortly after Lincoln's election. By February of 1861, six other Southern states had joined South Carolina: Mississippi, Florida, Alabama, Georgia, Louisiana, and Texas. These states formed their own nation, the **Confederate States of America,** and elected **Jefferson Davis** to be their president.

Though Abraham Lincoln begged the North and the South not to become enemies, the states had already chosen sides. As the Southern states began to withdraw from the Union, it became evident that only war could bring the country back together again.

Comprehension Check 10A

Identify
1. The invention of Eli Whitney.
2. A name for people who worked to make slavery illegal.
3. The compromise made in 1820 admitting Missouri to the Union and establishing law concerning the admission of new slave states.
4. The secret network of escape routes and hiding places between the Southern states and Canada.
5. The sixteenth President.

Think
6. Why did Southern planters begin owning more slaves? How did Northerners respond to the growing numbers of slaveholders in the South?
7. What lessons can you learn from the life of Abraham Lincoln?

10.2 THE CIVIL WAR BEGINS

The First Battle

The United States Army had several forts within Confederate territory. When the Confederates demanded that these forts and their guns be surrendered to the Confederate states, the Union refused. By April of 1861, only two significant forts had not fallen into Confederate hands: Fort Pickens, at Pensacola, Florida, and Fort Sumter, in the harbor of Charleston, South Carolina. <u>The war began when Confederate forces fired on</u> **Fort Sumter** <u>on April 12, 1861</u>.

The Union troops inside Fort Sumter had few supplies and were forced to surrender after two days of fighting. A Confederate flag soon flew over the fort. <u>The Confederates had won the first battle of the war</u>. Little did they realize that a long, horrible fight lay before them. They mistakenly believed that the North would give up. They also thought that England and France would come to help them. But the Confederates were wrong.

Call for Soldiers

The Battle of Fort Sumter saddened President Lincoln, for he knew that the Union must be preserved at all costs. When he called for soldiers to defend the Union, thousands volunteered. Black statesman **Frederick Douglass,** an outspoken and active opponent of slavery, helped Lincoln recruit blacks. The **Union** soldiers, sometimes called "Yankees," wore blue uniforms and marched beneath the Stars and Stripes. The **Confederate** army wore gray and proudly waved their own Confederate battle flag.

Some states in the South had not yet joined the Confederacy. When President Lincoln called for soldiers, however, they could not bear the thought of fighting against their own Southern neighbors. Instead, they left the Union and joined the Confederate states. These states were Virginia, North Carolina, Tennessee, and Arkansas. The Confederate government now consisted of 11 states. Twenty-two states stayed with the Union.

A Blockade against the South

Because the North had many factories and many small farms which grew large supplies of food, it had sufficient food and supplies to last throughout the war. The South had few factories, however, and it had depended mainly on cotton and tobacco for its economy. The people could not eat tobacco, nor could they wear cotton unless it was turned into cloth by factories in the North or in Europe. President Lincoln knew that the South now depended on trade with Europe to supply her with guns, ammunition, war supplies, and even some food. Without these things, the South did not have a chance of winning the war. To stop the South's trade with Europe, President Lincoln sent Union ships to block all major seaports in the South. A few ships managed to slip through the **blockade,** but most Southern ships were stopped.

The Merrimac *and the* Monitor

The South badly needed to break through the blockade and obtain important supplies. Because the Confederate navy had very few ships compared to the Northern navy, they decided to develop at least one powerful ship. Thus the Confederates raised the **Merrimac,** an old ship that the Union had sunk, and covered it with iron plates. Cannon balls and gun shells would simply bounce off these thick plates. They fitted guns to the sides of the ship and mounted a sharp piece of iron to the ship's bow. With this iron ram, the *Merrimac* could crash into the sides of the Union's ships.

At this time, ships were made of wood. It would be simple for an **ironclad** ship to destroy wooden ships without receiving any harm itself. Within a short time, the *Merrimac* had destroyed two of the best ships in the Union navy.

The Union then built an ironclad ship, the **Monitor.** Soon the *Merrimac* met the *Monitor* in battle. People have described the *Merrimac* as looking like an upside-down bathtub, while the *Monitor* has been described as looking like a cheesebox on a raft. For

U.S. during Civil War

Free states
Slave states
Border states
Territories

the battle between the Merrimac *and the* Monitor

Division and Reunion 187

hours, the two ships fought in vain. But because neither vessel could do more than dent the other, neither side won. Still, the battle did have an important result. It proved the value of ironclad ships to the navy. Gradually, the wooden ships of the world became outdated. In the future, ships would be built with iron and steel.

The Emancipation Proclamation

The plight of the slaves concerned President Lincoln. If he set them free, what would happen to them after the war? Very few of them had any education. How could they get jobs in order to buy homes, food, and clothing? How could a nation, already weak from war, help them? But as the war dragged on, President Lincoln decided that he could weaken the South and shorten the war by setting the slaves free. Thus he made the **Emancipation Proclamation,** an announcement that on January 1, 1863, all slaves would be considered free in any states that were fighting against the North.

Although the Emancipation Proclamation declared the slaves in the South free, it could not really free the slaves until the North won the war. And it did *not* free any slaves who were owned in states that were not fighting against the Union. After the war, Congress would make an *amendment* or change in the Constitution (the **13th Amendment**) giving all slaves in the United States and her territories their freedom.

But the Emancipation Proclamation did have two immediate results. For many people, it changed the reason for fighting the Civil War. Before, the Union army was fighting to keep our country from dividing, and the Confederate army was fighting for states' rights. Now the Union army was also fighting to free the slaves. Before the proclamation, England had considered helping the South become a separate country. England opposed slavery, however, and had no desire to help the South continue slavery. Thus the Emancipation Proclamation ended the chance of England helping the South.

Heroes of the Civil War

Many brave men fought on both sides of the Civil War. These men endured great hardships—hunger, cold, sickness, pain, and sometimes death. But they kept on fighting to defend what they thought was right. One courageous Union soldier, a black American by the name of **William Harvey Carney,** rescued the "Stars and Stripes" from a wounded color sergeant (flag bearer) in the heat of the Battle of Fort Wagner. Before fainting from wounds he had received while recovering the flag, Carney proclaimed, "The old flag never touched the ground!" Soldiers on both sides wrote letters home to their wives, parents, or sweethearts, telling them that times were hard but they knew God would help them. Great leaders also arose during this time, notably General **Ulysses S. Grant,** leader of the

Abraham Lincoln reads the Emancipation Proclamation to his cabinet.

Union troops, General **Robert E. Lee,** head of the Confederate army, and General **Stonewall Jackson,** General Lee's most valuable assistant.

Ulysses S. Grant, Union general. General Ulysses S. Grant, Lincoln's most valuable general, began his rise to prominence when he took control of Tennessee in 1862. With the support of a fleet of gunboats, Grant's army moved against Fort Henry and Fort Donelson in the interior of the state. Although Fort Henry fell quickly, the Confederate troops at Fort Donelson resisted the Union forces. Grant surrounded the fort, determined to take it or starve the Confederates out in the process. When asked for terms of surrender, Grant sent his famous reply: "No terms except unconditional and immediate surrender can be accepted." By February, 40,000 Confederate soldiers had surrendered and 40 cannons had fallen into Union hands. The courageous Union general soon became known as **"Unconditional Surrender" Grant.**

Ulysses S. Grant's greatest victory came at the Battle of Vicksburg in 1863. For six weeks, Grant's troops besieged this city along the Mississippi River until the Confederates finally surrendered. After the fall of Vicksburg, Union forces quickly took control of the Mississippi, dividing the Confederate states in two. Grant's many victories did not go unnoticed in Washington. In 1864, President Lincoln made him the commander of all Union armies.

Robert E. Lee, Confederate general. The thought of war greatly troubled Robert E. Lee, because he loved the United States. Lee also loved his home state of Virginia, however. When Virginia left the Union, Lee felt it was his duty to follow his state. Robert E. Lee became the most amazing general in the Civil War. He is remembered today as a gentleman, a great military general, and a man who always placed duty and responsibility above his personal feelings. "Duty is the sublimest word in our language," he said. "Do your duty in all things. You cannot do more. You should never wish to do less." Whenever Robert E. Lee had a decision to make, he first asked himself, "What is my duty as a gentleman and a Christian?" Once he knew the answer, he went ahead and did the thing that needed to be done.

"Stonewall" Jackson. One of the greatest military heroes of the Civil War and one of the greatest generals of all time was Thomas ("Stonewall") Jackson, who fought under Robert E. Lee. Jackson earned the nickname of "Stonewall" at the **Battle of Bull Run,** where he and his soldiers fought against overwhelming odds. Another Confederate general, seeing Jackson's great courage, shouted to his own men, "There is Jackson standing like a stone wall. Let us determine to die here, and we will conquer."

Stonewall Jackson had an outstanding Christian testimony that he shared with the men under him and around him. Church services were held in his camp whenever possible, and he handed out gospel tracts to his troops and encouraged them to pray and read their Bibles faithfully. Before the war, he taught a Sunday school class for black slaves, and during the war he continued to send money for the support of this class.

Stonewall Jackson lost his life in the Civil War when, as he came riding into camp one

Division and Reunion

evening, one of his men mistook him for the enemy and shot him. In a last attempt to save his life, doctors amputated Jackson's left arm. General Lee, who greatly valued Jackson as a general and a Christian companion, declared sadly, "He has lost his left arm, but I have lost my right arm." General Stonewall Jackson died a few days later. On his deathbed, he was offered brandy and water in an attempt to revive him, but he refused to drink, crying out, "It tastes like fire, and cannot do me any good!"

News of Stonewall Jackson's death spread quickly to other parts of the world. The people of England called him a "heaven-born general," and in Scotland the train conductors opened the doors of the passenger cars to tell passengers that the great Confederate general had died. General Stonewall Jackson has gone down in history as a great general and a great Christian.

Comprehension Check 10B

Identify
1. The first battle of the Civil War.
2. The black statesman who helped President Lincoln recruit blacks to fight for the Union.
3. President Lincoln's announcement that all slaves would be considered free in any states fighting against the North.
4. The leader of the Union troops.
5. The leader of the Confederate troops.

Think
6. What can we learn from General Stonewall Jackson's Christian testimony?

10.3 Important Civil War Battles

During the first two years of the Civil War, the North lost more battles than it won. Most of the fighting took place in the South. The Confederates fought hard to keep the North from sweeping across their land.

The Battle of Gettysburg. In the spring of 1863, the Confederates decided to push their troops to the North. In a bold move, General Robert E. Lee marched 70,000 men from Virginia to Pennsylvania. Union and Confederate troops met in a bloody battle at Gettysburg, Pennsylvania. Three days of fighting resulted in the deaths of over 7,000 Union and Confederate men, and the South lost the **Battle of Gettysburg,** the turning point of the war.

The Battle of Vicksburg. On the fourth of July 1863, General Grant had defeated the Confederates at Vicksburg, Mississippi. By gaining control of Vicksburg, the Union army won control of the Mississippi River. No longer could the Confederates on one side of the river send supplies to Confederates on the other side. Although the South was cut in two, she still would not give up.

the Battle of Gettysburg

Sherman's march to the sea. Everyone was tired of fighting. General Grant made plans which he hoped would hasten the end of the war. In 1864, he sent **General William T. Sherman** to capture Atlanta, Georgia, an important city to the Confederates. From there, he wanted Sherman to march to Savannah, Georgia, on the Atlantic Coast.

Believing that the only way to make the South surrender was to discourage her even further, Sherman gave orders for his Union troops to burn or destroy everything they found, including homes, barns, animals, food, and crops. The South could not possibly keep fighting much longer after such terrible destruction.

General Lee surrenders to General Grant at Appomattox Court House.

The Civil War Comes to a Close

Meanwhile, General Grant had been fighting General Lee to capture **Richmond,** Virginia, the capital of the Confederate States. After many months of hard fighting, the Union troops surrounded the Confederate army. The Confederates had been beaten in too many places. General Lee knew there was nothing else he could do but surrender.

On April 9, 1865, Lee met Grant in a farmhouse in the town of **Appomattox Court House, Virginia.** Grant wrote very generous terms of surrender. Like President Lincoln, Grant had no desire to hurt the South further. In his terms of surrender, Grant wrote that the North would take no prisoners of war. General Grant allowed the Confederate soldiers to keep their horses, because he realized that the Southern farmers would need these animals to help plant crops. He also allowed the officers of the Confederate army to keep their guns and General Lee to keep his sword.

When Lee read the terms of surrender that Grant had written, he said gratefully, "You have been very generous to the South." Now that the Confederate army had surrendered, Grant ordered that food be taken to the starving Confederate soldiers.

EVENTS IN HISTORY
The Gettysburg Address

The Battle of Gettysburg took a terrible toll on both the Northern and the Southern armies. Thousands of men died in this battle. After the battle, Gettysburg became a great cemetery. A special ceremony was held to honor the men who had been killed at Gettysburg. Many famous men were scheduled to speak, including President Lincoln.

The main speaker at Gettysburg on November 19, 1863, was a famous orator (speaker) named Edward Everett. For two hours, he held the audience spellbound as he described in flowery language the events of the recent battle. Then came the President's turn to speak. But instead of a long speech, Lincoln spoke for less than three minutes. He spoke 10 simple, direct sentences and then sat down. But those 10 sentences—now known as the Gettysburg Address—make up one of the most famous and familiar speeches in American history. Edward Everett's long speech has been forgotten, but everyone is familiar with the Gettysburg Address.

Division and Reunion

After the War

Results of the war. At last, the soldiers could return to their homes. Peace had come after four years of bitter fighting (1861–1865). The war had settled two important issues: (1) no state could leave the Union, and (2) there would be no more slavery in the United States.

Plans for peace. Just before the war ended, the people of the United States elected Abraham Lincoln to his second term as President. President Lincoln made it clear that he looked forward to the time when our nation would be whole again. *He did not intend to punish the South.* He spoke these words to our nation: "With malice [hatred] toward none, with charity [love] for all." He then asked the people "to bind up the nation's wounds; to care for him who shall have borne the battle, and for his widow, and orphan—to do all which may achieve . . . a just and lasting peace."

Lincoln did not say "only the North" or "only the South." Instead, he referred to "all." President Lincoln planned to bring peace again to our whole country. Unfortunately, he did not live to carry out his plans.

President Lincoln is shot. The Civil War had been over for only five days when a very tired but happy President Lincoln took his wife to see a play at Ford's Theatre in Washington, D.C. While they were watching the play, a half-crazed actor named **John Wilkes Booth** slipped through the theater to where the President sat and shot Lincoln, probably because he blamed Lincoln for the Civil War.

Men carried the President to a house across the street from the theater, where he died the next morning. Our whole nation mourned the death of this great man. Even the South was beginning to realize the friend they had in President Lincoln.

A bitter peace. Vice President **Andrew Johnson** became President in Lincoln's place. Although Johnson wanted to carry out Abraham Lincoln's wishes, many men in Congress felt bitter toward the South. These men were able to make Congress strong enough to stop President Johnson's plans. As a result, for several years Congress passed laws that punished the South. Fortunately, with the passing of time, the bitterness caused by the Civil War was forgotten. Once again, the men from the North and the South were willing to stand side by side to help their country.

Comprehension Check 10C
Identify
1. The battle that was the turning point of the war won by the North.
2. The importance of the Battle of Vicksburg.
3. The town in which Lee surrendered to Grant.
4. The man who shot President Lincoln.

10.4 Other Events of Civil War Times

Our Nation Gets a New Motto

During the Civil War, the motto "In God We Trust" first appeared on United States coins. The man most responsible for the adoption of the motto was Secretary of the Treasury Salmon Chase, who sent the following memo to the director of the Mint at Philadelphia (one of the places where our nation's money is made):

> No nation can be strong except in the strength of God, or safe except in His defense. The trust of our people in God should be declared on our national coins. You will cause a device to be prepared without unnecessary delay with a motto expressing in the fewest and tersest words possible this national recognition.

The director of the mint composed several mottoes, from which Chase chose

"In God We Trust." Since that time, coins issued by the United States have borne testimony to the nation's dependence on God. "In God We Trust" became the official national motto in 1956.

Americans Sing New Songs

Many songs were either written or became popular during the Civil War. Julia Ward Howe's "Battle Hymn of the Republic" and Dan Emmett's "Dixie" are the best remembered, but there were many others. Some were lively tunes that soldiers sang as they marched to war; others were quiet melodies that they sang around campfires. Many of these Civil War songs remain popular today because of their patriotic themes and their distinctly American flavor.

In the North, George Frederick Root wrote "The Battle Cry of Freedom" and nearly thirty other Civil War songs. In the South, "Bonnie Blue Flag" and "The Yellow Rose of Texas" became popular. "Goober Peas," a song about Confederate soldiers passing the time by eating peanuts, helped Southerners make light of the hardships they faced during the war. "When Johnny Comes Marching Home," and "Tenting on the Old Campground" were heard in the camps of both Northern and Southern troops. Even though war divided the nation, songs reflected the common bonds that remained between the people of the North and the South.

The Gospel Continues to Spread

Most churches, in both the North and the South, put themselves wholeheartedly into the war effort. Churches donated financial and medical aid to the cause and gave moral support to troops. Thousands of Bibles and tracts were distributed to both Union and Confederate soldiers. Many tracts were written specifically for the soldiers. During the war, in both North and South, many preachers served as chaplains. Church organizations devised various ways to help people in need. After the war, churches helped to heal the wounds, rebuild the country, return citizens to peacetime work, and prepare the freed slaves for citizenship.

Because war forces men to face death, it also forces them to think upon spiritual matters. In both North and South, there were many spiritual revivals during the course of the war among both civilians and soldiers. The revival was especially noted among the Southern troops, at least partly through the testimony of General Stonewall Jackson.

Clara Barton Founds the American Red Cross

Soon after the war began, **Clara Barton** (1821–1912), a native of Massachusetts, went to the battlefield to nurse wounded soldiers. By 1864, she had been appointed superintendent of a division of Union nurses. Her courage and skill earned her the respect of the nation. Soldiers called her the "Angel of the Battlefield." After the war, at President Lincoln's request, Clara Barton organized a bureau to locate missing soldiers.

Clara Barton

In 1869, Clara Barton went to Europe, where she served as a nurse on the front lines during the Franco-Prussian War. The work of the International Committee of the Red Cross in Europe greatly impressed her. When she returned to the United States in 1873, she immediately began efforts to establish an American branch of the Red Cross. In 1881, Clara Barton founded the American National

Division and Reunion

Red Cross. Clara Barton became its first president and served in that capacity until 1904.

The Pony Express Speeds the Mail

Now that people lived all over the United States, they needed a faster way of communicating across the miles. To meet this need, some men developed a mail route between St. Joseph, Missouri, and Sacramento, California, called the **Pony Express.** The Pony Express opened in 1860, shortly before the Civil War, and lasted only 19 months. The mail was carried by boys or young men who were small and light and were willing to ride through Indian country alone. The mail carrier rode a pony as fast as he could for a 15-mile stretch. At a way station, he would switch to a fresh pony and be on his way again in less than two minutes. Riders covered from 75 to 100 miles in a day. A letter sent by Pony Express could travel from coast to coast in 10 days. But the Pony Express was expensive (it cost $5.00 to send a letter) and very dangerous. Once telegraph lines linked the East to the West, there was no more need for it.

a Pony Express rider passes men working on telegraph lines

be laid across vast prairies and plains and over rugged mountain ranges. In 1862, during the Civil War, two railroad companies were chosen to begin this tremendous job. Within a couple of years, the **Union Pacific Company** began work in **Omaha, Nebraska.** (A railroad had already been built to Omaha from the East.) The Union Pacific workers laid their tracks westward from Omaha. At the same time, the **Central Pacific Company** started in **Sacramento, California,** and began laying tracks toward the East. Thousands of people from China moved to California to help lay these tracks. Somewhere in the middle, these two railroad companies would meet and join to form our first transcontinental railroad.

The Railroad Spans the Nation

Little by little, the railroads had improved, and some people began to dream of a railroad that could connect the East with the West. Building a **transcontinental railroad** would be a long, difficult job. The track would have to

The East and West meet at the completion of the transcontinental railroad.

Men labored many years to build this railroad. There were no stores along the way to buy supplies and food. As far as the new tracks were finished, trains carried supplies to the workers. The workers shot buffalo for fresh meat. Summer days were hot and winter days were cold. Indians often attacked the working men. Day by day, the two sets of tracks came closer and closer to joining each other. The two railroad companies raced each other to see which company would finish the most miles of tracks. Finally, on May 10, 1869, a Union Pacific locomotive traveling west met a Central Pacific locomotive traveling east at **Promontory Point, Utah.**

One more spike would finish the job. No ordinary spike would do for such a great event. Amidst the sound of cheers and the blows of sledge hammers, railroad officials drove a **gold spike** into the last rail.

The transcontinental railroad brought tremendous changes to our country. Settlers began traveling West in trains rather than in wagons, and people from the East were now able to visit people who had moved West. Farmers and businessmen from the West could send their products back East by train to sell them and order supplies in return from the East.

Comprehension Check 10D

Identify
1. Our nation's motto.
2. The founder of the American Red Cross.
3. The mail route between St. Joseph, Missouri, and Sacramento, California.
4. The railroad that stretched from the Atlantic Ocean to the Pacific. The two railroad companies that worked together to connect the East and the West.

Think
5. How did the transcontinental railroad benefit people in the East? In the West?

10.5 REBUILDING THE SOUTH

After the Civil War, much of the South lay desolate. Many farms had been ruined, and millions of slaves had been freed who had no jobs, no property, no homes, and no education. Two black men, both born into slavery, who spent their lives trying to improve conditions for the people in the South were Booker T. Washington and George Washington Carver.

Booker T. Washington: Famous Black Educator

Booker T. Washington (1856–1915) grew up with a deep love of learning. As a boy, he taught himself to read using an old, battered copy of Webster's "Blue-Backed Speller." Later, a teacher came to his town, and Washington was able to attend school. At the age of 15, he left his home in Malden, West Virginia, to go to a school called Hampton Institute. There he learned to love reading the Bible. He also learned many valuable skills.

In 1881, a group of people from the town of Tuskegee, Alabama, asked Booker T. Washington to teach a school there. The idea of having his own school building, his own books, and his own students thrilled Washington. But when he reached Tuskegee, he found no building, no books, and just a handful of students. Washington worked hard to build a school, but he did not mind, because he knew that his work would be worthwhile. "Nothing ever comes to one, that is worth having, except as a result of hard work," he said.

Washington was right about hard work. Although the Tuskegee school started out in a leaky, ramshackle old building, it grew rapidly as more and more students came to learn. Washington wanted to teach his students that they should work hard to support themselves

Division and Reunion 195

and prosper. He and his students planted a garden at the school. They used the crops for food and sold the surplus to get money for books. When the school needed more buildings, Washington taught the students to make bricks and build their own buildings. They sold the extra bricks. The school, which came to be known as **Tuskegee Institute,** prospered and grew. Known today as the Tuskegee University, it continues to provide excellent training for men and women. Booker T. Washington was elected to the Hall of Fame for Great Americans in 1945. A bust of him created by black sculptor Richmond Barthé is displayed at the hall at New York University. Washington's autobiography, *Up from Slavery,* has been ranked one of the top 50 books of the 20th century and still inspires people today.

Booker T. Washington

George Washington Carver: The Plant Genius

In 1896, Booker T. Washington, hoping to find a good chemistry teacher for his school, wrote a letter to a graduate of Iowa State College, inviting him to Tuskegee for a lifetime of "hard, hard work." **George Washington Carver** was not at all afraid of hard work. Though he had been born a slave, he had been blessed with kind masters who allowed him to read and study all he wanted. Fascinated by nature, he taught himself about the plants of the forest. His knowledge of trees and plants amazed his teachers in college. Carver decided that he could put his knowledge to good use at Tuskegee and accepted Washington's invitation.

George W. Carver

George Washington Carver amazed the world with his accomplishments. It seemed that he could do anything with plants. He studied the chemistry of plants very thoroughly and knew what could be done with them. For example, he found 118 uses for the sweet potato. He invented flour, starch, paste, vinegar, ink, rubber, chocolate, dyes—all made from sweet potatoes! From the peanut, he made over 285 products, including milk, butter, cheese, candy, coffee, shaving lotion, lard, soap, shampoo, and ink! Carver once served a delicious meal to a group of visitors. After the meal, the guests complimented Carver on his cooking. Only then did Carver reveal that the entire meal had been made from peanuts!

Carver loved the Bible and lived according to its precepts. At one time, he taught a Sunday school class which numbered over 300. In conducting his research, Carver placed so much confidence in God and His principles that his laboratory became known as **"God's Little Workshop."**

But we do not remember George Washington Carver simply because he stayed in his laboratory and did amazing things with peanuts and sweet potatoes. He did far more valuable work when he helped struggling farmers in the South become prosperous. For years, cotton was practically the only crop planted by Southern farmers. But cotton wears out the soil. Carver found crops which helped the soil, and he traveled around the South convincing farmers to plant them. He encouraged farmers to plant peanuts, which nourished and enriched the soil instead of wearing it out. He urged farmers to grow soybeans, one of the most profitable crops a farmer can grow today. Years and years of growing cotton had exhausted the soil and had made Southern farmers poor. George Washington Carver encouraged farmers to diversify their crops and helped restore the South to prosperity. In 1973, George Washington Carver was elected to the Hall of Fame for Great Americans.

Comprehension Check 10E

Identify

1. The man who founded Tuskegee Institute and said, "Nothing ever comes to one, that is worth having, except as a result of hard work."
2. The botanist who found 118 uses for the sweet potato.

Think

3. How did the students at Tuskegee Institute earn money for books? What did they do when they needed more buildings?

CHAPTER 10 CHECKUP

I. Define these **terms.**

cotton gin	tariff	Pony Express
abolitionist	Union	transcontinental railroad
Underground Railroad	Confederate	Union Pacific Company
compromise	ironclad	Central Pacific Company
Missouri Compromise	Emancipation Proclamation	Tuskegee Institute

II. Explain the importance of these **battles.**

Fort Sumter	Battle of Bull Run	Battle of Vicksburg
Merrimac and *Monitor*	Battle of Gettysburg	

III. Tell why these **people** are important.

Eli Whitney	Jefferson Davis	General William T. Sherman
Sojourner Truth	Frederick Douglass	John Wilkes Booth
Harriet Beecher Stowe	William Harvey Carney	Andrew Johnson
Harriet Tubman	Ulysses S. Grant	Clara Barton
Abraham Lincoln	Robert E. Lee	Booker T. Washington
Stephen A. Douglas	Stonewall Jackson	George Washington Carver

IV. Give the importance of these **cities.**

Richmond, Virginia	Omaha, Nebraska	Promontory Point, Utah
Appomattox Court House, Virginia	Sacramento, California	

Division and Reunion

chapter 11
United States History:
The NATION GROWS and PROSPERS

11.1 THE WESTERN FRONTIER

Over 100 years had passed since Daniel Boone led many of the first pioneers into Kentucky. Since then, pioneers had been traveling westward by the scores. By the middle of the 1800s, California and Oregon had already begun settlement. The Great Plains and the area around the Rocky Mountains remained the last frontier to settle. By 1900, settlers had pushed the West all the way to the Pacific Ocean, and what was once called the West became known as the Midwest.

The Indians of the Great Plains

As the pioneers moved westward, they settled on land that belonged to the American Indians. Our government had given the Indians the Great Plains for their own land, but little by little, the Indians watched this land disappear. Then the white men began to kill off the buffalo herds that had provided the Indians with food, shelter, and clothing. First, men came from the East to hunt the buffalo for its hide. Then men began to shoot the buffalo for sport. The buffalo herds dwindled rapidly.

Many Indians decided to fight for their land. Indian raids plagued the settlements. Homes were burned, and many men, women, and children were killed. Indian wars followed. Both sides showed great cruelty in this sad chapter in our country's history. The Indians had many false religions which made it difficult for them to get along with the

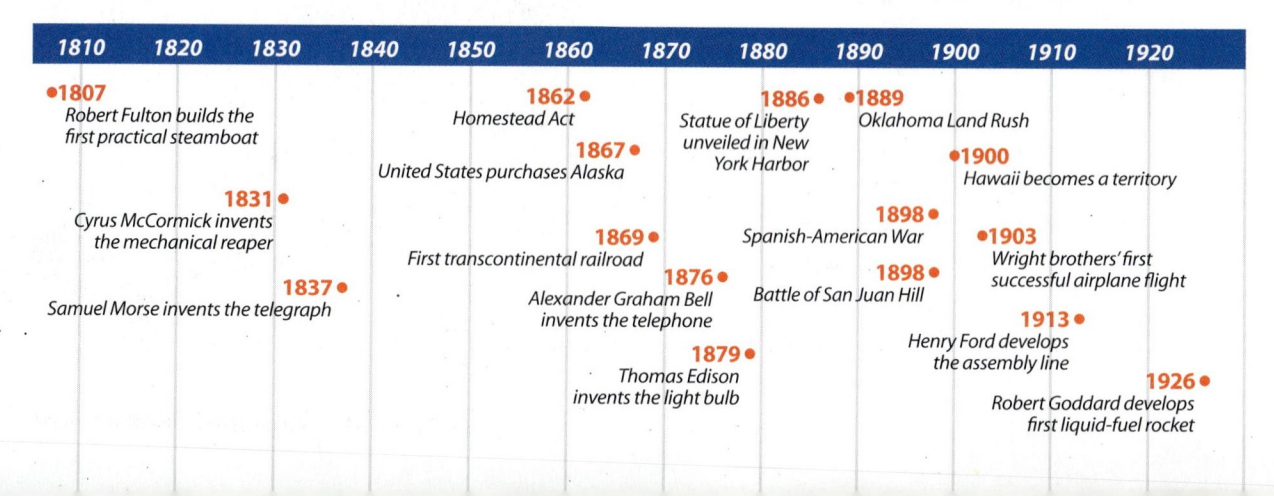

1810 | 1820 | 1830 | 1840 | 1850 | 1860 | 1870 | 1880 | 1890 | 1900 | 1910 | 1920

- **1807** Robert Fulton builds the first practical steamboat
- **1831** Cyrus McCormick invents the mechanical reaper
- **1837** Samuel Morse invents the telegraph
- **1862** Homestead Act
- **1867** United States purchases Alaska
- **1869** First transcontinental railroad
- **1876** Alexander Graham Bell invents the telephone
- **1879** Thomas Edison invents the light bulb
- **1886** Statue of Liberty unveiled in New York Harbor
- **1889** Oklahoma Land Rush
- **1898** Spanish-American War
- **1898** Battle of San Juan Hill
- **1900** Hawaii becomes a territory
- **1903** Wright brothers' first successful airplane flight
- **1913** Henry Ford develops the assembly line
- **1926** Robert Goddard develops first liquid-fuel rocket

The wonderful new technology of automobiles and flying machines symbolized the progress of America in the late 1800s.

white men. Yet few white men tried earnestly to teach the Indians Christianity, and the Christian Indians, particularly the Cherokees, sometimes suffered the greatest persecution. Although missionaries tried to help the Indians, conditions grew worse.

Finally, the United States government sent soldiers to the West to fight the Indians. One by one, the troops defeated the Indian tribes and moved them to **reservations** (land which the United States has set aside for Indians). In 1924, our government passed a law which made the American Indians official citizens of the United States. Happily, since that time, there has been a greater understanding and friendship between whites and Indians.

Cyrus McCormick and the Mechanical Reaper

Most farmers who moved to the Midwest planted wheat. The plains filled up with wheat so fast that farmers could not find enough workers to harvest it all. Once again, an ingenious American came up with a solution for the difficult problem. In 1831, **Cyrus McCormick,** a Virginian, invited his neighbors to watch the first demonstration of his mechanical reaper. He hitched horses to the reaper, climbed aboard, and headed into a wheat field. The reaper cut down the wheat neatly and evenly. Though it would have taken several men hours and hours to cut the wheat in that field, Cyrus McCormick did it by himself in a brief time.

McCormick set up a factory in Chicago for producing reapers, and soon there were many mechanical reapers ready to make the harvesting fast and efficient. Cyrus McCormick used the money he made from his inven-

The United States forced many Indian tribes to leave their land and move to reservations.

The Nation Grows and Prospers 199

tion wisely and generously. Much of it he gave to good causes, including very large sums to the great evangelist D. L. Moody for the building of a YMCA building and a Christian Bible college.

The American Cowboy

Settlers quickly found that the Great Plains is an ideal place to raise beef cattle. By the time of the Civil War, many ranchers in Texas were raising large herds of half-wild cattle called **longhorns**. Over the next few years, ranches spread to other parts of the Great Plains, including Wyoming, Montana, Colorado, Nebraska, and Kansas. In those days, there were no fences to confine the cattle. They roamed where they pleased. Often, a herd consisted of a thousand or more cattle. The rancher needed help in looking after a herd this size. <u>The men that the rancher hired to take care of his cattle were the American cowboys.</u>

Texas cattle crossing a stream on a cattle drive

The cowboys practically lived with the cattle, providing food, water, and protection for the animals. To keep one rancher's cattle from mixing with cattle from another ranch, the cowboys **branded** the cattle with a hot iron. Every ranch had its own special brand, different from that of surrounding ranches. During the spring, the cowboys would round up all of the new calves for branding.

The long drive. The coming of the transcontinental railroad provided a way for the ranchers to transport their cattle east for sale. Because the railroad did not pass through every city or even every state, however, most ranchers had to drive their herds over several hundred miles to the nearest railroad town that would handle cattle. Such towns with railroads were called **cow towns**. The three or four months' journey to a cow town was called the "long drive." Because the rancher had to stay with his ranch, he usually hired cowboys for the long, difficult trip. During the long drive, the cowboys had many dangers to look out for—Indian attacks, wild animals, storms. Any one of these dangers, or even a sudden noise, could cause a **stampede** in which the cattle would wildly run.

At night, the cowboys would take turns keeping watch over the herd. To soothe the tired animals and prevent stampedes, the cowboys often sang soft lullabies. During the day, when the herd moved slowly, the cowboys sang songs to keep the cattle moving at a good pace, such as:

> Whoopee ti yi yo, git along, little dogies;
> It's your misfortune and none of my own.
> Whoopee ti yi yo, git along, little dogies;
> For you know Wyoming will be your new home.

The rancher and the farmer disagree. As farmers settled in the West and planted fields of wheat and corn, trouble arose between the farmers and the cattle ranchers. Of course, the cattle preferred young, tender wheat and corn to the grass they could eat every day on the plains, and the farmers would not allow their crops to be trampled and ruined.

200 *New World History & Geography*

When there were few farms, the cowboys simply drove their herds away from the farms. But as the West became more settled, this became impossible. The ranchers did not own the land on which they grazed their cattle. The United States government owned this land and had begun selling it to farmers. As the owners of the land, the farmers had the right to protect their crops. Soon, farmers enclosed their fields with barbed-wire fences. Eventually the ranchers realized that they must buy their own land and fence in large pastures for their cattle to graze.

Two Famous Westerners

Two of the most famous men of America's West were William F. ("Buffalo Bill") Cody and James Butler ("Wild Bill") Hickok. By the age of 20, **Buffalo Bill** had already been a Pony Express rider, an army scout, and an Indian fighter. He earned his nickname when he had the job of supplying meat for the railroad workers. Within 18 months, he killed over 4,200 buffaloes (about seven buffaloes per day). In 1883, Buffalo Bill opened a traveling variety show about the West. Known as Buffalo Bill's Wild West Show, it starred famous western heroes such as Wild Bill Hickok and **Annie Oakley** (an amazing markswoman; she could hit a dime tossed into the air from 30 paces away), as well as many American Indians and a black cowboy. The show traveled throughout the Eastern United States and Europe demonstrating Indian battles and Buffalo Bill's sharpshooting skills. His most popular act featured the great Sioux Indian chief, **Sitting Bull,** who helped reenact an Indian attack on a stagecoach.

James Butler Hickok worked as a stagecoach driver, wagon train master, and a scout for the Union army; but he is best remembered as **Wild Bill Hickok,** the Indian scout and town marshal. He was respected for his courage among the Western outlaws, and he had a reputation for never shooting a man unless it was in the line of duty or in self defense. Hickok served as town marshal in two Kansas towns and also toured the East with Buffalo Bill's Wild West Show.

An advertising poster for Buffalo Bill's Wild West show depicts Annie Oakley, Buffalo Bill, and Sitting Bull.

The Homestead Act

In 1862, our government passed the **Homestead Act,** which said that any family that settled in certain areas of the West could receive 160 acres of land. To keep this land, the head of the family had to live on that land, farming or making other improvements to it, for five years. After the Civil War, many people were ready to accept this offer. By this time, Indians were being placed on reservations, and new methods of farming with less water made it possible to grow crops on the dry, windy plains. As the years passed, the government had less and less land to give away in the West. Whenever the government made land available for settlement, there would be a great **land rush.** People would line up in wagons and on horses, waiting to claim their 160 acres.

The Oklahoma Land Rush

Originally, the government had given the territory of Oklahoma to the American Indians. But once again the Indians had to move. The government set a date for settlers to claim land in Oklahoma. The day came for the great **Oklahoma Land Rush** in 1889. Many thousands of people lined up along the borders of Oklahoma. Some were in carriages, some in wagons, and some in trains. Some were on horseback, and some were on foot. Soldiers guarded the borders. No one could cross the border until a signal was given. When the signal finally came, eager settlers scrambled over the border to claim some land of their own. You can see why this was called a "land rush." Before the day was over, most of the land in the Oklahoma Territory had been claimed.

the Oklahoma Land Rush

People in History
James A. Garfield: From Canal Boy to President

James A. Garfield (1831–1881) was born in a log cabin in Ohio on November 19, 1831. His father died soon after, leaving his mother to care for her children's physical and spiritual needs.

At the age of 17, Jim left home and found a job as a canal hand. But he had never learned to swim, and with the barge's constant jerking there was always the danger of falling overboard, which he did—14 times.

The last time Jim fell overboard, there was no one nearby to pull him out. As he slipped beneath the water, he frantically grabbed for the tow line, only to find that it lay limply in the water.

"Oh God, help me!" he pleaded.

Miraculously the sinking rope became taut in his hands. Somehow the rope had caught on the edge of the barge. Hand over hand the exhausted boy slowly worked his way back onto the barge's deck, realizing that the Lord had answered his frantic prayer.

After this experience, Jim Garfield returned home. He knew God had saved his life for some special purpose. Jim went to school, and graduated from college. He became a college president, and during the Civil War, he rose to the rank of major general in the Union army.

In 1860, Garfield became a state senator. Two years later, he was elected to the United States House of Representatives, and he was reelected eight more times. In 1881, <u>James Garfield became the 20th President of the United States</u>. Many years before, President Andrew Jackson had begun a policy of awarding governmental jobs to people who voted for him. President Garfield decided to give the jobs only to men who were qualified. Becoming upset at this decision, one man shot President Garfield.

For almost 12 weeks, the President hovered between life and death. Then on September 19, 1881, President Garfield died.

Even though President Garfield's death greatly saddened the nation, the American people learned a valuable lesson. Within two years, the Civil Service Administration (the office responsible for assigning government jobs) was reorganized. No longer could jobs be given away in exchange for personal favors. Only qualified people could be hired to fill the positions. This is exactly the way James Garfield, the canal boy who became President, wanted it.

<u>James Garfield was the fourth Republican President. He was the last President to be born in a log cabin, the fourth President to die in office, and the second President to be assassinated</u>.

In 1890, the government announced that there was no more frontier land left in the United States. Large, unsettled areas remained, and some homesteads would still be given away, but one could no longer draw a clear line between an unsettled area and a settled area.

Comprehension Check 11A
Identify
1. Land set aside by the government for Indian tribes.
2. The man who built the first mechanical reaper.

Think
3. How did the mechanical reaper benefit farmers on the plains?
4. What conflict arose between the farmers and the cattle ranchers? How was it resolved?
5. Explain the Homestead Act. What occurred every time the government made more land available for settlement?

The Nation Grows and Prospers

11.2 IMMIGRATION, REVIVAL, AND INDUSTRY

Land of Second Chance

In 1870, the American population stood at 38 million; by 1916, there were nearly 100 million Americans. The population almost tripled in 46 years! Where did all of these people come from? Some of them were born in America, but most of them were immigrants.

An **immigrant** is a person who leaves his own country to make his home in another country. The United States has attracted more immigrants to its shores than any other country in the world. Because of our heritage of freedom and our free economic system, many people from all over the world have come here to live. The French people realized this when they sent us the Statue of Liberty as a gift of friendship for our 100th anniversary. The poem on the base of the Statue of Liberty reads in part:

> Give me your tired, your poor,
> Your huddled masses yearning to breathe free,
> The wretched refuse of your teeming shore.
> Send these, the homeless, tempest-tost to me,
> I lift my lamp beside the golden door!

This poem was written by Emma Lazarus, an American who helped immigrants adjust to their new world. The United States has become a new home to so many people that the American Indians now make up only one percent of the population. Because people from all over the world make up the United States and have influenced it in many ways, it is often called a **"melting pot."**

Most of the people of the world are referred to by the name of their country, such as French, English, Brazilian, or Canadian. The United States is such a mixture of many countries that it is the only country in the world whose citizens are not commonly called by their country but by their continent, Americans.

From the days of early colonization, people had come to America from Europe for freedom of religion, freedom to work and own land, and freedom from oppressive governments. As the years passed, the reasons for coming to America grew. Immigrants came for other freedoms that America had to offer—such as freedom of speech and press.

an Italian immigrant family at Ellis Island

204 *New World History & Geography*

Some came from poor families where they faced starvation. Many came because they could not own homes, businesses, or farms in their old homelands, but in America, if they worked hard, they could. Along with all of these hopes, they wanted education for their children. This may have been impossible in their homelands, but in the United States, every child could have a good education. So many people have come to the United States to find greater opportunity to reach their goals that our country has been called the "Land of Second Chance" or "Land of Opportunity."

The new Americans came from many different countries. Originally, almost all immigrants had been from northwestern Europe—England, Ireland, Scotland, Germany, Scandinavia, Switzerland, and France. Now many came from southern and eastern Europe—Italy, Poland, Russia, Austria-Hungary—and from Asia—China and Japan. Many of these new Americans had a difficult beginning. Few knew how to speak English. They had few possessions and very little money. But most had a great desire to work and build for themselves a home in a new and free country. By their work and determination, they helped build an even stronger United States.

Age of Great Revivals

Almost every family that traveled westward brought a Bible. The Bible molded the lives of many frontier families, and most of the pioneers were godly people. But religion also played an important role in the East. During the 1800s and in the early 1900s, great revivals swept through America's large cities, bringing salvation to immigrants as well as to long-time residents. These revivals were so successful that they reminded people of the Great Awakening. **Charles Finney** (1792–1875), a brilliant lawyer who became one of America's greatest revival preachers, had great influence in his day; usually, the buildings could not hold the crowds that came to hear him preach. He also brought revival to London, England.

Charles Finney

Dwight L. Moody (1837–1899), who began preaching several years after Finney, was America's most famous evangelist during the 19th century. When Moody, a shoe salesman from Massachusetts, came to know Christ, he was stirred by an urgent desire to share the gospel with as many people as possible. His historic revival services in America and England drew thousands upon thousands of people. He also founded Moody Bible Institute in Chicago.

Dwight Moody

In the early 1900s, **Billy Sunday** (1863–1935), a famous baseball star, captured America's attention. People from all walks of life flocked to hear this man of God preach. Some people came because they were concerned about their souls; some people came simply because they were curious. But no matter why they came, before they left they would hear the gospel presented in a clear and simple style. Many were saved.

Billy Sunday

Evangelists like Charles Finney, D. L. Moody, and Billy Sunday did much to mold and shape American life. When Finney, Moody, or Sunday held a meeting in a town, the town would experience a genuine change. Saloons and theaters would close. Businessmen found that people became more honest and came in to pay their bills. People responded in large numbers to the preaching

The Nation Grows and Prospers 205

of the evangelists. Many desired to obey the Bible and to let the Bible change their lives. They showed their love for others by sending out missionaries to other lands. Many hymns that we love to sing today were written during this time. So great were the advances made by Christianity during this time that one history writer called the 19th century "the greatest century which Christianity had thus far known."

Era of Industry

The 19th century saw great prosperity and growth in industry. Two main products caused American industry to grow rapidly: steel and oil. America was blessed with the materials needed for the mass production of steel and oil and enterprising businessmen who were eager to provide the money needed by the growing industry. The leaders of these two industries, Andrew Carnegie and John D. Rockefeller, became giants in American history.

Andrew Carnegie sees the future of steel. For many years, iron had been the chief metal used by industry, but it was heavy, expensive, and brittle (easily breakable). Around 1856, an Englishman named Sir Henry Bessemer developed a method of turning iron ore into steel, a metal which is just as strong as iron but is much lighter and more flexible. **Andrew Carnegie** (1835–1919) brought the steel industry to America.

In 1847, as a boy of 12, Andrew Carnegie came with his family to Pennsylvania from Scotland to find a better life. Andrew's father got a job in a mill factory and soon secured a position for his son as well. At first, Andrew earned only $1.20 a week, but because he was an able and willing worker, he soon moved on to better jobs. He became a messenger boy, then a telegraph operator, then a railroad clerk, and finally a railroad supervisor. As he earned more money, he used it wisely. He bought iron factories and prospered. When he saw Bessemer make steel from iron, Carnegie converted his factories to steel production. Some people thought he was being foolish, but Carnegie knew better. "The age of iron is over; the age of steel is here," he said. "All of the railroads will want steel rails because their old iron rails break too easily. Bridges will be built of steel, and ships and tall buildings and many other things that we don't even know about yet. The future is in steel."

As Carnegie predicted, the steel industry became a huge success, and Carnegie's steel company was the most successful of all. After many years, Andrew Carnegie had grown very

a steel mill

wealthy. But he felt it would be wrong to use his money selfishly. He believed that the best thing to do with money is to give it away for worthy causes. "The man who dies rich dies disgraced," said Carnegie, who spent the last years of his life giving away his fortune. Because he loved good church music, he donated over 7,000 pipe organs to churches. He also paid for schools and colleges. As a boy, he had loved to read. Because he wanted all boys and girls to have books to read, he built libraries in towns throughout America. He eventually paid for the construction of over 3,000 public libraries. By the time of his death in 1919, Carnegie—who had once earned $1.20 a week—had given away over $350 million.

John D. Rockefeller organizes the oil industry. Early settlers in Pennsylvania were often bothered by a sticky, black liquid which muddied their streams. When they heard that the Indians believed that the substance had magical powers, they bottled the liquid and sold it as medicine. Soon people discovered that this substance—oil—made a good fuel. People flocked to Pennsylvania to pump oil out of the ground, establishing dozens of small petroleum companies.

John D. Rockefeller (1839–1937) began to unite small companies into one big company, providing lower prices and better service. Rockefeller's company, Standard Oil, made him the first billionaire in history. For many years he was the richest man in the world.

Rich as he was, John D. Rockefeller learned that all of the money in the world could not give him happiness. His mental distress soon led to terrible health problems. When Rockefeller realized that his money could bring him joy only if he used it to help others, he created the Rockefeller Foundation, an organization which gave millions of dollars to worthy causes. Rockefeller recovered his health and lived to be 98 years old. He gave away over $550 million during his lifetime.

the first oil well in Pennsylvania

Although both Andrew Carnegie and John D. Rockefeller were born poor, both were free to work hard and to be rewarded for their work because America is a land of freedom. As a result of their labor, both became wealthy. Through the efforts of Carnegie and Rockefeller, American industry grew and prospered. And through their generosity, the lives of millions have been improved in many different ways.

Comprehension Check 11B

Identify

1. Three of America's famous evangelists during the 1800s and early 1900s.
2. The man who controlled much of America's steel business in the late 19th century.
3. The man who controlled much of America's oil industry in the late 19th century.

Think

4. What brought many immigrants to America in the 19th century?
5. How did revivals affect the American people during the 1800s and early 1900s?

The Nation Grows and Prospers

11.3 INVENTIONS: NEW WAYS TO DO THINGS

Each of us has been an inventor at one time or another. God has given us minds which enable us to think of better or faster ways of getting jobs done. Man has been inventing since Creation.

A good invention is never really finished. Someone else is bound to improve it. For example, look at pictures of the first cars and airplanes. Can you imagine yourself riding around in those early models instead of the modern ones? People will continue to invent new ways to improve the car and plane as well as every other important invention. This process of improvement is called *progress*—moving forward to improve our way of life. We have already learned about several inventors: Benjamin Banneker, Eli Whitney, George Washington Carver, and Cyrus McCormick. They are just a few of the inventive people of the United States. We must go back to the beginning of the 19th century for the story of one great American inventor, Robert Fulton.

Robert Fulton and the Steamboat

By the early 1800s, many factories used steam engines to run machines. The steam engine, which burned wood or coal, interested several Americans who wondered if steam could also be used to propel a boat. Although several men attempted to build a steamboat, their inventions were too expensive to operate for practical purposes. Then **Robert Fulton** (1765–1815) set his mind to the task. In 1807, just 31 years after America became a nation, Fulton finished building his steamboat, the ***Clermont,*** in a New York shipyard. Eager to test it, he scheduled a trial run.

When the day arrived, crowds of people gathered on the banks of the Hudson River to watch. Many mocked the *Clermont* before they even had a chance to see if it worked. Some were frightened by the smoke and sparks which poured from the *Clermont's* smokestack. But everyone cheered when the paddle wheels began to turn, propelling the *Clermont* up the river. Robert Fulton had invented the world's first successful steamboat.

Men began working to improve the steamboat. Within a few years, steamboats replaced sailboats on large rivers, and soon steamboats were traveling across the oceans.

Samuel Morse and the Telegraph

Steamboats and railroads speeded up communication somewhat, but some men still felt there had to be a faster way. **Samuel Morse** (1791–1872), a Christian man from Massachusetts, believed that messages could be sent over long distances through a wire by electricity.

Samuel Morse needed money to build and test his **telegraph.** To prove that his invention worked, he would need to spread telegraph lines over long distances. Morse, a poor

the Clermont

man with a family to support, often went without food himself so that he could work a little longer on his experiments. Morse believed that with his telegraph important messages could be sent from city to city in a matter of seconds instead of days. Knowing that such an invention would greatly benefit our country, he decided to ask the United States Congress for money to test his invention. At first, Congress said no. Though Samuel Morse became discouraged, he would not give up. After several years, he again asked Congress for the money, and this time Congress voted to give $30,000 to build a telegraph line from Washington, D.C., to Baltimore, Maryland, a distance of about 40 miles.

Because Morse knew he could not send words over his telegraph wire, he devised a code of short and long dots and dashes. <u>By this system of dots and dashes, known as the **Morse code,** the letters of the alphabet and numbers could be tapped over the telegraph wires.</u>

In May of 1844, Morse sat with a telegraph set in Washington, D.C., while another man sat with a telegraph set in Baltimore. Morse tapped out a simple message: "What hath God wrought!" Within seconds, the assistant waiting in Baltimore received the message on his telegraph set. He promptly returned the message to Morse in Washington.

Soon telegraph wires stretched from city to city and state to state. By 1861, a telegraph wire stretched from the East Coast to the West Coast of the United States.

When workers completed the transcontinental railroad in 1869, telegraphs sent the message of the railroad's success to cities across the United States. Now, newspapers in cities that were hundreds and even thousands of miles apart could print the nation's news the same day that it happened, thanks to the telegraph. People who were moving West no longer felt out of touch with those in the East. The telegraph had brought the East and the West together.

Alexander Graham Bell and the Telephone

Alexander Graham Bell (1847–1922), who sailed to America from Scotland as a young man, loved America and the opportunities he had as an American. Bell worked in the city of Boston, Massachusetts, as a teacher of students who were deaf and *mute* (unable to speak). Usually, these students could not talk because they had never heard words or sounds.

Bell once made the comment, "If I can make a deaf-mute talk, I can make iron talk." Already the idea and plans for a telephone were developing in his mind. The fathers of two of his students offered him money to help continue his work.

In March 1876, Thomas Watson, Bell's friend and assistant, heard Bell call him over a telephone wire from the inventor's attic workshop. "Mr. Watson, come here, I want you!" Excitedly, Mr. Watson came running. The telephone worked!

Americans were slow to realize the importance of Alexander Graham Bell's invention. They thought of the telephone more as a toy than as an important invention that could change their way of living.

In 1876, a world's fair was held in Philadelphia, Pennsylvania, to celebrate our country's 100th birthday. Our country had changed greatly since the Declaration of Independence had been written. <u>Many new inventions were shown at the world's fair,</u>

The Nation Grows and Prospers 209

Alexander Bell making the first New York to Chicago call in 1892

including Alexander Graham Bell's telephone. One English scientist described Bell's telephone as "the most wonderful thing in America." Americans finally began to see the telephone's usefulness. One year later, the first Bell Telephone Company came into being.

In 1915, another important telephone conversation took place between Bell and Watson. Again Bell said, "Mr. Watson, come here, I want you!" But Bell was joking this time, for he was calling from New York to Mr. Watson in San Francisco, California! It was the first coast-to-coast telephone conversation.

Alexander Graham Bell became a citizen of the United States in 1882. Although we remember him as the inventor of the telephone, he wanted to be remembered first of all as a teacher of the deaf, for he greatly loved his students.

Thomas Edison—A Man of Many Inventions

Few Americans have not been affected by the work of **Thomas Alva Edison** (1847–1931), probably the greatest inventor in history. Edison was so interested in inventing that he built a large invention factory at Menlo Park, New Jersey, where he often worked both day and night, stopping only for naps. The electric light, motion pictures, the phonograph, and office machinery are just a few of Thomas Edison's 1,000 or more inventions.

At first, even Edison's workers did not believe that his strange-looking **phonograph** could talk. As his workers watched, Edison leaned toward the mouthpiece and began turning the handle. "Mary had a little lamb; its fleece was white as snow . . . ," he said and finished the nursery rhyme. His workers waited as he adjusted the machine and began turning the handle again. The machine repeated, "Mary had a little lamb. . . ." Laughter and cheers filled the room. This invention would make Edison famous.

Thomas Edison also worked on the **electric light bulb.** Although several different men had attempted to invent one, their bulbs would burn out in only a minute or two. Edison struggled with the same problem. After two years of experimenting, however, Edison invented a successful bulb. He watched excitedly as the bulb kept burning hour after hour.

Thomas Edison with his phonograph

His first successful light bulb burned for 40 hours. Edison and his workers kept working to make light bulbs that would burn even longer.

Electric lights soon lit American streets. Stores and other buildings in big cities installed electric lights. Gradually, electric lights spread to homes throughout America. No longer did people have to use candles or kerosene lanterns to light their homes at night.

Edison could never put one of his successful inventions aside. He always worked to improve them. Many people called him a "genius." To that remark, Edison replied, "Genius is one percent inspiration and 99 percent perspiration." He meant that a good idea still needs many hours of hard work to make it successful.

Although Thomas Edison's attempts at inventing often failed, he never became a failure. Instead, he chose to learn from his mistakes. Edison once tested a special battery 10,000 times without a single success.

"Aren't you discouraged?" asked his friends, wondering why he wouldn't give up.

"Discouraged?" he asked. "Why I've made progress! I have found out 10,000 things that won't work!" And with that, he went back to work.

Comprehension Check 11C

Identify
1. The man who invented the first successful steam-driven boat.
2. The system of dots and dashes used to tap letters of the alphabet and numbers over telegraph wires, and its inventor.
3. The inventor of the telephone.
4. The man often thought to be the greatest inventor in history.

Think
5. What is progress? How do inventions contribute to progress?

Henry Ford and the Automobile

Today, nearly every American family owns a car, but when the car, or "the horseless carriage," was first invented in Germany, only the very wealthy could afford to buy one. Men had to make each car completely by hand. You can imagine how long it took them to build one car.

Fortunately, a man named **Henry Ford** (1863–1947) became interested in building cars. As a boy in Michigan, he saw that few people could afford to own cars. Ford's dream was to make an inexpensive car that nearly every American family could afford.

The first cars were run by steam engines or electricity. Then someone invented the gasoline engine. "Why not use a gasoline engine to run a car?" Ford asked himself. To answer this question, he first had to learn how to build a gasoline engine.

After he built a gasoline engine, Ford built a box-shaped car body and set the engine in it. His first car had four bicycle wheels for tires and a stick instead of a steering wheel. Ford finished his first gasoline-engine car in 1896. It ran successfully, but like the rest, it was completely handmade and would be expensive to buy.

Henry Ford built other cars, making improvements on each one. In 1903, when the Ford Motor Company began, still only the wealthy could afford to buy cars. But Ford remained determined to find a way of building a car for a low price.

At last, Ford developed the **assembly line** method, which he used to produce his Model T. On an assembly line, each person has his own special job to do. The worker becomes very skilled in this job and can work quickly. To make the work even faster, the car comes to the workers on a moving belt,

The Nation Grows and Prospers

Henry Ford's Model T assembly line

Model T

which moves at just the right speed to allow each worker to finish his job.

By hand, it took many days to assemble one car. With the assembly line, one car could be completely assembled in less than two hours! Because it took less time to build cars, they could be made at a much cheaper price—a price most American families could afford. By 1914, there were more than a million cars on the roads.

Ford's dream did come true. He may not have been the inventor of the car itself, but he was the first to use the idea of the assembly line to build cars. By using the assembly line, Henry Ford made his own reasonably priced car that most Americans could afford to buy. Soon other factories were using the assembly line to create other kinds of goods faster and cheaper. As manufacturers put this good idea to work, Americans began to enjoy a better way of life.

Black American Inventors

One black inventor, **Jan Ernst Matzeliger** (1852–1889), was a shoemaker in Lynn, Massachusetts. In 1883, he patented the first shoe-lasting machine. His invention meant that the shoemaker no longer had to stretch and shape each shoe by hand and then nail it to a sole.

Norbert Rillieux (1806–1894) traveled from New Orleans to France, where he became an engineering professor. After returning to New Orleans, he invented a sugar-refining process which greatly reduced the cost of refining (removing impurities from) sugar and revolutionized the sugar industry.

Inventor **Granville T. Woods** (1856–1910) was working for the Danville and Southern Railroad when he became interested in improving methods of communication and transportation. He opened a factory and invented a steam boiler furnace, automatic air brakes, an egg incubator, a telegraph device for communication between moving trains and train stations, and more than 15 electrical devices for railroads.

Garrett A. Morgan's (1877–1963) first famous invention, a gas mask, quickly became standard equipment for fire departments and police forces across the nation. The traffic signal with red, yellow, and green lights was also invented by Morgan, and the General Electric Company paid him $40,000 for rights to manufacture the invention.

The Wright Brothers and the Airplane

In 1878, two brothers, **Wilbur and Orville Wright,** began making toy helicopters from bamboo, cork, and paper. Eleven-year-old Wilbur (1867–1912) and 7-year-old Or-

212 New World History & Geography

ville (1871–1948) experimented with several designs, but they found that the bigger they made their helicopters, the less easily the toys would fly. The two disappointed brothers wondered why.

Some men who were also interested in flying were asking themselves another question. Would it ever be possible for a man to fly? Men had flown in balloons, but a balloon is not the same as a flying machine. Some men had tried to fly by strapping wings to their arms. Some had built strange-looking machines. But all had failed.

After the Wright brothers grew up, they became the owners of a bicycle shop, but they were still interested in flying. Their bicycle shop became a laboratory.

Several men had experimented with *gliders,* and the Wright brothers decided to build their own. After several years of work, they were finished. On the advice of the United States Weather Bureau, they decided to test their glider at Kitty Hawk, North Carolina, where sandy beaches would give their glider a soft landing and good ocean winds would help it fly. Their glider was successful, but the brothers were not satisfied. They built a second glider and then a third. The third flew more than 600 feet. Again and again they tried their third glider until they had made almost one thousand flights. This was the best glider any man had ever made.

Now they were ready to build an airplane with an engine. Gasoline engines were already being used in cars, but they were not light enough to be used in a plane. The brothers had to build a lighter gasoline engine. They also had to design special propellers for their plane.

It took the Wright brothers almost a year to build their first airplane. On December 17, 1903, they were ready to test it. Orville warmed up the engine. The airplane started forward, slowly lifting itself into the air. That first airplane ride lasted 12 seconds. Orville had flown 120 feet. The brothers made two more flights that day. Wilbur made the third flight. It lasted 59 seconds, and he flew 852 feet! <u>These three flights were the first *powered* flights in a machine that was heavier than air</u>, but only a few newspapers across the nation carried the story. People just could not believe that man could really fly. They thought the story was a joke.

The Wright brothers would not give up. They continued their work on the airplane and made improvements. By 1908, people finally became interested in the airplane.

Although Wilbur Wright died in 1912, Orville lived until 1948. During his lifetime,

Wilbur and Orville Wright's first flight

213

he saw great improvements that other men made on the airplane. By the time of Orville's death, large airline companies had been formed, and some men were even beginning to talk about flying to the moon.

Robert H. Goddard and the Rocket

Even as a boy, **Robert Goddard** (1882–1945) dreamed of one day sending an object high into space. At that time, however, men were still experimenting with the airplane. The thought of sending a rocket into outer space seemed ridiculous. People laughed at young Robert's dream, but when he graduated from college, Robert set out to make his dream come true. Although people continually mocked his efforts, he would not give up his experiments. He began work on a rocket that would burn liquid fuel, using a combination of gasoline and liquid oxygen. This was a new idea. Goddard and his workers had to be very careful, because liquid oxygen is highly explosive.

In 1926, Goddard launched the first successful liquid-fuel rocket ever built. In the following years, he built bigger and better rockets. For many years to come, people would not realize the importance of his work. Goddard himself realized he probably would not live long enough to build a rocket big and fine enough to fly to the moon, because it often took years of work to make one improvement on the rocket. Robert Goddard must have realized that other scientists would follow in his steps, as indeed they did. As a result, we have seen rockets carry astronauts to the moon.

Other American inventors. History shows that practical, hardworking Americans have probably produced more inventions than any other people of modern times. A few other American inventions of the 19th century include the following:

1836	**Samuel Colt**—revolver
1839	**Charles Goodyear**—vulcanization of rubber, a process which improved its strength and durability and did away with its stickiness
1846	**Elias Howe**—lock-stitch sewing maching
1867	**P. D. Armour**—meat packing
1868	**George Westinghouse**—railroad air brake
1868	**C. L. Sholes**—typewriter
1888	**George Eastman**—Kodak box camera

Comprehension Check 11D
Identify
1. The man who made the automobile affordable.
2. Inventor of the traffic signal.
3. The inventors of the airplane.
4. The man who launched the first successful liquid-fueled rocket ever built.

Think
5. How did the assembly line make cars more affordable?

Robert Goddard and his liquid-fueled rocket

11.4 New Frontiers

Alaska: The 49th State

England, France, and Spain were not the only countries to have a part in the history of America. At the time the 13 colonies won their independence from England, Alaska belonged to Russia. People called it Russian America. The Russians were interested in the furs and the fish they could find in Alaska. In 1867, our country's Secretary of State, **William H. Seward,** received a visitor from the Russian government. During that visit, it became evident that Russia wished to sell Russian America for $7,200,000.

Most Americans thought of Russian America as a worthless land of ice and snow. But these people had never been to Alaska. Alaska had rich farmland and much natural beauty to offer. At that time, no one knew of the great riches in gold and natural resources such as coal and petroleum that would one day be found in Alaska. These riches would make $7 million seem a very small price.

Seward urged our government to buy Russian America. He knew the wealth of valuable furs that could be trapped there. The purchase would also open the way for a large and profitable fishing industry. At last our government accepted the offer, although many Americans scoffed at the purchase. They called Russian America "Seward's Folly" and "Seward's Icebox."

The United States changed the name of Russian America to **Alaska.** Fishing and furs soon proved to be very valuable. In the year 1896, gold was discovered and the Alaskan Gold Rush began. Alaska soon paid for itself many times over. No longer could Americans mock the purchase of Alaska.

Alaska did not become a state when it was purchased. It became a **territory** of the United States. Because they lived in a territory, the people of Alaska could not vote in our national elections or choose their own governor. Instead, the President of the United States appointed a governor for Alaska. The governor could then tell our government what Alaska needed. Alaska became the 49th state in January of 1959.

Hawaii: The 50th State

The state of Hawaii consists of 8 large islands and over 110 smaller islands. The largest island is named Hawaii, from which the islands get their group name. This beautiful group of islands in the Pacific Ocean is more than 2,000 miles away from the coast of California. How then did Hawaii become our 50th state? To answer that question, we must go back in time about 200 years.

The English explorer, **Captain James Cook** discovered Hawaii, which he named the Sandwich Islands, in 1778. For the next 40 years, British and American explorers, adventurers, and whalers stopped at the Hawaiian Islands for food and supplies on their way to and from China. These visitors had a deep influence on the Hawaiian people, who had for years been worshiping false gods. Contact with people who believed in the one true God made the Hawaiian people want to find out more about God.

In 1820, Christian missionaries began arriving in the Hawaiian Islands from America. Ready for the message of salvation, many Hawaiians accepted Christ. Many Christian churches and schools were started.

Other Americans came to Hawaii to raise **pineapple** and **sugar cane.** They hired islanders to work their plantations. Most of the crops were sold to the United States. Soon the islanders began to depend on their trade with the United States.

The Nation Grows and Prospers

As the years passed, the Americans who were living in Hawaii wanted the islands to become a part of the United States. In 1900, the United States Congress voted to make Hawaii a United States Territory like Alaska. But like the people of Alaska, the people of Hawaii wanted to become a state. In 1959, the United States Congress finally voted to accept Hawaii as our 50th state.

The Spanish-American War

The island of **Cuba,** located ninety miles south of Florida, was one of Spain's last possessions in the New World. Though Spain struggled to keep Cuba, the people of Cuba constantly fought for their independence. In an effort to stop the fighting, the Spanish sometimes treated the Cubans cruelly. In time, the people of the United States grew sympathetic toward the Cubans.

"Remember the Maine." In February of 1898, our government sent the United States battleship *Maine* on a peaceful trip to Cuba to protect Americans living there. All went well until a great explosion sank the *Maine* off the shores of Cuba. Most of her sailors were killed or drowned.

The people of the United States blamed the Spanish for the explosion, although the Spanish claimed they did not do it. "Remember the *Maine*" became the slogan of many Americans who felt we should go to war with Spain. On April 25, 1898, our government declared war on Spain. The purpose of the Spanish-American War was to set Cuba free from Spain.

Because the only way to get to Cuba from either the United States or Spain was by water, the navies of both countries became very important. When the war began, **Admiral George Dewey** of the United States Navy was sent to the **Philippine Islands.** Although these islands are in the Pacific Ocean, near China, they also belonged to Spain. Admiral Dewey sailed into a bay of the Philippine Islands where a fleet of Spanish ships was docked. There, the United States Navy destroyed the Spanish ships, receiving only minor damage to U.S. ships.

The Rough Riders. Meanwhile, Americans were fighting the Spanish in Cuba and on the seas nearby. A group of American men known as the Rough Riders was headed by **Theodore Roosevelt** (1858–1919), who would one day become President of the United States. The Rough Riders played

Theodore Roosevelt and his Rough Riders were victorious at the Battle of San Juan Hill.

an important part in winning the most important land battle fought in the Spanish-American War, the Battle of **San Juan Hill**. The entire war lasted only three and a half months. It was the shortest war the United States had ever fought until the Persian Gulf War in 1991, which lasted only two and a half months.

Results of the Spanish-American War. As a result of the Spanish-American War, Spain gave Cuba her freedom, and the United States received several islands that had previously belonged to Spain: the **Philippines** and **Guam** in the Pacific Ocean, and **Puerto Rico,** an island near Cuba. In return for these islands, the United States paid Spain $20 million.

During the years after the war, the United States tried to help the people of these islands by building hospitals and schools. Many missionaries from the United States went to the Philippine Islands and set up churches, schools, hospitals, and colleges.

Since then the Philippines have become independent. The people of Puerto Rico and Guam now govern themselves but are also considered citizens of the United States.

Comprehension Check 11E

Identify

1. The title and name of the man who urged our government to buy Russian America.
2. Two crops that Americans went to Hawaii to raise.
3. The American ship that mysteriously sank off the shore of Cuba.
4. A group of Americans who were led by Theodore Roosevelt and who played an important role in the Battle of San Juan Hill.

Think

5. How and when did the Alaskan Purchase first prove to be profitable?
6. Name the two results of the Spanish-American War.

Chapter 11 Checkup

I. Define these **terms.**

reservation	stampede	immigrant	Morse code	Hawaii
longhorns	Homestead Act	"melting pot"	electric light bulb	"Remember the *Maine*"
branded	land rush	*Clermont*	assembly line	San Juan Hill
cow town	Oklahoma Land Rush	telegraph	Alaska	

II. Tell why these **people** are important.

Buffalo Bill	James A. Garfield	Andrew Carnegie	Admiral George Dewey
Annie Oakley	Charles Finney	John D. Rockefeller	Theodore Roosevelt
Sitting Bull	Dwight L. Moody	William H. Seward	
Wild Bill Hickok	Billy Sunday	Captain James Cook	

III. Know these **inventors** and their **inventions.**

Cyrus McCormick	Thomas Edison	Jan Ernst Matzeliger
Robert Fulton	Henry Ford	Norbert Rillieux
Samuel Morse	Wilbur and Orville Wright	Granville T. Woods
Alexander Graham Bell	Robert Goddard	Garrett A. Morgan

IV. Identify the locations from **Map Masteries 13–14.**

The Nation Grows and Prospers 217

chapter 12
United States History:
Into the
TWENTIETH CENTURY

12.1 OUR COUNTRY IN 1900
A Major World Power

By 1900, just 124 years after declaring its independence from Britain, the United States had become <u>the richest, most productive country in the world</u>. No other country had made such a rapid advance in such a short period of time. The United States in 1900 ranked as <u>one of the five major world powers</u> along with Great Britain, France, Germany, and Russia.

The population of the United States had grown from about 5 million in 1800 to about 76 million in 1900. (By 2000, it would be over 280 million.) The territory of the nation had grown from about 800,000 square miles in 1800 to over 3 million square miles. The Union now included 45 states (Alaska, Arizona, Hawaii, New Mexico, and Oklahoma had not yet become states). The Philippines, Guam, and Puerto Rico were United States possessions, and the United States was beginning negotiations with Denmark to purchase the Danish West Indies, now called the United States Virgin Islands.

Imports had grown from a few million dollars in 1800 to nearly a billion in 1900, and exports had almost tripled. The United

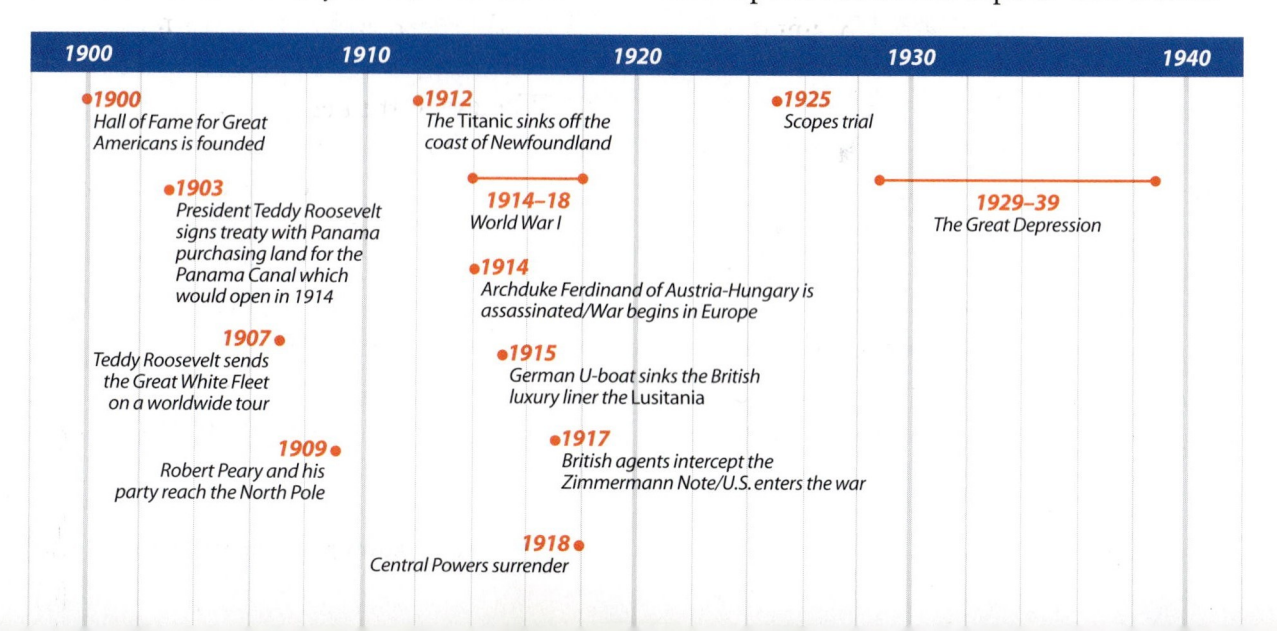

Timeline 1900–1940:

- **1900** Hall of Fame for Great Americans is founded
- **1903** President Teddy Roosevelt signs treaty with Panama purchasing land for the Panama Canal which would open in 1914
- **1907** Teddy Roosevelt sends the Great White Fleet on a worldwide tour
- **1909** Robert Peary and his party reach the North Pole
- **1912** The Titanic sinks off the coast of Newfoundland
- **1914–18** World War I
- **1914** Archduke Ferdinand of Austria-Hungary is assassinated/War begins in Europe
- **1915** German U-boat sinks the British luxury liner the Lusitania
- **1917** British agents intercept the Zimmermann Note/U.S. enters the war
- **1918** Central Powers surrender
- **1925** Scopes trial
- **1929–39** The Great Depression

The turn of the 20th century saw the "golden age" of the railroad in America.

States produced more than half of the world's cotton, corn, copper, and oil, and about a third of the steel, iron, silver, coal, and gold.

American farmers produced everything necessary for feeding the nation, including all varieties of grain, all common vegetables, all common fruits except bananas, and every kind of popular meat and fish. Such extras as cocoa, coffee, tea, and pepper were the only foods that had to be imported. Vast stores of timber still stood in American forests, however, and important minerals needed at that time could be found beneath American soil. Rubber was one of the few items essential for industry that had to be imported.

Daily Life and Work

Families. The American home in 1900 was a place where most children learned to honor their parents, to be courteous and honest in their dealings, to be obedient and submissive to authority, and to distinguish right from wrong. The father was the head of the house, and the mother was his honored companion and helper. Children were lovingly taught what was expected of them and lovingly punished when they disobeyed.

The Bible was read daily in many homes, and families usually prayed before meals as well as at other times. Many families were poor by today's standards, but they were happy, because they had values more important than money.

Children often heard the old familiar sayings whose truths had helped to make America great:

*A penny saved is a penny earned.
*Waste not, want not.
*Cleanliness is next to godliness.
*Early to bed and early to rise makes a man healthy, wealthy, and wise.
*Honesty is the best policy.
*A stitch in time saves nine.
*Never put off till tomorrow what you can do today.
*A man's word is his bond.

These and other sayings, most of which had been part of the American character since the time of Benjamin Franklin and before, helped the children of 1900 to become hon-

Into the Twentieth Century 219

Boys watch two icemen deliver ice in Harlem, NY.

est, hard-working individuals who would help our country continue prospering.

Homes. Most homes in the early 1900s still had fireplaces or wood stoves. In the big cities, however, *central heating systems* pumped steam, hot air, or hot water through some houses from a furnace in the basement. Many homes were lighted at night by *gas lights*. Mothers had no electric stoves, irons, or vacuum cleaners to lighten their workload. Families did not yet have electric refrigerators. Every few days, an iceman would deliver a huge block of ice to the home. The ice was put in the top compartment of a wooden icebox, where it would keep food cold until the ice melted.

Work. The United States had become the largest industrial nation in the world by 1900, and many people worked in the nation's bustling factories. Conditions were difficult and the hours were long, but people were thankful to have good jobs. Most people worked 10 hours a day, 6 days a week. Farm families usually went to town on Saturday to do their shopping, take care of other business, and visit friends. In most communities, Sunday was strictly a day of rest and worship.

Life expectancy. The number of years that a group of people can be expected to live on the average is called **life expectancy.** Life expectancy was much lower than it is now. Boys born in 1900 could expect to live to be about 46, girls about 48. In the years since 1900, life expectancy in the United States has increased by over 25 years. This means that today, on average, men live about 74 years and women live about 79.

In 1900, many important medical discoveries had not yet been made, and others had not had time to affect people's lives. People had been using antiseptics to kill bacteria for just 33 years, and x-rays had been discovered only 5 years earlier in 1895. Yellow fever, tuberculosis, measles, influenza, polio, diphtheria, smallpox, and typhoid fever claimed the lives of many children and young adults. Medical scientists had yet to discover the means of preventing or curing many of these diseases, and treatment was often difficult even when a cure was known.

the lathe room of a large New York factory

Education

American education was second to none in 1900. Ninety percent of all Americans were literate, or able to read, and it was widely recognized that Americans in general were more interested in books and in reading than were people in other parts of the world. Parents could send their children to the public

People in History
Mary McLeod Bethune: Famous Black Educator

Not every American child in 1900 had the opportunity for a good education. In many places, public schools were closed to black children. One educator who devoted her life to seeing that black children received a good education was Mary McLeod Bethune (1875–1955), the first American black woman to head a federal agency.

As the daughter of sharecroppers, Mary spent much of her childhood working in the cotton fields of her South Carolina home. Her Christian parents, who were former slaves, taught her to love God. Even though no one in the McLeod family could read, they kept a Bible on a special shelf in their home and waited eagerly for the times when the circuit-riding preacher would come teach them God's Word.

Mary longed to be able to read the Bible. At that time in her part of the country, black children were not allowed to attend the schools for white children, so when a teacher came to her town to start a school for black children, 9-year-old Mary was thrilled. In the months between planting and harvesting, she attended the school, and soon she could read the family Bible to her parents. God had answered her prayers.

After graduation from grade school, Mary was awarded a scholarship to Scotia Seminary, a Presbyterian high school and junior college for black women, in North Carolina. She diligently finished her studies there, and then she attended the Moody Bible Institute in Chicago, where her burden for the mission field of Africa grew. But God had different plans for Mary. When the time came for Mary to leave Moody, the mission board to which she had applied told her that they had no openings for a black missionary in Africa. Though disappointed, Mary trusted the Lord to show her His plan for her life.

Returning home, Mary became a teacher and discovered that she loved teaching. After a year, she went to Augusta, Georgia, where she taught for one more year. Then the mission board sent Mary to Kindell Institute in Sumter, South Carolina. Gradually, God revealed His plan for Mary. Though she was not serving in Africa as she had once hoped, Mary was indeed a missionary and had a special mission field—her classroom.

While teaching at Kindell, Mary married Albertus Bethune, and in 1899, the Bethunes moved to Florida. There, Mary McLeod Bethune heard about a railroad project in Daytona, Florida, and decided to build a school there for the children of the black laborers. In 1904, she opened a school for black girls, and within a year, the school's enrollment had grown from 5 to 100 hundred.

Mary McLeod Bethune taught her students to work "as unto the Lord, and not unto men." If her students wanted to attend college, she made sure they were prepared, but she also taught them practical skills such as sewing, cooking, and cleaning.

By 1923, the Bethune school had an enrollment of 600 students. That year, it merged with a boys' school to form Bethune-Cookman College, and Mrs. Bethune became the college president. In 1935, she became President Franklin D. Roosevelt's Special Advisor on Minority Affairs, and a year later, Mary became the director of the Negro Affairs Division of the National Youth Administration.

As a teacher, school administrator, college president, and director of a federal agency, Mary McLeod Bethune accomplished much for her people. When Mrs. Bethune died in 1955, she left behind a legacy of schools, hospitals, and associations for black Americans; and she had earned the respect and admiration of people all over the world.

Into the Twentieth Century 221

schools with confidence, knowing that the values they taught at home would also be taught at school. Many schoolteachers were Christians who honored the Bible. Bible reading and prayer were part of the daily routine in each schoolhouse. Character training played an important part in the school curriculum, and children were expected to learn the important facts about their world, as well as to be diligent, polite, honest, trustworthy, obedient, and reverent. Teachers encouraged patriotism among their students.

A favorite children's magazine, *The Youth's Companion,* published the **Pledge of Allegiance,** or Flag Salute, by Francis Bellamy, in 1892. It was such an excellent statement of loyalty to the United States that it was printed in leaflet form and distributed to every school in the nation. By 1900, each classroom had a flag, and millions of children throughout the nation recited the Pledge of Allegiance each morning. In 1954, the words "under God" were added to the Pledge to show that no nation can remain great without God's blessing.

Comprehension Check 12A
Identify
1. The 5 major world powers in 1900.
2. The average life expectancy for men and for women in 1900. Life expectancy today.
3. The statement of loyalty to America first published in 1892.
4. The first black American woman to head a federal agency.

Think
5. List 2 familiar sayings children often heard in 1900.

Religion

The Bible was the nation's most honored book. About 100,000 churches dotted the land, and nearly half the people were church members. The majority of the churches were true to the Bible. There were 6 million Methodists, 5 million Baptists, 1.5 million Lutherans, and 1.5 million Presbyterians, as well as many members of smaller denominations. William McKinley, the President of the United States, was a devout Christian who attended the Methodist church regularly. He took a courageous stand against liquor, swearing, and off-color stories, and he was known for his personal purity.

By 1914, more missionaries were being sent out from the United States than from any other nation on earth, and Americans were giving more money for missions than were any other people. Most Protestant missionaries in Japan, the Philippines, Korea, and Latin America came from the United States.

The great revivalist **D. L. Moody** died in 1899, but his work for God was continued by other dedicated Christians. Moody's assistant, **R. A. Torrey,** a great champion of the Bible, had served as the first superintendent of the Chicago school that would later be called Moody Bible Institute and took over Moody's responsibilities for a time after his death. Soon **Billy Sunday** would begin his great revival campaigns. Three great English preachers, **Gypsy Smith, G. Campbell Morgan,** and **F. B. Meyer,** also preached in the United States. Churches and revival preachers did much to keep the level of morality high in the United States. One noted advance was that people were becoming more and more aware of the evils of alcohol. By 1900, liquor was outlawed in many counties across the country.

Masters of Invention and Technology

Americans were known throughout the world in 1900 as inventors and users of many labor-saving devices. Because they understood the importance of work, Americans

a 30-horse harvester in the field

were masters at coming up with ways to get work done more quickly and efficiently. Farmers all over the world used American farm machinery, including mowers, reapers, and such marvels as the 30-horse harvester. (Motor-powered farm equipment would come later.) The typewriter hastened the work of many businesses, and the sewing machine, which was invented by Elias Howe and later improved by Isaac Singer, greatly increased the nation's capacity as a manufacturer of textiles. Electric typewriters and electric sewing machines had not yet been developed.

Infancy of automobiles and airplanes. Though transportation was still difficult for most Americans, that would soon change. Because only the extremely wealthy could afford automobiles at the turn of the century, there were fewer than 8,000 automobiles in the United States and less than 10 miles of concrete pavement. Most cars were powered by steam or electricity. Henry Ford would not develop the assembly line method for the construction of his Model T until 1913. Most people walked or rode horses, mules, bicycles, streetcars, steamships, or trains. There were about 18 million horses and mules in the United States in 1900 and about 10 million bicycles. A bold new form of transportation, the airplane, was on its way, but it would not be used for personal travel for many years. As you have learned, in September of 1900, the Wright Brothers flew their first glider at Kitty Hawk, North Carolina, and in 1903 they flew their first airplane.

The golden age of the railroad. America was enjoying the golden age of the railroad. Because Americans were leaders in the production of steel and pioneers in modern business management, the United States led the world in railroading. Over 190,000 miles of railroad track crisscrossed the country—as much as existed in the rest of the world put together. America had five transcontinental rail lines. Because of the emphasis on good equipment and efficient handling, American railways were able to handle loads averaging two or three times the weight of those in Europe. Passenger trains served meals, and passengers who had enough money could spend their nights comfortably in **Pullman sleeping cars** designed by American inventor George Pullman.

Some of the nation's most popular legends were railroad engineers. In the spring of 1900, **Casey Jones** died at the throttle while trying to slow down his crashing "Cannonball" to save the lives of his passengers.

Into the Twentieth Century 223

Ballads and folk tales would commemorate the brave engineer for years to come.

Before the 1900s, people in different locations set their clocks by the sun; thus, time differed from town to town. To reduce the confusion caused by differing standards of time, the railroads instituted standard time. The trains had to be coordinated to the second, or crashes could occur. Every railroader had a big pocket watch to help him keep the trains running according to a strict time schedule. His watch had to be officially approved and checked often for accuracy. Americans began using schedules in their homes and businesses to help them get more things done in a shorter amount of time, and people became conscious of being "on time" and "making good time" in all of their affairs. This time consciousness greatly increased the efficiency of businesses and led to greater prosperity for our nation.

Railroads carried the mail from city to city and from coast to coast. One famous **mail train,** the *Fast Mail,* made its run from New York to Chicago in only 24 hours. As the mail trains moved across the country, clerks sorted the mail in special cars. Many people on farms were able to take advantage of the new free rural delivery; they would no longer have to go to town to pick up their mail. Magazines, newspapers, and bulletins, as well as letters, came directly to farms and kept the farmers better educated and more informed than ever before. Catalogs from two new companies—Montgomery Ward and Sears and Roebuck—enabled farm families to do much of their shopping by mail.

Communication. The United States led the world in communication. Distant parts of the country were connected by more than 200,000 miles of telegraph lines— three times as many as any other country.

telephone switchboard operators c.a. 1900

224 *New World History & Geography*

Over a million **telephones** were already in use, and another million would be added in the next few years. There were no radios yet, but the wireless telegraph had been invented in 1895 by an Italian, **Guglielmo Marconi** [gōō·lyĕl′mō mär·kō′nē], and Americans were working hard to make it practical.

The Hall of Fame for Great Americans

Americans were justly proud of the great heroes of their country's history, and they searched for a way to honor them. In 1900, New York University founded the Hall of Fame for Great Americans. The Hall of Fame is a semicircular covered walkway lined with high columns and spaces for 102 bronze busts (a bust is a statue showing a person's head and shoulders). Twenty-nine people were elected to the Hall of Fame in 1900, including the following:

George Washington   *Robert Fulton*
Abraham Lincoln   *Henry W. Longfellow*
Daniel Webster   *Jonathan Edwards*
Benjamin Franklin   *Samuel F. B. Morse*
Ulysses S. Grant   *Robert E. Lee*
Thomas Jefferson   *Eli Whitney*

About every 5 years after that, other names were added to the hall. How many of the following do you recognize?

John Quincy Adams   *Booker T. Washington*
James Madison   *Alexander Graham Bell*
John Greenleaf Whittier   *Theodore Roosevelt*
Elias Howe   *Wilbur Wright*
Daniel Boone   *Stonewall Jackson*
Patrick Henry   *George Westinghouse*
Roger Williams   *Thomas Alva Edison*
John Paul Jones   *George Washington Carver*
Matthew F. Maury   *Clara Barton*
James Monroe   *Andrew Carnegie*
Grover Cleveland

the Hall of Fame for Great Americans

Comprehension Check 12B

Identify

1. Three famous American gospel preachers who preached in the United States during the late 1800s and early 1900s.
2. The form of transportation that increased the speed and efficiency of mail delivery.
3. The inventor of the wireless telegraph.

Think

4. Why did the United States lead the world in railroading? How many miles of railroad track were there in 1900?
5. How did standard time originate?

Into the Twentieth Century

12.2 President Theodore Roosevelt

The best-loved President of the early 1900s was **Theodore Roosevelt,** who was affectionately called "T. R." or "Teddy" by the American people. Theodore Roosevelt became Vice President of the United States in 1900 when William McKinley was reelected President. Six months after the election, President McKinley was assassinated by an anarchist (a person who believes all government should be done away with). McKinley was the third President to be assassinated. Theodore Roosevelt became the 26th President of the United States. At the age of 42, he became the youngest American President. (In 1961, John F. Kennedy would become the youngest President ever elected.)

A happy childhood. Teddy Roosevelt was born in New York City in 1858, just two and a half years before the Civil War began. His family tree was rich with American heroes. He was related by blood or marriage to nine other men who have been President of the United States—John Adams, James Madison, John Quincy Adams, Martin Van Buren, Zachary Taylor, Ulysses S. Grant, Benjamin Harrison, William Howard Taft, and Franklin D. Roosevelt—as well as to the Confederate leaders Jefferson Davis and Robert E. Lee. Young "Teddy," as he was called, was close to his family as he was growing up. He considered his father the grandest man he ever knew, and he spoke of his mother as being always gentle and kind. Each morning, the family began the day by gathering around the Bible for family devotions. Teddy's father, knowing that a strong spiritual life was important to all young people, helped found the YMCA (Young Men's Christian Organization).

A small, weak child, Teddy had poor eyesight and suffered from asthma, a disease of the lungs that hinders breathing. Many times in his childhood diary, he mentioned his asthma and the problems it caused. Mr. Roosevelt built an indoor gymnasium for 9-year-old Teddy and told him, "Theodore, you have the brains; you have got to make your body. It lies with you to make it, and it's dull, hard work, but you can do it." From that day forward, the determined Theodore Roosevelt began to build his weak body. Even when he was tired and wanting to quit, he pressed on, exercising faithfully every day. As the months passed, he grew stronger. Breathing became easier, but more important, he had learned the importance of determination, a lesson he applied throughout his life.

Public servant. Because of his weakness, Teddy was mostly taught at home by tutors and did not go to school. He was strong enough to enter Harvard University at the age of 18, where he proved to be an excellent scholar. After graduation from Harvard in 1880, he entered law school to become a lawyer. While attending law school, he wrote *The Naval War of 1812,* the first of more than 20 books. After only months in law school, Theodore Roosevelt decided to enter politics and become a public servant. In the fall of 1881, he was elected to his first political office, New York State assemblyman. His courage, determination, and intelligence earned him the respect of all who knew him, and he was reelected to office two more times.

Teddy had married shortly after gradu-

Theodore Roosevelt

226 *New World History & Geography*

Theodore Roosevelt on horseback at Yellowstone National Park

ating from college; 4 years later his young wife died after giving birth to their daughter, Alice. Teddy's mother died of typhoid fever on the same day as his wife, adding to his deep sorrow. He left politics and bought two cattle ranches in the Dakota Territory. The busy life of a rancher helped him to overcome his grief. Several years later Theodore Roosevelt married again. He and his wife reared a fine family of four boys and two girls, including his daughter from his first marriage. Theodore Roosevelt loved his children and enjoyed playing with them frequently.

Once again he entered politics and public life. He was named assistant secretary of the navy but resigned when the Spanish-American War of 1898 broke out because he wanted to fight for his country. He recruited former college athletes and western cowboys to create the First Volunteer Cavalry Regiment, later known as the Rough Riders. As you have already learned, Teddy Roosevelt and his Rough Riders became famous for their part in the war—the taking of San Juan Hill in Cuba.

After the war, Roosevelt was elected governor of New York. His famous motto, "Speak softly and carry a big stick," described his policy of government. He believed that America needs to be diplomatic with other nations but that we also need to be prepared for enemy attack by having a large, well-equipped army and navy.

The 26th President. Theodore Roosevelt became President in 1901 after the tragic death of President McKinley. In 1904, the Republicans nominated him for President, and he won the election by the greatest popular margin up to that time. He was popular, well-respected, and a capable leader. Even as President, he continued the physical fitness program he had begun as a young boy. When he refused to shoot a bear cub on a hunting trip, toy makers began making a special stuffed animal, the **teddy bear,** in honor of Teddy Roosevelt.

As President, Theodore Roosevelt stood for honesty in business, strength and courage in dealing with other countries, and wisdom in conserving our forests and other natural resources. In 1906, he received the Nobel Prize for peace because of his negotiations to end a war between Russia and Japan. He was the first American to win a Nobel Prize. (The Nobel Prize is awarded each year to people from all over the world who are judged

Into the Twentieth Century 227

to have achieved something "for the good of mankind." The prize money was willed by Swedish chemist Alfred Nobel, the inventor of dynamite.)

Roosevelt strengthens our country's defenses. Because he loved peace, President Roosevelt wanted to do all within his power to make sure that no other country could become a threat to American security. He announced that the United States was responsible to protect the countries of the Western Hemisphere from foreign invasion and persuaded Congress to authorize the construction of 10 battleships and 4 armored cruisers to build up the United States Navy. President Roosevelt knew that this "big stick" would make other nations very cautious about interfering with our freedoms. He wisely understood that the way to prepare for peace is to be prepared for war in case it should come.

The Panama Canal. To allow United States battleships to move rapidly between the Atlantic and Pacific Oceans, President Roosevelt made plans for the building of the Panama Canal. In 1903, he signed a treaty with Panama which gave the United States control of a strip of land 10 miles wide across the Isthmus of Panama. The United States paid Panama $10 million for the Canal Zone, plus $250,000 a year beginning in 1913. President Theodore Roosevelt visited Panama while the canal was under construction. This was the first time that a United States President had ever traveled to a foreign country while in office.

Building the canal kept 40,000 people busy for 10 years. It was one of the greatest engineering achievements of all time. When the Panama Canal opened in 1914, all nations not at war with the United States were allowed to use it. Because the United States had bought the right to build this canal, because the United States first had the approval of the people of Panama to build this canal, and because the United States had paid over $300 million to build the Panama Canal, the United States now had the right to control the canal and protect it from enemies.

The Great White Fleet. In 1907, President Roosevelt sent 16 new battleships on a tour around the world. These ships were called the **"Great White Fleet"** because they were painted white. This goodwill tour received

the Panama Canal

President Roosevelt visits construction of the Panama Canal.

228 New World History & Geography

Events in History
The Titanic

One of the greatest sea disasters in history took place in 1912. It was then that the new British luxury liner, the *Titanic*, collided with an iceberg and sank, leaving over 1,500 men, women, and children dead. Many of the people who died were United States citizens, and others were immigrants on their way to a new life in America.

Called the "Millionaires' Special," the *Titanic* was the largest, most luxurious ship in the world. It was approximately 175 feet tall (as tall as an 11-story building) and almost 900 feet long (the length of three football fields put end to end). Each of the vessel's four gigantic smoke stacks was big enough for a train to pass through.

It was the *Titanic's* maiden voyage (first trip), and when the ship left England, bound for New York City, she carried 915 crew members and more than 1,320 passengers. The passengers enjoyed the first swimming pool ever built on a ship, a fully-equipped gymnasium, a squash court for playing a game similar to tennis, fine restaurants, and elegant dining rooms. And if they needed medical attention, the ship had a hospital, complete with an operating room.

Because of the way the *Titanic* was constructed, it was considered to be unsinkable. One crew member foolishly said that not even God Himself could sink this ship.

The *Titanic* cruised along at a high rate of speed, trying to set a record for crossing the Atlantic. However, on April 14, around 11:40 P.M., the ship's lookout spotted a dark object in the water. He called the bridge to report, "Berg dead ahead." But because the ship was traveling at top speed, it could not slow down to turn quickly enough. Just as the *Titanic* reached the huge mass of ice, she turned, scraping against the iceberg.

The *Titanic* began to take on water, but no one panicked. Everyone believed the ship to be unsinkable. They knew that the *Titanic* could stay afloat with 4 holds (large compartments) flooded. However, they didn't realize that 5 holds were rapidly filling with water.

On the deck, passengers watched in disbelief as lifeboats were lowered. Then came the cry, "Women and children first!" For a moment, no one moved. Could it be true that this "unsinkable" giant was going under? Finally, one woman climbed into a lifeboat, and then other women began to follow her example. But the ship did not have enough lifeboats for everyone. Although there were 2,235 people onboard the *Titanic* that night, there was room for only 1,178 people in the lifeboats.

The *Titanic* started sinking more rapidly. As family members in the lifeboats said goodbye to those left on the ship, the band on deck played lively tunes, trying to keep spirits high. When the last lifeboat was towed away, the people left aboard the *Titanic* climbed to the top deck at the stern (rear end of the ship). Even as the bow (front end) of the ship sank lower and lower, the band members continued to play.

The survivors in the lifeboats stared in horror as the massive stern rose straight up out of the ocean. Then the ship disappeared beneath the water. In just $2^1/_2$ hours, the *Titanic* had sunk, and over 1,500 people had slipped into eternity.

Since the sinking of the *Titanic*, sea travel regulations have changed. Ships are now required to have enough lifeboats for all passengers onboard, and they also have to provide 24-hour wireless (radio) operators. Also, the International Ice Patrol has been formed to alert ships of dangerous icebergs floating in the North Atlantic.

In 1985, scientists discovered the shipwrecked *Titanic*, lying southeast of Newfoundland, at a depth of over 12,000 feet. After exploring the sunken vessel with deep-sea cameras, the scientists determined that the iceberg had split the seams in the vessel's hull. And thus it was that the great oceanliner sank.

Into the Twentieth Century

enthusiastic welcomes in many parts of the world. It showed countries that might feel hostile toward our nation that we were a major force that they could not attack without putting themselves in grave danger.

The Discovery of the North Pole

President Theodore Roosevelt's determination and love of adventure were reflected in other Americans of his day. **Robert Peary,** a United States naval officer and Arctic explorer, led the expedition that discovered the North Pole. During Peary's first attempt, he got as far north as Greenland's northern coastline and was forced to turn back. Seven years later, in 1907, Peary tried once again to reach the North Pole. He had a special ship, the *Roosevelt,* built to travel among the Arctic ice floes. He sailed to the northern coast of Canada's Ellesmere Island and then sledded across the ice toward the North Pole. Extreme hardships proved to be too much, however, and the exploration party was forced to turn back once again, after coming within 200 miles of the North Pole. On his third try, Robert Peary successfully led the remaining members of the exploration party—4 Eskimos and his black friend, **Matthew Henson**—to the North Pole on April 6, 1909.

Comprehension Check 12C
Identify
1. The toy that was made in honor of the 26th President of the United States.
2. The first American to be awarded the Nobel Prize for peace.
3. The year the Panama Canal opened and the countries eligible to use it.
4. The leader of the first expedition to reach the North Pole and the members of the group that accompanied him.
5. The "unsinkable" ocean liner that sank off the coast of Newfoundland in 1912.

12.3 WORLD WAR I

Civilization had progressed so far by 1900 that many people thought the world could only get better and better. Little did they realize that in Europe the stage was being set for two of the greatest wars the world had ever known—**World War I** (1914–1918) and **World War II** (1939–1945). These wars reminded Christians of Christ's words of prophecy and comfort:

And ye shall hear of wars and rumors of wars: see that ye be not troubled: for all these things must come to pass, but the end is not yet. Matt. 24:6

Both wars began with events that took place in Germany. The German people had for the most part rejected the Bible and embraced the teachings of modernist preachers, who said that Jesus is not God, that the Bible is not always true, and that a person's conscience should be his only guide. Without the true guide of the Bible, the Germans were in great danger of making unwise decisions.

The World Prepares for War

Kaiser Wilhelm II, the ruler of Germany in 1914, sought to control more land. Britain had the greatest navy in the world, but the German ruler also wanted to gain control of the seas. With this in mind, he began building up Germany's army and navy.

Other countries became fearful of Germany's might and decided to form alliances against Germany. An **alliance** is a promise between two or more countries to fight together against their enemies in time of war.

The countries that sided against Germany were called the Allied Powers or the **Allies.** Those countries that sided with Germany were called the **Central Powers.** The few countries that decided not to take any side were called **neutral nations.**

Archduke Ferdinand and his wife

European countries were preparing themselves for war. The only thing they lacked was an excuse to begin a war. The excuse came on June 28, 1914.

Archduke Ferdinand, heir to the throne of **Austria-Hungary,** was visiting the small country of Bosnia with his wife. The control of Bosnia was causing much ill will between Austria-Hungary and the small country of Serbia. A young man, under the influence of a Serbian secret society, decided to get even with Austria-Hungary. As the archduke and his wife rode by in an open car, this youth shot them both to death.

Austria-Hungary blamed everyone in Serbia for the assassination. Germany's ruler, eager for an excuse to begin war, told Austria-Hungary that it could count on Germany's help if it went to war against Serbia. Austria-Hungary soon declared war on tiny Serbia. Meanwhile, Russia told Serbia that the Russians would help Serbia. This angered the Germans, who then declared war on Russia. Because France had promised to help Russia, Germany declared war on France, too.

One by one, the countries of Europe declared war on one another. Soon England declared war on Germany. One Englishman said, "The lamps are going out all over Europe; we shall not see them lit again in our lifetime." Indeed, gloomy days lay ahead for all of Europe.

Woodrow Wilson was President of the United States at that time. Most Americans felt that the United States should stay out of the war in Europe. For the first 3 years of war, President Wilson kept our country neutral, which meant we would not take sides.

Woodrow Wilson

German U-boats

Germany's powerful army successfully defeated several countries. The Germans had to think of a different plan for defeating Great Britain. Because England is an island, she depended on ships to bring her food and supplies. Germany knew that if she could destroy England's ships, she could starve the people of England into giving up.

With this plan in mind, the Germans used their new weapon of war, the **U-boat** (underwater boat, or submarine). The Germans used the U-boats to destroy any ships that could be carrying food or

a German U-boat

231

American soldiers fighting near Mezy, France

supplies to England. The United States continued to send ships to England. As a result, the Germans began sinking American ships sailing in the waters around England.

The Sinking of the *Lusitania*

In May 1915, a British passenger liner, the **Lusitania** [lo͞o′sĭ-tā′nē-ə], left New York on its way to England. As the ship neared England, a German U-boat fired a torpedo into the side of the *Lusitania*. The ship sank quickly. Over 1,000 men, women, and children lost their lives—including over 100 Americans. Americans became very angry. Although many called for war, the United States remained neutral.

The United States Enters World War I

After a time of calm, the German government announced that after February 1, 1917, it would follow a policy of unrestricted submarine warfare. German submarines would sink, without warning, all ships entering the waters around the British Isles. Americans were enraged at this renewed threat to innocent human lives. Then, in March of 1917, British agents discovered a German letter asking Mexico to enter the war on the German side. This letter, called the **Zimmermann Note,** promised Mexico land from the states of New Mexico, Texas, and Arizona in return for help with the war. In other words, Germany was promising Mexico part of the United States if Germany won the war! Although Mexico did not help Germany, you can imagine how angry Americans became at the German threat to break up and divide the United States. The German ruler would stop at nothing. If he won in Europe, he would go after America. Our country was being threatened.

In April 1917, the United States declared war on Germany. President Wilson read a war message in which he said, **"The world must be made safe for democracy."** The United States joined the Allies.

In France, the French cheered the American soldiers as French bands played "The Star-Spangled Banner." The coming of the American troops gave a new hope to the Allies of Europe.

232 *New World History & Geography*

Thus the Germans met a brand new, fresh army. The German army began to weaken. With American help, the French and British began to defeat the Germans. Each day, both sides lost hundreds of men. But these men believed that their countries were worth dying for.

The End of the Great War

Finally the Central Powers surrendered. On **November 11, 1918,** World War I came to an end. (Today, November 11 is celebrated as **Veterans Day,** honoring those who have fought for our country in any war and all who have served in our nation's armed forces.)

Comprehension Check 12D

Identify

1. A binding agreement between 2 or more countries to help each other in time of war.
2. The name for the group of countries that fought against Germany during World War I. The group of countries that fought with Germany. The countries that did not take sides.
3. The event that began World War I.
4. The name for the German World War I submarines.

Think

5. Why did the Zimmermann Note enrage the United States?

12.4 BETWEEN THE WORLD WARS

The Roaring Twenties

By the beginning of 1920, most Americans turned their thoughts from war to happier times. Factories stopped making war supplies and began making products that would change the style of living in America. In a few years, a housewife would not have to scrub her clothes on a washboard anymore. She could buy a washing machine. Later, families could buy toasters, vacuum cleaners, and refrigerators to make their lives a little easier.

The invention of the **radio** brought another change to American life. In the evenings, many American families sat quietly around their radios listening to news, music, and programs. The radio was exciting, but everyone had to listen quietly. The first radios made a crackling sound which sometimes made it difficult to hear the program.

For the first time, many families were able to enjoy beautiful music and interesting programs on the radio. They could now hear the latest news even while it was happening. They could all listen to the President and other leaders give speeches, no matter where they lived.

In 1925, **Calvin Coolidge** (1872–1933) became the first President to give his inaugural address over the radio. Families gathered to hear the new President talk about America's history and America's future. "Because of what America is and what America has done," President Coolidge said, "a firmer courage, a higher hope

two boys listen to a crystal radio set in 1920.

Into the Twentieth Century 233

inspires the heart of all humanity." He then gave Americans a challenge to learn from their history. "We cannot continue these brilliant successes in the future," he said, "unless we continue to learn from the past."

The radio also brought the gospel message to many people who could not or would not go to church, as great preachers spread the message of salvation over the airwaves.

Automobiles, made cheaper by Henry Ford's assembly lines, became popular. The special highways built for automobile traffic amazed the people of the 1920s. How surprised these people would have been if they could have looked ahead to see the modern highways of today filled with millions upon millions of cars in every size, shape, and color! Henry Ford had said that any color was fine for a car, as long as it was black.

It became a tradition for the whole family to go for a drive in the country on Sunday afternoons. It also became much easier to visit grandparents and other relatives who lived in a different part of the country.

During the 1920s, business thrived. Factories made more and more products. More workers were hired to make more products. For many Americans, the "Roaring Twenties" was a prosperous decade.

Challenges to Christianity

During the 1920s, some people in the United States began listening to the arguments of unbelieving preachers and teachers, many from Germany. These men were called *modernists* or *liberals*. Many of the modernist ideas began with the teachings of **Charles Darwin** (1809–1882), a British naturalist

People in History
Calvin Coolidge: A Man of Good Sense

Calvin Coolidge, the President of the United States during most of the 1920s (1923–1929), was known for his scholarship, character, frugality, quiet humor, and good sense. Coolidge, a native of Vermont, understood the people of the United States. He knew their strengths and their weaknesses, and he often said that *the strength of the nation depended upon the character of the people.*

From his Puritan ancestors and his study of the Bible, Calvin Coolidge learned the character traits that made generations of Americans great. President Coolidge did not talk much and because of this, people often called him "Silent Cal." The things he did say were so filled with good sense and quick wit that they have been remembered for over half a century. Calvin Coolidge's famous sayings include the following:

- Industry, thrift, and self-control are not sought because they create wealth, but because they create character.
- There is no dignity quite so impressive, and no independence quite so important, as living within your means.
- If you see 10 troubles coming down the road, you can be sure that 9 will run into the ditch before they reach you.
- Prosperity is only an instrument to be used, not a deity to be worshiped.
- The meaning of America is not to be found in a life without toil. Freedom is not only bought with a great price; it is maintained by unremitting effort.
- If all the folks in the United States would do the few simple things they know they ought to do, most of our big problems would take care of themselves.

who rejected the Scriptures and said that man had evolved from animals. Bible-believing Christians all over the country banded together to affirm (declare positively) the fundamental teachings of Christianity:

1. The Bible is the Word of God and true in every detail.
2. Jesus is God.
3. Jesus was born of a virgin.
4. The miracles recorded in the Bible were real, historical events.
5. Jesus shed His blood for the sins of mankind.
6. Jesus arose bodily from the grave.
7. Jesus will return to earth some day.

Because they still believed the fundamental truths of Christianity, many of the people who affirmed the truth of the Bible were called **Fundamentalists.** About 75 percent of the churches in the United States in the 1920s were fundamental in their beliefs.

God sent many great speakers, teachers, and preachers to help Americans from all walks of life take a firm stand for the Bible. **William Jennings Bryan** (1860–1925), a famous lawyer and statesman who ran for President three times, was the most popular speaker in the country. His powerful speeches earned him the title "Silver-tongued Orator." Bryan, a devout Presbyterian, victoriously defended the Bible in a famous court case against a teacher who was illegally teaching evolution in the classroom. This case was called the Scopes trial, or the "monkey trial." William Jennings Bryan won the case against evolution.

Dr. Harry Rimmer (1890–1952) spoke in the universities and wrote several books that effectively refuted the error of evolution. A brilliant Greek professor from Princeton University, **J. Gresham Machen** (1881–1937), gave radio talks about the truth of the Bible and the falseness of modernism. The books that he wrote are still read today.

J. Gresham Machen

R. A. Torrey, Moody's assistant, helped people see that modernism is not true scholarship and that it will eventually lead to the loss of the values that have made our country great.

Billy Sunday preached to the masses in both the United States and England at this time, and the English preachers Gypsy Smith, G. Campbell Morgan, and F. B. Meyer also traveled back and forth between the two countries teaching and preaching. These men and many others like them helped save our country from the despair and hopelessness that was spreading over much of Europe.

Americans were still so firmly grounded in the Bible and its teachings that people who wanted to follow a worldly lifestyle often left the United States to live in Paris or London. This was true especially of authors who had bitter feelings against the United States and Christianity. At least 85 American authors lived in Europe at this time, and many of these attacked the Bible in their writings. Some writers in our country and abroad taught the ideas of socialism and Communism, and some of their ideas spread to the teachers' colleges. Fortunately, the majority of the American people listened to the positive Bible teachers and preachers rather than to the negative writers.

William J. Bryan

Into the Twentieth Century

Unemployed men being served soup by charity workers during the depression.

The Great Depression

In October 1929, hard times came to America. Banks ran out of money, and people did not have money to buy things. Factories closed down, and many people lost their jobs.

As weeks turned into months, people began to go hungry. Even though prices had dropped drastically, people still could not afford to buy food, clothing, or factory goods. People began to lose their homes because they could not pay their bills.

These difficult years from 1929 to 1939 became known as the **Great Depression.** Millions of United States citizens suffered. Their spirits were good, though, and families and individuals worked together to make the best of what they had. Many people who went through these years look back on them as a time when God helped in special ways when all else seemed to fail.

The government began working to see how it could end the Great Depression. President **Franklin D. Roosevelt** thought of a way to create jobs through projects such as building highways, dams, and bridges. The men who worked on these projects were paid by the government. But the government was just as poor as everyone else. Where did the money come from to pay these men? In a risky move, the government began to spend more money than it had. Though the government may have helped people temporarily during the Depression, some of the policies set up then have caused serious problems that still plague us today.

Sometimes it seemed as though the Great Depression would never end. By the late 1930s, however, things had begun to improve. Men found jobs and earned money to buy food, clothes, and other products. But only when America went to war again did the economy boom and the last traces of the Great Depression disappear.

During the Great Depression people often had to sell what they had to pay bills.

Plans for Peace That Failed

Peace-loving countries remembered World War I with horror. The United States, Great Britain, France, and several smaller countries decided on a plan to reduce the number of weapons and the size of the armed forces that a country has. They agreed that no new battleships should be built for 10 years. Italy and Japan also joined the agreement, although the leaders of those countries did not sincerely seek peace.

Immediately, the United States, England, and France began to cut back on their weapons. They felt sure of peace. They did not realize that Italy and Japan had no intention of keeping their promise. <u>While the United States was making her navy smaller and less powerful, Japan was secretly making hers stronger.</u>

To make matters worse, Germany began to build an even stronger navy and army than she had during World War I. <u>Secretly, Germany's factories began producing powerful bombs and planes to carry them.</u>

Comprehension Check 12E

Identify

1. The first American President to give his inaugural address over the radio.
2. The British naturalist who rejected the Scriptures and developed a theory that tried to prove that man had evolved from animals.
3. People who still believed the fundamental truths of Christianity and the Bible.
4. Eight men who fought against evolution and for Biblical principles.
5. The period from 1929 to 1939 when Americans had severe economic difficulties.

Think

6. What happens to a family that spends money it does not have? Could the same thing happen to a government? Explain.

Chapter 12 Checkup

I. Tell why these **people** are important.

Noted Individuals
- Mary McLeod Bethune
- Casey Jones
- Guglielmo Marconi
- Theodore Roosevelt
- Robert Peary
- Matthew Henson
- Kaiser Wilhelm II
- Archduke Ferdinand
- Woodrow Wilson
- Calvin Coolidge
- Charles Darwin
- Franklin D. Roosevelt

Preachers and Defenders of the Bible
- R. A. Torrey
- Gypsy Smith
- G. Campbell Morgan
- F. B. Meyer
- D. L. Moody
- Billy Sunday
- William Jennings Bryan
- Dr. Harry Rimmer
- J. Gresham Machen

II. **Identify** the following.

- life expectancy
- Pledge of Allegiance
- Fast Mail
- Great White Fleet
- *Titanic*
- alliance
- Allies
- Central Powers
- neutral nation
- U-boat
- *Lusitania*
- Zimmermann Note
- modernism
- fundamentalist
- Great Depression

III. Give the noted events for these **dates**.

1914	April 1917	1929–1939
May 1915	November 11, 1918	

IV. Identify the locations from **Map Mastery 15**.

Into the Twentieth Century 237

chapter 13 United States History:

NO SUBSTITUTE for VICTORY

13.1 THE WORLD BETWEEN THE WARS

The United States was not the only country to suffer from the Great Depression. The war-torn countries of Europe also knew much hunger and poverty as they worked to rebuild their cities after World War I.

Having forgotten God, the people of Russia, Germany, and Italy began listening to men who wanted to become more powerful, even if by war. Eager to see better times, many people believed the promises of prosperity that these men made. New forms of government came to power. **Dictators, people who rule by force and do not allow their subjects any freedoms**, took control in Russia, Germany, and Italy. In Japan, which had been ruled by an emperor for many years, military leaders became more and more powerful.

Russia—Communism

In 1917, a year before the end of World War I, the Communist Party took control of Russia. Under the leadership of **Nikolai Lenin,** they built a cruel empire, the **Soviet Union,** that threatened to take control of many other countries, too. In a free country, people can own their own businesses, homes, and land. When **Communism** takes over a country, the government takes these things from the people and claims to own them.

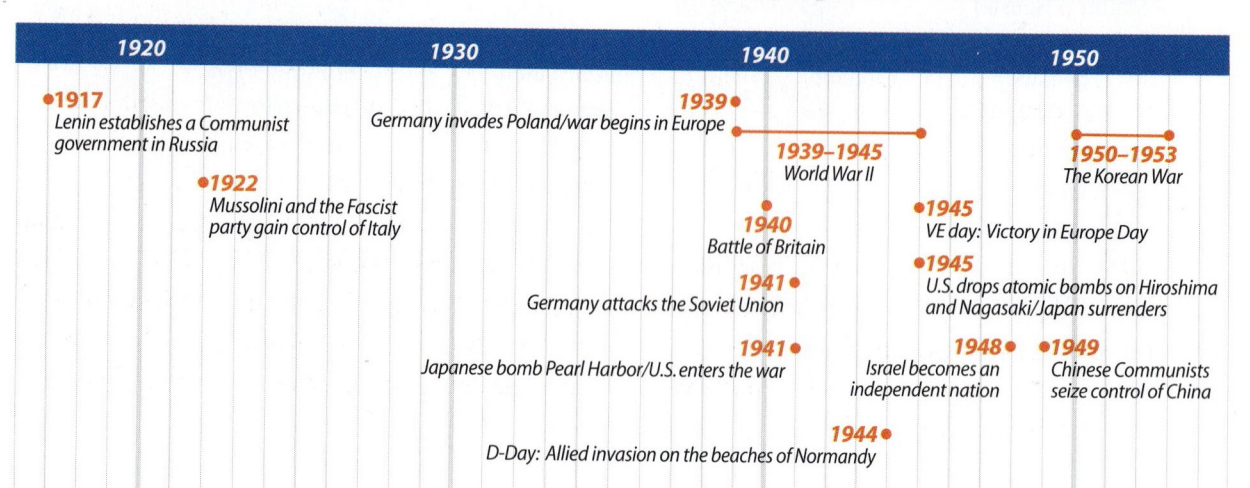

| 1920 | 1930 | 1940 | 1950 |

- **1917** Lenin establishes a Communist government in Russia
- **1922** Mussolini and the Fascist party gain control of Italy
- **1939** Germany invades Poland/war begins in Europe
- **1939–1945** World War II
- **1940** Battle of Britain
- **1941** Germany attacks the Soviet Union
- **1941** Japanese bomb Pearl Harbor/U.S. enters the war
- **1944** D-Day: Allied invasion on the beaches of Normandy
- **1945** VE day: Victory in Europe Day
- **1945** U.S. drops atomic bombs on Hiroshima and Nagasaki/Japan surrenders
- **1948** Israel becomes an independent nation
- **1949** Chinese Communists seize control of China
- **1950–1953** The Korean War

The "flying tigers" (U.S. pilots) run to their fighters at the sound of an air raid siren during World War II. They painted tiger shark faces on their planes to intimidate the Japanese.

The people must work for the Communist government or suffer great losses. Although the people in the Soviet Union were allowed to vote, they usually had only one candidate to vote for—the Communist candidate!

The Communist Party allowed no freedom of speech, press, or religion. In 1929, **Joseph Stalin** became the Communist dictator of the Soviet Union. Stalin was one of the cruelest dictators the world has ever known, eliminating by force and terror anyone who opposed him. He had millions of his own people either executed or sent to concentration camps in Siberia. In 1939, he made an agreement with Adolf Hitler, the dictator of Germany, to help the Germans if Germany went to war.

Joseph Stalin

Italy—Fascism

The people of Italy believed **Benito Mussolini's** [bə·nē′tō mōō′sə·lē′nē] promise that he would protect them from Communism with his own form of socialism. The Italians made Mussolini their leader.

Mussolini became a harsh dictator. He allowed no other political party in Italy but his, the **Fascist** [făsh′ĭst] **Party.** Although the people owned their own property, they lost their freedoms. Those who dared to disobey Mussolini were killed or put into prison. The Fascist Party was very much like the Communist Party in its oppression of the people. The Italians listened as Mussolini told them that Italy would become powerful, and they watched as he began building one of the strongest armies in Europe.

Germany—National Socialism

The German people, impoverished and discouraged by their losses in World War I, wanted a leader who could deliver them from their problems and protect them against a Russian invasion. The **Nazi (National Socialist) Party** promised to make Germany a powerful nation, free from problems. Hearing these promises, many German people became eager to follow the Nazi leader, **Adolf Hitler.** In doing so, they gave up their freedom and came under the rule of a cruel, ungodly dictator.

No Substitute for Victory 239

Benito Mussolini (left) and Adolf Hitler (right) pictured at Munich, 1937.

National socialism taught (1) that the leader and the government of a country are all powerful and are more important than the people of that country; (2) that all people are not equal in worth, but some groups of people (such as Jews) are inferior; and (3) that the leader could do no wrong. Hitler and his Nazi government used brutal tactics to punish or even kill those who opposed them. Again, in its oppression of the people, National Socialism was much like Communism.

Hitler demanded absolute loyalty from everyone. He hated anyone who was loyal to someone else. Hitler especially hated the Jews, God's special people, because of their loyalty to God, and he blamed the problems of Germany on them. In one of his most horrible crimes, Hitler had millions of people executed, including several million Jews.

Hitler tried to make the German people think that Germans were superior to other peoples of the world. "The Germans should conquer and rule the world," Hitler told his people. With this in mind, Hitler built a powerful army, navy, and air force.

Japan—Militarism

Before and during World War II, **Emperor Hirohito** [hē′rō·hē′tō] ruled Japan. Japan had a very powerful army and navy. But as military leaders—especially a general named **Tojo**—became more powerful than the emperor, Hirohito had no choice but to go along with their wishes. Japan's military leaders planned to conquer and rule Asia. As early as 1931, Japan began attacking China.

Tojo

Comprehension Check 13A

Identify

1. Russia's first dictator under its Communist government.
2. The Communist who became dictator of the Soviet Union in 1929.
3. The Italian dictator and leader of the Fascist Party.
4. The Nazi dictator of Germany.
5. The Japanese emperor during World War II.

Think

6. What happened in Russia when the Communist Party took over?

240 New World History & Geography

13.2 WORLD WAR II

The Attacks Begin

The government leaders of the Soviet Union, Italy, Germany, and Japan gained powerful control over the people of their countries. Although each ruler represented a different kind of government, each had the same selfish desire to control other countries and thus make his country the most powerful country in the world. Germany began attacking the small, weak countries of **Europe.** Italy attacked **Ethiopia** in Africa. Japan attacked **China.** The Soviet Union watched and waited.

The rest of the world criticized these countries for attacking others, but they did nothing to stop them. They told themselves that Germany would soon stop on her own. China and Ethiopia seemed so far away that the people of Europe were not concerned. No one wished to begin another war.

The world's apathy delighted Hitler. With each new country he conquered, he lied to the world, saying that he was satisfied and he would stop the attacks. Then suddenly his army would conquer another country. Once again, the lights were going out all over Europe.

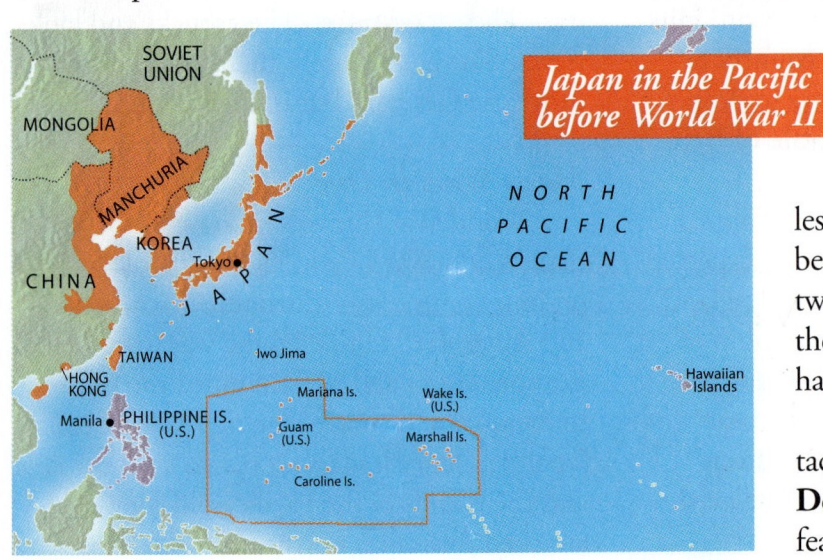

Aggression in Europe 1936-1940

Germany Conquers

By 1939, Hitler's army had taken over the small countries of Austria and Czechoslovakia. When Hitler demanded that Poland give up a piece of her land to Germany, Poland refused. Hitler and Stalin made a secret agreement to divide Poland once the Germans had conquered it. The Germans then invaded Poland.

Troubled by Hitler's desire to conquer, both France and Great Britain warned Hitler to withdraw from Poland. When the Nazis did not stop, France and Britain declared war on Germany. Canada and other Commonwealth nations quickly followed suit. World War II (1939–1945) had begun. Soon, the Russian army marched into Poland. With two powerful armies attacking Poland, Britain and France could do little to help the country. In less than 3 weeks, Poland had been defeated and divided between her enemies, Germany and the Soviet Union. Another light had been snuffed out in Europe.

In April 1940, Germany attacked and defeated **Norway** and **Denmark.** In May, Germany defeated the countries of **Belgium,**

Japan in the Pacific before World War II

No Substitute for Victory 241

the **Netherlands,** and **Luxembourg.** Germany then invaded **France** and defeated her.

The free countries of the world were alarmed when France fell under German rule. Now, Great Britain was the Nazis' last powerful European enemy that was not occupied by Germany. Great Britain begged the United States for help.

The United States Builds Its Armed Forces

At that time, **Franklin D. Roosevelt** was President of the United States. The defeat of France shocked the American people, and our country's factories began to produce war supplies. The armed forces, though not yet at war, began to strengthen the navy, army, marines, and air force. Guns and war supplies were sold or loaned to Great Britain and other countries struggling against the enemies. President Roosevelt called the United States "the great arsenal of democracy."

Franklin Roosevelt

Germany Attacks England

Because England is an island nation, Hitler's armies could not invade the country by land. Instead, Hitler sent airplanes to drop bombs over the country. The **Battle of Britain** began.

For 8 months, German planes dropped bombs on England. Each day, Hitler expected Britain to give up, but the people of England fought bravely, inspired by the leadership of their Prime Minister, Sir Winston Churchill. England's air force was finally able to beat back the Germans. Although the war was far from over, the United States was relieved. Great Britain had not been conquered.

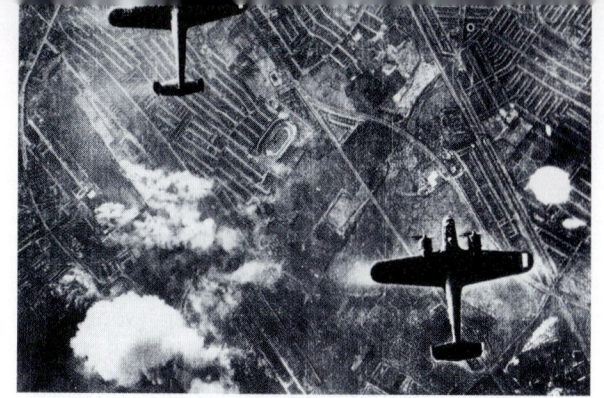

German bombers over England during the Battle of Britain

Hitler Surprises the Russians

Even though Germany and the Soviet Union had signed a 10-year nonaggression pact in 1939, Hitler had been planning a surprise attack on the Russians. If he defeated the Soviet Union, Hitler could force the Russians to provide Germany with food and war supplies. Great Britain warned the Soviet Union that Germany would turn on them, but the Russians did not listen.

In June 1941, Germany attacked the Soviet Union. Joseph Stalin, the Russian dictator, now turned and asked for aid from Great Britain and the United States. In order to keep the Germans from gathering Russian supplies, Britain agreed to help.

However, it was the cold Russian winter that helped the Soviet Union most of all. The German soldiers had no warm winter clothing. Their food froze. Their trucks and tanks froze. Slowly but surely, the Russian army drove the Germans out of their country.

Many Wars in One

World War II involved more of the world than World War I had. Fighting took place on four continents—**Europe, Africa, Asia,** and **Australia.** Hitler led the war to conquer Europe; Hitler and Mussolini led the war to conquer and control the riches of Africa. Japan's military leaders set out to conquer Asia and the islands of the Pacific, and they even attacked Australia's northern coast. Together,

242 New World History & Geography

Germany, Italy, and Japan were known as the **Axis Powers.**

Those countries that struggled against them were called the Allied Powers, or **Allies.** At first, Britain and the Commonwealth nations stood almost alone. Soon, the United States, China, and many other nations joined the Allies. It became clear to the Allies that Germany, Italy, and Japan would all have to be defeated if World War II were to come to an end.

Comprehension Check 13B

Identify

1. The event that began World War II.
2. The President of the United States at the time World War II began.
3. The collective name given to Germany, Italy, and Japan.
4. The name given to the countries which fought against Germany, Italy, and Japan.

Think

5. How did the rest of the world react at first to Hitler's aggression in eastern Europe? When did the free countries of the world begin to take action?

Smoke and flames billow from the USS Shaw after the Japanese attack on Pearl Harbor.

13.3 THE UNITED STATES ENTERS WORLD WAR II

On the beautiful island of **Oahu** in Hawaii, the United States Navy had an important base called **Pearl Harbor.** Now that airplanes had been improved and were being used for war as well as peace, it was important that the Hawaiian Islands be protected. If an enemy took control of Hawaii, it would not be long before the west coast of the United States would be in danger of enemy air attacks.

You will remember that Japan wanted to control Asia and the islands of the Pacific. "The power of the United States Navy must be destroyed," the Japanese military leaders told each other. "If Pearl Harbor is destroyed, it would be too hard for the Americans to bring other ships to the Pacific Ocean. Besides," the Japanese boasted, "Americans would rather give up than fight."

To trick the Americans, Japan sent officials to Washington, D.C., to talk about making peace. Meanwhile, the Japanese secretly planned an air raid on Pearl Harbor.

Early on Sunday morning, **December 7, 1941,** nearly 200 Japanese planes took off from aircraft carriers and flew over Pearl Harbor. This first wave of the attack swept across Oahu. Taking the Americans by surprise, they quickly destroyed the planes sitting on the airfields and then attacked eight battleships which were important to the Pacific navy. In a second wave, 170 more Japanese planes arrived. In less than 2 hours, seven of the eight battleships, as well as many other ships of the Pacific Fleet, were either sunk or badly damaged. Over 2,000 Americans were killed.

Later that day, Americans who were listening to their radios were shocked to hear their programs interrupted by an

No Substitute for Victory

World War II

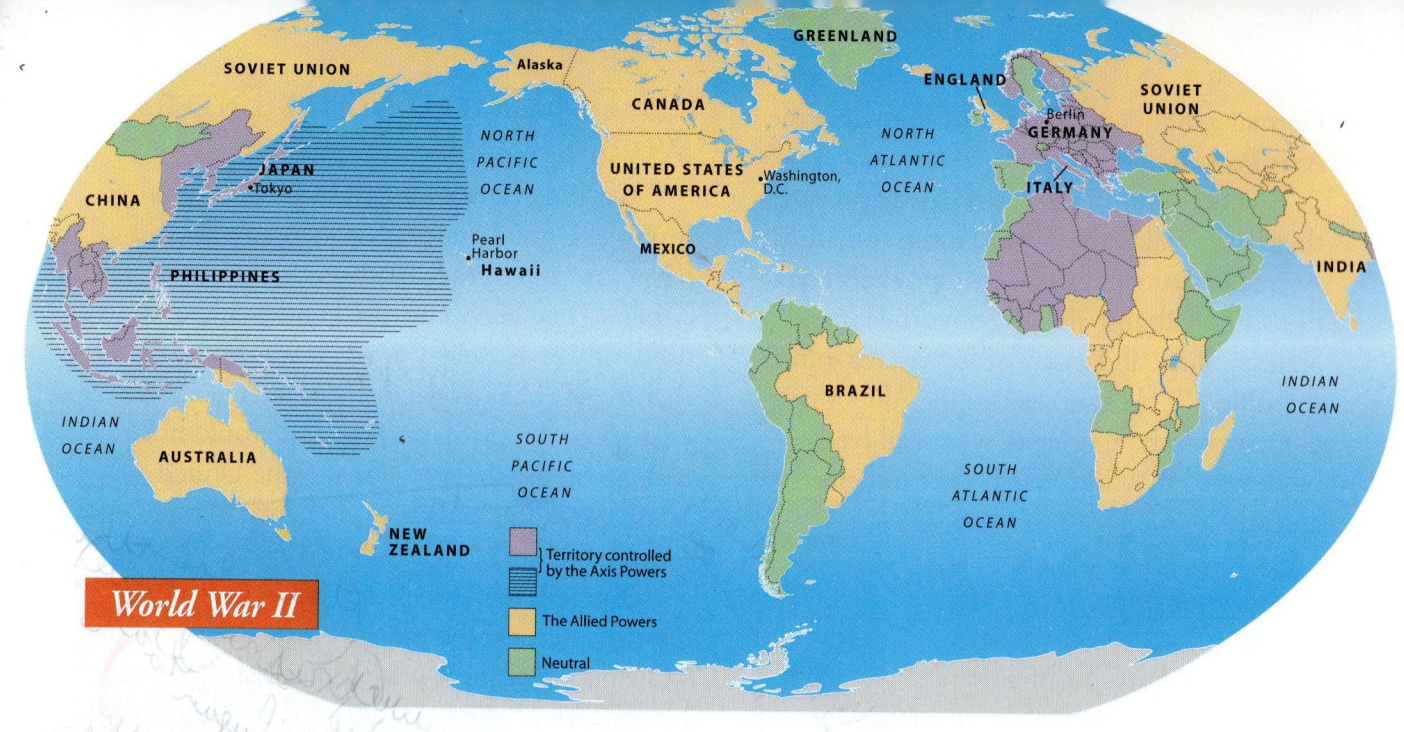

Map Legend:
- Territory controlled by the Axis Powers
- The Allied Powers
- Neutral

emergency news report—"Pearl Harbor has been bombed." The Japanese would soon find that their attack on Pearl Harbor had not brought the results they anticipated. Instead of destroying American military power, the attack brought American power into action. On December 8, 1941, the United States and Canada declared war on Japan. (Canada had already been at war with Germany.) A few days later, Germany and Italy declared war on the United States.

Victory Comes at Last

The Allies had before them the gigantic job of defeating three powerful enemies—Italy, Germany, and Japan. Different battles were fought in different places of the world at the same time. American men fought in the Pacific Ocean, China, the Mediterranean Sea, Africa, Europe, Australia, and the Atlantic Ocean.

In 1943, after gaining victory in North Africa, the Allies attacked the Axis Powers in Italy. In 1944, Italy removed Mussolini from power.

While troops fought in Italy, more Allied forces focused on freeing France. They planned a great invasion of the country to be led by American General Dwight D. Eisenhower. The Germans closely guarded French borders, but Allied troops landed on the beaches of Normandy in northern France on June 6, 1944, or **D-Day**. In a bold, swift action, men came by air and by sea, storming the beaches for several weeks. Once they hit the coast, Allied soldiers fought fiercely against the Germans in northern France. The Allies freed Paris in August of 1944, and their ground troops then marched to Berlin, Germany. Germany surrendered on May 7, 1945. May 8 was declared **V-E Day** (Victory in Europe Day).

Japan remained the only enemy for the Allies to defeat. She had learned since Pearl Harbor that Americans were hard, courageous fighters. Although the attack on Pearl Harbor had severely damaged the United States Navy in the Pacific, within a year the navy was ready to do battle once again.

The Japanese had suffered much loss during the war, but they refused to surrender.

People in History
The Nisei of the 442nd: Japanese-American Patriots

By World War II, thousands of Japanese immigrants had settled in the United States. The Japanese-Americans loved America and faithfully supported her through the war, despite being distrusted and even persecuted by some other Americans. Many patriotic Japanese-Americans enlisted in the United States Army after the bombing of Pearl Harbor. They formed the 442nd Regimental Combat Team. The men of the 442nd were American-born, American-educated sons of Japanese immigrants and were called **Nisei** [nē′sā′] or *second generation,* the name for all those born in the United States of Japanese parents.

Throughout the war, the Nisei displayed unflinching devotion and courage. By the end of the war, they had earned the distinction of being the most decorated infantry unit in all of the United States Army. Together, the Nisei received 7 Presidential unit citations and 18,143 individual awards and decorations. One particular battalion of the 442nd, the 100th Infantry Battalion, became known as the "Purple Heart Battalion" because so many of its members died or were wounded in battle. The Nisei played an important part in many battles and fought with unquestionable loyalty for their country, the United States of America.

The military leaders of Japan seemed to care little about the Japanese civilians who were being killed in each air raid upon their cities or the thousands of Japanese soldiers who died fighting for their power-hungry leaders. Yet the Allies knew that Japan must surrender if the countries of Asia were to remain free.

The United States had to make a difficult decision. The powerful **atomic bomb** had been invented. Should it be used to bring the war in Japan to a quick end? On August 6, 1945, an American bomber dropped an atomic bomb on the Japanese city of **Hiroshima.** A few days later, another bomb was dropped on **Nagasaki.** Both cities were destroyed. The Japanese quickly surrendered. World War II, the largest war in history, had come to an end.

the atomic bomb at Hiroshima

No Substitute for Victory

After the war, the Allied soldiers found German prison camps (called **concentration camps**) where men, women, and children had been penned up under horrible conditions with very little food. In Germany and other lands held by Hitler, millions of people had been cruelly massacred. Included in these numbers were 6 million Jewish people, as well as many Germans and people of other nationalities. The murder of the Jews and others became known as the **Holocaust**.

a Nazi concentration camp

People in History
Colonel Benjamin O. Davis, Jr. AND THE FIGHTING RED TAILS

Benjamin O. Davis, Sr. (1877–1970), who served in the Spanish-American War, World War I, and World War II, was the first black American to reach the rank of general in any branch of the United States military. Following in his father's footsteps, in 1959 **Benjamin O. Davis, Jr.,** became the first black officer in history to attain the rank of major general in the United States Air Force.

In the spring of 1942, Lieutenant Colonel Davis (1912–) became the commander of the 99th Pursuit Squadron. He trained the squadon's 13 young black American men at Tuskegee Institute in Alabama, and after training, the men of the 99th entered World War II in North Africa. There, they fought heroically under the leadership of Major George "Spanky" Roberts, while Colonel Davis returned to the United States to train new black cadets.

In June 1944, the 99th joined Colonel Davis once again and, together with the 332nd Fighter Group, formed the **Fighting Red Tails.***

The Fighting Red Tails quickly distinguished themselves as courageous, skillful pilots, who destroyed 261 enemy aircraft and damaged 148. They flew a total of 1,578 missions and 15,553 sorties (short missions, often flown by a single plane). The Fighting Red Tails became the first pilots to shoot down the new German jet fighter *ME-262* and the only pilots to sink a German destroyer singlehandedly. They also flew 200 bomber escort missions during the war, without losing a single bomber plane to enemy fighters.

After achieving the rank of general in 1959, General Davis served as chief of staff for the United States Forces in Korea (1965–1967), commander of the 13th Air Force at Clark Air Force Base in the Philippines, deputy commander in chief of the U.S. Strike Command at MacDill Air Force Base in Tampa, Florida, and when he retired as a lieutenant (3-star) general in 1970, continued to serve our nation in the U.S. Department of Transportation. On December 9, 1998, General Benjamin O. Davis, Jr., with a line of Fighting Red Tails standing by him was awarded his 4th general's star.

*To read more about Colonel Benjamin O. Davis, Jr., and the Fighting Red Tails, see *Of America,* Volume 1, from *A Beka Book.*

Once again, the United States left the war as the most powerful nation in the world. The war had done much to unite the American people. Everyone had wanted to do his part to aid in the war effort. American women had gone to work in factories to produce weapons and supplies for the soldiers. Americans knew that they had been fighting for a good, just cause, and their spirit throughout the war years was one of unity and patriotism.

Leaders of the Allies

During World War II, several Allied leaders became famous to people around the world. The leaders of the **Big Four**—the four most powerful Allied countries—were **Chiang Kai-shek** [jē·äng′ kī′shĕk′] of China, **Joseph Stalin** of the Soviet Union, **Sir Winston Churchill** of England, and **President Franklin D. Roosevelt** of the United States. There were many important American generals, including **General Douglas MacArthur, General Dwight D. Eisenhower, General George S. Patton, General Omar Bradley,** and **General George C. Marshall.** General Eisenhower, who was often called "Ike," later became President of the United States.

Douglas MacArthur: Hero of the Pacific

One of America's greatest World War II generals was **General Douglas MacArthur** (1880–1964). By December 7, 1941, the Japanese controlled many important islands in the Pacific Ocean. General MacArthur and the few men who were with him gallantly defended the Philippines against tremendous odds when the Japanese took over the Philippines after their attack on Pearl Harbor. For his heroic defense, General MacArthur received the Medal of Honor—the highest United States military award. His citation read in part:

> He mobilized, trained, and led an army which has received world acclaim for its gallant defense against tremendous superiority of enemy forces in men and arms. His utter disregard of personal danger and under heavy fire and aerial bombardment, his calm judgment in each crisis, inspired his troops, galvanized the spirit of resistance of the Filipino people, and confirmed the faith of the American people in their armed forces.

The Medal of Honor was especially meaningful to Douglas MacArthur because his father, Arthur MacArthur, had received the same award many years earlier for acts of heroism in the Civil War. It is the only time in history that a father and his son have both received this distinguished award.

In March of 1942, President Roosevelt ordered General MacArthur to leave the Philippines and go to Australia as commander of the Allied forces in the Southwest Pacific. MacArthur left his men with great reluctance.

Churchill, Roosevelt, and Stalin at the Yalta Conference

No Substitute for Victory

General MacArthur wades ashore as he returns to the Phillippines in 1944.

He and his wife and their young son, Arthur, were removed by night in a navy torpedo boat, and later sent by plane to Australia. From Australia, MacArthur made his famous promise to the Filipino people: **"I shall return."** This promise gave the people of the Philippines hope and courage to keep fighting.

MacArthur showed great personal bravery and military genius as he led the troops that freed New Guinea, New Britain, the Solomon Islands, and the Admiralty Islands from the Japanese. Then, on October 20, 1944, he kept his promise to the Filipinos by returning to their islands to free them from the Japanese. <u>He became a 5-star general of the Army and later took command of all American forces in the Pacific</u>.

After the Japanese surrendered, President Truman made General MacArthur <u>supreme commander for the Allied Powers</u>. MacArthur officiated at the Japanese surrender ceremonies aboard the battleship *Missouri* in Tokyo Bay on September 2, 1945. (Because Japan is west of the International Date Line, the date was September 1 in the United States.)

MacArthur gave a moving speech to the people of the United States on this occasion:

My Fellow Countrymen:

Today the guns are silent. A great tragedy has ended. A great victory has been won. . . . I thank a merciful God that He has given us the faith, the courage, and the power from which to mold victory. We have known the bitterness of defeat and exultation of triumph, and from both we have learned there can be no turning back. We must go forward to preserve in Peace what we have won in War. . . .

We stand in Tokyo today, reminiscent of our countryman, Commodore Perry, 92 years ago. His purpose was to bring to Japan an era of enlightenment and progress, by lifting the veil of isolation to the friendship, trade, and commerce of the world. But, alas, the knowledge thereby gained of Western science was forged into an instrument of oppression and human enslavement. . . . The energy of the Japanese race, if properly directed, will enable expansion vertically, rather than horizontally. If the talents of the race are turned into constructive channels, the country can lift itself from its present deplorable state into a position of dignity. . . .

In the Philippines, America has evolved a model for this new free world of Asia. In the Philippines, America has demonstrated that peoples of the East and peoples of the West may walk side by side in mutual respect with mutual benefit. The history of our sovereignty there has now the full confidence of the East.

And so, my fellow countrymen, today I report to you that your sons and daughters have served you well and faithfully, with the calm, deliberate, determined fighting spirit of the American soldier and sailor, based upon a tradition of historical truth, as against the fanaticism of an enemy supported only by mythological fiction. Their spiritual strength and power have brought us through the victory. They are homeward bound—take care of them.

After a war, the winning side often takes command of the losing countries until the losers can recover their resources and learn to live peaceably. General Douglas MacArthur became the leader of the military government in Japan. The Japanese people feared his rule at first, but his firm fair leadership soon made him the most popular man in Japan. He brought about many changes in Japan that helped it turn away from its militant philosophy to become the fastest growing industrialized nation in the world.

General MacArthur wisely recognized that the greatest need of the Japanese people was to hear the gospel. He sent out an urgent plea for over 1,000 missionaries to go to Japan. "The more missionaries we can bring out here," he said, "and the more occupation troops we can send home, the better." At his request, the Pocket Testament League distributed 10 million Bibles in Japanese. The Japanese people gathered in eager crowds to hear the returning missionaries and to receive a copy of the Bible, and for a while there was a spiritual awakening in Japan.

One missionary to Japan made headlines all over the world. **Jacob De Shazer,** an American soldier during the war, had been captured by the Japanese in the famous bombing raid of Tokyo led by General James Doolittle. For 3 years, De Shazer was tortured in Japanese prisons. Then someone gave him a Bible, and through reading the Bible De Shazer came to accept Christ as his personal Savior. His hatred of the Japanese turned to love, and as soon as possible after he was free he returned to tell them about the love of Christ. Through his testimony, Mitsuo Fuchida, the commander of the Japanese squadron that had bombed Pearl Harbor, became a Christian on April 14, 1950.

General Douglas MacArthur administered Japan from 1945 until 1951. In 1950, he was selected to command the United Nations forces in the Korean War. President Truman later sent MacArthur home because MacArthur wanted to pursue the Communists into China. The people of the United States gave him a hero's welcome upon his return to the States. When MacArthur died at the age of 84, President Lyndon B. Johnson called him "one of America's greatest heroes" and proclaimed a week of public mourning.

Comprehension Check 13C

Identify

1. The first day of the Allied invasion of Nazi-occupied France.
2. The first black officer to attain the rank of major general in the United States Air Force.
3. The most decorated infantry unit in all of the United States Army and the name for its Japanese-American members.
4. The Big Four and their countries.

Think

5. What tragedy did Allied soldiers find in German prison camps after the war? What was the Holocaust?
6. What promise did General MacArthur make to the Filipino people? Did he keep his promise?

No Substitute for Victory

13.4 CONTINUING WORLD PROBLEMS

The United Nations and the Spread of Communism

Dreams of peace. As World War II came to an end, many Americans hoped for a lasting peace. Yet many had hoped for peace at the close of World War I. What was there to prevent a third world war? At the closing of World War I, President Woodrow Wilson had planned a League of Nations wherein the countries of the world could talk out their problems peaceably. When the League of Nations was formed, however, the people of the United States did not want to become part of it. Many of them realized that not every country in the world can be trusted, even if it promises to be friendly. Now President Franklin Roosevelt and other world leaders began to dream of another world organization in which the nations of the world would work together to settle their problems. This organization would be called the **United Nations,** or the UN.

The false science of humanism. Franklin Roosevelt died before World War II came to an end, and Vice President **Harry S. Truman** took his place. Before President Roosevelt died, he wrote a speech saying that a United Nations organization could help people by using "scientific" methods. ". . . [W]e must cultivate the science of human relations," he wrote, "the ability of all people, of all kinds, to live together and work together, in the same world, at peace." Science can bring us wonderful things, but peace comes from a kind of understanding that science can never bring. Roosevelt did not understand this, and neither did many people around the world.

In 1945, representatives of 50 nations met in San Francisco and formed what President Roosevelt envisioned, the United Nations (UN). Later, a building was built for the UN in New York City. Unfortunately, the United Nations failed to end wars and bring about world peace. Since 1945, over 100 wars have been fought around the world. Over 1 billion people have been slaves under Communism, and more than 40 million people have been executed by the Communists. The United Nations has not been able to preserve the rights of these people. Many people think it has actually helped to spread Communism.

the United Nations headquarters

Communism becomes a growing problem. Although World War II defeated Nazism in Germany, Fascism in Italy, and militarism in Japan, it did not defeat atheistic Communism in the Soviet Union. You will remember that Stalin agreed to fight on Germany's side if Germany went to war. It was only after the Germans attacked the Soviet Union that the Russians decided to join the Allies. Although the Soviet Union supposedly fought with us to free Europe from Nazi rule, it soon became clear that she meant to control the small, helpless countries of Eastern Europe and many other countries throughout the world.

China Falls to Communism

Chiang Kai-shek's brave struggle against Communism. The Communists soon spread their influence from Europe into Asia, taking control of China. China's leader, **Chiang Kai-shek,** a Christian and one of the greatest heroes of the 20th century, had led China to victory against the Japanese invaders during World War II. Exhausted by the struggle against the Japanese, Chiang's army was unable to resist a new attack by the Chinese Communists. In addition, the Soviet Union gave the Chinese Communists large amounts of captured Japanese weapons and supplies. With help from the Russians, the Chinese Communists drove Chiang Kai-shek out of China and took over that huge country for Communism.

Chiang Kai-shek

The betrayal of China. Despite a clear Communist threat to the liberties of the Chinese people, the United States Congress refused to help Chiang Kai-shek in his struggle against the Communist tyrant **Mao Zedong** [mou′ dzə′dŏng′: also Mao Tse-tung]. The Communists murdered Christian missionaries and many Chinese Christians. At least 800,000 opponents of Communism were murdered by the Chinese Communists between 1945 and 1949. Chiang Kai-shek and his followers fled to the island of Formosa, where they set up the **Republic of China (Taiwan).** For many years, the United States and many other nations recognized the Nationalist government on Taiwan as China's legal government. Taiwan grew and prospered as a free republic, while Red China became poor and backward under Communism.

Berlin Is Divided

After World War II, Germany was divided. West Germany became free and independent, but East Germany fell under the Communist rule of the Soviet Union. The city of Berlin was located within Communist East Germany but was divided into free West Berlin and Communist East Berlin. Robbed of their freedom, many of the people of East Berlin tried to escape to West Berlin. In 1961, the Communists built a wall that divided the city in two. People who tried to escape over the wall to freedom in West Berlin were shot and killed by Communist soldiers. The **Berlin Wall,** called the "Wall of Shame," became a dark and frightening symbol of Communism. By 1989, the Soviet Union had become so desperate for money and technology from free West Germany that it permitted the "Wall of Shame" to be torn down and allowed East Germany to unite with the rest of Germany.

The Berlin wall became a symbol of the lack of freedom that people have under Communism.

251

The 23rd U.S. Infantry Combat Team breaking through Chinese forces during the Korean War.

Israel Becomes a Nation

The persecution that the Jewish people had suffered under Hitler in World War II convinced the world that a home for the Jews should be made in **Palestine.** God's chosen people had been wandering for centuries all over the earth, but the Bible prophesied that they would return to their homeland. In May of 1948, **Israel** once again became a nation. It developed factories, schools, and towns, and quickly became the most advanced country in the Middle East. Christians all over the world saw this as a major step in the unfolding of God's plan for the ages.

The Korean War

Divided Korea. At the end of World War II, the small Asian country of **Korea** was divided into 2 parts, with the northern half under the control of the Soviet Union and the southern half under the control of the United States. The people of South Korea were allowed to hold elections, and they set up a free republic. In North Korea, the Russians set up a Communist government. The United Nations again failed to protect the rights of these people against Communist invaders.

The Communists had made it clear that they desired to gain control of other countries. In 1950, Communist North Korea invaded South Korea. The UN ordered North Korea to stop fighting, but the Communists would not obey. The United Nations sent an army to South Korea. Although men from the United States made up most of this army, 15 other nations also sent troops to help South Korea. This struggle became known as the **Korean War.**

"No substitute for victory." The commander of the United Nations troops in Korea was General Douglas MacArthur. The Communists had virtually taken over all of South Korea when, in the summer of 1950, General MacArthur staged a brilliant military maneuver which caught the Communists off guard. He drove the Communists out of South Korea and then proceeded to invade North Korea. When the

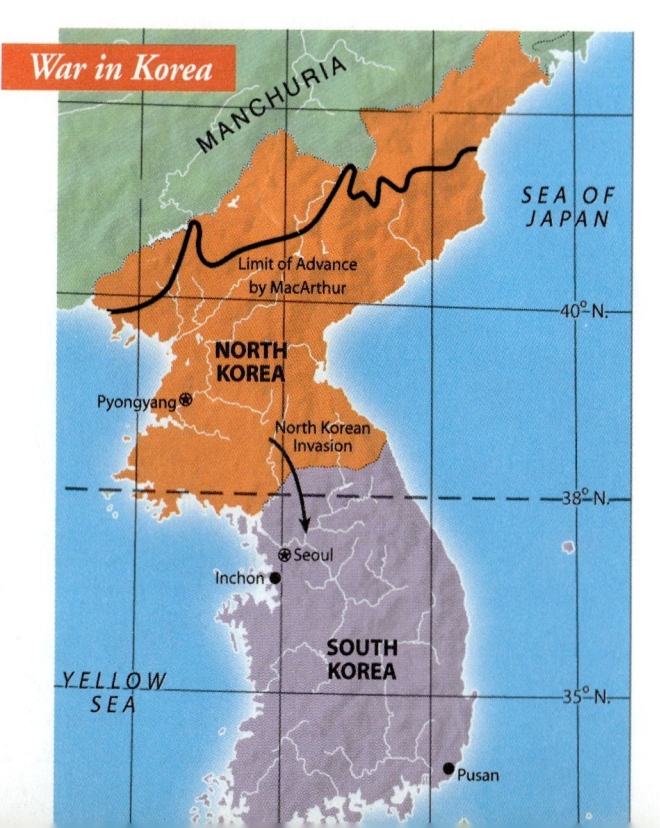

War in Korea

252 *New World History & Geography*

Chinese Communists began to send troops into North Korea to drive MacArthur out, the General asked President Truman for permission to invade China and wipe out Communism once and for all in that part of Asia.

President Truman believed in a foreign policy known as **containment,** which committed American troops to stay on the defensive and simply prevent Communism from spreading. The President ordered General MacArthur to return to South Korea and let the Communists keep North Korea. The liberal Congress of the United States, having already abandoned the Free Chinese under Chiang Kai-shek, firmly opposed an invasion of Communist China. They felt that a war with China would be unpopular with the American people, and some officials in our State Department, which is responsible for foreign policy, even sympathized with the Communist cause.

General MacArthur told President Truman that the policy of containment was a weak one which encouraged Communist aggression. He wanted to go on the offensive and insisted that *"there is no substitute for victory."* Because of his criticism, President Truman released MacArthur from his command. The United States withdrew from North Korea, allowing the Communists to keep that part of Korea enslaved under a cruel dictatorship. Meanwhile, Christian missions work began to bear much fruit in the free Republic of South Korea.

Comprehension Check 13D
Identify
1. The organization, similar to the League of Nations, which was formed after World War II to help nations live together peacably.
2. The leader of China during World War II.
3. The Communist tyrant who took over China after World War II.
4. The German city that was divided after World War II.
5. The year Israel became a nation once again.
6. The foreign policy which forced American troops to stay on the defensive and simply prevent Communism from spreading.

Think
7. Why did President Truman release General MacArthur from his command?

Chapter 13 Checkup

I. Tell why these **people** are important.

Nikolai Lenin	Emperor Hirohito	Chiang Kai-shek	General Douglas MacArthur
Joseph Stalin	Tojo	Mao Zedong	Jacob De Shazer
Benito Mussolini	Franklin D. Roosevelt	Sir Winston Churchill	Harry S. Truman
Adolf Hitler	Benjamin O. Davis, Jr.	General Eisenhower	

II. Define these **terms.**

dictator	D-Day	Hiroshima	"Big Four"	containment
Communism	Axis Powers	Nagasaki	United Nations	
Fascist Party	Allies	Nisei	Republic of China	
Nazi Party	Fighting Red Tails	concentration camps	Berlin Wall	
Battle of Britain	atomic bomb	Holocaust	Korean War	

III. Give the noted event for these **dates.**

1917	1939–1945	December 7, 1941	May 7, 1945
1939	1940	December 8, 1941	May 1948
	1941	June 6, 1944	1950–1953

IV. Know these **countries** and the role they had in and around WWII.

Soviet Union	Germany	Great Britain	China	Israel
Italy	Japan	United States	France	Korea

chapter 14　United States History:

Time for FREEDOM *and* RESPONSIBILITY

14.1 YEARS OF PROSPERITY AND OPPORTUNITY

Baby Boom and Economic Boom

The United States emerged from World War II as the most powerful and prosperous country in the world. Between 1945 and 1965, many young couples made down payments on houses and started families. America experienced a **baby boom** as the birthrate soared. More children meant that more schools and teachers were needed as well as more goods. Because America had a healthy private enterprise system, factories were able to produce the needed goods, stores were able to sell them, and the people could afford to buy them. Sales of everything from bicycles to clothing increased. The **economy,** or system of producing and distributing goods, was healthy. The prosperity of the United States during these years laid the foundation for the research and development of today's **computers, lasers,** and **medical wonders.** People were working hard and had the money to improve their lives, support their families, and invest in the future.

Suburbs, Skyscrapers, and Shopping Malls

Soon, two out of every three people in the United States lived in or near a large city. Some lived in apartments within the city, but most lived in communities called **suburbs** which ringed the central cities. In the center of the city stood the **skyscrapers** where people

1950 | **1960** | **1970** | **1980** | **1990** | **2000**

- **1956** Interstate Highway Act
- **1961** Cuban patriots are defeated by Castro at the Bay of Pigs
- **1962** Cuban Missile Crisis brings the world to the brink of nuclear war
- **1964** Civil Rights Act
- **1965** President Johnson sends U.S. troops to South Vietnam
- **1965–73** The Vietnam War
- **1969** Neil Armstrong walks on the moon
- **1969** President Nixon begins to withdraw U.S. troops from Vietnam
- **1974** Watergate Affair: President Nixon resigns
- **1979** Iranian terrorists take 52 Americans hostage
- **1979** President Carter negotiates Camp David Peace Accords
- **1983** U.S. troops liberate Grenada from a Cuban invasion
- **1986** Space shuttle Challenger explodes
- **1991** Soviet Union dissolves
- **1991** Persian Gulf War
- **1993** World Trade Center in New York City is bombed by Muslim terrorists
- **1994** Republicans win majority in Congress for the first time since 1950s
- **1995** Oklahoma City federal office building is bombed
- **1998** President Clinton is impeached

Boston, Massachusetts skyline

worked during the day. On the outskirts of the city, pleasant houses with lawns and gardens made up the suburban areas. Living in the suburbs was made possible by widespread use of the automobile for transportation. For the first time in history, people had the mobility to go wherever they pleased with a minimum of time and effort. By the 1960s, most families lived in their own homes and owned a car or were buying these items.

In the 1960s and 1970s, many businesses moved to the suburbs. **Industrial parks** were clustered about the main city. These new urban areas featured parks, recreation facilities, and **shopping malls,** where people could take care of all of their needs in one place and not have to worry about the weather. Indeed, by the 1990s, a trip to the mall with its glassed-in courtyards, lush tropical foliage, and cascading fountains and waterfalls was a source of outside entertainment for many Americans.

Supermarkets and Better Health

Better and faster transportation, including **jet airplanes,** made fresh fruits, vegetables, meat, and dairy products available to all. New **technology** (practical science) increased the production of food and also resulted in better ways to preserve food. Before the 1950s, fresh vegetables were available only during the short local growing season. In the northern cities, foods like orange juice or bananas were considered luxuries. But new **supermarkets** now overflowed with healthful products.

The advance of medical technology also contributed to better health. The average life span had been 47 years in 1900; by the year 2000, it increased to about 77 years. The **polio vaccine,** developed by **Dr. Jonas Salk** in the early 1950s, ended the spread of that dreaded disease. Vaccines were later developed against measles, mumps, diphtheria, tetanus, whooping cough, and other diseases. Unfortunately, unhealthful eating habits as well as smoking and drinking led some people to ruin their health. In the 1960s, President John F. Kennedy launched a national campaign of exercise and physical fitness. Most Americans began to take better care of their bodies by the 1970s.

Time for Freedom and Responsibility 255

A 1950s family enjoy their first television set.

Time for Leisure and Recreation

Because of new technologies in the workplace, many Americans began to work fewer hours per week. New inventions for the home, such as automatic washers, dryers, dishwashers, and garbage disposals made chores at home less time consuming. Later, microwave ovens would make cooking much faster. The resulting leisure time was often spent in family activities such as bowling and outdoor sports ranging from baseball to hunting and fishing. Millions of people also attended major league sports events in the stadiums and arenas of many cities.

Increasingly, people began to spend more time at home watching **television.** Television sets became popular in the 1950s. They had very small screens and offered only a few channels to the viewer. Color sets became popular in American homes in the 1960s.

Increased leisure time made it possible for millions of Americans to take vacations, making tourism a major industry in some of the more scenic regions of the United States. Many Americans took to the new interstate highways and toured the country, and more and more Americans began to travel by jet airplane. The National Park System was further developed, and places like Yellowstone, Yosemite, and the Great Smokies received millions of visitors. Large numbers of Americans visited such places as the Grand Canyon, Washington, D.C., or the beaches of Florida for the first time. All of this activity tended to create a greater feeling of unity among Americans from all parts of the country.

Freedom and Opportunity for All Americans

The years after World War II witnessed the increased participation of people of Asian, African, Latin American, and American Indian descent in all areas of American life. These minority groups had served their country during the war by working and fighting for freedom, and many Americans were convinced that now was the time to overcome racial prejudice. The first group to achieve more opportunities were black Americans, who wanted to guarantee a better life for their children under the legal protection of their government.

Jackie Robinson and the Brooklyn Dodgers

Jackie Robinson (1919–1972), a young man from a sharecropper's farm in Georgia, signed on as a player for the Brooklyn Dodg-

256 *New World History & Geography*

ers in 1947 and became the first black major league baseball player. He led the way for many other black athletes to become major league sports stars. Jackie Robinson was elected to the Baseball Hall of Fame in 1962. Black athletes became role models for millions of young Americans.

Jackie Robinson

Marian Anderson: One of the World's Ten Most Admired Women

At the age of six, **Marian Anderson** (1897–1993) displayed such talent as a member of the choir in Philadelphia's Union Baptist Church that the church established a trust fund known as "Marian Anderson's Future" to pay for her professional training. By 1939, she was recognized throughout Europe as one of the greatest opera singers of the age. But in that same year, misguided officials in Washington, D.C., denied her the privilege of singing in Constitution Hall.

On Easter Sunday morning of 1939, Marian Anderson stood on the steps of the Lincoln Memorial before 75,000 Americans of all races and walks of life who came to hear her marvelous voice. The acceptance of Marian Anderson in the world of arts was a milestone in racial progress. She was the first black American to be a performing member of New York City's Metropolitan Opera. She received many awards, including the prestigious Spingarn medal, which is awarded annually to honor the outstanding achievements of a black American. By 1961, she was

Marian Anderson

recognized by the American Institute of Public Opinion as one of the world's 10 most admired women—and to think that only 22 years earlier she had been told she could not sing at Constitution Hall! Marian Anderson used her God-given talent and honest character to peacefully bring about change, and Americans responded to her personal appeal. Although a master of the classical opera, Marian Anderson always included spirituals as a major part of her musical performances.

The Civil Rights Movement

Desegregation of the schools. In the 1950s and 1960s, black Americans made considerable political and economic gains through the **civil rights movement.** When seven-year-old Linda Brown was denied admission to a neighborhood public school because of her color, court proceedings resulted in a 1954 Supreme Court ruling known as *Brown vs. The Board of Education,* which called for the desegregation, or racial integration, of all public schools.

Rosa Parks. Just a year after the Supreme Court's important decision, **Rosa Parks,** a black American woman, refused to give up her seat on a Montgomery, Alabama, bus to a white passenger. This was a violation of the city's segregation laws, and Rosa Parks was arrested. In response to the incident, a group of black Americans in Montgomery organized a bus boycott, in which they refused to use the city bus system. In 1957, the Supreme Court ordered Montgomery to desegregate its bus system, providing equal privileges for all passengers.

Dr. Martin Luther King, Jr. By 1955, a young black minister had organized the Montgomery bus boycott, and a civil rights campaign spread nationwide. As a result of **Dr. Martin Luther King, Jr.'s** efforts and those

Time for Freedom and Responsibility 257

Martin Luther King, Jr. giving his famous speech on the steps of the Lincoln Memorial in 1963

of many others, Congress passed legislation that guaranteed voting, housing, and job rights for ethnic minorities. This legislation became known as the **1964 Civil Rights Act.**

"I have a dream!" Perhaps the most dramatic moment of the civil rights movement came in 1963 when Dr. King addressed some 200,000 people from the steps of the Lincoln Memorial. Standing where Marian Anderson stood on Easter Sunday morning in 1939, Dr. King called for an end to discrimination:

> I have a dream that one day this nation will rise up and live out the true meaning of its creed, "We hold these truths to be self-evident, that all men are created equal."
>
> ... I have a dream that my four little children will one day live in a nation where they will not be judged by the color of their skin, but by the content of their character.

Dr. King insisted on nonviolent demonstrations to end racial discrimination. He said, "Don't let anyone pull you so low as to hate them." Many Americans supported what he stood for. However, Communism and other radical ideas hurt the civil rights movement. Dr. King's teaching that people should break the law in nonviolent ways to bring about change opened the door to other kinds of lawbreaking. Power-hungry individuals stirred up the people, and riots terrorized black neighborhoods in the late 1960s. As violence began to take over, Dr. King found he could not control all radical groups. In 1968, while on a visit to Memphis, Tennessee, Dr. King was assassinated by a gunman who used the violent atmosphere to justify his action. Today, people of all ethnic groups are striving to realize Dr. King's dream that people be judged by their character rather than by their skin color. It is a dream shared by all Americans of goodwill, and great progress has been made.

Black Americans have served in the United States Congress, Presidential Cabinets, and the Supreme Court, among many other positions. In 1966, **Edward C. Brooke** was elected to the United States Senate, and in 1989, **L. Douglas Wilder** was elected governor of Virginia. **Robert C. Weaver** was the first black cabinet member, appointed head of the Department of Housing and Urban Development in 1966. The first black American woman senator was **Carol Moseley-Braun,** elected in 1992 to represent Illinois. In 1994, **J. C. Watts, Jr.** became the first black American Republican to win a seat in the U.S. House of Representatives since shortly after the Civil War.

Asian Americans

As a result of Communist oppression in Asia, large numbers of Asians began arriving in the United States and Canada during the 1970s. Asian Americans have been noted for their willingness to work and to make great sacrifices to give their children a good education. Some of the top computer engineers and programmers have been Asian Americans, as well as many medical doctors and business people. Asian Americans have also participated in American politics, and many have been elected to high offices. The first Japanese-American woman to serve in the United States Congress was Representative **Patsy Takemoto** [tä·kə·mō·tō] **Mink,** from the state of Hawaii. Senator **Daniel Ken Inouye** [ē·nō·ŏŏ·yĕ], the first Japanese-American to serve in the U.S. Congress, represented the state of Hawaii. In 2001, Asian-Americans assumed new leadership in the Presidential Cabinet as Japanese-American **Norman Mineta** [mĭn′ĕt′ə] was appointed Secretary of Transportation, and Chinese immigrant **Elaine Chao** [chou] was appointed Secretary of Labor.

American Indians

With a population of nearly 2 million, American Indians are a significant American presence. It has been projected that their population will nearly double in the next 50 years. By the 1800s, Indians had been placed on reservations; however, by 2000, over half of the total Native American population would live away from reservations. By the 19th century, Americans Indians held national public office, and **Charles Curtis,** a Kaw Indian from Kansas, served as Vice President under Herbert Hoover. **Ben Nighthorse Campbell,** chief of a Cheyenne tribe and prominent United States Senator from Colorado, was first elected in 1992, becoming the only American Indian to serve in the Senate at the time.

Hispanic Americans

The fastest growing and possibly the largest minority ethnic group in the United States is made up of Spanish-speaking, or **Hispanic,** Americans. The largest number of Hispanic Americans have come from Mexico, Puerto Rico, Central America, and Cuba. **Puerto Rico** is, of course, an American commonwealth and is represented in the United States Congress. After the **Communist dictator Fidel Castro** overthrew the government of **Cuba** in 1959, several hundred thousand Cubans sought political and economic freedom in the United States. Hispanics have achieved much success in American life. Many states have had Hispanic governors, and Hispanic Americans have served in a wide range of political positions including city mayor, Surgeon General, and member of Congress. Cuban-born **Melquiades ("Mel") Martinez** [mär·tē′nəz] was appointed the Secretary for Housing and Urban Development in 2001. In a speech before the Senate, Martinez talked of the success he has achieved in this nation:

> ". . . regardless of where you are from, what language you speak, or the color of your skin, if you share the American Dream of a brighter tomorrow, if you pursue it with respect for the law and for others, and with an abiding faith in God, all things are possible."

The Future for Minorities in America

In the future, minority populations will continue to increase, and people of minority groups will continue to contribute to American life in many significant, positive ways. Important strides have been made to ensure that American freedoms are extended to all citizens

Time for Freedom and Responsibility 259

People in History
Huber Matos: For a Free Cuba

A fine example of the Hispanic contribution to the cause of freedom is the story of **Huber Matos,** a former major in Castro's army who suffered 20 years of imprisonment for his stand against Communism. His story illustrates what happened to thousands of Cubans who dared to disagree with the Communists.

Betrayed by Castro. Major Matos joined Fidel Castro to bring about a revolution in Cuba, believing Castro's statements that he would bring freedom and justice to the Cuban people. But Major Matos soon discovered that Castro was a tyrant who would enslave them to Communism. Matos, one of Cuba's top military commanders, bravely stood up to Castro and told him to his face, "Now *you* have become a tyrant, and the people have no chance for justice."

Jailed and tortured. Castro, enraged that anyone would so boldly confront him with the truth about Communism, sentenced Matos to 20 years in prison. Castro was afraid to kill him because Matos still had many friends in Cuba. For years, he suffered brutal treatment in prison. Prison officials allowed Matos no visitors or mail, though his wife and family wrote hundreds of letters and tried to visit him countless times. Eventually his wife, Maria Luisa, fled to America with their children. In 1976, his son, Huber Matos, Jr., was murdered by Castro's Communist agents.

Free at last! Huber Matos had been in jail since 1959, but at any time he could have gone free if he had simply confessed that he had been wrong and that Communism and Castro were good for the Cuban people. He refused to tell such a lie. Finally, on October 21, 1979, after being severely beaten, he was released from prison. Maria Luisa Matos had worked tirelessly telling people around the world of the terrible tortures her husband and other Cuban prisoners were suffering. Fidel Castro, fearing world exposure as a cruel tyrant, decided to let Matos go.

Freedom and family. Huber Matos stepped off the plane in Costa Rica and was reunited with his wife and his four children, who were now grown men and women. Ten young grandchildren, whom he had never seen before, proudly came forward to meet their grandfather—Huber Matos, a genuine Cuban hero.

---

of the United States. It should not matter where a person was born, the color of his skin—or eyes, or hair—or with what accent he speaks, "For there is no respect of persons with God" (Rom. 2:11). The principles upon which this nation was founded should unite all Americans. Moral character—honesty, diligence, kindness, patience, service, among other qualities—should be the standard by which people are measured.

The importance of moral character in America was expressed in a statement made by **Justice Clarence Thomas.** For several weeks in the fall of 1991, Clarence Thomas, a black American who upheld conservative family values, endured an extensive examination by liberal senators who opposed his nomination to the Supreme Court, which was eventually confirmed. Like Jackie Robinson, Justice Thomas was born to poor sharecroppers in Georgia. Through his own hard work and God-given ability, he earned a law degree and served in several legal and government positions, including assistant attorney general for Missouri and judge for the U.S. Court of Appeals for the District of Columbia. When he was confirmed a Justice of the Supreme Court, Thomas said:

Clarence Thomas

> . . . I'd like to thank America. I'd like to thank this country for the things it stands for and the people for the things that we stand for—our ideals. . . I give God thanks for our being able to stand here today, and I give God thanks for our ability to feel safe, to feel secure, to feel loved.

In a speech given in February of 1998, Thomas emphasized the importance of good character:

> Having the character that will lead others to a path of virtue does not require extraordinary intelligence, a privileged upbringing, or significant wealth. Nor, for that matter, is character a matter of accomplishing extraordinary feats or undertaking magnanimous acts. . . . It is the small things we do each day, the often mundane and routine tasks, that form our habits and seem to have the most lasting impression on our fellow man.

Comprehension Check 14A

Identify
1. The system of producing and distributing goods.
2. The vaccine developed by Dr. Jonas Salk.
3. The first black major league baseball player.
4. The act that gave equal voting, housing, and job rights to ethnic minorities.

14.2 Preserving Freedom in an Age of Big Government

The Proper Role of Government

Though Supreme Court Justice Clarence Thomas clearly benefited from the advances made in the area of civil rights, he insisted that any success he had achieved was due to the help of God, his own hard work, and the help of private individuals. In other words, although government can help an individual, government is not responsible for that individual's success or failure. Even in America, everyone is ultimately responsible for his own actions.

Since 1950, American history has been marked by much individual initiative and success, but it has also been a time of increased government interference in people's lives. <u>Our Founding Fathers believed that the role of government was to **protect** the life and private property of the individual and his family.</u> From the 1950s to the 2000s, American leaders have shown both strength and weakness in protecting the American people from the great threat to national freedom—international Communist aggression.

<u>By the 1960s, some politicians were saying that the government should **provide** food, shelter, and other goods for large numbers of people.</u> They were actually echoing the words of Communist and socialist leaders. Rather than encouraging people to be responsible for their own affairs, these politicians made many people entirely dependent on the government, gradually taking away their self respect, initiative, and civil liberties. People could no longer make certain decisions for themselves without the heavy hand of government dictating their choices. Because money for government handouts must come from working citizens, millions of hard-working Americans faced higher taxes.

Time for Freedom and Responsibility 261

Thus, private individuals no longer had the money to invest in private businesses and the nation's economic future.

As you study the political events from the 1950s to the 2000s on the next few pages, look for ways that government policies helped and hindered the well-being of Americans. Also look for ways that the strength or weakness of American leaders in the face of Communist aggression helped to strengthen or weaken world Communism.

President Eisenhower: Peace through Strength

Alliances for freedom. General **Dwight David Eisenhower** (1890–1969), a Commander of the Allied Forces in World War II, became President of the United States in 1952. President Eisenhower's main goal was to ensure American economic prosperity while building up our defenses against Communism. The Soviet Union had enslaved all of Eastern Europe. To prevent the spread of Communism to the West, Eisenhower strengthened the military alliance of **NATO**, the North Atlantic Treaty Organization, an alliance of Western European nations, Canada, and the United States against Communism. NATO had begun in 1949 under the Presidency of Harry Truman. President Eisenhower also formulated plans to defend Southeast Asia from Communism by establishing **SEATO**, the Southeast Asia Treaty Organization. The strength and success of these commitments (especially NATO) played a major role in the eventual collapse of the Communist government in the Soviet Union.

Dwight Eisenhower

Advances for a strong America. Under President Eisenhower, free enterprise thrived. The economy prospered: unemployment was low and Americans' average income increased. Great roadways were built to link together the entire country, creating an **Interstate Highway System.** The completion of the **St. Lawrence Seaway** fostered close relations between the United States and Canada by opening up the Great Lakes region to ocean shipping. These are examples of government projects built by private enterprise. The prosperity of private businesses also made it possible for our government to develop atomic weapons with which to protect the free world from the Communist threat of the Soviet Union and China.

Triumphs in space. Moreover, President Eisenhower was able to bring the United States into the **space age** because of the ingenuity of private research and the tax revenue generated from healthy private businesses. The National Aeronautics and Space Administration (**NASA**), started in 1958, soon launched America's first satellite and put the first astronauts into space. The first American to fly in space was **Alan B. Shepard, Jr., in 1961.** In **1962, John Glenn** became the first American to orbit the earth. John Glenn later served as a senator for the state of Ohio.

In **1969, Neil Armstrong** became the first man to walk on the surface of the moon. The American space program is a fine example of how government and private enterprise can work together. Much of NASA's effort was motivated by the need to strengthen American defenses against Communism through space age weapons technology, but many peaceful applications, especially in computer software, were developed.

262 New World History & Geography

The United States was the first country to land a man on the moon.

John F. Kennedy's "New Frontier"

Prosperity without hard work. When President **John Fitzgerald Kennedy** (1917–1963) took office in 1961, he represented the liberal wing of the Democratic party. (A **liberal** in modern America is a person who endeavors to break away from traditional beliefs and values. Because liberals often seek freedom from personal responsibility, they believe that the government should provide for people's everyday needs. A **conservative** wants to preserve traditional beliefs and values. Conservatives believe that the government should protect the nation from invaders and let the people be free to handle their own everyday responsibilities. American conservatives want to preserve the nation's heritage of freedom and responsibility by upholding the Constitution's original meaning and promoting traditional values.) Under President Kennedy, government welfare programs were expanded to gain more votes and expand the influence of liberal politicians. Because it is human nature to try to get something for nothing, Americans saw the government borrow more and more money to try to take care of people with needs. Before this time, families, churches, and private charities had taken care of these needs. John F. Kennedy called his welfare program the **New Frontier.**

John Kennedy

A liberal Supreme Court. During 1962 and 1963, the Supreme Court ruled that prayer and Bible reading were illegal in the public schools. The Founding Fathers who wrote the Constitution had great respect for both prayer and God's Word, and because of our Christian heritage it had always been a common practice to include prayer and Bible reading in the daily routine of most schools. The Supreme Court, ignoring our Christian heritage, interpreted the Constitution in a way that its writers would not have agreed with. Later, as public schools declined in many ways, many parents began to enroll their children in Christian schools, and thus the **Christian school movement** saw tremendous growth. The 1960s and 1970s saw many liberal court decisions, including *Roe vs. Wade* (1973), which legalized **abortion,** the killing of unborn babies.

Time for Freedom and Responsibility 263

Success and failure in Cuba. Since 1959 Cuba had been under the control of Communist dictator Fidel Castro. Large numbers of freedom-loving Cubans fled to the United States. On April 17, 1961, an American-trained force of Cuban freedom fighters invaded Cuba at the **Bay of Pigs.** President Kennedy had promised these brave men United States air cover and support, but at the last minute the President backed away from this promise. The invasion failed, and President Kennedy was humiliated.

Still smarting from the Bay of Pigs failure, Kennedy decided that he would have to take a strong stand against Communism if America was to remain strong. In October 1962, President Kennedy ordered a naval blockade around Cuba to keep the Soviet Union from shipping missiles and nuclear warheads to the island. With Cuba only 90 miles from Florida, Soviet missiles in Cuba posed a grave threat to the United States.

The Soviet leader Nikita Khrushchev [nĭ·kē′tə kroosh′chôf] at first refused to back down, and the **Cuban Missile Crisis** had the entire world on the brink of nuclear war. But President Kennedy remained firm, and the United States, thanks to wise military planning and economic prosperity, had a clear weapons advantage over the Soviet Union at that time. Thus, the Communists were forced to stop sending nuclear weapons and even to remove the nuclear weapons which were already in Cuba. In return, President Kennedy showed his old weakness for compromise by promising that no American President would ever invade Cuba and deliver it from Communist slavery.

Assassination of President Kennedy. On November 22, **1963,** President Kennedy and his wife Jackie visited Dallas, Texas. While traveling in a motorcade through downtown Dallas, President Kennedy was shot and killed. His successor, **Lyndon B. Johnson** (1908–1973), became President.

President Johnson: Welfare and Vietnam

The Great Society. President Johnson believed that education and government planning could solve our social problems. He called his social reform program the **Great Society.** As Congress taxed private individuals and businesses and gave the money to local and state governments, local governments became dependent on these financial handouts. Many people looked to Washington for schools, food, housing, and medical care rather than to their families, their local communities, and private charities. People became dependent on big government to support these social programs. American businesses became less competitive as money for research dwindled.

Lyndon Johnson

Heroism and tragedy in Vietnam. President Johnson decided to make a major commitment to fighting Communism in the southeast Asian nation of **South Vietnam.** From 1964 to 1968, he unsuccessfully urged Congress, which was then controlled by liberal Democrats, to allow American forces to invade Communist North Vietnam and take the offensive. But as in the days of General Douglas MacArthur, Congress opposed a clear military victory.

Under President Johnson, some 500,000 Americans were sent to South Vietnam to defend freedom in what became unofficially known as the **Vietnam War.** Although the men in the armed forces fought bravely, they were not allowed to fight to win. Many people think that if the military had been al-

264 New World History & Geography

◀ Troops jump from a "Huey" during an operation in Vietnam.

▼ The Vietnam Veteran Memorial in Washington, D.C., memorializes the many who lost their lives in Vietnam.

lowed to fight the war as it should have been fought, fewer people would have been killed and Communism would have been defeated.

Nixon: From China to Watergate

Abandonment of Vietnam. **President Richard M. Nixon** (1913–1994) promised to defeat Communism in South Vietnam and bring all of the American troops home. Because of pressure from a liberal Congress and his desire to befriend Communist China, President Nixon pulled all American troops out in 1973, leaving the South Vietnamese helpless against the Communists.

Watergate brings down a President. By the summer of 1974, several of the President's closest advisors were found guilty of criminal charges involving an illegal break-in of the Democratic National Headquarters in 1972, during Richard Nixon's campaign for re-election. Because this break-in occurred in the Watergate complex in Washington, D.C., the incident became known as the

Richard Nixon

Watergate affair. It appeared that the President had been involved in a "cover-up" to keep the American people from knowing about the incident. When Congress threatened to impeach President Nixon and possibly remove him from office, he decided to resign. Richard Nixon was the first President ever to resign from office. Upon the resignation of Richard Nixon on August 9, 1974, the Vice President, **Gerald R. Ford** (1913–) became President.

President Gerald Ford

Congress, still controlled by liberal politicians, refused to cooperate with President Ford's plan to cut back on government spending and social welfare, and the economy suffered. In 1975, the Communists took over all of Vietnam. Soon there was a terrible bloodbath of Communist-inspired murder and torture in the neighboring nation of Cambodia. Communists also took control of the country of Laos.

Gerald Ford

Time for Freedom and Responsibility 265

President Carter: International Problems

United States gives up the Panama Canal. In 1977, **President Jimmy Carter** (1924–) followed the desire of the United Nations and signed a treaty with the military dictator of Panama to surrender the canal to Panama on December 31, 1999. This gave the Communists the idea that the United States was giving up on its protection of Central America from Communism and led to increased terrorism in **El Salvador** and to the Sandinista Communist Revolution in **Nicaragua.**

Jimmy Carter

American hostages are taken. After these failures in Central America, many nations believed the United States was becoming a weak nation. When the anti-Communist **Shah of Iran** was overthrown in 1979, the new revolutionary government of Iran took American diplomatic personnel hostage. President Carter and Congress failed to help the Shah restore the legitimate government in Iran. And President Carter did not take the necessary military action to secure the release of the American hostages.

By December 1979, the United States reached a historic low in its ability to defend freedom. The Soviet Union, perceiving our weakness, felt confident enough to invade the nation of Afghanistan.

Treaty between Egypt and Israel. President Carter achieved the foreign policy success of the Camp David Peace Accords (1979), signed at the Presidential retreat of Camp David, Maryland. He was able to get the leader of Egypt, Anwar el-Sadat [än′wär ĕl-sə·dät′] and Israeli Prime Minister Menachem Begin [mə·näk′əm bā′gĭn] to agree to a peace treaty. This was the first time in 2,000 years that Jews and Arabs had officially talked together peaceably.

Comprehension Check 14B
Identify
1. The first man to walk on the surface of the moon.
2. The year the Supreme Court made abortion legal and the name of the decision.
3. The two practices that the Supreme Court made illegal, contributing to the growth of the Christian school movement.

Think
4. Describe a "liberal" in modern America. Describe a "conservative" in modern America.
5. What forced President Nixon to resign from office in 1974?
6. Which President negotiated the surrender of the Panama Canal Zone to Panama? What message did this send to the other nations of the world?

14.3 RETURN TO PEACE THROUGH STRENGTH

Ronald Reagan: A Return to Patriotism and Family Values

Americans approached the Presidential elections of 1980 with the feeling that something had to be done to restore America's image at home and abroad. The hostages were still being held in Iran, Communism was making gains throughout the world, especially in Latin America, and heavy taxation and social welfare spending had created serious economic problems.

A patriotic and spiritual revival. The Republican party put forth **Ronald Reagan** (1911–), former governor of California, as their candidate for President to oppose Jimmy Carter. Ronald Reagan told

Ronald Reagan

266 New World History & Geography

the people that he wanted to return America to her traditional Christian values and end the killing of unborn children. He emphasized the need for America to rebuild its defenses and to take a strong stand against Communism in the world. He said that he wanted to revive America's strength, dignity, and pride because America was meant to be a "city on a hill" putting forth the "beacon of liberty" for all the world to see.

Christians become politically active. In the 1980 Presidential election, large numbers of Bible-believing Christians became actively involved in the political process. They became involved by educating people on the issues, by encouraging people to vote, and by taking responsibility to vote themselves. They realized that Ronald Reagan represented a return to traditional and family values. America was in danger of being washed away by a tide of immorality, drug abuse, and Communism.

Peace, Opportunity, and Prosperity under God

Ronald Reagan, the first President since Dwight Eisenhower to serve two four-year terms, was elected by a landslide in 1980. On March 30, 1981, just two months after his inauguration, President Reagan was shot by a young man named John Hinckley, Jr., while walking from a Washington hotel to his car. After being rushed to surgery, Reagan made a rapid recovery and was soon back at work in the White House.

The Reagan Revolution. Reagan was able to make long-range plans that put America on a more stable and conservative course. The attempt to return America to the traditional values of church, family, and free enterprise became known as the **Reagan Revolution.**

The President's first confrontation with liberal values was his attempt to cut government welfare spending and restore the ability of the family to make its own financial decisions. Although he was forced to compromise with the politicians who controlled Congress, the President succeeded in cutting taxes, which spurred American job growth and productivity while bringing down inflation. This cutting of taxes was very important. If individuals are taxed too much, they cannot buy the things they need for themselves and their families, and businesses cannot sell the things they make. And if businesses cannot sell their goods and have to pay heavy taxes, they have to charge higher prices for their goods and they have to lay people off their jobs. Lower taxes helped all Americans.

The Reagan Doctrine. President Reagan restored the strength of the American army, navy, and air force, enabling the nation to exercise peace through strength. He believed in stopping Communism before it could attack and enslave a country—an idea which became known as the **Reagan Doctrine.**

The United States liberates Grenada. In 1983, President Reagan received some alarming news concerning the island nation of **Grenada** in the West Indies. Cuba's dictator Fidel Castro planned to invade this defenseless island and use it as a military base to invade the mainland of South America. Castro felt that the United States would be too cowardly to resist his plans to enslave Latin America.

The people of Grenada and other Caribbean islands called on the United States for help. A small force of Cuban military men had already arrived in Grenada; to wait for an all-out Communist invasion would be folly. President Reagan decided to use his full authority as Commander in Chief of the armed forces to send American troops to Grenada and liberate the people from the Communists. The Grenadians welcomed the Ameri-

Time for Freedom and Responsibility

American soldier sitting on the street in Grenada

can soldiers who landed on their island. With the help of armed forces from neighboring islands, the Americans quickly rounded up the advance guard of Cubans and shipped them back to Cuba.

Defending Traditional Values

Ronald Reagan appointed three conservative justices to the Supreme Court of the United States, which began to interpret the Constitution of the United States more in line with the traditional values of the Founding Fathers. Among these was Justice **Sandra Day O'Connor,** the first woman justice ever appointed to the high court.

Space Shuttle Challenger Explodes

Millions of Americans, as well as people all over the earth, watched by television as one of the latest technological marvels of the space age, the **space shuttle *Challenger*,** was launched from Cape Canaveral, Florida, on the bright, sunny morning of January 28, 1986. The space shuttle was designed to be a "space plane" that could enter space and return, carrying cargoes such as satellites, telescopes, or space stations. The *Challenger* carried seven crew members, including a schoolteacher, Christa McAuliffe, the first ordinary citizen to fly in a space vehicle.

Within 73 seconds of takeoff, the beautiful shuttle had risen 10 miles above the earth. Suddenly, as the *Challenger* prepared to escape the atmosphere, a gigantic fireball engulfed the plane. Millions of horrified viewers watched as the space shuttle exploded, killing all seven people onboard. The explosion of the *Challenger* shocked the nation and the world. This accident slowed down the space program for a few years.

Decline of the "Evil Empire"

As America built up its defenses and strengthened its research in new space-age technology, the Soviet leaders knew they did not have the resources to keep up. Communism is a very **inefficient economic system** which gives its workers little incentive to work hard or to become more skillful. The Soviet Union spent so much time and money building weapons that it had little left to provide basic food, shelter, and clothing for its citizens. The Soviet government also paid terrorist groups and armies throughout the world to attempt to overthrow free governments, though their own people remained poor and backward in living standards. The standard of living for most Soviet people was lower than the American standard had been before World War II.

By 1985, the Soviet Union was in deep economic trouble. The enslaved people of the Soviet Union, unable to satisfy the basic needs of their families, began to show their unrest and their dissatisfaction with the Communist system. The Evil Empire was collapsing eco-

268 *New World History & Geography*

nomically because of its own false Communist system and because America (under Ronald Reagan) had stood up to Communist aggression.

Frightened Communists. In 1987, President Ronald Reagan visited the Soviet leader **Mikhail Gorbachev** [mĭ·kāl′ gôr′bə·chôf′]. Gorbachev was alarmed by the progress the United States was making in the development of laser weaponry, especially the program known as the Strategic Defense Initiative (**S.D.I. or "Star Wars"**), a system of space-age weaponry designed to destroy enemy rockets in the air before their missile warheads could be released. President Reagan had equipped the American military with technological marvels that the bankrupt Soviet economy could not match.

the space shuttle Challenger

Communist Perestroika. Desperate to save the Soviet Union from complete collapse, Mikhail Gorbachev agreed to reduce Soviet weapons strength, to free the enslaved nations of Eastern Europe, and to stop encouraging revolution and bloodshed throughout the world. In return, the United States and other free nations promised to help the Soviet Union rebuild its economy and political system on a democratic, free enterprise model—a plan which the Soviets called **Perestroika** [pĕr′ə·stroi′kə], which means "restructuring."

The Soviet people begin to stir. Once Gorbachev's reforms began to take place, the Communists lost control of Eastern Europe. Communist leaders in Moscow managed to keep things under control in the Russian Republic until 1991, when the power of the Soviet Communist Party finally collapsed.

The Reagan Legacy

The Presidency of Ronald Reagan set into motion a chain of historic events. His appointment of three conservative Supreme Court justices held the promise of helping to restore traditional values. The buildup of the American defense systems aided in the collapse of the Soviet economy, and Reagan's support of private enterprise caused an economic boom that further weakened the appeal of Communism around the world.

Comprehension Check 14C
Identify
1. The name given to President Reagan's policy against Communism.
2. The first woman justice ever appointed to the Supreme Court.
3. The tragedy that shocked the nation in 1986 and interrupted the space program.

Think
4. How was the "Reagan Revolution" good for the United States?

14.4 ADVANCES FOR FREEDOM

President Bush: Filling Reagan's Shoes

The American people overwhelmingly elected Reagan's Vice President, **George H. W. Bush** (1924–), to the Presidency in 1988. President Bush promised to continue the job that Ronald Reagan had begun.

Operation Desert Storm

In August 1990, **Saddam Hussein** [sä·däm′ hoō·sän′], the dictator of **Iraq**, invaded the tiny, oil-rich kingdom of **Kuwait**. Confident that he would get away with his aggression, the Iraqi dictator planned to conquer all the Arab nations surrounding the Persian Gulf. President Bush compared Saddam Hussein to Adolf Hitler—both were cruel and evil men intent on conquering innocent people and stealing their wealth.

George H. W. Bush

A threat to world peace. Because the European nations and Japan received most of their oil from the Middle East, they also condemned Saddam Hussein, who could cut off the supply of oil or greatly raise its price. Other Arab nations worried that they would be the next victims of Hussein's aggression. Finally, Israeli secret agents revealed that Saddam Hussein was very close to developing an atomic bomb. President Bush convinced the United Nations to send troops to liberate Kuwait and protect the other Arab nations.

The fighting begins. As in past actions of the United Nations, the United States provided most of the military muscle. By early 1991, 500,000 American troops were stationed in the Arabian Desert. Once President Bush had obtained the support of Congress, **Operation Desert Storm** (later called the **Persian Gulf War**) began. UN forces began round-the-clock bombing of Iraqi troop positions. New technology enabled the air force to select and destroy military targets without harming the civilian population of Iraq. President Bush meant to win, echoing General MacArthur's sentiment that "there is no substitute for victory."

Saddam Hussein was totally unprepared to fight a "high-tech" war on such a large scale. The American military was more powerful than the Iraqi military because President Bush was now using the weapons that Presi-

The F-117A Stealth fighter was used during the Persian Gulf War. It's stealth capabilities made it invisible to the Iraqi radar defenses.

dent Reagan had developed and stockpiled. President Bush also insisted that the war in the Persian Gulf be directed by military men rather than by politicians. He realized that soldiers, not politicians, knew how to fight and win a war.

Bush placed **General Colin Powell** in command of Operation Desert Storm. General Powell, the son of hard-working Jamaican immigrants, grew up in New York City's South Bronx and served in Vietnam, where he was wounded in action and received a Purple Heart. Later, he won the Soldier's Medal for risking his life by rushing into a burning helicopter and pulling two men to safety. Hard work and love of country helped him become the chairman of the Joint Chiefs of Staff—second in military command only to the President. He insisted on pushing toward total victory to liberate Kuwait. For the first time since World War II, the U.S. Congress followed the wise counsel of a military commander. Because of his excellent leadership skills and military experience, General Powell became the first black American Secretary of State in 2001.

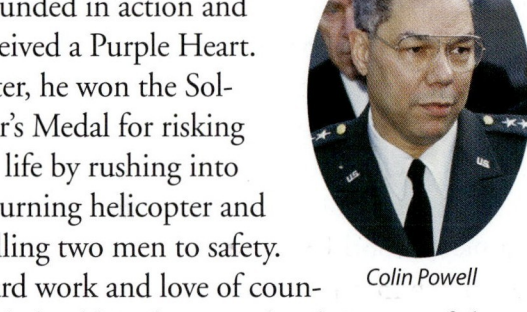

Colin Powell

President Bush appointed **General Norman Schwarzkopf** [shwôrts′kŏf] to lead the troops into combat. General Schwarzkopf inspired great devotion and bravery in his men, who affectionately called him "Stormin' Norman," or "the Bear." He often stated that his main goal in combat was to "minimize risks and save soldiers."

Invasion and victory. On February 24, 1991, American, British, and French ground troops, assisted primarily by the Saudi Arabians and the Egyptians, invaded Iraq with

General Norman Schwarzkopf with some American ground troops

armored tanks. The army of Iraq crumbled before General Schwarzkopf's brilliant moves on the battlefield. Tens of thousands of Iraqi troops threw down their weapons in mass surrender or fled in the wake of the general's advance.

Within a few days, Kuwait had been liberated and Saddam Hussein had retreated to a bunker in Baghdad. Operation Desert Storm was a great triumph for the American military and the cause of freedom. The war lasted only two and a half months—from January 16 to April 6, 1991—making it the shortest war our nation has fought.

The Collapse of the Soviet Union

Before his defeat, Saddam Hussein appealed to the Soviet Union for help. But the Soviet Union was in no position to help Iraq. Much of Eastern Europe had by now declared its independence from Moscow and thrown off the yoke of Communism. The Baltic Republics, once enslaved by the Soviet Union, had rejected Communism and were recognized as the independent countries of Latvia, Lithuania, and Estonia. Other Russian republics in Asia began to assert their right to independence from the Soviet Union as well.

Time for Freedom and Responsibility

protestors taking down the statue of Lenin in Russia

A military coup. In August 1991, fearing that Mikhail Gorbachev's policy of Perestroika would lead to the downfall of Communism, a group of Communist leaders and military men staged a *coup* [koo: an overthrow of an established government]. The Soviet military put Gorbachev under house arrest and attempted to take control of the nation.

Then several key members of the Soviet military decided to back Gorbachev and Boris Yeltsin, the President of the Russian Republic, rather than support the coup. The free nations of the world immediately cut off all economic aid to the Soviet Union. Even the young men who drove the tanks, after killing three people in the streets, decided not to fire any more guns and joined the citizens in supporting Yeltsin.

Independence for Russia. Following the coup, Boris Yeltsin assumed control of Russia and declared it an independent nation. The other Soviet republics were then free to govern themselves. In 1991, Gorbachev resigned, making Yeltsin's power official. By 1992, the Communist flag of the Soviet Union no longer flew over the Kremlin Fortress in Moscow. It had been pulled down and replaced by the tricolor red, blue, and white flag of the Russian Republic.

The Commonwealth of Independent States

With the fall of the Soviet Union, all of the former member states of the Soviet Union declared their independence. In order to coordinate their economic policies and determine the ownership of former Soviet properties, most of the independent republics agreed to join together in a loose organization called the **Commonwealth of Independent States.** Christians in the United States and Europe rushed to get the gospel to the new nations and to help the churches, which had been persecuted for so long, to reach more people for Christ.

The collapse of the Soviet Union and its properties showed the world the failure of Communism politically, morally, and economically. Although it was a victory for freedom, Communism was not dead. Communists still controlled China, North Korea, Cuba, and other countries, and Communist parties still troubled Eastern Europe and many other parts of the world.

Comprehension Check 14D

Identify

1. Ronald Reagan's Vice President who was elected President in 1988.
2. The dictator of Iraq who invaded Kuwait in 1990.
3. The American general in command of Operation Desert Storm.
4. The American general appointed to lead the troops into combat.

Think

5. How was Saddam Hussein a threat to Japan and the nations of Europe? To neighboring Arab nations and Israel?
6. Explain the collapse of the Soviet Union. What weakened the economy?

272 *New World History & Geography*

14.5 INTO THE NEXT MILLENIUM
President Bill Clinton

Before the Presidential election in 1992, both Democratic party candidate Bill Clinton and independent candidate Ross Perot [pəˈrōw] claimed that the nation was in an "economic crisis." With the conservative vote split between President Bush and Ross Perot (who had campaigned as a conservative), **William "Bill" Clinton** (1946–) won the election with only 43 percent of the popular vote. He became the nation's 42nd President.

Bill Clinton

During his Presidency, Bill Clinton involved the United States in several world conflicts. He sent American troops on UN and NATO "peace-keeping missions" to the nations of **Somalia, Bosnia,** and **Haiti.** He worked for greater cooperation with Communist China, permitting the transfer of valuable missile technology, and attempted to open relations with Communist Cuba. President Clinton hosted peace talks in Washington with the Israeli and the Palestinian leaders in 1993. As a result of the negotiations, they agreed to create an independent Palestinian state in the Gaza Strip and Jericho. Meanwhile, the Clinton administration reduced the American military dramatically, decreasing the numbers of ships, aircraft, weapons, and troops.

Terrorism in America

During the 1990s, Americans witnessed increased instances of violence. Two acts of terrorism threatened Americans' sense of security. On February 26, 1993, Muslim terrorists planted a bomb at the **World Trade Center,** a large building in New York City, killing 6 people and injuring over 1,000. On April 19, 1995, a bomb exploded outside the Alfred P. Murrah Federal Building in downtown **Oklahoma City.** This deadly blast took the lives of at least 167 people and was the work of American terrorist Timothy McVeigh.

The Information Age

The 1980s ushered in an age of increased computer technology; by 2000, half of all U.S. households owned a computer.

The development of the World Wide Web, a new "information superhighway" introduced in 1991, enabled computer access to the Internet, or the World Wide Web. The Internet is a high-speed network of information that can be transferred via computer around the world.

Nationwide Moral Decline

White House scandals. Bill Clinton's integrity was first questioned during the 1992 presidential campaign when rumors of an immoral affair with a woman circulated nationwide. In 1994, the President and his wife, Hillary Rodham Clinton, were linked to questionable business dealings involving Arkansas real estate in the **Whitewater Investigation.** In 2000 they were finally cleared of any criminal charges.

the Alfred P. Murrah Federal Building in Oklahoma City

In 1998, a special legal prosecutor, called the Independent Counsel, discovered that Clinton lied to a grand jury regarding his immoral conduct with a young White House intern named Monica Lewinsky. Congress impeached him for perjury (lying to a jury) and obstruction of justice. If a President is impeached (charged with a crime) by the House, the matter goes to trial before the Senate to determine if he should be removed from office. The Senate voted not to remove him from office. <u>President Clinton became the second President in United States history to be impeached; Andrew Johnson was impeached in 1868</u>.

An ever-changing America. In many ways, Bill Clinton set a tone for America—one that denied principles of honesty and integrity. Many Americans throughout the 1990s turned to alcohol, drugs, and material goods to make them "happy." The crime rate increased in suburban and rural areas—where many Americans raise their families. Gambling was made legal in more areas of the country, and immoral behavior became even more popular. Abortions increased as President Clinton lifted abortion restrictions imposed during the Reagan-Bush years, and doctor-assisted suicides became more common.

Declining academics and school violence. Public schools continued to decline rapidly in the academic areas. Students did not learn as much as they had, and, instead of ensuring that students learn, schools often lowered their standards. As a result, the Christian school movement was strengthened, and the **home-school movement** experienced dramatic growth. Morality also declined drastically. On the morning of April 20, 1999, two students walked into Columbine High School in Littleton, Colorado, and opened fire, killing 12 classmates and a teacher, wounding 21 other students, and then killing themselves. The incident at Columbine was the most severe of numerous instances of school violence.

Crossroads of the Millennium

Election 2000. In 2000, the American people had a choice to make. President Clinton's second term was nearly over, and a national election loomed on the horizon. Early in the race for the White House, **Vice President Al Gore** emerged as the top candidate on the Democratic ticket. The Republican party nominated Texas **Governor George W. Bush.**

George W. Bush advocated "compassionate conservatism" based on his faith in the American people to do what is right without government aid. Bush, the son of former President Bush, campaigned on promises of reforming welfare, cutting taxes, and strengthening the military. Al Gore, a skilled politician, alienated many with his confidence in more government to solve problems.

On November 7, 2000, after the votes had been cast, <u>each candidate needed to win Florida to win a majority of the votes and claim the Oval Office</u>, but the Florida vote was very close. The Gore campaign questioned the narrow margin of Bush's win in Florida. For the next 36 days, as several precincts recounted their votes manually, the nation waited to hear who would become the next President. Finally, on December 12, the Supreme Court ended the vote recountings. A day later, <u>George W. Bush (1946–) was declared the nation's 43rd President</u>. Later recounts verified that Bush had the majority of votes in Florida.

Inauguration of a new era. On January 20, 2001, George W. Bush took the oath of office. During his speech, President Bush drew from the richness of our nation's past to call

274 *New World History & Geography*

Americans to a fresh commitment to "live out our nation's promise through civility, courage, compassion, and character." He spoke of taking responsibility for the condition of the United States because the "stakes for America are never small. If our country does not lead the cause of freedom it will not be led." With high hopes, numbers of Americans listened as the new President talked of improving education, reforming the welfare system, and rebuilding the nation's military defenses. Many people felt renewed faith in the highest office in the land as President Bush promised to live by the principles of which he spoke so highly. In the closing of his speech, President George W. Bush reminded Americans that God is sovereign over the United States, and it is to Him they offer their service.

George W. Bush

Our Job Today

In his first official act as President, George W. Bush declared January 21, 2001, a national day of prayer and thanksgiving. As Christians, we should take the opportunity daily to pray for our national leaders that we "may lead a quiet and peaceable life in all godliness and honesty" (1 Tim. 2:2). Although there can never be true world peace until Jesus returns, we should be thankful to live in a country where we still have such great freedoms, and we should do all we can to keep those freedoms from passing away.

Comprehension Check 14E

Identify

1. Two acts of terrorism that took place in the 1990s.
2. The investigation into allegations that President Clinton was involved in questionable business dealings.
3. The state that became the deciding vote in the 2000 Presidential elections.

Chapter 14 Checkup

I. *Tell why these people are important.*

Dr. Jonas Salk
Jackie Robinson
Marian Anderson
Rosa Parks
Dr. Martin Luther King, Jr.
Fidel Castro
Huber Matos
Justice Clarence Thomas
Alan B. Shephard, Jr.
John Glenn
Neil Armstrong
Sandra Day O'Connor
Mikhail Gorbachev
Saddam Hussein
General Colin Powell
General Norman Schwarzkopf

II. *Define these terms.*

baby boom
economy
technology
civil rights
1964 Civil Rights Act
NATO
SEATO
liberal
conservative
New Frontier
abortion
Roe vs. Wade
Bay of Pigs
Cuban Missile Crisis
Vietnam War
Watergate Affair
Camp David Peace Accords
Reagan Revolution
Reagan Doctrine
S.D.I. or "Star Wars"
Operation Desert Storm
Whitewater Investigations

III. *Tell what these Presidents are noted for.*

Dwight D. Eisenhower
John F. Kennedy
Lyndon B. Johnson
Richard M. Nixon
Gerald R. Ford
Jimmy Carter
Ronald Reagan
George H. W. Bush
William Clinton
George W. Bush

Time for Freedom and Responsibility

chapter 15
Mexico and Central America

15.1 Middle America

Mexico, Central America, and the West Indies are often called *Middle America*, because they lie between the United States and South America. All three regions are considered part of the North American continent. In this chapter, you will study the mainland regions of Middle America—Mexico and Central America.

Latin America

Canada and the United States are called **Anglo-America,** because English is the main language of these countries. The part of the New World that lies south of the United States is called **Latin America.** That is because **Spanish** and other languages developed from Latin are the main tongue of most nations there today. Besides the language difference, other factors distinguish Latin America from Anglo-America. For example, **Roman Catholicism** is the main religion in Latin America, while **Protestantism** prevails in Canada and the United States.

Land of Geography

Middle America is the location of some of the most spectacular landforms in the Western Hemisphere. Peninsulas, plateaus, mountains, volcanoes, islands, deserts, jungles, rain forests, and beaches combine to make it a region of variety and natural beauty.

rainforest in Costa Rica, Central America

276 *New World History & Geography*

Popocatépetl is a volcano 40 miles east of Mexico City, Mexico.

The map on pp. 102–103 will show you that Middle America is nearly surrounded by water. It is bounded on the north by the United States, on the west and south by the Pacific Ocean, and on the east by the Atlantic Ocean and Colombia, South America. With the exception of El Salvador, every country of Middle America has a coast on the Caribbean Sea.

Locate **Baja California** (Lower California), the **Gulf of California,** and the **Isthmus of Panama** on the map. As you can see, the Isthmus of Panama is between North America and South America. Locate the **Panama Canal,** which allows ships to travel between the Pacific Ocean and the **Caribbean Sea.**

Comprehension Check 15A
Identify
1. The region formed by Mexico, Central America, and the West Indies.
2. The two large countries that form Anglo-America.
3. The term used for the countries of North and South America whose people speak a Romance language.

15.2 MEXICO: LAND OF THE AZTECS
Early Indian Civilizations

The rise of the Aztecs. Mexico, the southern neighbor of the United States, was first inhabited by Indian tribes. A tribe of Indians called the Toltecs [tōl′tĕks] built a civilization north of Mexico City around A.D. 900. Their civilation was short-lived, however, and within a few hundred years the **Aztecs,** a nomadic tribe from the south, had come to power. The early Aztecs settled in central and southern Mexico in an area called the Valley of Mexico. By the 1400s, they had established a powerful empire with a magnificent capital, **Tenochtitlán** [tĕ·nôch′tē·tlän′], on the site where Mexico City stands today.

Capital city. Tenochtitlán was built on two small islands in a shallow lake. The Aztecs used rocks and debris to fill in the marshes around the islands and thus expand their city. Although the buildings and many of the streets were built on dry ground, some of the streets were actually canals. A huge, flat-topped pyramid stood in the center of the city.

Mexico and Central America

Mexico and Central America

On the top of the pyramid was a temple to the Aztecs' false gods. Priests climbed to this temple by a set of stairs that were built up the side of the pyramid. In addition to the king's private rooms, the royal palace contained a zoo, a library, and workshops where artisans could create beautiful items. The ruins of Tenochtitlán can still be seen in Mexico City today.

Food and clothing. The Aztecs had a culture similar to that of the people who live in remote Mexican villages today. Corn, or maize, was one of their main foods; they used it to make *tortillas* [tôr·tē′yəs]. The people also ate beans and chili and drank a chocolate-flavored drink. (We get the English words *chocolate* and *cocoa* from the Aztec language.) The Aztecs wore clothing made of brightly dyed cotton and lived in huts made of poles or *adobe* [ə·dō′bē: sun-dried bricks].

Education. The Aztecs had no alphabet, but they invented **pictures** and **symbols** for their words. A few Aztec boys and girls were trained to work in the temple. Some boys learned history, crafts, and Aztec traditions and religious beliefs in schools called "Houses of Youth." Many Aztec children received their education at home, learning how to make a living.

Hernando Cortés meets Montezuma

278 New World History & Geography

OF SPECIAL INTEREST
The Spanish Language

More than 250 million people around the world speak Spanish as their first language, making it the most widely used Latin language. (A Latin language is one that developed from the Latin spoken during the Roman Empire.) Besides Spanish, some other languages included in the Latin language group are Italian, French, and Portuguese. You will learn in chapter 18 about one huge country in South America where Portuguese is the official language. The Latin languages are also called the **Romance** (from Roman) **languages.**

Today, the standard form of Spanish is called **Castilian Spanish,** and most Spanish-speaking people use some variation of Castilian. **Latin-American Spanish** is the variation spoken in Middle America. The different varieties of Spanish have developed some differences in pronunciation and in vocabulary over the centuries.

The English language has adopted many Spanish words into its vocabulary. *Alligator, cargo, cork, lasso, mosquito, ranch, rodeo, tomato, tornado,* and *vanilla* are just a few. The state names of Colorado, Florida, Nevada, and California are also Spanish in origin. Many people in the United States speak Spanish as either their first or their second language.

Common Spanish Words

Days of the Week
Sunday	**domingo**	[dō·měng′gō]
Monday	**lunes**	[lōō′nās]
Tuesday	**martes**	[mär′tās]
Wednesday	**miércoles**	[mē·ār′kō·lās]
Thursday	**jueves**	[hwā′vās]
Friday	**viernes**	[vē·ār′nās]
Saturday	**sábado**	[sä′bä·t͟hō]

Numbers
one	**uno**	[ōō′nō]
two	**dos**	[dōs]
three	**tres**	[trās]
four	**cuatro**	[kwä′trō]
five	**cinco**	[sēn′kō]
six	**seis**	[sā′ēs]
seven	**siete**	[sē·ā′tā]
eight	**ocho**	[ō′chō]
nine	**nueve**	[nōō·ā′vā]
ten	**diez**	[dē′ěs]

Geographic Terms
mountain	**montaña**	[mōn·tä′nyä]
low, lower	**bajo**	[bä′hō]
north	**norte**	[nôr′tā]
western	**occidental**	[ôk′sē·t͟hän·täl′]
city	**ciudad**	[syōō·t͟häth′]
eastern	**oriental**	[ô·ryān·täl′]
town, village	**pueblo**	[pwä′blō]
mountain chain	**cordillera**	[kôr′t͟hē·yä′rä]
port, harbor	**puerto**	[pwěr′tō]
coast	**costa**	[kŏs′tə]
river	**río**	[rē′ō]
desert	**desierto**	[dā·sē·ěr′tō]
mountain range	**sierra**	[syěr′rä]
equator	**ecuador**	[ā′kwä·t͟hôr′]
earth, land	**tierra**	[tyěr′rä]
large, great	**grande**	[grän′dā]

Common Phrases
Thanks.
Gracias. [grä′syäs]

What is your name?
¿Cómo se llama usted?
[kō′mō sā yä′mä ōō·stěd′]

Merry Christmas.
Feliz Navidad.
[fā·lēs′ nä′vē·däd′]

What time is it?
¿Qué hora es?
[kā ōr·ə′ ās]

God is love.
Dios es amor.
[dē·ōs′ ās ä·mōr′]

Spanish Discovery

Spanish explorers discovered Mexico in 1517. The Spanish explorer **Hernando Cortés** [hər·năn′dō kôr·těz′] sailed to Mexico in 1519 to find gold and silver. Because the Aztecs had never seen white men or horses before, they worshiped the Spanish soldiers as gods. **Montezuma,** the Aztec emperor, gave Cortés and his men gifts of gold and silver. Cortés was not satisfied, however. With the help of the Aztecs' enemies, the Spanish conquered Montezuma and the Aztecs. Because of Cortés, Mexico became a Spanish colony.

The Mexicans served Spain for the next 300 years. Then, in 1810, the Mexicans re-

Mexico and Central America

volted. Mexico won its independence in 1821 and set up a new government. In 1846, the United States and Mexico fought a war over the control of the Texas territory, which was held by Mexico. The war ended in 1848 when the United States paid Mexico for the land.

Mountains, Plains, and Plateau

Horn of plenty. Mexico is a land of mountains, deserts, and tropical jungles. It is shaped like a cornucopia (horn of plenty) with two large peninsulas—**Baja California** (*Lower California* in English) and the **Yucatán Peninsula**—tacked on. In the north, Mexico stretches along the southern border of the United States for 1,833 miles. The Rio Grande ("Great River") forms part of this border. Near the southern end of Mexico, the **Isthmus of Tehuantepec** [tə·wän′tə·pĕk′] is only 137 miles wide. This narrow isthmus separates the Gulf of Mexico from the Pacific Ocean. From north to south, Mexico is about 1,900 miles long.

Land of mountains. Mexico is one of the most mountainous countries in the world. The entire central region, from the United States border to the Isthmus of Tehuantepec, is a high plateau rimmed by two mountain ranges. The **Sierra Madre Occidental,** or western mountain range, includes some of the country's most rugged land. Canyons almost a mile deep cut through the western mountains, and parts of this region are so wild that they have never been explored except by air.

At the point in the south where the Sierra Madre Occidental meets the **Sierra Madre Oriental,** or eastern mountain range, there are many high peaks and a number of volcanoes.

Sierra Madre Mountains

Citaltépetl [sē′tläl·tā′pĕt′l], a dormant snow-capped volcano sometimes called Orizaba, is Mexico's highest point (18,555 feet) and the third tallest mountain in North America. Two other famous volcanic mountains, **Iztaccíhuatl** [ēs′täk·sē′wä·t′l], or "White Woman," and **Popocatépetl** [pō′pə·kăt′ə·pĕt′l], or "Smoking Mountain," are both more than 17,000 feet high. According to legend, Popocatépetl is a warrior guarding Iztaccíhutal, a beautiful woman. Although Iztaccíhuatl is extinct, Popocatépetl, which is only 40 miles from Mexico City, has been active for several years, spewing gas, ashes, and hot rocks. Tens of thousands of people have been forced to evacuate their homes as officials continue to monitor the volcano's periodic eruptions.

The **Mexican Plateau,** which lies between the mountain ranges, is where most of Mexico's people live. In the north, this vast plateau is 1,500 miles across. The country's agricultural regions and principal cities are located on this plateau, including its capital, **Mexico City.** The plateau begins at an elevation of about 3,000 feet in the north and rises to 8,000 feet around Mexico City.

Many Climates

The **tropic of Cancer** runs through the middle of Mexico; thus half of the country lies in the Tropics and half in the temperate zone. The northern half of Mexico is mostly desert. Here, the **Chihuahuan Desert,** the **Sonoran Desert,** and semidesert (partly desert) areas cover most of the land. In the south, especially along the Caribbean coastal plain, there are lush tropical jungles filled with some of the most colorful birds in the world.

Mexico's climate is greatly affected by altitude (height above sea level). The coastal plains are very hot. Along the slopes of the mountains, the climate is mild and pleasant, with little change in temperature from winter to summer. High on the plateau, such as at Mexico City, the nights are cool and the days are warm and sunny almost all year long. The crops that can be grown in Mexico depend much upon altitude.

Natural Resources

Minerals. Mexico leads the world in the mining and producing of **silver.** **Gold** is also abundant, as are sulfur, lead, zinc, and copper. Petroleum is one of Mexico's greatest natural resources.

Flora. There are more than 1,000 kinds of cactus plants in Mexico's deserts. The **candelilla** [kăn′dl·ē′ə: "little candle"], a desert plant which looks like a candle, has many thin, pencil-like stems that are coated with wax that helps conserve its moisture. Mexicans boil the wax off and sell it for use in shoe polish, car and floor wax, candy, and crayons. Thousands of kinds of flowers grow in the varied Mexican climate, including azaleas, chrysanthemums, geraniums, orchids, and poinsettias.

About a fifth of Mexico is covered with forests. The largest forests are found in the northwestern and central mountains and in the rainy south and southeast. Ebony, mahogany, rosewood, walnut, and other hardwood trees found in these forests are valuable in furniture making. **Tropical forests** include hardwoods, palms, and plants that receive their moisture and nutrients from the air and rain. **Pine forests** grow in the mountains and supply timber for Mexico's pulp and paper industry. In the south, the **sapodilla** [săp′ə·dē′ə] trees ooze sap that is the source of chicle, a major ingredient in chewing gum.

Fauna. The tropic of Cancer is the dividing line between the North American realm of animal life and the South American realm.

a Mexican worker climbing a sapodilla tree

Thus, Mexico has many animals that are also found in South America as well as many that live in North America. In the mountains, bears, deer, and mountain lions live. Coyotes, lizards, prairie dogs, and rattlesnakes are found in the northern deserts. Alligators, jaguars, opossums, rodents, monkeys, armadillos, tapirs, anteaters, pumas, and wolves also live in Mexico.

Montezuma had an aviary (large building that houses many birds) that surprised and delighted the Spanish explorers. The Indians bred **macaws** [mə·kôz′], **parrots,** and **turkeys.** They worshiped birds, used their feathers for decoration and trade, and ate their meat. Beautifully colored **quetzals** [kĕt·sälz′] live in southern forests. Some other birds of Mexico are **flamingos, hummingbirds, herons,** and **pelicans.**

Mexico Today

People. The people of Mexico are of three main groups: **Indians, Europeans,** and **mestizos** [mĕs·tē′zōz]. Most Mexicans are

Events in History
Paricutín: The Corn Field That Became a Volcano

On February 20, 1943, a Tarascan Indian and his young son were plowing their small corn field west of Mexico City.

"Father, Father, the earth is grumbling," cried the boy as he came running.

Dionisio Pulido, the father, had not heard any noise because he had been yelling at the oxen pulling his plow. Now he stopped and listened. There! He, too, heard it. It sounded as if something underground had growled. He spun around to see a thin spiral of smoke escaping from the ground. Grabbing his son, Dionisio ran the two miles to his village to warn the priest and another two miles to the next village to warn the village mayor.

All night long, frightened villagers watched a glowing spiral of smoke shoot into the air as frequent explosions rocked the ground. What could be happening to their neighbor's corn field?

The next morning, a few of the braver villagers cautiously approached Dionisio's corn field. In the middle of his flat corn field rose a volcanic cone about 30 feet tall. The Mexican villagers were witnessing a rare event—the birth of a volcano. Many people have watched an old volcano come to life again, but very few people in the world have watched a new volcano develop. It had been over 170 years since the last Western Hemisphere volcano had formed.

For the next several weeks, the earth shook with violent explosions. Gases and smoke shot three miles into the air. Every night, the glowing mountain put on a tremendous fireworks display. Molten lava continued to pour out of the volcano's mouth and roll down the mountainside. It swallowed up trees, animals, homes, and two whole villages before the volcano quieted down. After nine years of explosions and rumblings, Dionisio Pulido's small corn field had become a mountain 1,500 feet tall! The world came to know of the volcano as **Paricutín** [pä·rē′koo·tēn′], but the Tarascan Indians have another name for it—*El Monstruo*, the monster.

The lava from Paricutín buried two villages. All that remains of one is the top of this church. Paricutín is the volcano in the background.

282 *New World History & Geography*

Mexico City

mestizos, a mixture of Indian and European ancestry. The Indians are the direct descendants of the ancient Indian tribes who lived in Mexico, especially the Aztecs, Mayas [māy′əz], and Toltecs.

Cities. **Mexico City,** the capital of Mexico, is the largest city and most advanced area in the entire country. In 2000, it was the third largest city in the world, containing well over 16 million people. It is the only heavily populated city in the world that has no river or sea nearby. Although modern skyscrapers, factories, offices, stores, and houses are common in Mexico City, there are still many old, traditional buildings. Many of the same retail stores and fast-food restaurant chains found in the United States can also be found scattered throughout the city.

Monterrey [mŏn′tə·rā′] is one of Mexico's largest cities and the center for Mexico's steel industry. Major iron ore deposits are located in the Sierra Madre Orientals around Monterrey. Another large city and favorite tourist spot is **Guadalajara** [gwŏd′l·ə·här′ə], located near the Pacific coast.

Mexican cities are built around a central area called a *plaza* [plä′zə]. The plaza is a public meeting place similar to the town squares in the American colonies. In or near the plaza is the marketplace where merchants and farmers sell their goods. Many people who live in the country's largest cities live in modern houses.

Villages. Villages in Mexico are often located in remote places—deep in the mountains or far into a barren area. Mexican villages are also built around a plaza, and some of the larger villages have a marketplace. Farmers who do not live near a market must travel each week to take their goods to market. Missionaries to Mexico sometimes use small airplanes to reach the people of the villages. Village people often live in simple adobe houses. They are farmers who plant, harvest, and prepare all of their own food.

People in the villages eat a large meal about two o'clock in the afternoon, after which many take a ***siesta*** [sē·ĕs′tə], or nap, to avoid activity during the hottest part of the day. Corn and beans are the main foods. Corn is often ground and made into ***tortillas.*** Beans are used in chili and as a filling for tortillas.

Mexican women making tortillas

Mexico and Central America 283

A young boy dressed in traditional clothing gets ready for his part in a rodeo.

Mexicans raise cattle, chickens, turkeys, and hogs for meat. Most Mexican dishes are flavored with spices and seasonings. Fruit juices, hot chocolate, milk, and coffee are favorite beverages.

Traditional Mexican clothes are made of wool or cotton. Men may wear a ***sombrero*** [sŏm·brâr′ō], a tall hat with a wide brim. Women wear cotton blouses and long, full skirts. A ***poncho*** [pŏn′chō] is a large square or diamond-shaped wool cloth with a hole cut for the head. It covers most of the upper body. During the day, men and women wear a brightly colored ***serape*** [sə·rä′pē] over one shoulder. At night they use the serape as a blanket. In the larger towns and cities, however, people wear modern clothes that they buy in stores and shopping malls.

Recreation. Mexicans celebrate special events with a ***fiesta*** [fē·ĕs′tə]. All of the people in a town come out for the fiesta, which may last several days. Eating, dancing, and playing games are the main attractions. **Bullfights** are very popular in Mexico. Children may play a game with a ***piñata*** [pē·nyä′tä] a hollow clay or papier-mâché container shaped in the form of an animal. The hollow is filled with candy and toys. The children take turns being blindfolded and trying to break open the piñata with a stick.

Mexicans enjoy such sports as baseball, swimming, and volleyball. Many outstanding American major league baseball players have come from Mexico and other parts of Middle America. By far the most popular sport is soccer, which the people enjoy both watching and playing.

Government. Mexico has a democratic form of government with a president and other national officials. The Mexican government has great power over the people—much more than that of the United States. In the past, Mexico's government has taken private farms away from their owners and given the land to the poor and has taken over many major industries including banking, railroads, and petroleum. Recently, however, the government has once again allowed people more freedom to own land and make their own economic choices. Communists, desiring Mexico's oil wealth, have posed a serious problem, because they deceive the people into believing that Communism can help them to escape from poverty.

Comprehension Check 15B
Identify

1. The Indian tribe that built a powerful empire in Mexico.
2. The two mountain ranges that rim the Mexican Plateau.
3. The precious metal that Mexico produces more of than any other country.
4. The Spanish explorer who came to Mexico in 1519 looking for wealth.

15.3 CENTRAL AMERICA: LAND IN BETWEEN

Location and Geography

Central America is the narrow strip of land lying between Mexico and South America. The Caribbean Sea is on its east and the Pacific Ocean is on its west. It stretches about 1,000 miles from north to south, but it is very narrow. Although the region is only about one-fourth the size of Mexico, it is made up of seven independent nations. Locate the seven Central American nations on the map of Middle America on pp. 102–103. They are **Belize** [bə·lēz′], **Guatemala** [gwä′tə·mä′lə], **Honduras** [hŏn·dŏŏr′əs], **El Salvador** [ĕl săl′və·dôr], **Nicaragua** [nĭk′ə·rä′gwə], **Costa Rica** [kŏs′tə rē′kə], and **Panama** [păn′ə·mä′].

Mountains run down the center of Central America. Some are 10,000 feet high or taller—over 2 miles high. Valleys between the mountains provide some of Central America's best farmland. There are a number of active volcanoes in the mountain ranges, and often there are earthquakes.

On each side of the mountains are *coastal plains.* The Pacific coastal plain is covered with grass, and the Atlantic coastal plain is mainly tropical jungle. **Lake Nicaragua** is the largest lake, and unlike other freshwater lakes, Lake Nicaragua is the home of certain animal species—such as sharks and swordfish—usually found only in the ocean. Two long rivers of Central America are the San Juan [săn wän′] and the Coco.

Mayas: Builders of Civilization

Over 1,000 years before the birth of Christ, the Mayas built the first great civilization of the Western Hemisphere. They lived in the area of the Yucatán Peninsula, Guatemala, and northern Belize for over 2000 years—long before the Toltecs and Aztecs inhabited the region.

The Mayas lived off the land. They built simple huts from poles and ate mainly corn, beans, squash, and chili peppers. Besides these foods, Mayan farmers grew sweet potatoes, cotton, and tobacco. Some families kept a hive of stingless honeybees for their honey. The Mayas made most of their clothing of woven cotton material, but they sometimes made clothing from pounded tree bark.

Recreation played an important part in Mayan life. The most popular game in every village was something like our modern game of basketball. A hoop was mounted vertically above the players' heads, and two teams competed to see who could get a rubber ball through it using only their knees or hips. This game was so popular that some of the larger villages built stadiums so spectators could enjoy the sport.

Mayan priests were the only scholars of the empire. They learned many things about astronomy and arithmetic. They devised a chart that predicted eclipses of the sun, and they de-

ruins of a Mayan observatory

veloped a 365-day calendar. The Mayas were the only ancient American people to develop a practical written numbers system and an advanced form of writing—a system of *hieroglyphics,* or special signs and symbols. The sons of chiefs and priests went to school and learned history, astronomy, hieroglyphics, and medicine.

The Maya built some structures that are still standing today. At **Chichén Itzá** [chē·chěn′ ē·tsä′] on the Yucatán Peninsula, tourists can see the ruins of a Mayan temple, observatory, and stadium.

The Mayan empire was at its height from A.D. 300–900. The civilization had already greatly declined before the arrival of the Spanish. In the 1500s, several Spanish explorers conquered parts of the area and defeated the Mayas.

Climate

Temperatures in Central America depend on the altitude. The low coastal areas have annual temperatures of around 75°F. Areas that lie 5,000 feet above sea level have temperatures between 60°F and 69°F. Rainfall is heaviest from May to October. Some regions along the Caribbean coast have rain almost the entire year. One part of Nicaragua receives more than 250 inches of rain annually, while Guatemala receives only about 50 inches per year.

Natural Resources

The mountains of Central America have small deposits of minerals such as copper, lead, gold, manganese, and silver. Tropical trees—especially mahogany—grow in the jungles near the Caribbean Sea. Balsa, pine, cedar, palm, and rubber trees also grow in the region, supporting the timber industry.

Today, most of Central America's power comes from hydroelectric plants. Mountain streams are used to produce electricity in all of the Central American countries.

Coffee, bananas, cacao [kə·kä′ō: chocolate], **cotton,** and **sugar** are the main agricultural crops today. Coffee is grown on the cool mountain slopes of every Central American country. In about half of the countries, it is the major export item. Farmers also raise cattle, citrus fruits, manioc (used in making tapioca), rice, and wheat.

Wildlife

Many animals make their home in Central America. A large number of these animals are also found in the rain forests of South America.

Mammals. The **jaguar** [jăg′wär′], the largest cat native to the Western Hemisphere, ranges from Mexico to Argentina. At one time it lived in parts of the United States as well. The **jaguarundi** [jăg·wə·rŭn′dē], one of the smallest wild cats in the Western Hemisphere, has a small head, short legs, and a long tail.

Five kinds of monkeys live in Central America. The **squirrel monkey** is very sensitive to its environment. If it is deprived of its normal light or warmth for even a short time, it could die. The **douroucouli** [dōō′rōō′kōō′lē], the only *nocturnal* (active at night) monkey, makes a good family pet. It is especially good at tracking down roaches and other insects in the home. Many naturalists consider the **capuchin monkey** to be the most intelligent monkey of the Western Hemisphere. Best known as the "organ grinder monkey," the capuchin has often been trained to collect money for organ grinders who play their instruments on street corners.

The **spider monkey** is best known for its three-foot long tail. When a branch is too narrow for the spider monkey to walk on, this animal swings under the branch and hangs upside down by its tail, feeding and relaxing in this position. This strong tail is as sensitive as our fingertips, and the spider monkey can use it to pick up an object as small as a peanut. The **howler monkey,** named for its loud, distinctive cry, howls at dawn, when it meets other monkeys, or when it is disturbed. It rarely leaves the trees.

The **coati** [kō·ä′tē], a small, tree-dwelling mammal, is similar in many ways to the raccoon and the ring-tailed cat. It is noted for its very long tail and its long, flexible snout.

Reptiles. The **caiman** [kā′mən], a crocodilian that greatly resembles both an alligator and a crocodile, lives in the lakes and rivers of Central and South America. The **common iguana** [ĭ·gwä′nə], a large lizard that can grow up to 6 feet long, lives in the tropical forests of Central and South America. The **bushmaster,** a large, poisonous snake, can be up to 11 feet long, although it usually measures about 6 feet. It has rough, light brown skin with black splotches.

Birds. Parrots, toucans, currasows [kōōr′ə·sōz], and hummingbirds are some of the colorful birds found in Central America. **Toucans** are distinguished by their enormous, colorful bills. The bills look heavy, but they are full of tiny air holes that make them light.

Comprehension Check 15C
Identify
1. The largest lake in Central America.
2. People who built the first great civilization of the Western Hemisphere.
3. The major export crop of Central American countries.

Think
4. What were some of the achievements for which the Maya are known?

Mexico and Central America 287

15.4 COUNTRIES OF CENTRAL AMERICA

Belize. Belize was granted independence from Great Britain in 1981, becoming a member of the Commonwealth of Nations. This Central American country with the fewest people is located on the Caribbean Sea near the Yucatán Peninsula. Belize is the only Central American country that does not have a Pacific coast. Because of its location, Belize is plagued by hurricanes. The capital used to be Belize City, which is located along the coast, before a major hurricane destroyed much of the city. Today the capital is **Belmopan** [bĕl′mō·păn′], a small city located farther inland.

Belize has one of the most racially diversified populations of any nation in the world. Mestizo, Africans, Maya Indians, English, Europeans, Chinese, East Indians, Mexicans, Lebanese, and a few German Mennonite farmers have made Belize their home. Unlike the rest of the countries in the region, Belize was colonized by the British instead of the Spanish, and this is why Belize is the only Central American country in which Spanish is not the main language. English is the major language, and Creole, Spanish, and Mayan are also spoken. Many of the children go to church-operated schools. Agriculture, garment production, and tourism are all important to the economy.

Costa Rica. *Costa Rica* means "rich coast." It was given the name by Christopher Columbus because he believed he would find much gold there. Costa Rica is a narrow country with white sandy beaches on the Caribbean Sea and the Pacific Ocean. Between these beaches is a mountainous backbone.

Costa Rica eventually came under Spanish control but gained its independence by the 1830s. Nearly all of its people are descendants of Spanish colonists. About 95 percent of the people can read and write—a higher percentage than in any other Central American country. The nation, which does not keep an army, has been much more peaceful and free than its neighbors. Coffee and bananas are its chief exports. The country has developed its mining and manufacturing industries, making it richer than most of the rest of Central America. **San José** [săn′ hō·zā′] is the capital and largest city.

El Salvador. The smallest country in the Western Hemisphere that is not an island is El Salvador. The country's name, *El Salvador*, is Spanish for "the Savior," a reference to Jesus Christ. Averaging approximately 730 people per square mile, mountainous El Salvador is also the most densely populated country on the mainland. It is the only Central American county without a Caribbean shore, but it has a fertile coastal plain on the Pacific. The people of El Salvador raise large quantities of coffee, cotton, and sugar.

For many years the Spanish ruled the area, where they raised indigo, a plant commonly used to dye cloth blue. El Salvador became completely independent in 1839. The country has suffered under military rule and recent civil war, yet it is the most industrialized nation in Central America. **San Salvador** is the nation's capital and largest city. The people of El Salvador, most of whom are mestizos, enjoy various sports, including auto racing, basketball, baseball, and the national favorite, soccer.

Guatemala. Guatemala is a beautiful place filled with lush rainforests and tall mountains. About two thirds of the country is covered with mountains, many of which are volcanoes. The land that is now Guatemala used to be the heart of the Mayan empire. About half of the Guatemalans today are American

288 New World History & Geography

As in most Latin America countries, soccer is a favorite sport in El Salvador.

Indian, and many of these are direct descendants of the Maya. Most of the rest of the people are mestizos. Guatemalans enjoy wearing traditional clothing made of brightly colored fabrics. Agriculture is the main industry. Guatemalan farmers raise coffee, bananas, and sugar cane.

The Spanish took over the area in the 1500s. Guatemala was able to become independent in the 1830s. The country is poor, and the people have been troubled by military takeovers and civil war. Guatemala has the largest population of any Central American country. **Guatemala City,** the nation's capital, is also Central America's largest city.

Honduras. Honduras is one of the poorest Central American countries. Much of the region is mountainous and covered with trees, which the people use for lumber and other wood products. The land with its hot, humid climate is also ideal for bananas and coffee, two of the country's chief exports. The capital of Honduras, **Tegucigalpa** [tə·gōō′sə·găl′pə], is also the largest city. Most Hondurans live in or near small rural settlements, where they can raise crops and livestock. In 1998, a fierce hurricane devastated the country, killing over 5,550 of its people.

Christopher Columbus came to Honduras in 1502, and more Spanish followed soon after, eager for a share of gold mined in the area. Honduras became fully independent in 1838. The country has had problems, however, with dictators and revolutions.

Tourists that come to Honduras can enjoy the impressive, partially reconstructed **Copan** [kō·pän′]. This ancient Mayan city includes plazas, monuments, sculptures, ballcourts, and pyramids. Diving and snorkeling along the Bay Islands coral reefs are also popular.

Nicaragua. Managua [mə·nä′gwə] is the capital of Central America's largest country, Nicaragua. Along the Caribbean is a swampy region called the "Mosquito Coast," where there is lush tropical rainforest. Beautiful mountains and volcanoes are farther west, as is Lake Nicaragua, the largest lake in the region.

Farmers harvest bananas for export in Honduras.

Events in History
The Panama Canal: A Milestone of Transportation

North and South America stretch almost all the way from the North Pole to the South Pole. Before the Panama Canal was built, a ship traveling from New York City to San Francisco, California, had to sail around South America, passing through the Strait of Magellan—over 13,000 miles!

By 1900, the United States had realized the need for a shorter route. A French company had started building a canal across the narrow Isthmus of Panama, but had run out of money. A few years later, the United States expressed interest in taking over the canal-building effort. At that time, Panama was part of Colombia, South America, and Colombia did not want the United States to build the canal. The United States helped Panama to become independent of Colombia, and in 1903 Americans started building the canal.

The men who built the Panama Canal faced a difficult task—cutting through mountains while controlling the dreaded and deadly disease, malaria. Using shovels and dynamite, they conquered the mountains. **Colonel William Gorgas** worked for 10 years to conquer the malaria. To do this, he had to drain the swamps where mosquitoes, which carry this disease, bred. He also installed sewer lines and built hospitals to treat people who had contracted malaria and other tropical diseases.

The canal opened in 1914. Fifty-one miles long from end to end, it cut the trip from New York to San Francisco from 13,000 miles to only 5,200 miles—making it 7,800 miles shorter.

The Panama Canal was built with U.S. money and engineering skill. The United States operated the canal and controlled the 10-mile-wide Canal Zone until 1977, allowing countries friendly to the United States to pay tolls to use it. In that year, a treaty was signed which gave Panama control of the canal on December 31, 1999. Many Americans think this was a serious mistake for America. They are concerned about the problems our country could face if the Communists gain control of this important area.

Interesting Facts:
- It takes 8–12 hours for the average ship to pass through the canal.
- It takes 52 million gallons of water for each ship to pass through the canal.
- The largest toll ever paid was $141,344.91 by the *Crown Princess*.
- The smallest toll ever paid was 36¢ by a man who swam the canal in 1928.

Much like the other Central American countries, Nicaragua came under Spanish control in the 1500s. During Nicaragua's early European history, pirates frequently raided the towns along Lake Nicaragua. After gold was discovered in California in 1848, the lake became part of a route that used boats and stage coaches to transport gold seekers across Central America to the Pacific, where they could continue to California by ship. During its history of independence, frequent earthquakes, dictatorships, and war have rocked the country. Cotton, the most productive crop—as well as coffee, sugar, bananas and gold—contribute greatly to Nicaragua's economy.

Panama. The country of Panama is known as the "Crossroads of the World" because the **Panama Canal,** which connects the Atlantic and Pacific Oceans, is located there. This canal is one of the most important man-made waterways in the Western Hemisphere.

Like Costa Rica, Panama is composed of central mountains and coastal plains; much of this land is covered with the Western Hemisphere's largest tropical rainforest outside of the Amazon. After the Spanish took over the area in the 1500s, Panama quickly became a center for trading and shipping. It was freed from Spain in 1821 and joined Colombia in South America; Panama became completely independent in 1903.

Most Panamanians are mestizos, although there are also many whites, American Indians, and people from the West Indies. The largest city, **Panama City,** is also the country's capital. The economy relies heavily on bananas, coffee, sugar, manufacturing, and income that comes from operating the Panama Canal.

Comprehension Check 15D

Identify
1. The country that is the home of the ancient Mayan city, Copan.
2. The Central American country that is both the smallest and the most densely populated on the mainland.
3. The peaceful Central American country whose name means "rich coast."
4. The country that links North and South America.

Think
5. Why was the Panama Canal needed?

Chapter 15 Checkup

I. Define these terms.

silver	Mexico City	plaza	sombrero	fiesta	Chichén Itzá
petroleum	Monterrey	siesta	poncho	bullfights	Panama Canal
candelilla	Guadalajara	tortillas	serape	piñata	

II. Tell why these people or tribes are important.
- Aztecs
- Montezuma
- William Gorgas
- Hernando Cortés
- Mayas

III. Give a noted fact about these animals.

jaguar	douroucouli	howler monkey	common iguana
jaguarundi	capuchin monkey	coati	bushmaster
squirrel monkey	spider monkey	caiman	toucan

IV. Define these geographical terms.

Baja California	Rio Grande	Sierra Madre Occidental	Iztaccíhuatl	Lake Nicaragua
Yucatán Peninsula	Isthmus of Tehuantepec	Sierra Madre Oriental	Popocatépetl	
Gulf of Mexico	Mexico Plateau	Citaltépetl	Paricutín	

V. Know these Central American capitals and countries.

| Mexico City, Mexico | Guatemala City, Guatemala | Managua, Nicaragua | Panama City, Panama |
| Belmopan, Belize | Tegucigalpa, Honduras | San José, Costa Rica | |

VI. Identify the locations found in Map Mastery 14.

Mexico and Central America 291

chapter 16
The WEST INDIES
Islands of the Caribbean

16.1 LAND OF DISCOVERY
Rich Heritage

Discovery by Christopher Columbus. On August 3, 1492, the Italian navigator **Christopher Columbus** set sail from Spain with a fleet of three tiny ships—the *Niña* [nē′nyə], the *Pinta* [pēn′tə], and the *Santa Maria* [săn′tə mə·rē′ə]—and ninety men. He hoped to reach a group of islands near Japan and set up a great city for trade between the East and the West. He did not realize that two great continents, North and South America, lay in the way.

Using the North Star to measure latitude, Columbus sailed due west from the Canary Islands (west of Africa). The trade winds carried him along at a good speed, but land was not as near as he had expected. He and his crew sailed for over four weeks, longer than anyone had ever sailed before in one direction out of sight of land. The men grew frightened and threatened to mutiny. Finally on **October 12, 1492,** land was sighted. Columbus and his men landed on an island that Columbus named **San Salvador.** Christopher Columbus had discovered America!

Early peoples. The people who met Columbus on San Salvador were the **Arawak** [ăr′ə·wäk′], a gentle tribe who gave us our words *maize, potato,* and *tobacco.* Another tribe, the fierce **Carib** [kăr′ĭb], were named by Columbus after the Spanish word for cannibals. Our word *canoe* is from the Carib language, and the **Caribbean Sea** was named for the Carib. Columbus called the Arawak and Carib "Indians," because he thought he had arrived in the Indies, a term which at that time referred to India, China, the East Indies, and Japan. When people learned of the mistake later, they named the islands the **West Indies** to avoid further confusion. The native people of the Americas are still often referred to as *Indians.*

Search for gold. Columbus asked the Indians where the gold ornaments they wore had come from. One of the places the Indians mentioned was **Cuba.** Thinking he was near Asia, Columbus understood the Indians to be saying *Cipango,* another name for Japan. Columbus and his men sailed along the coast of Cuba, **Hispaniola** [hĭs′pən·yō′lə], and several other islands, observing the cus-

292 *New World History & Geography*

view of Martinique

toms of the Indians and continuing their search for gold. When the *Santa Maria* sank off the coast of present-day **Haiti** (on Hispaniola), a friendly Indian chief helped save the cargo. Columbus built a fort there and left about forty men on the island to look for gold. He then sailed back to Spain with the *Niña* and the *Pinta,* taking several captive Indians with him.

The return voyage, sailing against the trade winds, was extremely rough, but Columbus and his crew finally arrived in Spain. They were given a grand reception by **Ferdinand** and **Isabella**, the Spanish king and queen who had paid for the trip, and Columbus was given the titles **"Admiral of the Ocean Sea"** and **"Viceroy of the Indies."**

Columbus's later voyages. In September of 1493, Columbus set out on his second voyage. This time he brought seventeen ships and 1,500 men. Arriving at Hispaniola, he founded **Isabela**, the first European city in the Americas, and set up a government there. He also discovered **Puerto Rico** [pwĕr′tə rē′kō], **Jamaica** [jə·mā′kə], and some smaller islands.

On his third voyage, in 1498, Columbus sailed farther south and was caught in the doldrums (a region of calm waters and light, variable winds near the equator) for eight days. The men suffered from the intense heat until a wind finally arose and carried them to **South America,** where they discovered the mouth of the Orinoco River. On his fourth voyage, in 1502, Columbus reached the coast of Honduras and discovered the **Isthmus of Panama.**

Although Christopher Columbus died in Spain in 1506, he lives on in history as one

Voyages of Columbus

of the greatest seamen the world has ever known. Soon after his first voyage, other Europeans began sailing west and making one discovery after another. Columbus, by finding the West Indies and returning to Spain to tell the world, opened the way for the Old World settlement of the New World.

From Colonial Days to Modern Times

Colonial days. After Columbus claimed the West Indies for Spain, **Spanish colonies** were established in the islands. The Spaniards forced the American Indians to work in their sugar cane and tobacco fields. Most of the Indians died because of overwork and diseases the Spanish carried, and black slaves from Africa were imported to take their place. The Spaniards taught the Catholic religion to both the Indians and the blacks.

Many **English, French,** and **Dutch** explorers also claimed land in the West Indies and colonized some of the islands. **Danish** colonists (from Denmark) settled some of the Virgin Islands.

Trade flourished between Europe, the West Indies, and the thirteen colonies that

slaves at a sugar mill in the West Indies

would eventually become the United States of America. The West Indies played an important role in colonial days because of the sugar and tobacco plantations owned by the European colonists there. During the 1600s and 1700s, pirates terrorized trading ships laden with gold that sailed to the islands. A tiny island in the Caribbean's Virgin Islands, Dead Chest Island, was the place where Blackbeard left fifteen mutinous members of his crew to die.

Modern times. When slavery was abolished in the West Indies during the 1800s, Chinese,

PEOPLE IN HISTORY
Balboa's Discovery of the Pacific Ocean

After Columbus discovered the West Indies, Vasco Núñez de **Balboa** [băl·bō′ə: 1475–1519], like many other young Spaniards, decided to leave his homeland and seek his fortune in the new land. On September 26, 1513, he became the first European to view the Pacific Ocean.

After sailing with a Spanish exploration party along South America's northern coast, Balboa decided to become a farmer on the Spanish-controlled island of Haiti. Later, he sailed to what is today southern Panama and established a settlement there.

When Spain's King Ferdinand heard about the new settlement, he made Balboa the governor. Balboa learned from the natives that a huge sea and a land of gold lay to the south. (They were describing the Inca Empire in Peru.) After three weeks of traveling west over the rough terrain of the Isthmus of Panama, Balboa climbed alone to the top of a mountain to take his first view of the Pacific Ocean. Three days later, he and his party worked their way to the ocean's edge, where Balboa waded into the water up to his knees. He named the ocean the "South Sea" and claimed it for Spain. About seven years later, the Spanish explorer **Magellan** renamed the South Sea the **Pacific Ocean** (*Pacific* means "peaceful") because of its seeming calmness.

crowded marketplace on Saint Lucia

Portuguese, Spanish, and East Indian laborers went to the islands to work in the plantations. Thousands of East Indians (from India) went to the Lesser Antilles [ăn·tĭl′ēz], especially Trinidad, Jamaica, Martinique [mär′tĭ·nēk′], and Guadeloupe [gwŏd′l-o͞op′]. They were hard workers and adapted well to the Caribbean climate. Today, more than one third of the people of Trinidad are of East Indian ancestry, and most of these are followers of the Hindu or Muslim religions. The majority of the people of the West Indies, however, are the descendants of black slaves and most are either Protestant or Catholic.

The United States gained control of Cuba and Puerto Rico as a result of the Spanish-American War in 1898. In 1916, Denmark transferred control of some of the Virgin Islands to the United States. Puerto Rico and the western Virgin Islands are still a part of the United States, but Cuba came under a Communist dictatorship. The people of Puerto Rico and the U.S. Virgin Islands are United States citizens, although these areas are not states. St. Croix, one of the Virgin Islands, is the easternmost point of the United States. The eastern Virgin Islands are a dependency of Great Britain.

Today, most of the larger islands in the West Indies are independent, with a wide variety of governments. Others belong to Great Britain, France, the Netherlands, and the United States.

With the opening of the Panama Canal in 1914, the Caribbean Sea became the busiest shipping route in the Western Hemisphere. Nearly half of all United States trade today passes through the Panama Canal or the Gulf of Mexico. Two thirds of the oil imported by the United States comes through these routes, as do more than half of the metals needed for building defensive weapons. This is one reason why the United States is interested in helping the West Indies to remain financially stable and free from further Communist dictatorships.

Comprehension Check 16A
Identify
1. The date Columbus first sighted land in the New World and the place where he landed.
2. The Spanish monarchs who funded Columbus's expedition.
3. The first European to view the Pacific Ocean.

The West Indies: Islands of the Caribbean Sea

16.2 EXPLORING THE WEST INDIES
Islands of Mountains and Coral

An archipelago. The West Indies form an *archipelago* [är′kə·pĕl′ə·gō: group or chain of many islands] about 2,500 miles long in the **Caribbean Sea.** They separate the Atlantic Ocean from the Caribbean Sea. There are thousands of islands in the West Indies, most of which are very small. Cuba, the largest, covers over half the land area. Cuba's coastline is 2,100 miles long. Many of the islands, in contrast, are only a few square miles in area.

The Antilles and the Bahamas. The West Indies are divided into three groups: the Greater Antilles, the Bahamas, and the Lesser Antilles. The **Greater Antilles** include Cuba, Hispaniola (today shared by Haiti and the Dominican Republic), Jamaica, and Puerto Rico. The **Bahamas** lie northwest of the Greater Antilles. The **Lesser Antilles** include the Virgin Islands, the Leeward Islands, the Windward Islands, Barbados [bär·bā′dōs], Trinidad, Tobago [tə·bā′gō], and the Netherlands Antilles.

A fourth group of islands, the **Bermudas** [bər·myoo′dəz], are not actually a part of the West Indies, but they are often included with the West Indies. The Bermuda Islands are in the Atlantic Ocean, about 580 miles southeast of North Carolina. (Locate them on the atlas map of North America.) Bermuda is a self-governing British dependency.

Mount Pelée is one of several active volcanoes in the Caribbean.

Volcanoes. The Greater and Lesser Antilles are mountainous and have fertile soil and great forests. They are actually the peaks of an underwater mountain chain that may have once linked North America and South America. Most of the islands are volcanic. Several volcanoes are still active, including **Mount Pelée** [pə·lā′] on Martinique. Mount Pelée erupted violently in 1902, destroying the town of St. Pierre [sănt′ pĭr′] and killing about 38,000 people.

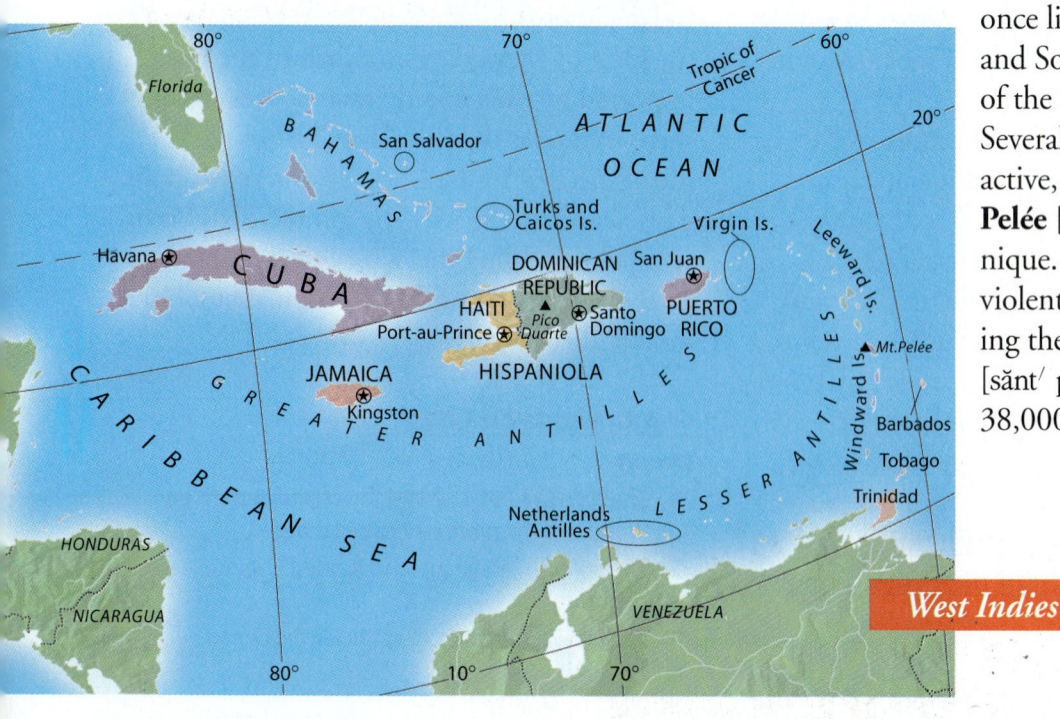

West Indies

296 New World History & Geography

Coral reefs. The Bahamas are flat and sandy because they are made of *coral*. Coral reefs also fringe the waters around many of the other islands. **Coral reefs,** which usually form in shallow tropical waters, are colorful formations created by millions of tiny animals called **polyps,** which secrete limestone (calcium carbonate) into the water. Common corals found in the Caribbean Sea are fire coral, finger coral, elkhorn, sea fans, and sea whips.

Colorful Creatures

Tropical fish. Many tropical fish swim among the coral reefs. Some of these fish eventually find their way to aquarium tanks around the world. Other tropical fish such as **guppies** and **angelfish** live in freshwater streams, lakes, and rivers along the tropical coasts. Guppies are some of the most common tropical fish found in the West Indies and South America.

Shellfish. The conch [kŏngk], a sea snail, houses its soft, meaty body in the world's largest shell, a beautiful spiral-shaped shell that is prized by people for many reasons. The **queen conch,** called *lambi* by the West Indians, can be over a foot long. The islanders pound its meat to make it tender and then eat it. When irritating particles get inside its rosy pink shell, the queen conch will produce pink pearls. The **horse conch** has the largest shell found in American waters—this snail produces shells that can be over two feet long! One type of **helmet shell** resembles a large, white helmet. Layers of white shell cover its inner brown shell. The helmet shell is often exported and used for cameos.

coral reef

Other sea life. Some large sea animals of the Caribbean waters include marlin, wahoo, barracuda, and dolphin. The **dolphin** is a mammal that looks like a whale or porpoise but has a beaklike snout. The **marlin** is a fish with a spearlike snout up to two feet long. The **wahoo** has a protruding snout and often grows over five feet long and weighs over 140 pounds. Commercial catches of the Caribbean include sardine, tuna, and spiny lobster. **Manta rays** and **sea turtles** are also common.

Life on land. Tropical plants such as **coconut palms,** mangoes, cacao, wild orchids, and sugar cane are plentiful on the islands, and **mangroves** stand around lagoons and *estuaries* (the wide mouths of rivers where the tide meets the current). The high islands—Cuba, Jamaica, and Puerto Rico—are topped by **tropical rain forests.** On the dry sides of many islands, cacti grow. **Parrots, parakeets,** and **toucans** add bright flashes of color to the landscape.

a man harvesting sugar cane

Pleasant Climate Punctuated with Hurricanes

The West Indies have a very pleasant climate. Although all of the islands but the Bahamas are located in the Tropics, they have a temperate climate all year long. Temperatures on the coasts average between 70° and 85°F. The pleasant temperature range is caused by the *trade winds,* winds that blow steadily toward the equator. In the Tropics north of the equator, such as the West Indies, trade winds blow from the northeast. South of the equator, they blow from the southeast.

Because of their location, the West Indies are occasionally hit by tropical storms called *hurricanes.* Hurricanes have some of the strongest winds on earth. They are violent storms (low pressure systems) that form over warm ocean water and usually move toward land. Many people may be killed when a hurricane strikes because of its heavy rains and winds of 74 to 125 (or more) miles per hour. Hurricanes hit the Caribbean Sea and the Gulf of Mexico about eight times a year. The hurricane season is from June to the end of November, and hurricanes occur most frequently in August and September.

In the North Pacific Ocean, a hurricane is called a *typhoon.* In the South Pacific Ocean or the Indian Ocean, it is called a *cyclone.*

Industry

Sugar cane. Sugar is made by all plants, but the sugar cane, a grassy plant that looks like bamboo, is an especially valuable commercial source of sugar. This plant grows in warm, moist areas around the world. Brazil, India, and Cuba are the world's leading cane sugar producers, but Hawaii actually produces the richest sugar cane crops. Sugar is the main product of the West Indies. *Bananas, coffee, cacoa, tobacco,* and *petroleum* are also important.

Tourism. The major industry of most of the islands is **tourism.** The islands of the West Indies are among the world's principal winter vacation areas. People visit the islands to enjoy the climate, the beautiful scenery, the sparkling beaches and turquoise blue water, the many good snorkeling areas, and the important historical sites.

Comprehension Check 16B

Identify
1. Three island groups that form the West Indies.
2. Four large islands that make up the Greater Antilles.
3. Name of the volcano that erupted in 1902, destroying St. Pierre.

Think
4. Why are hurricanes devastating to the islands of the West Indies?

16.3 People and Islands

Puerto Rico

Discovery. Did you know that Puerto Rico is the only part of the United States that Columbus ever visited? Columbus discovered this lovely island on November 19, 1493. In 1508, fifteen years after Columbus claimed Puerto Rico for Spain, Juan Ponce de León [wän pŏns′ də lē′ən], the discoverer of Florida, led Spanish settlers to the island.

United States citizens. Puerto Rico became a United States possession in 1898, after the Spanish-American War. In 1917, Puerto Ricans became citizens of the United States, and in 1952 the island became a self-governing territory, the Commonwealth of Puerto Rico. Like all United States citizens, Puerto Ricans are free to travel throughout the United States without passports and to move to any place they wish in the country. They do not pay federal income taxes, however, and while living on the island they do not vote in Presidential elections.

Most Puerto Ricans are Roman Catholic and are of Spanish ancestry. Although Spanish and English are both official languages, most people speak Spanish; English is taught in many of the schools.

Industrious island. Puerto Rico's economy is closely associated with that of the United States, and the people have a higher standard of living than the people in the rest of the West Indies. Manufacturing, agriculture, and tourism are the island's leading industries. The country exports large amounts of medicinal drugs; in fact, approximately half of the prescription drugs used in the United States are manufactured on this island. Sugar cane, coffee, and tobacco are among the most valuable crops. Every year, millions of tourists come to enjoy the island's tropical climate and such attractions as Luquillo [lōō·kē′yō] Beach, El Yunque [ĕl yŏong′kā] peak, and El Morro [ĕl môr′ō] Fortress. Because of the island's dense population, few wild animals roam the Puerto Rican countryside. One interesting animal resident, a small frog called the *coquí* [kō·kē′], sings like a bird through the night.

"John is his name." When Columbus discovered the island, he named it San Juan Bautista [săn wän bou·tēs′tä] after John the Baptist. The commonwealth's motto, *Juan Est Nomen Ejus* (Spanish for "John is his name"), is taken from Luke 1:63. **San Juan,** the capital and largest city, is also named for John the Baptist. San Juan became the capital

El Morro is a Spanish fort built in the 16th century to defend Puerto Rico against the Carib Indians.

The West Indies: Islands of the Caribbean Sea

in 1521, ninety-nine years before the Pilgrims landed in Massachusetts. The city was originally known as *Puerto Rico,* meaning "Rich Port." The island later inherited the name, and the city became known as *San Juan.*

This Jamaican is climbing down from a pimento tree. The berries of this tree are used to make pimento spice.

Jamaica

Jamaica's name comes from an Arawak Indian word meaning *"Island of Springs."* Over 120 rivers and streams flow from the mountains down to the island's coasts, creating much rich farmland.

Resources and industries. Jamaicans grow sugar cane, bananas, coffee, cacao, citrus fruits, and coconuts. Much of the world's supply of **pimento spice** (also called allspice or Jamaican pepper) comes from Jamaica. (This spice is not the same as the pimento that is used for stuffing green olives.) Jamaica is also one of the world's largest producers of *bauxite,* an ore used for making aluminum. Jamaica attracts many *tourists* with its sparkling Caribbean beaches and luxurious resorts.

Baptist missions. You have already learned that in 1779, a freed black slave from the United States named **George Liele** went to Jamaica to preach the gospel. He labored with his hands to earn his support. Although he and his followers were greatly persecuted, he kept preaching and eventually founded a number of Baptist churches for the black people of Jamaica.

One of the early English missions to Jamaica began in 1820 with the help of money that **Robert Boyle,** the great English scientist and Christian, had left in his will over a hundred years earlier. Boyle had said that he wanted the money to be used for spreading the gospel to foreign lands.

By 1839, there were close to 25,000 Baptists in Jamaica. The Jamaican Baptists established a school in Jamaica for training pastors and missionaries and sent a number of missionaries to Africa. Many Jamaican Christians made great sacrifices for the cause of Christ. In 1859, a great spiritual revival spread through the island. People crowded into the churches, and many came to Christ. Crime decreased, the practice of Christian standards increased, and old superstitions lost their grip on many people.

People of variety. The Jamaican national motto is "Out of Many, One People." The "many" include people of African, European, Asian, and Syrian descent. Most Jamaicans are black or mulatto and most speak a **dialect of English** which combines African, Spanish, and French words with English grammar and vocabulary.

British Commonwealth. Jamaica was a British colony until the country gained independence in 1962. The island is now a member of the British Commonwealth of Nations. **Kingston** is the capital city.

Hispaniola: Home of Haiti and the Dominican Republic

The second largest island in the West Indies, **Hispaniola,** was discovered by Columbus on his first voyage. This island is divided into two countries—**Haiti** in the west and the **Dominican Republic** in the east.

300 *New World History & Geography*

Haiti. Haiti is one of the oldest black republics in the world and the second oldest independent nation in the Western Hemisphere (after the United States). Haiti's name means "high ground"; the island is mostly mountainous. **Port-au-Prince** [pôrt′ō·prĭns′] is the chief seaport and the capital city. Most Haitians are the descendants of African slaves. The official languages are *French* and *Haitian Creole,* which is French that has been mixed with an African dialect. Many Haitians practice **voodoo,** a religion of sorcery and charms that originated in Africa. The country is poor, and many people live in deep poverty.

Dominican Republic. The Dominican Republic, which takes up the eastern two thirds of Hispaniola, is the most mountainous country of the West Indies. In its center stands the highest peak in the West Indies, **Pico Duarte** [pē′kō dwär′tā: 10,417 feet]. Columbus established the first European colony in the New World, Isabela, in the Dominican Republic. After a hurricane destroyed Isabela, the city was rebuilt in a different location and called **Santo Domingo** [săn′tō də·mĭng′gō]. Santo Domingo, the capital and largest city, is the home of the oldest university in the Western Hemisphere (established 1538). About one half of the people of the Dominican Republic work in agriculture. In the fertile plains, they grow sugar, tropical fruits, and tobacco. Mountain crops include coffee and cacao. Three fourths of the **sugar cane** crop, the most important crop, is exported to the United States.

The Bahama Islands

San Salvador, an island in the Bahamas, is probably the place where Columbus first landed in the New World before going to Cuba and Hispaniola. The Bahamas is an archipelago of approximately 700 islands and 2,300 islets [ī·lĕts: very small islands] and coral reefs. Their name comes from a Spanish word meaning *"shallow water."* The closest island is about 60 miles from Florida. Only about twenty-two islands are inhabited. The largest island is Andros, but almost all the people live on New Providence or Grand Bahama. The capital and largest city, **Nassau** [năs′ô], is on New Providence.

Because little of the land in the Bahamas is suitable for cultivation, only about two percent of the Bahamians are farmers, and most food must be imported. The Bahamas serve as a center for international banking, but **tourism** is the main industry of the islands. Every year thousands of tourists flock to the Bahamas from the nearby North American mainland to enjoy the warm climate, beautiful beaches, and luxury resorts. At Nassau's famous **straw market,** Bahamians sell straw mats, purses, baskets, and hats that they have made and decorated.

The majority of Bahamians have descended from either African slaves or British Loyalists. (Many Loyalists, American colonists loyal to the English king, moved to the

woman selling straw baskets and mats at Nassau's straw market, Bahamas

Bahamas

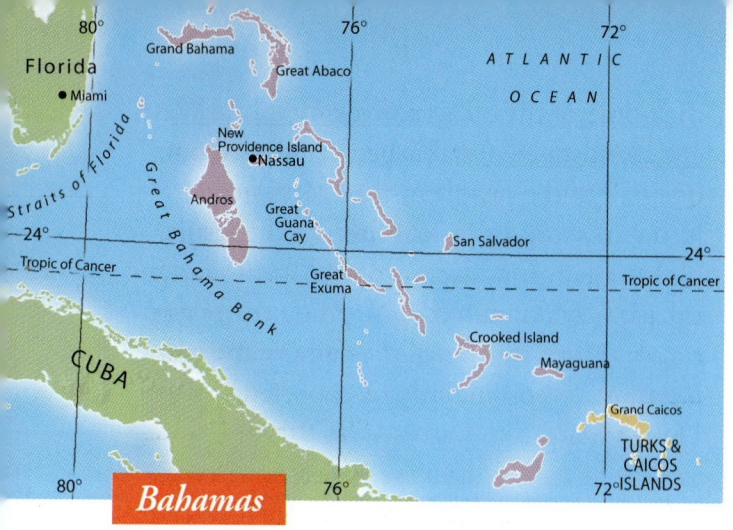

Bahamas after the American War for Independence.) More than four fifths of the inhabitants are black; most others are white or mulattoes. The main language of the Bahamas is English, the country's official language. <u>Many people belong to Baptist churches, which form the largest church group in the Bahamas.</u>

Spaniards shipped the native Arawak people to plantations elsewhere in the West Indies. The country later became a British colony, and cotton was grown on plantations. In 1973, the Bahamas became independent of Great Britain. The government is patterned after a constitutional monarchy, like England. As an independent member of the Commonwealth of Nations, the Bahamas are given a governor general to represent Britain. The governor general appoints a prime minister to rule as chief executive.

Comprehension Check 16C

Identify
1. The large island south of Cuba where George Liele preached.
2. The two nations that make up the island of Hispaniola.
3. An archipelago of 700 islands lying east of Florida.

Think
4. As citizens of the United States, what are some of the rights Puerto Ricans enjoy?

Virgin Islands

Discovery and settlement. Before Europeans came to the Virgin Islands, fierce Carib Indians lived there. Columbus discovered the islands in 1493 when, on his second voyage, he landed on St. Croix [kroi], which he called Santa Cruz [săn′tə kroōz]. However, the Spanish did not settle the islands. In 1672, the British gained control of the northeastern Virgin Islands. The first British to land on the islands were the settlers who came to Jamestown, the first successful colony in the United States. Denmark founded settlements on St. Thomas in 1625 and St. John in 1717 and bought St. Croix from the French in 1733. Combined, St. John, St. Croix, and St. Thomas were known as the **Danish West Indies.**

Moravian missionaries. In 1730, a black man from the Danish West Indies went to Copenhagen, Denmark, where he met **Count von Zinzendorf,** the great leader of the Moravian church. The West Indian told the count that missionaries would be welcome on his island. Count von Zinzendorf was deeply touched. When he returned to his home in Germany, he told his followers what he had heard. In 1732, two Moravian mission-

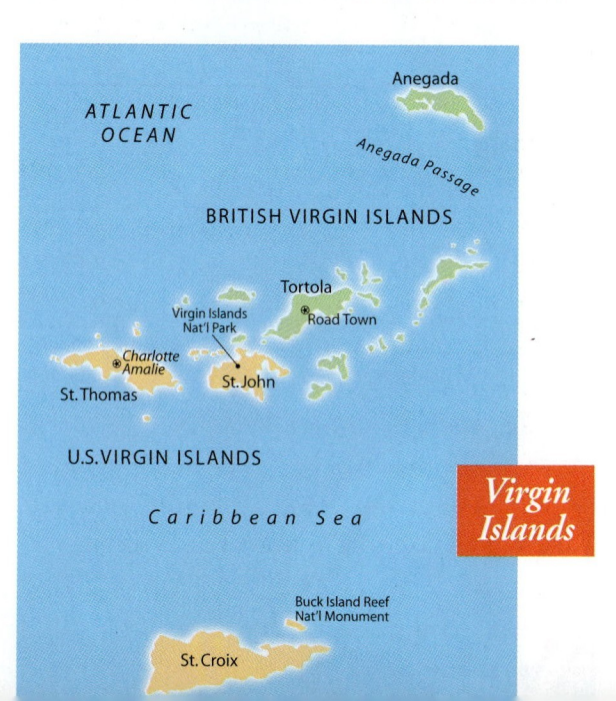

302 New World History & Geography

A diver is surrounded by yellow-tail snapper.

aries arrived on the island of St. Thomas. These two Moravians were some of the very first foreign missionaries of modern times. Others joined them later, and missionary stations were established on several islands.

The islands today. The northeastern Virgin Islands remained under British control and are known today as the **British Virgin Islands.** Denmark sold the southwestern Virgin Islands to the United States in 1917 for twenty-five million dollars. The United States later used the Virgin Islands as a base for protecting the Panama Canal during World War II. The **United States Virgin Islands** is made up of fifty tiny islands and three larger islands, **St. Croix, St. John,** and **St. Thomas.** The capital and largest city, Charlotte Amalie [shär′lət ə·mäl′yə], is located on St. Thomas. The U.S. Virgin Islands is the only United States possession where the people drive on the left side of the road. The people are of many racial backgrounds, but they speak one language—**English.**

Tourism. The economies of both the British and United States Virgin Islands depend heavily on tourism. **Virgin Islands National Park,** on St. John, St. Thomas, and some of the smaller islands, is part of the United States National Park System. It is a favorite tourist spot because of its sparkling waters and lush tropical growth, which includes mangoes, coconut palms, cacao, wild orchids, and sugar cane. **Buck Island,** near St. Croix, is a favorite place for scuba diving. Many tropical fish are taken from Buck Island.

Few natural resources. The Virgin Islands has few natural resources. The people sometimes have to buy imported bottled water because the islands are too small for many freshwater streams. There is little manufacturing, but the people do raise food crops and other crops, such as bananas and sugar cane, for exportation.

The Leeward Islands

The Leeward Islands, a portion of the Lesser Antilles, consist of the islands which lie east and southeast of Puerto Rico, including the Virgin Islands, Anguilla [ang·gwĭl′ə], Barbados, Antigua [ăn·tē′gə] and Barbuda [bär·bōō′də], Guadeloupe, Dominica, and a number of smaller islands.

Antigua and Barbuda. Antigua and Barbuda is a small country composed of three islands—Antigua, Barbados, and Redonda [rĭ·dän′də]. (Uninhabited Redonda is only half of a square mile, but it rises 1,000 feet above the ocean.) Antigua was one of the first Caribbean islands to promote tourism, which is now the economy's mainstay. Britain colonized the islands of Antigua and Barbuda in the 1600s; it became an independent country in 1981. The majority of the people are black and the official language is English.

Antigua, a British possession, became the strongest center of Christianity among the blacks of the West Indies during the late 1700s. This was largely due to the efforts of three men. Nathaniel Gilbert, a planter

The West Indies: Islands of the Caribbean Sea 303

and lawyer of Antigua who came to Christ under the ministry of the great English preacher John Wesley, returned to Antigua and preached to the slaves for many years. After he died, John Baxter went to Antigua to work as a ship builder and to preach during his spare time. By 1786, there were about 2,000 Methodists in Antigua, most of them blacks. That year, **Thomas Coke,** a good friend of John Wesley, visited the island. He was so excited by the Christian work he saw there that he visited the islands five times, each time bringing new missionaries from England. This great-hearted man, whom John Wesley called his "right hand," is remembered as the founder of Methodist missions. He died on his way to missionary work in India in 1814.

Guadeloupe. Guadeloupe, an overseas department (much like a state) of France, consists of two main islands, Basse-Terre [băs·târ′] and Grande-Terre [grăn′târ′], and a number of smaller islands. French colonists settled in Guadeloupe in 1635. British settlers followed, and black African slaves were brought to work on the plantations. Agriculture remains the main industry today. Guadeloupe exports bananas, sugar cane, coffee, and other products, but France has been forced to support the economy. The islands are governed by a prefect (much like a governor) and an elected council and are represented in the French National Assembly in France.

Dominica. Christopher Columbus discovered the mountainous island of Dominica on Sunday, November 3, 1493, and called it *Dominica,* the Latin word for "the Lord's Day," or "Sunday." The French, the British, and the Carib Indians fought over the island until Britain finally won control of Dominica in 1783. Like many of the European colonists in the West Indies, the British settlers on Dominica brought slaves from Africa to work on their banana and coconut farms. Britain granted Dominica its freedom in 1978 and the island became an independent republic. In 1979, a hurricane devastated the island. Today, most Dominicans are of African or mixed (French, British, African) descent. English is the country's official language.

The Windward Islands

The Windward Islands, also a portion of the Lesser Antilles, lie south of the Leeward Islands and include Martinique, St. Lucia, St. Vincent, Barbados, Grenada [grə·nā′də], and many smaller islands.

Grenada. Grenada, one of the Windward Islands, is sometimes called the Isle of Spice because of its leading world role in producing **nutmeg** and other spices. Nutmeg production is honored on Grenada's flag by a yellow and brown nutmeg design. Grenada became

304 *New World History & Geography*

independent of Britain in 1974, although it still keeps ties to the United Kingdom. In the early 1980s, Cuba tried to bring the people of this little island under Communist control. Surrounding island nations, realizing the threat to their own freedom, cried out to the United States for help. When President Ronald Reagan learned in 1983 that the Cubans were setting up an airstrip in Grenada to invade two South American nations, he sent American soldiers to free the islanders from the Communists. Several Caribbean nations assisted the United States in the liberation of Grenada, including Antigua, Barbados, Barbuda, Dominica, and Jamaica. The people of Grenada welcomed their rescuers as national heroes.

Barbados. Barbados lies the farthest east of all the West Indian islands, about 250 miles off the coast of Venezuela. With over six hundred people per square mile, it is one of the world's most densely populated countries. About eighty percent of the people are descendants of black slaves, but they follow an English way of life. The majority belong to the Church of England, and like the English people, they drive on the left side of the street. Barbados has one of the highest literacy rates in the West Indies—97 percent of the adults can read and write.

Netherlands Antilles

The Dutch West Indies, or Netherlands Antilles, consists of a small group of islands east of Puerto Rico in the Leeward Island chain and a larger group fifty miles north of Venezuela. **Aruba** [ə·rōō′bə], **Curaçao** [kōōr′ə·sou′], and **Bonaire** [bô·nâr′], all near Venezuela, are the largest islands. Important oil refineries located on Curaçao and Aruba refine oil shipped from Venezuela. Dutch, English, and Spanish are all spoken on the islands, as well as a mixture of the three languages called *Papiamento* [pä′pyə·měn′tō]. The Netherlands Antilles have a partnership with the kingdom of the Netherlands.

Trinidad and Tobago

The islands of Trinidad [trĭn′ĭ·dăd′] and Tobago lie just a few miles off the northeast coast of Venezuela. Columbus discovered Trinidad in 1498 and claimed the island for

These plant workers in Grenada peel the red-colored mace from the husked nutmeg.

Spain. The Spanish began to settle the island in 1592. The Dutch colonized the nearby island of Tobago shortly afterward. During the late 1700s, Spain offered land on Trinidad to Roman Catholic settlers from other countries, bringing many French colonists from Haiti and other islands in the West Indies. Britain took control of the island in 1797 and captured Tobago by 1802. For many years, African slaves made up the majority of the islands' work force. Then, in 1834, Britain abolished slavery and workers from India came to replace the African slaves, introducing yet another culture to the islands' diverse population. Trinidad and Tobago became a united British colony in 1888 and finally, in 1962, the islands won independence. In 1976, the islands became a republic and a member of the Commonwealth of Nations. Today, the nation's economy depends heavily on its oil production and refining. The population is a mix of blacks, East Indians, and whites. Many tourists come to enjoy the tropical beauty and colorful cultures of the islands. Some say that Tobago was the island Daniel Defoe had in mind when he wrote *Robinson Crusoe*.

Comprehension Check 16D

Identify

1. The two divisions of the Virgin Islands.
2. The large island group to which the Virgin Islands, Leeward Islands, and Windward Islands belong.

Think

3. How did the gospel come to the Virgin Islands?

16.4 CUBA: COUNTRY UNDER COMMUNIST DICTATORSHIP

Cuba, the largest island in the West Indies (about the size of Pennsylvania), is located only ninety miles south of Key West, Florida. **Havana** is the nation's capital and largest city. This city has a rich cultural heritage, as seen by the Spanish customs and architecture that still linger there. Cuba includes over a thousand smaller islands. Most Cubans live on the main island, although a few live on the Isle of Youth (formerly known as the Isle of Pines). About three fourths of the Cubans are Spanish; others are black or mulatto. The official language is **Spanish.** Among other things, Cuba is known as the home of the **bee hummingbird,** the smallest bird in the world. (It has a wingspan of only one inch, and its nest is the size of half a walnut shell.) Cuba is probably best known, however, as home of the first Communist government in the Western Hemisphere.

From Colony to Nation

Discovery and settlement. Columbus discovered Cuba and claimed the island for Spain on his first voyage to the New World. Within twenty years, Spanish settlers were farming

Cathedral Square in Havana, Cuba

Fidel Castro speaking to a crowd in Havana

the island's fertile soil. Soon Cuba was one of the wealthiest colonies in the West Indies. The desire for independence increased among the Cubans, and several revolts were attempted against Spain. The United States offered to buy the island, but Spain refused to sell. Finally, with help from the United States, the Cubans won independence from Spain in 1898 after the Spanish-American War.

Struggling young nation. For a while, the United States government ruled the island. In the early 1900s, the United States allowed Cuba to form its own government under American supervision. The new republic suffered several uprisings in the following years until a revolution in the early 1930s established a dictatorship under Fulgencio Batista [fool·hän′syō bə·tēs′tə]. The United States eventually supported Batista, and retained only one important naval base at **Guantánamo Bay.**

The Coming of Communism

Rise of Castro. In 1959, **Fidel Castro** [fē·thĕl′ käs′trō], backed by the Soviet Union, overthrew Batista's dictatorship. Castro told the Cubans that he wanted to make them free. They soon found out that he was not telling them the truth. Instead of giving the people a free government, Castro set up a Communist government with himself as the ruler. He called himself "prime minister," and later "president," but in reality he was a dictator far more cruel than the man from whom he had supposedly delivered the Cuban people.

Many refugees. Hundreds of thousands of Cubans left their land to escape the terrors of Communism. Most fled to the United States; others went to Spain, Mexico, and Puerto Rico. These intelligent, hard-working people did well in their new lands and enriched the countries to which they fled. Many became business owners, bank presidents, and medical doctors. Why did so many Cubans leave their lovely tropical island home? They left because of the terrible living conditions that Communism brings and the repression of liberty that always results from Communist rule.

Thought Control in the Church and School

Suppression of religion. Many Christians and church leaders fled Cuba in 1961, the year that Castro openly declared his country to be Communist. They knew that Communism always brings religious persecution. Be-

The West Indies: Islands of the Caribbean Sea

Cuban school children

cause Communists are **atheists** (people who do not believe there is a God), they cannot tolerate Christianity. Castro allowed a few churches in Cuba to stay open, but few people went to church anymore because they knew they would be fired from their jobs or persecuted in other ways if they did. Christmas celebrations were outlawed, and most signs of spiritual life disappeared. "Our people do not care anymore for religion," boasted the Communist bosses. "We are materialists."

Indoctrination of schoolchildren. Cuban children were put into boarding schools. From kindergarten up, they were taught atheism and other false Communist ideas in their schools and clubs. Communist teachers encouraged the children to spy on their parents and taught them that Cuba must fight to spread Communism around the world.

Living in Confinement

No freedom. Communist revolutions are called "liberation movements" by their leaders. *Liberation* means "freedom." But Communism does not *bring* freedom, it *takes freedom away.* When Castro took over Cuba, he took away many freedoms, including:
- freedom of the press
- the right to trial by jury
- the right to own property
- the right to make a profit
- the right to vote
- the right to fair treatment and freedom from fear.

A "big, dark jail." Communism always rules by force and fear. Once Fidel Castro gained power, there were no more real elections in Cuba. He chose all of the leaders and ruled the country by a system of fear and suppression. Castro sent Cuban leaders to Russia and Czechoslovakia to learn how to keep people under control in a Communist state. They learned so well that Cuba has been called a "big, dark jail." Specially trained Cubans in every city and village watched their neighbors closely and reported suspicious activities to the government. The secret police also watched everyone's actions and dealt harshly with anyone whom they suspected of disagreeing with Castro. Over five thousand people were shot to death for not accepting Communism, and many more were cruelly beaten in public places. "To live in Cuba is to live in fear," the people said.

Prisons and torture. At least twenty thousand people were put in Cuban jails for disagreeing with the Communist rule. These political prisoners were given long sentences—ten, twenty, or even thirty years. Sometimes when they finished serving one sentence, they were immediately given another. The prisoners were forced to work seventy or eighty hours a week, and many were tortured, some to death. Others died because they were denied medical aid, and some were experimented on by Communist doctors. Many prisoners developed terrible diseases because of deplorable conditions, lack of wholesome food, and cruel beatings.

Economic Disaster

No incentive to work. The Communist government in Cuba took over all industries, banks, and small businesses. Everyone in Cuba had a job, but that did not mean that everyone worked. Under a Communist system, everyone gets paid whether he works hard or not. Because the Cubans were not rewarded for good work, they spent much of their time just trying to avoid the harsh punishments given by the Communist Party bosses.

People usually work hard if they know they will profit from their work. Communism, however, causes people to become lazy and dishonest. They feel that the only way they can show that they do not accept Communism is by not caring how well or how fast they do a job. Many people are absent from work or late to work each day. Poverty, hunger, fear, and suspicion are the results.

Even Castro eventually had to admit that Cuban workers had become lazy and undisciplined. He complained that they were "more enthusiastic about serving in Angola or Ethiopia than in doing a day's work at home." One Cuban explained the reason: "We are willing to go to Africa because you can accomplish something overseas. At home, the Communist system frustrates us."

The young people suffered especially because they never learned the habit of honest work. They had schooling, clothing, and medical care provided; thus they saw no need to work for anything. Some young people became so bored with this lazy life that they committed suicide. Others turned to alcohol, drugs, or robbery.

Lack of food. Blessed with rich farmland and a warm, moist climate, Cuba had always produced fine crops of sugar cane, pineapples, rice, citrus fruits, and vegetables. Under Communism, however, Cuba suffered serious crop failures. This happens in any country ruled by Communism. The government takes over almost all private farmland and forces the people to work for the state. Without the incentive of personal profit, the farmers produce far less than they did when they were free.

Food in Cuba had to be **rationed,** meaning that the people were given a fixed daily allowance of food. They could have only the small amounts of food the government allowed, and no more. Many times, the rations ran out. People sometimes had to spend two hours a day standing in long lines in grocery stores where the shelves were almost empty, except for a few basic items. Children over seven were not allowed any milk to drink, and sometimes there was no milk for the babies. To keep from starving, the people bought food from the black market, an illegal, un-

Because food was rationed, it was common for people to wait in line for the arrival of things like produce. A ration card was needed to get vegetables. This photograph was taken in 1964.

derground system for the exchange of goods, developed to avoid governmental regulations.

Housing shortage. Communism also caused a severe housing shortage in Cuba. According to Communist teaching, people should not be allowed to buy houses—they must live in apartments owned by the government. Two or more families often had to live in the same small apartment. A family of four might have a tiny living room with a refrigerator and a table and chairs; a curtained-off cooking area; a tiny patio for washing and hanging clothes; and a bedroom with just enough room for a double bed for the parents, a bunk bed for the children, and one dresser for the whole family. Because of the housing shortage, the family might have to share these quarters with another family!

Waiting in line. Whatever the Cubans needed—food, medical care, mail delivery, clothing, housing repairs, permission to travel to the next town—had to be approved by the Committees for the Defense of the Revolution. If these Communist committees did not like a person, they could refuse to give him his needs, thus forcing all but the very strongest to bow to Communism. The common people in Cuba had to wait in line for everything. Few of them owned automobiles, and they sometimes had to wait four hours a day for buses to take them to work and back. Even after long waits for goods, the goods were sometimes not available. Gasoline and clothing were rationed, and books were not allowed unless they agreed with Communist teachings. Because of the Communist system, few new things were manufactured after Castro took over. Almost everything—cars, clothing, appliances, school materials, medical equipment—was old and shabby.

Inequality and Its Consequences

Unequal treatment. The Communist system was supposed to treat everyone as equals. In actuality, about one fifth of the people were treated far, far better than the rest. Such inequality has been the case in all countries that have been ruled by Communism. The

Communist Party bosses, people in high ranks in the armed forces, business managers, and students who were training to be Communist leaders made up this privileged class. They lived in luxury compared to the common people. They were treated to expensive clothing, plush vacation retreats, homes with private swimming pools, and the very best food. Unlike other Cubans, they were allowed to travel to other countries, and they were among the few who owned automobiles.

Increased crime. Because so few things were available in the stores for the common Cubans, stealing became widespread. To escape punishment, thieves bribed the police. Many robberies took place in the neighborhoods of the privileged class. Since the people had largely abandoned all religious principles, they simply took the things that they could not get any other way. The officials also worried that the widespread alcoholism that had plagued other Communist countries would infest Cuba.

The Desire and Need for Capitalism

Vision of a better life. Castro called the Cubans who left their island for a better life in free countries *gusanos* [gōō·sä′nōs], or "worms." When some of these exiles were allowed to return to Cuba for a short visit with their relatives, however, the Cuban people called them *gusanos de seda* [dā sā′də], or "silkworms." Castro had been telling the Cubans who stayed behind that those who fled to the United States were trodden underfoot and kept in poverty by the Americans. When these people returned for visits, it was obvious to all that they were living like rich people in America in comparison to Cuban standards. The exiles had better clothes, more luxuries, and of course, far more freedom than anyone who stayed in Cuba. Soon the Cubans were saying that the *gusanos* had been transformed into *mariposas* [mä·rē·pō′säs: butterflies]. "The Cuban Communist government is not for the people," they lamented. "The revolution brought us nothing but misery and fear."

A group of desperate Cubans set sail on a raft bound for Florida, fleeing the regime of Fidel Castro.

The West Indies: Islands of the Caribbean Sea

CONCEPTS TO CONSIDER
A Study in Contrasts between Free and Communist Countries

Free Countries	Communist Countries
1. **People are free to worship God in the way they think is right.** This is the most important right guaranteed to Americans by the Constitution of the United States.	**The Communists say that there is no God.** Because Communists do not believe in God, they do not allow religious freedom.
2. **People have the right to free speech and press.** Newspapers, televisions, and radio stations in the United States are free to report the news as they see it and to make their own comments on it.	**Communists control all newspapers, televisions, and radios in the countries they rule.** People are told by the government how to think and what to read and listen to.
3. **Families have the right to privacy in their homes.** In the United States, "a man's home is his castle," and no one can legally interfere with the responsibility parents have to care for their family in the way they believe is best.	**Families have very little privacy.** The Communists can go into homes at any time to make sure families are not listening to a non-Communist radio broadcast, reading the Bible, or speaking against Communism.
4. **People have the right to own private property.** Americans are allowed to own land, houses, businesses, and many other things and to use these things as they see fit.	**According to Communist teaching, property should be held in common, and there should be no private property.** The Communist Party takes homes, farms, businesses, and factories away from the people and forces them to work for the government.
5. **People have the right to move about freely at home or abroad.** Americans have great freedom in traveling within the United States and among other countries.	**People must get permission from the Communist Party to move from one place to another,** and only rarely are they allowed to travel outside the country. The people are like prisoners in their own country.
6. **People have the right to petition for grievances and expect fair and honest judgment.** If an American thinks he has been wronged or that something in the government needs to be changed, he can present his case to judges and expect to have a fair hearing.	**The benefit of the State is more important than the fair treatment of individuals.** People enslaved by Communism live in fear that the state will treat them harshly, no matter how they behave.
7. **People have the right to trial by jury; a person is innocent until proven guilty.** In America, every caution is taken to make sure a person is not punished for a crime he did not commit. An American is not responsible to prove his innocence; his accusers are responsible to prove his guilt.	**People do not have the right to trial by jury.** A person accused by the State is assumed to be guilty unless he can prove he is innocent. Even if a person is innocent, he can be punished.
8. **People have the right to free elections using personal secret ballots.** Americans have the privilege and responsibility to vote for their leaders without being pressured to vote any certain way.	**The people may sometimes vote, but they can only vote for Communists.** Sometimes they have only one Communist for which to vote. The Communist Party bosses watch them as they vote and punish them if they do not vote the "right" way. In some Communist countries, elections are not held at all.

Partial return to capitalism. By 1981, the Cubans had become so discontented with the Communist way of life that Castro allowed some capitalist (free enterprise) ideas to return to the island. He had to do this in order to prevent the whole island from sliding off into a sea of poverty. One official admitted, "For twenty years we made the mistake of rejecting everything capitalistic. Now we know that people won't work hard unless they have some incentive."

Had Castro given up on Communism? Not at all! He still suppressed religion as much as ever and controlled almost every area of the Cubans' lives. And he still tried to spread Communism to other parts of the world, even though it was a dismal failure in Cuba. He simply realized that he had to give up some of his principles in Cuba in order to survive. Without saying it, he was admitting what all thinking people know: **Communism does not work for the betterment of the people.**

Comprehension Check 16E

Identify
1. The largest island in the West Indies and its distance from Key West, Florida.
2. The smallest bird in the world.
3. Name of the Cuban dictator who established the first Communist nation in the Western Hemisphere.
4. The important document that guarantees certain rights to Americans.

Think
5. Why do Communists persecute Christians?
6. Explain why Communism is a bad economic system.

Chapter 16 Checkup

I. Identify the following.

October 12, 1492	Carib	Caribbean Sea	Pico Duarte	nutmeg
San Salvador	Isabela	Mount Pelée	Virgin Islands National Park	atheists
Arawak	Isthmus of Panama	Coral Reefs	Buck Island	rationing

II. Distinguish these **island** groups.

- Greater Antilles
- British Virgin Islands
- Netherlands Antilles
- Bahamas
- United States Virgin Islands
- Trinidad and Tobago
- Lesser Antilles
- Leeward Islands
- Virgin Islands
- Windward Islands

III. Tell why these **people** are important.

- Christopher Columbus
- Magellan
- Count von Zinzendorf
- Ferdinand and Isabella
- George Liele
- Thomas Coke
- Vasco Balboa
- Robert Boyle
- Fidel Castro

IV. Give the noted fact about these **animals.**

- queen conch
- horse conch
- marlin
- helmet shell
- dolphin
- bee hummingbird

V. Know these West Indies **capitals** and **countries.**

- San Juan, Puerto Rico
- Port-au-Prince, Haiti
- Nassau, Bahamas
- Kingston, Jamaica
- Santo Domingo, Dominican Republic
- Havana, Cuba

VI. Know the countries and important facts about them taught in this chapter.

VII. Identify the locations from **Map Mastery 16.**

The West Indies: Islands of the Caribbean Sea

VENEZUELA
COLOMBIA
Mackaw
GUYANA
SURINAM
FRENCH GUIANA

Cotopaxi volcano

ECUADOR

Ocelot

Hut by the Amazon River

Galapagos Tortoise

Hunter with poison arrows

PERU

Llama

Anaconda

BRAZIL

Tapir

Machu Picchu

Sacsahuaman Inca Fortress

Jaguar

Reed boat on Lake Titicaca

BOLIVIA

Giant anteater

Sloth

PACIFIC OCEAN

Villarica volcano

ARGENTINA

PARAGUAY

Iguacú Falls

URUGUAY

CHILI

Argentine Gaucho

Andes Mountains

Penguin

SOUTH AMERICA

Toucan

Rio Preto, Brazil

Rio de Janeiro

ATLANTIC OCEAN

- Mount Aconcagua (22,834 ft.) in Argentina is the highest peak in South America as well as the Western Hemisphere.
- South America's many waterfalls include the world's highest, Angel Falls, with a 3,212 foot drop.
- Peru and Boliva share the world's highest body of water–Lake Titicaca.
- The Amazon River is second only to the Nile River in length. However, it has the world's largest drainage basin, 2,400,000 square miles.
- Cape Horn is the southernmost point in the Americas.
- Cuzco is probably the most famous city in Peru. It was the capital city of the Incas and is home of Manchu Picchu.
- One of the driest places in the world is the Atacama Desert.
- The anaconda is the world's largest snake. The largest ever measured was 28 feet long, 44 inches around and was estimated to have weighed over 500 pounds!

chapter 17
SOUTH AMERICA
CONTINENT of NATURAL RESOURCES

17.1 EXPLORING SOUTH AMERICA

Tropical Climate and Opposite Seasons

South America, the fourth largest continent, is about twice the size of the United States. The **equator** passes through a wide region in the northern area of South America, and most of the continent lies between the Tropic of Cancer and the Tropic of Capricorn, or in the Torrid Zone. Thus the lowland regions of much of South America have year-round tropical temperatures. The southern tip of South America, however, is just six hundred miles from Antarctica and consequently has a very cold climate. Because South America is located mainly south of the equator, its seasons are opposite those of the United States and Canada: summer is from December to March, and winter is from June to September.

Many Nations and Varied Geography

Look at the map of South America on p. 318. In the north, South America is bordered by the Caribbean Sea and Panama; on the east by the Atlantic Ocean; and on the west by the Pacific Ocean. The continent is divided into twelve independent nations—**Argentina** [är′jən·tē′nə], **Bolivia** [bō·lĭv′ē·ə], **Brazil** [brə·zĭl′], **Chile** [chĭl′ē], **Colombia**, **Ecuador** [ĕk′wə·dôr], **Guyana** [gī·ăn′ə], **Suriname** [soor′ə·năm], **Paraguay** [păr′ə·gwā], **Peru** [pə·roo′], **Uruguay** [ūr′ə·gwā], and **Venezuela** [vĕn′ə·zwā′lə]—and one overseas department of France, French **Guiana** [gē·ăn′ə]. The countries vary in size from Brazil, which is as big as the continental United States, to French Guiana, which is about the size of Indiana. Each country of South America will be studied in chapter 18.

Like North America, South America has high mountains in the west, lower mountains in the east, and a great plain in the middle. Find the **Andes Mountains,** the **Brazilian Highlands,** and the **Guiana Highlands** on the map. South of the Guiana Highlands, you will see the mighty **Amazon River** and the great lowland area that it waters. Find two other lowland areas—the **Gran Chaco** [grän chä′kō] in Argentina and Paraguay and

316 New World History & Geography

The jagged peaks of the Andes pierce the clouds.

the **Pampas** in Argentina. Can you find the **Atacama Desert** along the coast of Chile? The Atacama Desert is the driest place on earth, rarely receiving a trace of rain.

Andes Mountains. The Andes Mountain Range is the longest and second highest mountain range in the world. The Andes extend from Cape Horn north for more than 5,500 miles to the Caribbean coast. If the Andes were stretched out in a straight line instead of being curved, they could reach from San Francisco across the U.S. to London! The range is 500 miles across at its widest point, and it has at least fifty peaks over 20,000 feet. Only the Himalaya Mountains of northern India and Tibet are higher. **Mount Aconcagua** [ăk′ən·kä′gwə] in Argentina is the highest mountain in the Western Hemisphere. Find it on the map. How high is it? Weather conditions vary drastically in the Andes. Tropical temperatures and year-round snows lie within a few miles of each other because of the great altitude changes. Precipitation also varies widely.

The Andes Mountain Range is not a single line of peaks but a collection of mountain ranges with intervening plateaus and depressions. The western range, near the coast, is the site of devastating volcanoes and earthquakes. Between the eastern and western ranges of Peru and Bolivia lies the famous *Altiplano* [äl′tē·plä′nō], a wide plateau that is

the Pampas

South America: Continent of Natural Resources 317

about 12,000 feet above sea level.

Islands near and far. Hundreds of islands surround South America, especially the southern part of it. At the tip of South America lies the archipelago **Tierra del Fuego** [tē·ĕr′ə dĕl fwā′gō]. The largest island in the group is separated from the mainland of South America by the **Strait of Magellan** [mə·jĕl′ən]. The **Falkland Islands** [fôk′lənd] and **South Georgia Islands** lie in the Atlantic Ocean. Much farther north, the **Galápagos Islands** [gə·lä′pə·gəs] and **Easter Island** are in the Pacific Ocean.

Varied Animal Life

South America provides a home for almost one fourth of all known kinds of animals. Although many animals live there, South America does not have any huge animals.

Mammals. The **tapir** [tā′pər], a hoglike mammal which does not grow much bigger than a pony, is the largest South American animal. The tapir's worst enemy is the **jaguar,** the largest cat in the Western Hemisphere. The **capybara** [kăp′ə·bä′rə], the largest rodent in the world, is four feet long and weighs 100 pounds. With light fur that encircles its eyes like glasses, the **spectacled bear** is the only bear in the world that lives south of the equator.

The **two-toed sloth** lives in trees in the tropical rain forests of South America. The sloth rarely comes down out of its tree because it cannot walk. It hangs upside down from tree branches and moves so slowly that its brownish fur turns green from algae. Because it spends most of its time hanging upside down,

318 New World History & Geography

◀ *two-toed sloth*
▼ *flesh-eating piranha*

the sloth's hair parts down the middle of its underside. The **giant anteater,** which weighs over 50 pounds, uses its long, sticky tongue to help trap the 30,000 ants and termites it eats every day. It also lives in the damp tropical forests.

Four types of camel-like mammals are native to South America. Although all of these are classified as camels, none of them has a hump. **Alpacas** [ăl·păk′əz], live in mountain areas of Peru and Bolivia. They have long necks and long, shaggy hair. Farmers raise alpacas for their wool, shearing them once a year and getting as much as seven pounds of wool per animal. **Guanacos** [gwä·nä′kōz] are wild animals that live in groups throughout the Andes. Like the other camel-like mammals, guanacos will spit if they are upset at something. **Llamas** [lä′məz], the largest South American camels, also live in the Andes. Adult male llamas are used as pack animals. Like Middle Eastern camels, they can be very stubborn. If a llama feels that its pack is too heavy or that it has gone far enough, it will sit down and refuse to go anywhere. **Vicuñas** [vĭ·koōn′yəz] live in the mountains of Bolivia, Chile, and Peru. These wild animals have excellent sight, speed, and endurance. Vicuñas were once hunted to the edge of extinction for their fine wool.

Reptiles and fish. Although not necessarily the longest, the **anaconda** [ăn′ə·kŏn′də] is by far the largest snake in the world because of how big it is around. The largest anaconda ever measured was 28 feet long, 44 inches around, and is estimated to have weighed over 500 pounds! **Galápagos giant tortoises** of the Galápagos Islands are among the world's oldest living creatures—they can live over 100 years. They weigh over 300 pounds each, and some weigh as much as 500 pounds. **Piranhas** [pĭ·rän′əz], small, bloodthirsty fish

South America: Continent of Natural Resources

cock-of-the-rock

of the Amazon, eat the flesh of animals. They usually attack small animals or ones that are wounded or dying, although they have been known to bite off the fingers of careless fishermen. People of the Amazon routinely bathe or swim in piranha-infested water, but they must be careful, especially if they have bleeding wounds that might attract these fish with the razor-sharp teeth.

Birds. The **Andean condor,** the largest flying land bird in the Western Hemisphere, is an average of about four feet long with a ten-foot wingspan. The **cock-of-the-rock** is a handsome bird with bright orange or red feathers and dark wings and tail that lives in the rain forests of the Andes from Peru to northern Brazil. The beautifully colored **macaw** also lives in tropical rain forests. Its feathers are blue, red, yellow, and green.

Abundant Natural Resources

If you were to ask a South American what his continent's most valuable natural resource is, he would probably answer "Soil!" The rich, black soil of the Pampas area is some of the best in the world. Many South Americans are farmers. Some tend their own small farms, while others work on large plantations owned by wealthy families. Farmers raise *wheat, barley,* and other grains on cultivated areas of the Pampas and graze *cattle* and *sheep* on uncultivated, grassy areas. *Sugar cane* and other crops thrive in the tropical climate along the seacoasts. The volcanic soil of the Andes Mountains is ideal for growing **coffee.**

Bananas need a hot, moist, climate to grow well, and they thrive in South America. It is the greatest banana-producing region in the world, and Brazil is the largest single grower. Bananas are one of the most popular fruits in the world.

Petroleum is another important natural resource to South America. Almost all of the countries have some petroleum, but *Venezuela* produces an enormous amount. *Copper, iron ore, nitrates, tin,* and *emeralds* are abundant in the Andes Mountains and the eastern highlands.

The mighty rivers and waterfalls of South America supply *hydroelectricity* to much of the continent. This is the most common energy source, because coal is scarce and petroleum is mostly exported. The Pacific Ocean along the west coast supports a major *fishing* industry.

Comprehension Check 17A
Identify
1. Highest peak in the Western Hemisphere.
2. Two highland areas in eastern South America.
3. Some of South America's common crops.

17.2 The Amazon and Its Peoples

The Amazon River

The mighty **Amazon River,** the second longest river in the world, begins high in the Andes Mountains of Peru and flows eastward through northern Brazil into the Atlantic Ocean. It is about 4,000 miles long, and is only a few miles shorter than the Nile. The Amazon, however, is considered the world's largest river, containing more water than the Mississippi, Nile, and Yangtze Rivers together. The Amazon ranges from 1½ to 6 miles wide and has an average depth of 40 feet, though it can be more than 300 feet deep in some areas. More than 1,000 known tributaries flow into the Amazon, six of which are over 1,000 miles long. The **Madeira** [mə·dĭr′ə] **River,** the Amazon's longest tributary, is over 2,000 miles long.

The Amazon Valley

The **Amazon River Basin,** or Amazon Valley, is the world's largest tropical rain forest, covering over two million square miles. Parts of these forests have never been explored. In South America, tropical rain forests are called *selvas* [sĕl′vəs]. The temperature stays about the same all year, averaging around 85 °F. Yearly rainfall ranges from 50 to 120 inches depending on the location and altitude; many places receive well over 100 inches annually. A wide variety of animals live in the Amazon Basin, including *jaguars, sloths, anteaters, snakes, parrots,* and *monkeys. Manatees, piranhas, crocodiles,* and *giant leeches* live in the Amazon River.

Plants of the rain forest. More than 2,500 kinds of trees grow in the selvas, including bamboo, rosewood, Brazil nut trees, cacao, and wax palm. Naturalists have counted more than 3,000 kinds of plants in one square mile. No one knows how many varieties of **orchids** grow in the Amazon Valley, because they are so numerous that they have never been counted. In some places, the tops of the trees are so close together that little sunlight can penetrate to the forest floor.

the Amazon River

MISSIONARY HEROES
Jim Elliot: A Yielded Servant

As the yellow plane flew over the tropical jungles of Ecuador's Amazon Basin, the two missionaries inside the plane looked down at the small village. "We like you; we want to be your friends," they called over a loudspeaker. From the plane, the men lowered a large metal cooking pot with a shirt and some beads inside. Earlier they had dropped machetes, combs, and articles of clothing. With their gifts they hoped to convince these **Auca Indians** that they were their friends.

Jim Elliot and his friend **Nate Saint,** the two American men in the plane, knew that Christ loved these Indians and had died for their sins, too. Jim Elliot strongly felt God's command to "preach the gospel to *every* creature," and he knew that God was leading him to tell the Aucas (today known as *Waorani*) of Christ.

From the day that he had accepted Christ at the age of six, Jim Elliot had been a "missionary." He had told his young friends about Christ and had made up his mind always to serve the Lord.

When he was in college, Jim kept a journal in which he wrote prayers to God. Once he wrote, "I seek not a long life, but a full one, like you, Lord Jesus."

Jim felt that God wanted him to go to Ecuador, so he studied the Quechuan [kĕch'wən] language and learned about the Quechuan tribe. When he heard that one of the Quechua missionaries had to leave because his wife had been injured in an accident, Jim volunteered to go tell the Quechua of Christ.

During their stay with the Quechua, Jim and his wife Betty (short for Elisabeth) learned of savage attacks made by the **Aucas,** another Indian tribe in Ecuador. Wanting to tell the Aucas of Christ, they founded Operation Auca, an endeavor to reach the lost souls of the Auca tribe. Four other dedicated missionary couples joined the Elliots in the work: Nate and Marj Saint, Pete and Olive Fleming, Ed and Marilou McCully, and Roger and Barbara Youderian.

The men developed a system in which gifts could be lowered from the plane by a rope. And after receiving some gifts that the Aucas tied to the end of the rope, the men made plans to try to make a friendly contact with the tribe. If the Aucas knew that the missionaries were their friends, perhaps they would listen when they told them of Christ's love.

Jim, Nate, and the other three men built a tree house on the beach of the Curaray River. Three men stayed there, while two returned in the plane to the mission compound for supplies each night. Daily the men flew over the Auca village, calling out greetings and inviting the Aucas to the river. Finally, two Auca women and a man came out to meet them. The missionaries gave them gifts and took the man for a ride in the plane. Surely now they had made friends. The three visitors left, but no one else came.

A few days later, as he and Jim were flying over the forest, Nate Saint saw a group of men coming toward the river. "Surely, they are coming to meet us," he called over the plane's radio to the wives waiting back at the station. "Looks like they'll be here for the early afternoon service. Pray for us. This is the day!" These were the last words anyone heard from either Jim Elliot or Nate Saint. The Auca men had come to kill, not to be friends.

The wives learned of their husbands' deaths a few days later. How easy it would have been to hate the men who had killed their husbands! But the love of Christ was greater than their grief.

Later Elisabeth, Jim Elliot's wife, and Rachel, Nate Saint's sister, met two Auca women coming out of the jungle and took the opportunity to tell them about Christ. These Auca women went back and told the tribe of the love they had seen in Elisabeth and Rachel. Elisabeth Elliot and Rachel Saint went into the Auca village and told the people of Christ. Many Aucas were saved.

Jim Elliot's prayers for the Aucas to believe in Christ had been granted. He had once said, "He is no fool who gives what he cannot keep to gain what he cannot lose." He had a short life, but a full one, as he had desired. He was truly one of God's faithful servants.

◀ family hut in a village along the Amazon

▼ Indian hunter with a blow gun

Wild **rubber** trees also grow in the Amazon Valley. Rubber, which originally came from Brazil's Amazon Basin, is an important product all over the world. It is used in manufacturing 40,000 to 50,000 different products. There are two types of rubber, natural and synthetic. Most natural rubber comes from rubber trees. Synthetic rubber is made by man, using chemicals.

Indians of the Amazon

Small tribes of Arawak and other Indians live in the rain forests of the Amazon Basin. At one time, they were among the world's most feared and savage Indian tribes, but most of them have given up such practices as cannibalism and head shrinking. Some have left the tribes to work on plantations, where they have adopted European ways. Many who remain in the jungle, however, are still controlled by superstitions, evil spirits, and traditions of self-torture.

Family living. The Amazon people live in small family units of forty to sixty members. They often wear nothing but tight bands of palm leaves or bark fibers tied around their upper arms, wrists, or calves. They believe this practice gives them extra strength in hunting and battle. They usually live in grass or palm-frond huts. Several families commonly share a hut, which may be 100 feet long and almost 100 feet tall. While the people of some tribal groups may sleep on mats on the floor, most of them sleep in hammocks.

Food. The people eat fish from the Amazon River and its tributaries; birds, monkeys, and other small animals from the jungle; and some garden vegetables such as *cassava,* a kind of tropical plant with edible, starchy roots. To plant their garden, a tribe will clear a patch of land by hand or burn away the underbrush. Once the soil is no longer rich enough to support plant life, the Indians clear a new plot of land.

To catch fish, they beat poles along the river bottom to scare the fish to the surface; then they spear or net their dinner. They sometimes beat the water with poisoned branches. When the fish die and float to the surface, the Indians gather them for food. The poison does not hurt the people, only the fish. To hunt in the jungle, the Indians use hollow bamboo or reed stalks as blow guns and small darts tipped in a poison called

South America: Continent of Natural Resources

curare [kū·rä′rē]. By blowing into one end of the tube, they can send the dart up to 120 feet through the air to their prey.

Finding food in the jungle is not easy. More insects live there than any other living creature. Many Indians starve to death or die from the bites of disease-carrying insects. Often the insects force the natives to spend their days indoors. Some Indian tribes paint their hair and bodies with insect-repelling dye. Because of the scarcity of food, the people are forced to live in small bands and move around frequently. Related tribes gather together only to celebrate special events.

Religion. The religion of the Amazon Indians is full of superstitions and evil spirits. To insure a good hunting or fishing trip, they cut their legs with razor-sharp fish teeth. They believe that spirits live within all of nature, and they are very fearful of these spirits. One tribe will grind up the bones of dead relatives and eat them so that the spirits of the dead can be released and will not bother the living. The people of some tribes have been known to bury themselves alive when near death.

Many brave men and women have given their lives to reach these Indians with the gospel, but there are still tribes deep in the jungle that have never heard the message of God's love for them.

Comprehension Check 17B

Identify
1. The river that is both the world's largest and second longest.
2. Location of the world's largest tropical rain forest.
3. Young missionary who said, "He is no fool who gives what he cannot keep to gain what he cannot lose."

Think
4. How were the Auca Indians reached with the gospel?

17.3 HIGHLIGHTS OF SOUTH AMERICAN HISTORY

The Incas

A great empire. People were living in all parts of South America when Spanish explorers came in the sixteenth century. The most famous group, the Incas, established a great empire in the Andes Mountains. As long ago as 2000 B.C., this empire extended from what is now northern Ecuador all the way to central Chile, but the heart of the empire was in Peru. About 1200 B.C., the Inca established **Cuzco** [kōōs′kō], which became the capital and center of their civilization. From Cuzco they conquered surrounding tribes and built an impressive empire (1438–1532). They left magnificent projects in art, architecture, and agriculture.

The Incas were great builders. They constructed thousands of miles of paved roads through the heart of the Andes, tunneling through mountains and building suspension bridges where necessary. These roads featured distance markers and rest stations where government messengers could relax. Because the Andes are so steep, the roads often zigzagged back and forth up a mountain to make it easier for travelers.

Social classes. The Inca people were divided into four classes: rulers, nobles, common people, and slaves. The rulers and nobles lived in luxurious palaces of stone and had many servants. Most of the Inca, however, were common people, and many of them were farmers. Criminals or people captured from other tribes were used as slaves.

Agriculture. Inca farmers grew grains, beans, and many kinds of vegetables. They were some of the first people to cultivate potatoes, one of their important foods. Another major crop was corn, some of which was made into popcorn. They also learned how

324 *New World History & Geography*

to dry meats, fruits, and vegetables, and they raised llamas, ducks, and guinea pigs for meat.

Education. In most ancient countries, only the boys went to school. But in the Inca empire, some girls as well as boys were chosen to be educated. In addition to studying religion, history, etc., the selected girls were trained to be servants in the emperor's palace or to be wives of nobles. The Incas had no alphabet or written language. They memorized all of their poetry and history and passed it down orally from one generation to the next.

Handiwork. Skilled Inca craftsmen wove beautiful fabrics with complicated patterns from the wool of llamas and alpacas and painted colorful designs on the pottery that they made. The Inca were also talented in stoneworking. Although they used no mortar (a mixture used to bind stones or bricks together) between the blocks of their buildings, the stones fit together so closely that a knife blade could not be inserted between them! Silver, copper, bronze, and especially gold were refined and fashioned into eating utensils, pieces of jewelry, and other items.

Spanish conquest. The Spanish discovered the Inca empire in 1532. **Francisco Pizarro** [frän·thēs′kō pē·thär′rō], a Spanish conquistador [kŏn·kwĭs′tə·dôr′] in search of gold and glory, kidnapped the Inca ruler **Atahualpa** [ä′tə·wäl′pə] and held him for ransom. Although the Incas gave Pizarro enough gold and silver to fill a room in the palace up to the height of a man, the Spaniards executed Atahualpa for rejecting Catholicism. Between 1532 and 1569 there were various uprisings among the Incas. Finally, in 1569, the Spaniards utterly defeated the Inca empire.

Today, the Incas do not exist as a nation, but a number of people can trace their ancestry back to the time before Pizarro. Many Peruvians still speak **Quechua,** the Inca language.

Rule by Spain and Portugal

Dividing the land. After Christopher Columbus discovered the New World in 1492, Spain and Portugal agreed to split South America. Spain claimed the western part of the continent. Portugal claimed the eastern part which eventually became the modern country of Brazil. This explains why Brazil is the only nation in the Western Hemisphere whose official language is Portuguese.

Exploring "the New World." In 1500, the Portuguese navigator Pedro Alvares **Cabral** [pä′throo äl′və·rĕsh kə·bräl′] discovered and claimed Brazil for Portugal. Between 1497 and 1503, **Amerigo Vespucci** [ä′mä·rē′gō vĕs·poo′chē], explored the coasts of Brazil, Uruguay, and Argentina. He was the first to realize that this land was not Asia, but a "New World." In 1507 a German mapmaker suggested that the New World be named *America* in honor of Amerigo Vespucci. In 1520, Ferdinand **Magellan** sailed south along the coast of Argen-

Inca stonework at Cuzco

Amerigo Vespucci

tina and discovered the strait that now bears his name. Magellan was the first European to sail from the Atlantic to the Pacific Ocean.

The conquistadors. By the middle of the 1500s, Spanish conquistadors Francisco **Pizarro** and Pedro de **Valdivia** [pä′thrō de väl·dē′vyä] had gained control over most of the South American Indians. The Araucanian [ä′rou·kä′nyä] Indians of Chile continued to resist the Spaniards for over 300 years. Spanish and Portuguese people poured into the new lands from 1500 to 1800. Some were looking for adventure and quick wealth, but others were looking for new lives. Thus South America was fairly well colonized before the first English settlers landed at Jamestown in North America in 1607.

Struggle for Independence

Paraguay leads the way. South American colonies remained under European control until the early 1800s. First Paraguay declared its independence in 1811. Then **José de San Martín** [hō·sā′ dǐ sän′ mär·tēn′] led his native Argentina and Peru in their revolts against Spain. He also helped **Bernardo O'Higgins** gain independence for Chile.

The George Washington of South America. The most famous patriot in South America's struggle for independence was **Simón Bolívar** [sē·môn′ bō·lē′vär: 1783–1830], who has been called the "George Washington of South America." Born in Venezuela and educated in Europe, Bolívar returned to South America after school and joined the fight for independence from Spain. Bolívar gave his own money to feed and clothe his troops. He crossed the Andes and freed Colombia, Venezuela, Ecuador, and part of Peru. The part of Peru that he freed became a separate country named Bolivia in his honor. By 1830, all of South America but the three Guianas (mod-

Simon Bolívar

ern Guyana, Suriname, and French Guiana) was free of European rule.

South America's Greatest Need

From nature worship to Catholicism. Before Europeans came to Latin America, the native Indians worshiped anything they could not understand—the sun, the moon, animals, trees, and water. The Spanish and Portuguese explorers brought Catholic priests who converted many South Americans to Catholicism, often at the point of a sword. For many centuries the Bible was almost an unknown book in South America. The Indians often accepted the outward form of Catholicism and combined it with their own pagan worship.

Today, between eighty and ninety percent of Latin Americans are Roman Catholic. The huge, lavishly furnished cathedrals contrast greatly with the poor houses of most of the people. One of the world's most expensive church buildings is in Salvador, an old city in Brazil. Much of the interior of the church is covered with gold leaf (a very thin layer of gold).

326 New World History & Geography

Bibles and missions. One of the first Protestant missionaries to South America, an Englishman named **James Thomson,** came in the early 1800s. He started schools in Argentina, Uruguay, Chile, and Peru, using the Bible as the main textbook. Thomson's schools were received warmly at first but were later persecuted by Catholic officials. Other missionaries also went through great hardships to get the Bible into the South American countries. One Argentine Christian, Francisco Penzotti, went as a missionary to Peru, where he was imprisoned for selling Bibles. South Americans who accepted Christ faced persecution from their friends and neighbors, but many stood firm in their new faith. By 1900, there was a Protestant witness in every country of South America.

Some of today's missionaries work in the large cities and towns; others go deep into the jungles to witness to native tribes. Christian radio broadcasts reach people in cities and jungles, and Christian literature printed in Spanish and Portuguese also reaches many people. Airplanes are used to bring supplies to missionaries in remote places or to transport them to where they need to go.

Despite missionary efforts, the people of South America and the other Latin American countries have had very little access to the Bible. In 1942, Latin American scholar Dr. W. Stanley Rycroft wrote the following:

> A truly great civilization can be built only on a spiritual foundation. Latin America needs all that Evangelical Christianity means and stands for: personal commitment to the Living God; strength of character and moral integrity in business, professional, social, and political relationships; the rehabilitation of multitudes of downtrodden men and women through the application of Christ's teachings, the principles of freedom and democracy, and the dedication of individuals and groups to a spiritual ideal in human life. . . .
>
> Jesus Christ who lived, died, and rose again—all that he was and is—this is the foundation of a great civilization in Latin America, and in the Western Hemisphere of tomorrow.

Comprehension Check 17C

Identify
1. Indians who established a great empire in the Andes Mountains.
2. The man after whom the Americas were named.
3. The "George Washington of South America" and the names of two other military men who helped free South America.

Think
4. Why did the Inca government need good roads across its empire?
5. Why do you think Simon Bolívar was called the "George Washington of South America"?

Chapter 17 Checkup

I. Tell why these **people** are important.

Jim Elliot	Ferdinand Magellan
Nate Saint	Pedro de Valdivia
Francisco Pizarro	José de San Martín
Atahualpa	Bernardo O'Higgins
Pedro Alvares Cabral	Simón Bolívar
Amerigo Vespucci	James Thomson

II. Define these **terms.**
   Incas   Quechua

III. Give the noted fact about these **animals.**

tapir	anaconda
capybara	piranha
spectacled bear	Andean condor
llama	

IV. Define these **geographical terms.**

South America	Amazon River
Andes Mountains	Madeira River
Mount Aconcagua	Amazon River Basin

V. Identify the locations found in **Map Mastery 17.**

South America: Continent of Natural Resources

chapter 18
NATIONS of SOUTH AMERICA

From what you already know about South America, you will not be surprised to learn that the continent is home to a wide variety of nations. Look at the map of South America again, pp. 104-105, and answer the following questions:

1. What two nations do not touch any ocean or sea?
2. In which nation is Patagonia?
3. Which nation has two capitals?
4. Which South American nation shares a border with Panama?

18.1 PERU, ECUADOR, AND BOLIVIA

Peru: Land of the Incas

Mountains, jungles, and deserts. The **Andes Mountains** run through the center of Peru, South America's third largest country. West of the Andes, the coastlands of Peru and Chile form the **Atacama** [ä′tə·kä′mə] **Desert**, one of the driest regions in the world. East of the Andes, thick rain forests and jungles dominate the landscape. Peru has one of the world's largest **commercial fishing** industries and is a leading producer of *copper, lead, silver,* and *zinc*. Valuable hardwoods thrive in the tropical rain forests. Yet, in spite of these valuable resources, most Peruvians are poor.

Descendants of the Incas. Almost half of Peru's population is Indian. More Indians live in Peru than in any other country in the world. The Indian population of Peru makes

Countries of South America

(ranked from largest to smallest in area)

Name	Capital	Rank in Population
Brazil	Brasília	1
Argentina	Buenos Aires	3
Peru	Lima	4
Colombia	Bogotá	2
Bolivia	La Paz; Sucre	8
Venezuela	Caracas	5
Chile	Santiago	6
Paraguay	Asunción	9
Ecuador	Quito	7
Guyana	Georgetown	11
Uruguay	Montevideo	10
Suriname	Paramaribo	12

Other Political Units
French Guiana (Overseas Dept. of France)   13
Falkland Islands (British dependency)   14

328 *New World History & Geography*

temple ruins, Machu Picchu

up more than one fifth of the total Indian population of the Western Hemisphere. It is easy to see why Peru has two official languages, Spanish and Quechua. **Quechua,** the language of the Incas, is the most common Indian language spoken in Peru. It became an official language in 1975.

Cities. Peru's capital, **Lima** [lē′mə], is located on the Pacific coast. It is Peru's largest and busiest city, and with its colonial style buildings, it is also one of South America's most picturesque cities. The University of San Marcos, the oldest university in South America, was founded there in 1551.

Probably the most famous city in Peru is **Cuzco** [ko͞o′skō]. Located in the Andes of southern Peru at an altitude of 11,207 feet, Cuzco was the thriving capital of the Inca empire for more than three centuries. In 1533, Francisco Pizarro took over the city. In 1650, earthquakes nearly destroyed Cuzco. After the earthquakes, the city was rebuilt and became famous for its production of art, particularly paintings, sculptures, and ornamental woodwork. Today, tourists visit many of its ancient ruins.

The Inca built many religious sites, the most famous of which is **Machu Picchu** [mä′cho͞o pēk′cho͞o], a well-preserved mountain city that was hidden from outsiders until 1911. This "lost city" is believed to have been built to honor the Inca sun god and is considered the most spectacular ruin in the Americas.

Ecuador

Part of the old Inca empire is now the country of Ecuador, which lies just north of Peru. Many Ecuadorean Indians speak Quechua, the language of the Incas, or other Indian languages and have very little contact with city dwellers. The name *Ecuador* is Spanish for *equator*. The equator passes just fifteen miles north of **Quito** [kē′tō], Ecuador's capital. Quito is Ecuador's second largest city and has been its capital since 1822. It is the oldest of all the South American capitals. Quito is located 9,350 feet above sea level, on the lower slopes of the Pichincha [pē·chēn′chä], a volcano that last erupted in 1666. Although Quito is very close to the

Nations of South America 329

equator, its altitude gives it a fairly cool climate, with an average temperature of 55°F.

Bananas grow so well in Ecuador's tropical climate that it has become the world's leading banana producer. The country's other main exports include *petroleum, coffee, cacao,* and *shrimp*. Ecuador also produces more **balsa wood** than any other country in the world. **Guayaquil** [gwä′yä·kēl′], Ecuador's largest city, is the country's chief port and center of trade. Quito is Ecuador's textile center. Other industrial products include art pieces made of leather, wood, gold, and silver. Although Ecuador is among South America's smallest and poorest countries, it has one of the fastest-growing populations in the world.

A Peruvian man paddles a totora reed boat through the marshes of Lake Titicaca.

Bolivia: Country with Two Capitals

Landlocked nation. Bolivia, which is about the size of California and Texas put together, is landlocked. That is, it has no seacoast. Many Amazon tributaries drain the country, however, giving it a water route to the Atlantic Ocean. The Andes Mountains form an uncrossable barrier in the west.

People and economy. Bolivia's economy relies on her large **forests** and deposits of **tin** and **petroleum**. Most of the people are Indian farmers who live in the valleys between the Andes Mountains. These Indians have lived in the same area for hundreds of years, and the soil is worn out from farming. Although eastern Bolivia is very fertile, the Indians do not want to leave their ancestral homelands.

Two capitals. The official capital of Bolivia is **Sucre** [soo′krə], but most of the government buildings are in **La Paz** [lä päs′], giving the country two capitals. La Paz, located near **Lake Titicaca** [tē′tē·kä′kä], is the world's highest capital city.

Lake Titicaca. Lake Titicaca lies on the border of Peru and Bolivia, 12,500 feet above sea level. Surrounded by the Andes Mountains, it is the highest navigable lake in the world. It is approximately 110 miles long, 35 miles wide at the widest point, and over

600 feet deep in spots. The Peruvian and Bolivian Indians who live near Lake Titicaca are famous for their **totora reed boats,** unsinkable boats made with reeds taken from the shore of the lake and tied together with grass twine.

Lake Titicaca is known for its changeable and often dangerous weather. Storm clouds can rumble down the mountainsides and in moments stir the calm water into nine-foot waves. The lake also is rumored to contain sea monsters. When Jacques Cousteau, the famous French underwater explorer, investigated the lake, he did not find a sea monster, but he did discover a variety of frog that can grow almost a foot in length. Approximately one billion of these frogs live on the bottom of Lake Titicaca!

Because Lake Titicaca is located two and one half miles above sea level, the air there contains less oxygen than the air at lower elevations. If you were to visit Lake Titicaca, you might become dizzy and nauseated, and you would tire faster than usual because of the difference in the oxygen level. Fires have never been a big problem there, because fire needs oxygen to burn. The Indians of the region have a much larger chest and lung capacity than most people, allowing them to take in more air in one breath. They also have up to one quart more blood and one million more red blood cells than people at lower elevations.

Comprehension Check 18A
Identify
1. The capital of Peru.
2. The landlocked country with two capitals. The world's highest capital city.
3. The highest navigable lake in the world.

18.2 COLOMBIA, VENEZUELA, AND THE THREE GUIANAS

Colombia: Emerald Capital of the World

Discovery. Notice on the map of South America that Colombia, the second largest country in South America in population, is connected to North America by the narrow Isthmus of Panama. Colombia was named for Christopher Columbus, who explored its northern coast in 1502. Although Santa Marta [sän′tä mär′tä], the oldest European settlement in Colombia, was founded in 1525, Spain did not defeat the native inhabitants and claim the country until 1536.

Abundant resources. Colombia has many valuable natural resources. **Coffee** trees grow in the rich volcanic soil of the Andes Mountains. Although Brazil produces more coffee than Colombia, Colombian coffee is often considered to be the finest in the world. Colombia also produces more than half of the world's **emeralds**. Petroleum, gold, and salt are other important mineral resources found in the country.

Bogotá. Colombia's capital, **Bogotá** [bō′gō·tä′], is located on the edge of a high-

coffee beans being ground and packaged

land basin 8,659 feet above sea level and is surrounded by mountains. The altitude gives Bogotá a cool, fresh climate. Until air travel came to Bogotá, it was the most inaccessible capital city in Latin America. Bogotá is the home of major tire, chemical, and pharmaceutical industries, and more than 30 bank headquarters. A large number of Indians, mestizos, and mulattos live in Bogotá.

Venezuela

Lakes and waterfalls. Located on the northern tip of South America is Venezuela, a land of scenic mountains, valleys, lakes, and waterfalls. South America's largest lake, **Lake Maracaibo** [mä′rä·kī′vô] lies in northern Venezuela. Venezuela is also the location of two of the most spectacular waterfalls in the world, Kukenaam [koo·kā·nän′] Falls and Angel Falls. **Angel Falls,** the world's highest waterfall, is 3,212 feet high. Because of the thick jungle surrounding the falls, they are easier to see from the air than from the ground. In 1935, an American pilot, James Angel, became the first white man to see the falls.

Settlement. Europeans established the settlement of Cumaná [koo′mä·nä′], the oldest permanent European settlement in South America, in northeastern Venezuela in 1523. The tropical region remained undeveloped, however, until oil was discovered under Lake Maracaibo in 1910. The discovery of **oil** brought many Americans and Europeans to Venezuela in the early 1900s.

Industries. Today, Venezuela is one of the leading producers of petroleum and natural gas.

Angel Falls in Venezuela

Much of the oil that Venezuela produces comes from deposits under Lake Maracaibo. The country also exports aluminum, steel, processed foods, and textiles. Since the rise of the petroleum industry, agriculture has decreased in Vene-zuela. Less than one fifth of the people are farmers; *sugar cane, coffee,* and *cacao* are the main crops. *Beef* and *dairy cattle* graze on ranches in the lowlands of central Venezuela.

Caracas. Most Venezuelans live in cities or towns in the Andes Highlands. **Caracas** [kə·rä′kəs], the capital and largest city, is located in this region. Caracas has grown rapidly in the 20th century because of Venezuela's booming oil industry and is one of

Caracas is one of the most developed cities in South America.

the most highly developed cities of South America.

The Three Guianas

The name Guiana, meaning "land of waters," was given to the marshy northeast coast of South America. Much of this land is near or below sea level, requiring dikes and drainage systems to keep it from flooding. Today, the term "the Guianas" refers to the countries of Guyana, Suriname, as well as to French Guiana. These three small countries were once controlled by Great Britian, France, and the Netherlands. Only one—French Guiana—is controlled by a European country today.

Guyana. Guyana, the largest of the three countries, was one of the first areas to be settled in the New World. Guyana became independent of Great Britain in 1966. Its official language is English. Most cities and towns in Guyana are located on the coast. The land has good *bauxite* deposites and grows *sugar cane* and *rice* well. The inland area is inhabited mostly by Indians. Beautiful waterfalls are found on some of the rivers. East Indians and mulattos are the two major groups in Guyana. They work the plantations as well as hold many of the business and government jobs.

French Guiana. The land of French Guiana is still an overseas department of France. For many years, it served as a prison camp for political prisoners. One famous prison was located on **Devil's Island.** Today, visitors can visit the old prisons and even sleep in parts that have been converted into an inn. French Guiana is also famous for a **satellite-launching base** from which the European Space Agency launches most of Europe's satellites.

Most of the people in French Guiana are descendants of black slaves who were taken there by the French in the 1600s and 1700s. The French government is trying to encourage more people to move there by building up the gold mining, food and lumber processing, and shrimping industries.

Suriname. Dutch Guiana was a prize colony of the Netherlands for over 300 years. In 1975, it became independent and the name was changed to Suriname. People of mixed European and black ancestry control most of the government business, while Hindustanis [hĭn′dōō·stä′nēz] and Indonesians do the farming and industrial work. Suriname has deposits of bauxite and aluminum and has swampy land that is good for growing rice.

Comprehension Check 18B

Identify

1. Country known for its fine coffee.
2. South America's largest lake.
3. The world's highest waterfall.
4. Term used for the countries of Guyana, Suriname, and French Guiana.

Think

5. Why is Lake Maracaibo important to the economy of Venezuela?

18.3 BRAZIL: GIANT OF THE SOUTH

Land of the Amazon

Brazil, the fifth largest country in the world in area, covers almost half of the South American continent. Northern Brazil is dominated by the **Amazon River** and its tributaries. Jungles cover much of this region. Farther south, the land rises to a range of fertile plateaus, where more than half of the country's people live. **Three rivers** water the southern plateaus—the **Paraguay,** the **Paraná** [pä′rä·nä′], and the **Uruguay.** Coffee plantations, cattle ranches, cotton fields, pine forests, and vineyards thrive in these highlands.

Historical Events

Slavery. Portuguese colonists began to pour into Brazil shortly after explorer Pedro Alvares Cabral claimed the land for Portugal. The colonists soon discovered that sugar cane, tobacco, cotton, and rice thrived in the fertile soil of the Brazilian coast. At first, the Portuguese landowners forced the native Brazilian Indians to work on their plantations. Many of the Indian laborers died, however, either in revolts against their masters or from disease.

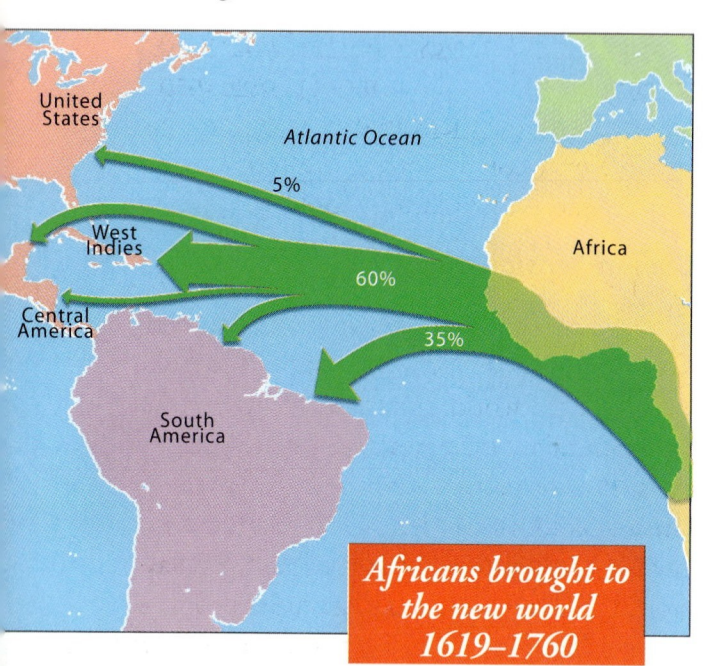

The colonists replaced their Indian slaves with black slaves from Africa. Thousands of black slaves were sold to Brazilian plantation owners between the 1500s and the 1800s—in fact, more than one third of the slaves brought from Africa to the New World were sold in Brazil (most of the other two-thirds were sold in the West Indies and Central America).

Independence. Members of Portugal's royal family ruled Brazil for 200 years until, in 1822, Pedro, son of the king of Portugal, declared Brazil to be independent. Thus Brazil gained its independence without bloodshed and became an empire. Pedro I ruled as emperor until 1831, when the Brazilians, dissatisfied with his rule, forced him to resign. His son, Pedro II, became emperor in 1840 at the age of 15.

The Age of Pedro. Pedro II proved to be a wise ruler and helped Brazil develop into a strong country. So much progress took place during his reign that the years 1840–1889 became known as the "Age of Pedro." During those years, Brazil's first highways, railroads, and telegraph lines were built, and the economy, culture, and education flourished. **Slavery** became an important issue during the Age of Pedro. While many Brazilians called for the complete abolition (doing away with) of slavery, slave owners clung to their valuable work force. Pedro II opposed slavery, but he realized the power of the landowners and planned to free the slaves gradually. First he granted freedom to the children born to slaves; later he freed the elderly slaves. In time he hoped to free them all, but the abolitionists continued to demand immediate abolition. Finally, in 1888, while Pedro II was away in Europe, his daughter **Princess Isabel** yielded to the pressure and declared all of the slaves in Brazil free. Though 700,000 slaves applauded

Africans brought to the new world 1619–1760

334 New World History & Geography

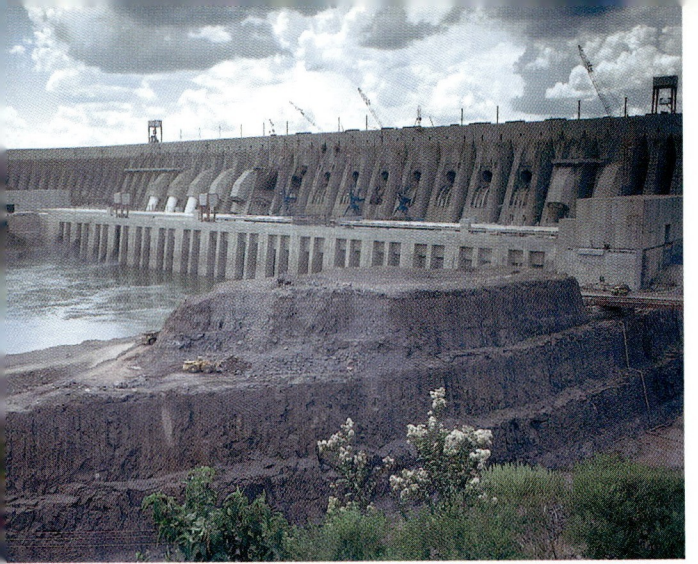

the Itaipú Dam on the Paraná River

her, the plantation owners revolted. Within a year, the royal family had been banished to Europe, though Pedro II is still honored as a national hero. Since 1889, Brazil has been ruled mostly by a succession of military dictatorships.

Twentieth century. Brazil has the distinction of being the only South American country that fought in World War I and World War II. During World War II, the Brazilian navy helped keep important Atlantic sea lanes open for the Allied ships. In recent years, many Brazilian leaders have struggled valiantly against Communist infiltration.

Prosperous Economy

Natural resources. Brazil has tremendous natural resources, including farmlands. It is the largest producer of **coffee** in the world, while the United States is the largest single consumer. Coffee comes from coffee trees which grow on mountainside coffee plantations called *fazendas* [fə·zĕn′dəz]. Each berry growing on a coffee tree contains two beans. The berries are removed by machines, then roasted to bring out the rich coffee taste and aroma.

Brazil also ranks as a leading producer of **cacao** beans or seeds. The bean-sized seeds grow inside a pod that is 6 to 10 inches long. After the ripe pods are picked, the beans are removed, allowed to ferment, and then processed into chocolate, cocoa, or cocoa butter. Although most of the world's cacao crop comes from West Africa, Central America and South America also produce significant amounts.

In addition to coffee and cacao, Brazil is a leading producer of **bananas, sugar cane, citrus fruits, cattle,** and **sheep.** Most of these crops and livestock are raised on sprawling plantations. Some of the plantations in Brazil are as large as the state of Oregon!

Brazil's natural resources also include forests, mineral deposits, and water power. It ranks among the leading producers of forest products. The country's mineral wealth includes quartz, graphite, iron ore, tin, petroleum, and many other valuable minerals. Most of the nation's electricity is produced by hydroelectric dams. The **Itaipú** [ĭ·tī·pōō′] **Dam** on the **Paraná River** is one of the most powerful hydroelectric plants in the world.

People

As the fifth largest country in the world in population, Brazil has more people than all other South American countries combined. It is the only country in the Western Hemisphere where Portuguese is spoken. (There are nearly 10 times as many Portuguese-speaking people in Brazil as in Portugal.) Almost 90 percent of all Brazilians are Roman Catholics, making Brazil the largest Catholic nation in the world. Despite the huge industrial potential of the Amazon River Basin, most Brazilians live along the coast where the first colonists settled. Only plantation owners and scattered Indian tribes live away from the cities. To encourage more people to move inland, the Brazilian government moved

Nations of South America 335

the capital from **Rio de Janeiro** [rē′ō dā zhə·nâr′ō] to **Brasília** [brə·zĭl′yə]. But still most of the people remain near the coast.

Cities

Rio de Janeiro. "Rio," as **Rio de Janeiro** is often called, is one of the most beautiful cities in the world. Its name means "River of January." The explorer who discovered the bay on January 1, 1502, gave it this name because he thought it was the mouth of a great river. Rio developed into a trading center because of its good harbor. Scenic **Guanabara** [gwä′nə·bär′ə] **Bay** is considered one of the seven natural wonders of the world. A cable car carries tourists over the bay to the top of **Sugar Loaf Mountain,** a rocky formation which rises from a peninsula on the harbor. Rio is one of South America's chief seaports as well as Brazil's cultural center. The city has 35 universities and 28 museums. Residents of Rio are called *Cariocas* [kä′rē·ôk′əs], an Indian word meaning "white man's house."

São Paulo. The largest city in South America and the fourth largest city in the world is São Paulo [soun pou′lō], Brazil. It was founded as an Indian settlement in 1554. Today, São Paulo is the industrial center of Latin America. Missionaries to Brazil often go to São Paulo first to study the Portuguese language. Many publishing companies are located there. They print books, Bibles, and Sunday school materials in Portuguese.

Manaus. Located in the heart of the Amazon jungle near the junction of the Negro and Amazon rivers, **Manaus** [mə·nous′] is the center of trade and commerce for the Amazon Basin. Ocean liners travel 1,000 miles up the Amazon to unload and pick up cargo at this busy port. Major exports include such forest products as rubber, lumber, and Brazil nuts.

a cable car carrying tourists ▲ up to Sugar Loaf Mountain

Guanabara Bay ▶

336 *New World History & Geography*

Seven Natural Wonders of the World

1. **Mount Everest,** on the Nepal-Tibet border in Asia—the world's highest mountain.
2. **Victoria Falls,** on the Zambia-Zimbabwe border in Africa—discovered by missionary David Livingstone.
3. **Grand Canyon** of the Colorado River in Arizona.
4. **Great Barrier Reef** of Australia—the world's largest coral formation.
5. **Northern Lights,** also known as the *aurora borealis*.
6. **Paricutín,** a volcano in Mexico.
7. **Guanabara Bay,** the harbor at **Rio de Janeiro**.

Brasília. The capital of Brazil, **Brasília,** is well known for its striking architecture and orderly arrangement. The Brazilian government moved from Rio de Janeiro to Brasília in 1960 after five years of planning and construction. The officials chose an inland location for their capital in an effort to draw Brazilians away from the coastal cities to settle the country's wild interior. From the air, Brasília looks like a drawn bow and arrow. Residential districts form the bow. Government buildings form the tip of the arrow, while businesses, cultural centers, and recreational facilities make up the shaft. Because most of the city's residents work for the government, the city economy relies heavily on government activities. Other city residents work for the construction industry, the second leading employer, or various service industries.

Comprehension Check 18C

1. What is the largest country in South America?
2. Rain forests surround what important river in Brazil?
3. What is the capital of Brazil today? Where was the capital before the Brazilian government moved it? Why did they move the capital?
4. Which of the seven natural wonders of the world will you see in the Americas?

18.4 ARGENTINA, CHILE, PARAGUAY, AND URUGUAY

Argentina: Land of the Pampas

Fertile grasslands. Argentina is the second largest country in South America in area, and the third largest in population. Spanish explorers seeking silver named the land *La Plata,* meaning "silver." When the Argentines won their independence from Spain in 1816, they first called their land the United Provinces of La Plata but later changed the name to *Argentina* after the Latin word for silver, *argentum.* Although the Spaniards did find some silver, their most valuable discovery was the **Pampas,** an area of fertile grasslands that extends across central Argentina. Stretching from the Atlantic coast to the foothills of the Andes, the Pampas covers an area of 295,000 square miles. *Pampa* is an Indian word meaning "flat surface." Although the Pampas appears to be flat, it actually slopes from 1,640 feet above sea level in the northwest to 66 feet in the southeast. In the west, the Pampas is dry and barren, but in the east, it is humid, temperate, well watered, and consequently very productive. The **pamperos** [päm·pâr′ōs], violent gales and heavy rains created by cool winds from the south meeting warm air from the tropical north, periodically sweep across the Pampas.

"Granary of the South." Because of the great volume of **wheat** grown on the Pampas, Argentina is known as the "Granary of the South." Huge herds of cattle roam the **estancias** [ĕ·stän′syäz: ranches], watched by the **gauchos** [gou′chōz: South American cowboys]. Argentina is one of the world's largest **beef** producers. **Sheep** are raised on Tierra del Fuego for their wool. Argentina is the location of one of the world's highest active volcanoes, Volcán Antofalla [bôl·kän′ än′tō·fä′yä], which is 21,162 feet above sea level.

Nations of South America 337

gaucho with a herd of sheep on the Pampas

The people and their government. Most Argentines are descendants of Spanish colonists. They live in Spanish-style homes with tile roofs and have a higher standard of living than most other South Americans. About 90 percent of Argentina's population is Roman Catholic. Argentines do not have many of the freedoms that are so precious to Americans. The government even tells parents what they may and may not name their children. Argentina has one of the highest literacy rates in South America—96 percent of the population can read and write.

Resources and industries. Petroleum and natural gas are pumped along the Atlantic coast. Meat packing, food processing, and textiles are based in the cities. **Tourism,** however, is the biggest industry. Millions of people vacation in Argentina every year. Some go to see spectacular **Iguaçú** [ē′gwä·sōō′] **Falls,** stay at a seaside resort, ski in the Andes, or hike to the famous monument **Christ of the Andes.** Most of them visit **Buenos Aires** [bwā′nəs âr′ēz], the beautiful capital city.

Buenos Aires. About one third of the Argentines live in Buenos Aires, the tenth largest city in the world. It has been nicknamed the "Paris of America" because of its wide boulevards, its general beauty, and its role as the Latin American cultural center. Buenos Aires is located near the Atlantic coast on the banks of the **Rio de la Plata** [rē′ō dā lä plä′tä] in central Argentina. The mouth of this river has been dredged so that Buenos Aires, 170 miles inland, is a seaport.

Buenos Aires has 80 percent of Argentina's investment in industry, labor, and business. Argentina's railroad system spreads out from Buenos Aires like a fan, carrying produce from the city's flour mills, grain elevators, meat-packing plants, and other industries. Buenos Aires is one of the leading publishing centers of all Spanish-speaking countries. The University of Buenos Aires is one of the largest educational institutions in South America; more than 200,000 students enrolled for classes in 2000!

Patagonia. The southern part of Argentina's mainland is called **Patagonia** [păt′ə·gōn′yə], or "Land of the Big Feet." It was named for the Indians of the region, a very tall people who wore large boots stuffed with grass. Although much of Patagonia is desert, parts of the region are useful for grazing sheep. Deposits of coal, petroleum, and iron ore have been found there.

Falkland Islands. The Falkland Islands, called the *Islas Malvinas* [ēz′läs mäl•vē′näs] by the Argentines, lie in the Atlantic Ocean, 300 miles east of the Strait of Magellan. The islands have a damp, cool climate with strong winds that inhibit the growth of trees. Most of the people are of British origin. They raise sheep and export the wool. Fishermen from the Falklands get oil from whales that are killed nearby and ship it to **South Georgia Island** to be exported. British Captain John Strong claimed the islands in 1690, naming them for Viscount Falkland, the British treasurer of the Navy. Although several other European countries laid claim to the Falklands, Britain eventually took control in the 1800s. Argentina, however, continued to claim ownership of the islands.

Finally, in 1982, Argentina invaded the islands. After **British Prime Minister Margaret Thatcher** appealed to the patriotism of her people on behalf of the several thousand British citizens in the Falklands, thousands of Britons volunteered to go and fight for English liberty. Within three months, the British had defeated the Argentine forces and freedom had been restored to the Falklands. Many Argentines saw the foolishness of this war and demanded an end to their military dictatorship.

OF SPECIAL INTEREST
The Miracle of Tierra del Fuego

Tierra del Fuego is a group of islands just off the southern tip of South America. Magellan named the islands *Tierra del Fuego,* or *land of fire,* because as he passed by, he saw many campfires dotting the shoreline.

The **Ona** and **Yahgan** Indians who lived on these islands were the southernmost people of the world. Neither of these primitive tribes wore much clothing. Even in snow, many would wear only a cape made of animal skins.

The Indians of Tierra del Fuego rarely stayed in the same place for more than two days. Many Yahgan families actually lived out at sea in canoes. Some of them became deformed because of the cramped living conditions.

When the evolutionist **Charles Darwin** saw these people during his voyage around South America, he mistakenly thought he had found a missing link between man and ape! He had actually found a group of people who had wandered so far away from God and other people that they had lost most of their heritage.

After the world heard about the Indians of Tierra del Fuego, people became burdened to tell the Indians about Christ. A British naval officer, **Captain Allen Gardiner,** was the first to try. He died of starvation only a few months after arriving because the Indians would not let him leave his ship. Other missionaries followed, eight of which were killed by the Indians. Christians would not give up their attempts to help these people, however. After many years of Christian witness, over 4,500 Indians became Christians. Their lives were so greatly changed that even Darwin admitted his mistake and gave money to the missionary work.

The Indians of Tierra del Fuego became very active for the Lord. They collected large amounts of money for other missionaries around the world, and even sent some of their own people as missionaries to other tribes. They were not half animals as Darwin had thought, but people who needed to hear the gospel.

Nations of South America 339

Chile: Where the Land Ends

Long and narrow. Chile, the southernmost country of South America, has a coastline that stretches 2,500 miles. If you saw a large map of Chile on a wall, it might be only one foot wide but reach from the floor to the ceiling. Chile's name comes from the Spanish word *chilli*, which literally means "where the land ends."

Mineral wealth. Four fifths of the people live in Chile's modern cities. Many Chileans work in the mining industry, because Chile has huge mineral deposits. It produces more **copper** than any other nation in the world. Other mineral exports include petroleum, lead, silver, gold, nitrates, and iron ore. Because of the long coastline, **fishing** is also a major industry. Agriculture is limited greatly by the country's rugged terrain. **Valparaíso** [bäl′ pä·rä·ē′ sō] is an important seaport and center of industry in Chile.

Santiago. Chile's capital, **Santiago** [sän·tyä′ gō], lies in a fertile valley between the Andes Mountains and the Pacific coastal range about 90 miles east of the Pacific Ocean. Santiago is Chile's largest city and its industrial center. Its major products include foods, textiles, shoes, and clothes. Nearly a third of the country's population lives there. The people of Santiago are mostly Spanish, but some are French, German, or Italian, and many are mestizos.

Paraguay: From Prosperity to Poverty

War's destruction. Through the first half of the 19th century, Paraguay, the first of the South American countries to declare its independence from Spain, prospered as a young nation. Then, in the 1860s, Paraguay made the grave mistake of declaring war on her most powerful neighbors—Brazil and Argentina. Within five years, the nation's population dropped from 1,000,000 to 221,000. When Paraguay finally surrendered, both her people and her land had been devastated.

Montevideo, the capital of Uruguay, is known for its beautiful parks.

Struggling economy. Today, Paraguay is one of the poorest countries in South America. About half of the Paraguayans are poor farmers. They raise corn, sugar, soybeans, cotton, and other crops on a piece of land until the soil wears out and then move on to another piece of land with more fertile soil. Most farmers raise only enough food for their families. Those who produce enough to export face another problem: like Bolivia, Paraguay is landlocked. Goods must be sent through Argentina, and relations between Paraguay and Argentina are poor. Paraguay's two most valuable resources—its forests and its hydroelectric potential—remain largely undeveloped. Paraguay is the only country whose flag has different pictures on the front and the back; the national coat of arms adorns the front, and the treasury seal decorates the back.

Uruguay: Industrious Little Country

Prosperous economy. Uruguay is one of the smallest countries on the South American continent, but it is also very prosperous. The

Pampas land extends from Argentina into Uruguay, giving the country good farmland. The Uruguayan economy depends heavily on agriculture and related industries. Although Uruguay has no mineral fuels of its own, it profits greatly by refining the petroleum of neighboring countries. Uruguayan industries can export their products from one of several seaports on the country's coast. Railroads connect many remote towns and villages to the busy port cities. Hydroelectricity provides almost all of Uruguay's energy. Uruguay is noted for its clean, modern cities.

"City of Roses." Montevideo [mŏn′tə·vĭ·dā′ō], the capital and largest city, is called the City of Roses because of its flower-filled squares and beautiful parks. This thriving seaport serves as the center of government, education, and trade. About 97 percent of the Uruguayan population can read and write.

Comprehension Check 18D

Identify

1. The area of fertile grasslands that extends across central Argentina.
2. Islands belonging to Great Britain that Argentina invaded in 1982.
3. One of the smallest, but most prosperous, countries in South America.

Chapter 18 Checkup

I. *Define these* **terms.**
   Inca Indians   fazendas   estancias   Ona Indians   totora reed boats
   Quechua   pamperos   gauchos   Yahgan Indians

II. *Tell why these* **cities** *are important.*
   Cuzco, Peru   Guayaquil, Ecuador   Rio de Janeiro, Brazil   Manaus, Brazil
   Machu Picchu, Peru   Cumaná, Venezuela   São Paulo, Brazil   Valparaíso, Chile

III. *Tell why these* **people** *are important.*
   Pedro I   Princess Isabel   Charles Darwin
   Pedro II   Margaret Thatcher   Captain Allen Gardiner

IV. *Know these South American* **capitals** *and* **countries.**
   Lima, Peru   Bogotá, Colombia   Buenos Aires, Argentina
   Quito, Ecuador   Caracas, Venezuela   Sucre and La Paz, Bolivia
   Santiago, Chile   Brasília, Brazil   Montevideo, Uruguay

V. *Define these* **geographical terms.**
   Atacama Desert   Uruguay River   Falkland Islands   Sugar Loaf Mountain
   Lake Titicaca   Angel Falls   Christ of the Andes   South Georgia Island
   Lake Maracaibo   Itaipú Dam   Rio de la Plata   Patagonia
   Devil's Island   Paraná River   Pampas   Tierra del Fuego
   Paraguay River   Guanabara Bay   Iguaçú Falls

VI. *Tell which South American country is known for being the major producer of these* **resources.**
   bananas   emeralds   oil   beef
   balsa wood   fine coffee   most coffee   copper

VII. *Identify the locations from* **Map Mastery 17.**

Document Memorization

> Elementary students are at the peak of their ability to memorize, and they will easily learn the documents in this section if just two or three minutes a day are set aside for class recitation. Students should also learn the states and capitals and the Presidents of the United States. The suggested number of weeks to spend on each document or list is given.

THE AMERICAN'S CREED *(4 weeks)*

I believe in the United States of America as a government of the people, by the people, for the people, whose just powers are derived from the consent of the governed; a democracy in a republic; a sovereign Nation of many sovereign States; a perfect Union, one and inseparable; established upon those principles of freedom, equality, justice, and humanity for which American patriots sacrificed their lives and fortunes.

I therefore believe it is my duty to my country to love it, to support its Constitution, to obey its laws, to respect its flag, and to defend it against all enemies.

—*William Tyler Page*

Document Memorization

from THE DECLARATION OF INDEPENDENCE *(6 weeks)*

In Congress, July 4, 1776

When, in the course of human events, it becomes necessary for one people to dissolve the political bands which have connected them with another, and to assume, among the powers of the earth, the separate and equal station to which the laws of nature and of nature's God entitle them, a decent respect to the opinions of mankind requires that they should declare the causes which impel them to the separation.

We hold these truths to be self-evident:—That all men are created equal; that they are endowed by their Creator with certain unalienable rights; that among these are life, liberty, and the pursuit of happiness. That, to secure these rights, governments are instituted among men, deriving their just powers from the consent of the governed; that, whenever any form of government becomes destructive of these ends, it is the right of the people to alter or to abolish it, and to institute a new government, laying its foundation on such principles, and organising its powers in such form, as to them shall seem most likely to effect their safety and happiness. Prudence, indeed, will dictate that governments long established should not be changed for light and transient causes; and, accordingly, all experience hath shown that mankind are more disposed to suffer, while evils are sufferable, than to right themselves by abolishing the forms to which they are accustomed. But, when a long train of abuses and usurpations, pursuing invariably the same object, evinces a design to reduce them under absolute despotism, it is their right, it is their duty, to throw off such government, and to provide new guards for their future security. . . .

PREAMBLE TO THE CONSTITUTION *(2 weeks)*

We the people of the United States, in order to form a more perfect Union, establish justice, insure domestic tranquillity, provide for the common defense, promote the general welfare, and secure the blessings of liberty to ourselves and our posterity, do ordain and establish this Constitution for the United States of America.

FIRST AMENDMENT TO THE CONSTITUTION *(2 weeks)*

Congress shall make no law respecting an establishment of religion, or prohibiting the free exercise thereof; or abridging the freedom of speech, or of the press; or the right of the people peaceably to assemble, and to petition the government for a redress of grievances.

THE RIGHTS OF AMERICANS *(2 weeks)*

1. **The right to** worship God in one's own way.
2. **The right to** free speech and press.
3. **The right to** petition for grievances—in fair and honest judgment.
4. **The right to** privacy in our homes.
5. **The right to** own private property.
6. **The right to** own, keep, and bear arms.
7. **The right to** move about freely at home or abroad.
8. **The right to** habeas corpus—without excessive bail.
9. **The right to** trial by jury—innocent until proven guilty.
10. **The right to** free elections and personal secret ballots.
11. **The right to** the service of government as a protector and referee.
12. **The right to** freedom from arbitrary government regulation and control.
13. **The right to** work in callings and localities of our choice.
14. **The right to** bargain for goods and services in a free market.
15. **The right to** contract about our affairs.
16. **The right to** go into business, compete, and make a profit.

Lincoln's Gettysburg Address *(6 weeks)*

Fourscore and seven years ago our fathers brought forth upon this continent a new nation, conceived in liberty, and dedicated to the proposition that all men are created equal.

Now we are engaged in a great civil war, testing whether that nation, or any nation so conceived and so dedicated, can long endure. We are met on a great battlefield of that war. We have come to dedicate a portion of that field as a final resting place for those who here gave their lives that that nation might live. It is altogether fitting and proper that we should do this.

But, in a larger sense we cannot dedicate—we cannot consecrate—we cannot hallow—this ground. The brave men, living and dead, who struggled here, have consecrated it far above our poor power to add or detract. The world will little note nor long remember what we say here, but it can never forget what they did here. It is for us, the living, rather, to be dedicated here to the unfinished work which they who fought here have thus far so nobly advanced. It is rather for us to be here dedicated to the great task remaining before us—that from these honored dead we take increased devotion to that cause for which they gave the last full measure of devotion; that we here highly resolve that these dead shall not have died in vain; that this nation, under God, shall have a new birth of freedom; and that government of the people, by the people, for the people, shall not perish from the earth.

The Nifty Fifty States and Capitals *(6 weeks)*

Memorize states and capitals.

State	Capital	Abbreviations	Date of Admission	Order of Admission
Alabama	Montgomery	Ala., AL	1819	22
Alaska	Juneau	Alaska, AK	1959	49
Arizona	Phoenix	Ariz., AZ	1912	48
Arkansas	Little Rock	Ark., AR	1836	25
California	Sacramento	Calif., CA	1850	31
Colorado	Denver	Colo., CO	1876	38
Connecticut	Hartford	Conn., CT	1788	5
Delaware	Dover	Del., DE	1787	1
Florida	Tallahassee	Fla., FL	1845	27
Georgia	Atlanta	Ga., GA	1788	4
Hawaii	Honolulu	Hawaii, HI	1959	50
Idaho	Boise	Idaho, ID	1890	43
Illinois	Springfield	Ill, IL	1818	21
Indiana	Indianapolis	Ind., IN	1816	19
Iowa	Des Moines	Iowa, IA	1846	29
Kansas	Topeka	Kans., KS	1861	34
Kentucky	Frankfort	Ky., KY	1792	15
Louisiana	Baton Rouge	La., LA	1812	18
Maine	Augusta	Maine, ME	1820	23
Maryland	Annapolis	Md., MD	1788	7
Massachusetts	Boston	Mass., MA	1788	6
Michigan	Lansing	Mich., MI	1837	26
Minnesota	St. Paul	Minn., MN	1858	32
Mississippi	Jackson	Miss., MS	1817	20
Missouri	Jefferson City	Mo., MO	1821	24

New World History & Geography

Document Memorization

State	Capital	Abbreviations	Date of Admission	Order of Admission
Montana	Helena	Mont., MT	1889	41
Nebraska	Lincoln	Nebr., NE	1867	37
Nevada	Carson City	Nev., NV	1864	36
New Hampshire	Concord	N.H., NH	1788	9
New Jersey	Trenton	N.J., NJ	1787	3
New Mexico	Santa Fe	N. Mex., NM	1912	47
New York	Albany	N.Y., NY	1788	11
North Carolina	Raleigh	N.C., NC	1789	12
North Dakota	Bismarck	N. Dak., ND	1889	39
Ohio	Columbus	Ohio, OH	1803	17
Oklahoma	Oklahoma City	Okla., OK	1907	46
Oregon	Salem	Oreg., OR	1859	33
Pennsylvania	Harrisburg	Pa., PA	1787	2
Rhode Island	Providence	R.I., RI	1790	13
South Carolina	Columbia	S.C., SC	1788	8
South Dakota	Pierre	S. Dak., SD	1889	40
Tennessee	Nashville	Tenn., TN	1796	16
Texas	Austin	Tex., TX	1845	28
Utah	Salt Lake City	Utah, UT	1896	45
Vermont	Montpelier	Vt., VT	1791	14
Virginia	Richmond	Va., VA	1788	10
Washington	Olympia	Wash., WA	1889	42
West Virginia	Charleston	W. Va., WV	1863	35
Wisconsin	Madison	Wis., WI	1848	30
Wyoming	Cheyenne	Wyo., WY	1890	44

*The standard abbreviation is given first. The second abbreviation should be used with ZIP code.

United States Presidents *(6 weeks)*

Memorize Presidents in order.

No.	Name	Born / Died	Years in Office	State of Birth	State of Residence When Elected
1	George Washington	1732–1799	1789–1797	Va.	Va.
2	John Adams	1735–1826	1797–1801	Mass.	Mass.
3	Thomas Jefferson	1743–1826	1801–1809	Va.	Va.
4	James Madison	1751–1836	1809–1817	Va.	Va.
5	James Monroe	1758–1831	1817–1825	Va.	Va.
6	John Quincy Adams	1767–1848	1825–1829	Mass.	Mass.
7	Andrew Jackson	1767–1845	1829–1837	S.C.	Tenn.
8	Martin Van Buren	1782–1862	1837–1841	N.Y.	N.Y.
9	William Henry Harrison	1773–1841	1841	Va.	Ohio
10	John Tyler	1790–1862	1841–1845	Va.	Va.
11	James K. Polk	1795–1849	1845–1849	N.C.	Tenn.
12	Zachary Taylor	1784–1850	1849–1850	Va.	La.
13	Millard Fillmore	1800–1874	1850–1853	N.Y.	N.Y.
14	Franklin Pierce	1804–1869	1853–1857	N.H.	N.H.
15	James Buchanan	1791–1868	1857–1861	Pa.	Pa.
16	Abraham Lincoln	1809–1865	1861–1865	Ky.	Ill.
17	Andrew Johnson	1808–1875	1865–1869	N.C.	Tenn.
18	Ulysses S. Grant	1822–1885	1869–1877	Ohio	Ill.
19	Rutherford B. Hayes	1822–1893	1877–1881	Ohio	Ohio
20	James A. Garfield	1831–1881	1881	Ohio	Ohio
21	Chester A. Arthur	1830–1886	1881–1885	Vt.	N.Y.

348 New World History & Geography

Document Memorization

No.	Name	Born/Died	Years in Office	State of Birth	State of Residence When Elected
22	Grover Cleveland	1837–1908	1885–1889	N.J.	N.Y.
23	Benjamin Harrison	1833–1901	1889–1893	Ohio	Ind.
24	Grover Cleveland	1837–1908	1893–1897	N.J.	N.Y.
25	William McKinley	1843–1901	1897–1901	Ohio	Ohio
26	Theodore Roosevelt	1858–1919	1901–1909	N.Y.	N.Y.
27	William Howard Taft	1857–1930	1909–1913	Ohio	Ohio
28	Woodrow Wilson	1856–1924	1913–1921	Va.	N.J.
29	Warren G. Harding	1865–1923	1921–1923	Ohio	Ohio
30	Calvin Coolidge	1872–1933	1923–1929	Vt.	Mass.
31	Herbert Hoover	1874–1964	1929–1933	Iowa	Calif.
32	Franklin D. Roosevelt	1882–1945	1933–1945	N.Y.	N.Y.
33	Harry S. Truman	1884–1972	1945–1953	Mo.	Mo.
34	Dwight D. Eisenhower	1890–1969	1953–1961	Tex.	N.Y.
35	John F. Kennedy	1917–1963	1961–1963	Mass.	Mass.
36	Lyndon B. Johnson	1908–1973	1963–1969	Tex.	Tex.
37	Richard M. Nixon	1913–1994	1969–1974	Calif.	N.Y.
38	Gerald R. Ford	1913–	1974–1977	Nebr.	Mich.
39	James E. Carter	1924–	1977–1981	Ga.	Ga.
40	Ronald Reagan	1911–	1981–1989	Ill.	Calif.
41	George H. W. Bush	1924–	1989–1993	Mass.	Tex.
42	William J. Clinton	1946–	1993–2001	Ark.	Ark.
43	George W. Bush	1946–	2001–	Conn.	Tex.

Document Memorization 349

Dictionary of Geographical Terms

> Terms that are further explained by the landform models or in this dictionary are often printed in italics when they appear in the text.

altitude [ăl′tĭ·tūd]: elevation; height above sea level.

archipelago [är′kĭ·pĕl′ə·gō]: a group or chain of many islands.

arid [ăr′ĭd]: dry and barren; lacking sufficient water for things to grow.

atoll [ăt′ŏl]: a coral reef surrounding a central lagoon.

aurora borealis [ô·rôr′ə bôr′ē·ăl′ĭs]: brilliant lights that sometimes light up the night sky in the Northern Hemisphere; northern lights.

basin: a region drained by a river; land largely enclosed by higher land.

bay: part of a body of water which reaches into the land, generally with a wide opening.

canal [kə·năl′]: a narrow, man-made channel of water that joins other bodies of water. It is used for navigation or irrigation.

canyon: a deep, narrow valley with steep sides.

cape: point; a piece of land extending into the water.

cataract [kăt′ə·răkt]: a natural bridge or rock deposit in a river that forms a waterfall.

channel: a deep, narrow body of water connecting two larger bodies of water; also, the deepest part of a river or harbor.

chasm [kăz′m]: a deep crack in the earth's surface.

cliff: a high, steep wall of rock.

cordillera [kôr′dĭl·yâr′ə]: a system or chain of mountains, especially the principal mountain range of a continent.

crater: a bowl-shaped cavity, as at the mouth of a volcano or on the surface of the moon.

dam: a man-made barrier designed to hold back flowing water.

deciduous [dĭ·sĭj′oo·əs] **trees:** trees that lose their leaves in fall.

delta: the land deposited at the mouth of a river.

depression: a lowland area, often below sea level, without a drainage outlet.

desert: a land too dry or too cold to grow many plants.

divide: a height of land which separates river basins.

downstream: the direction toward which a river flows.

drainage: the carrying away of waters; a region or area drained by a river.

drought [drout]: a dry season; a time of little or no rain.

earthquake: a shaking or trembling of the crust of the earth, caused by underground volcanic forces or by breaking or shifting rock beneath the surface.

environment: surroundings, including climate, land forms, and other forms of life.

eruption [ĭ·rŭp′shən]: a bursting forth as of lava from a volcano.

escarpment [ĕs·kärp′mənt]: a steep slope or cliff.

estuary [ĕs′choo·ĕr′e]: an inlet or arm of a sea; especially the wide mouth of a river, where the tide meets the current.

fall line: the area where rivers descend from piedmont to plain and form waterfalls or rapids.

fault: a crack in the earth's surface.

Dictionary of Geographical Terms

fiord [fyôrd]: a narrow inlet of the sea with steep banks, made by a glacier.

fissure [fĭsh′ər]: a long, narrow, deep cleft or crack.

gap: a narrow opening, especially through a mountain.

geyser [gī′zər]: an opening in the earth's surface from which hot water and steam shoot up at certain times.

glacier [glā′shər]: a large mass of ice that moves slowly down a valley from highlands toward sea level.

gorge [gôrj]: a deep, narrow pass between steep heights.

ground water: water found underground in porous rock layers and soils.

gulf: a part of an ocean or sea which reaches into the land. It generally has a narrower opening than a bay.

harbor: a sheltered place where ships may anchor safely.

highland: hills, mountains, or plateaus.

horizon [hə·rī′zən]: the line where the sky seems to meet the earth.

hot spring: a spring which produces water above 98 °F.

ice shelves: large floating sheets of ice.

iceberg: a mountain of ice floating in the sea.

intermountain: between mountains.

irrigation [ĭr′ĭ·gā′shŭn]: supplying water to land for growing crops.

island: an area of land completely surrounded by water.

isthmus [ĭs′məs]: a narrow strip of land which connects two larger bodies of land.

key (or cay): a low island, usually composed of sand; a reef.

lagoon [lə·goon′]: a shallow lake or pond; an area of shallow salt water separated from the sea by sand dunes.

lake: an inland body of water.

lava plain: a plain covered by lava.

lava [lä′və]: melting rock issuing from a volcano.

marsh: an area of low, wet, soft land; a swamp or bog.

mesa [mā′sə]: a small high plateau or flat tableland with steep sides.

migration: the movement of one group of people or animals to another part of the world.

mountain chain: connected ranges of mountains.

mountain range: a long row of mountains.

mouth (of a river): the place where the river flows into a larger body of water.

oasis [ō·ā′sĭs]: a desert area made fertile by the presence of water.

ocean current: a stream of water moving in a definite direction through the ocean. Some currents are warm, some cold.

ocean trench: a deep furrow in the ocean floor where earthquakes begin.

ocean: one of the large, continuous areas of the earth into which the water surface is divided.

pass: a narrow passage or opening between mountains.

peak: the highest point of a mountain; a mountain that has a pointed top.

peninsula: a piece of land that is nearly surrounded by water.

permafrost: permanently frozen ground.

piedmont [pēd′mŏnt]: hilly land at the foot of mountains.

plain: a flat or level area of land.

plateau [plă·tō′]: tableland; a highland plain or elevated area of generally level land, sometimes containing deep canyons.
port: a city or town with a harbor where ships can load and unload cargo.
prairie: level or hilly land covered by grass but no trees.
precipice [prĕs′ə·pĭs]: a vertical or overhanging rock face; a steep cliff.
rapids: a part of a river where the current is very swift.
ravine [rə·vēn′]: a long, deep hollow in the earth's surface.
reef: a ridge of rock, coral, or sand at or near the water's surface.
reservoir [rĕz′ər·vwôr]: a tank, lake, or other place for collecting and storing water.
river basin: the area drained by a river and its tributaries.
river valley: a lowland through which a river flows.
sand bar: a ridge of sand built up by the waves of the sea or by a river current.
savanna: a tropical region of long, thick grasses.
sea: a large area of salt water smaller than an ocean that is partly or completely enclosed by land.
sea level: the level of the ocean waters. Sea level is used as a starting point to measure the height or depth of a location on earth
seacoast: land next to the sea.
semiarid [sĕm′ĭ·ăr′ĭd]: dry, but not as dry as a desert.
silt: sand and soil that is carried by moving water.

snowline: the mountain altitude above which the snow never melts.
sound: a wide channel or strait linking two large bodies of water or separating an island from the mainland.
source (of a river): the place where a river begins.
steppe: a region of short grasses.
strait: a narrow body of water connecting two larger bodies of water.
swamp: a low area of wet, spongy ground, usually containing reedlike vegetation.
tableland: a high, broad, level region; plateau.
terrain: land, especially referring to its geographical features.
timberline (or treeline): a point on a mountain or in polar regions beyond which trees cannot grow because of the cold.
topography [tə·pŏg′rə·fē]: the surface features of a region, including its land height, rivers, lakes, etc.
tributary: a river or creek which flows into a larger river.
upstream: the direction from which a river flows.
valley: a lowland between hills or mountains.
volcanic island: an island composed of volcanoes.
volcano [vŏl·kā′nō]: a mountain with openings in the earth's crust through which lava escapes. A volcano is **active** when erupting, **dormant** during a long period of inactivity, and **extinct** when all activity has finally ceased.

Index

Page numbers for illustrations are indicated by a *p* and printed in *italic type*.

A

A.D. 108
abolitionists 182–183
abortion 263
absolute monarchy 153
Acadia 33
Acadians 36
Adams, John 157
adobe 278
Africa 2
African Baptist Missionary Society of Richmond 169
Alamo 175, *p175*
Alaska 215
Alberta 41
Allen, Ethan 145
Allen, Richard 166
alliance 230
Allies 230, 243
Alline, Henry 37
Altiplano 317–318
Amazon River 8, *p8,* 316, 321, *p321,* 334
Amazon River Basin 321
American Bible Society 169
American Indian tribes (*see also* Indians):
  Middle American
    Arawak 292
    Aztec 6, 277–278
    Carib 292
    Maya 6–7, 285–286, *p285*
  North American
    Apache 92
    Beaver 24
    Bella Coola 88
    Blackfoot 70
    Cayuga 57
    Cayuse 91
    Cherokee 58
    Cheyenne 70
    Chinook 88
    Chippewa (*see* Ojibwa)
    Comanche 70
    Cree 24
    Creek 58–59
    Crow 70
    Dakota 70
    Delaware 59
    Flathead (*see* Salish)
    Havasupai 79–80
    Hopewell 57
    Hopi 80, 92
    Keres 92
    Mohawk 57
    Mojave 92
    Navajo 80, 92
    Nez Percé 89, 91
    Nootka 88
    Ojibwa 24, *p24, 25*
    Oneida 57
    Onondaga 57
    Ottawa 24
    Pueblo 91–92
    Salish 91
    Seminole 59
    Seneca 57
    Shawnee 58
    Shoshone 89
    Sioux 70, *p70*
    Tewas 92
    Tlingit 88
    Ute 91
    Wampanoag 59
    Yellowknife 24
    Zuñi 92
  South American
    Auca 322
    Inca 8, 324–325
    Ona 339
    Waorani (*see* Auca)
    Yahgan 339
American's Creed 342
Anderson, Marian *p257*
Andes Mountains 8, 316, 317, *p317,* 328
Angel Falls 332, *p332*
Anglo-America 276
animals 4–5, *p4*
  alpaca 319
  anaconda 319
  Andean condor 320
  angelfish 297
  antelope jack rabbit 83
  appaloosa 89
  arctic fox 18
  arctic tern 17
  arctic wolf 17
  bald eagle 23, 55
  bat 84
  beaver 22–23
  bee hummingbird 306
  bighorn sheep 76
  bison 65–67, *p67*
  black bear 56, *p56*
  bobcat 84
  buffalo (*see* bison)
  bushmaster 287
  cacomistle (*see* ringtail)
  caiman 287, *p287*
  California condor 84, *p84*
  California gull 85
  Canada goose 17
  capuchin monkey 286
  capybara 318
  caribou 17, 18, 22
  chuckwalla 83
  coati 287, *p287*
  cock-of-the-rock 320, *p320*
  collared peccary 84
  common iguana 287
  conch 297
  cony (*see* pika)
  coquí 299
  cougar (*see* mountain lion)
  coyote 84
  crow 23
  desert tortoise 83
  dipper (*see* water ouzel) 77, *p78*
  dog 19–20
  dolphin 297
  douroucouli 286
  elk (*see* wapiti)
  ermine 23
  flamingo 282
  fur sea 15
  Galápagos giant tortoise 319
  giant anteater 319
  gila monster 83
  golden eagle 23, *p23*
  gooney bird (*see* wandering albatross)
  gray whale 85
  grizzly bear 77
  guanaco 319
  gulls 17
  guppies 297
  helmet shell 297
  heron 282
  horned toad 83, *p83*
  horse conch 297
  howler monkey 287
  hummingbird 282
  jaguar 286, 318
  jaguarundi 286
  kangaroo rat 83
  kit fox 84
  lemming 18, *p18*
  llama 319
  macaw 282, 320
  manta ray 297
  marlin 297
  marten 23, *p23*
  mink 23
  moose 22
  mountain goat 76–77, *p76*
  mountain lion 77, *p77*
  musk oxen 17
  narwhal 15
  pack rat 83
  panther (*see* mountain lion)
  parakeets 298
  parrot 282, 298
  pelican 282
  pika 77, *p77*
  piranha 319–320, *p319*
  pocket mouse 83
  polar bear 15, *p30*
  prairie chicken 67, *p67*
  prairie dog 65, 67
  ptarmigan *p16,* 17
  puffin 15
  puma (*see* mountain lion)
  queen conch 297
  quetzal 282
  ram 76
  raven 23
  ringtail 84, *p84*
  roadrunner 84
  salmon 85–86
  sea lion 85
  sea turtle 297
  seal 18, 85
  snow goose 17
  snowy owl 17
  spectacled bear 318
  spider monkey 287
  spotted skunk 84
  squirrel monkey 286
  tapir 318

Index 353

toucan 287, 298
two-toed sloth 318–319, *p319*
vicuña 319
wahoo 297
wandering albatross 85, *p85*
wapiti 56
water ouzel 77
weasel 23
whistling hare (*see* pika)
white-tailed deer 56, *p56*
wild turkey 55, *p55*, 282
wolverine 23
Antigua 303–304
Apache Indians 92
Appalachia 51
Appalachian Mountains 5, 30, *p30*, 50–52
Appomattox Court House 191, *p191*
Arawak Indians 292
archery 10
archipelago 296
Arctic 14
Arctic Islands 26
Arctic Ocean 14–15
arctic willow 17, *p17*
Argentina 316, 337–339
Arizona 176
Ark 126
Armistead, James 148
Armour, P. D. 214
Armstrong, Neil 262
Articles of Confederation 152
Aruba 305
Asbury, Francis 165
Asia 2
Asian Americans 259
assembly line 211–212, *p212*
Atacama Desert 8, *p8*, 317, 328
Atahualpa 325
atheists 11, 307
Atlantic Coastal Plain 52–53
Atlantic Ocean 53–54
Atlantic Provinces (*see* Maritime Provinces)

atomic bomb 245, *p245*
Auca Indians 322
aurora borealis 14, *p15*
Australia 2
Austria-Hungary 231
automobiles 223, 234
Axis Powers 243
Aztec Indians 6, 277–278

B

B.C. 108
baby boom 254
Badlands 68, *p69*
Baffin Island 26
Bahamas 296, 301–302, *p302*
Baja California 6, 277, 280
Balboa, Vasco Núñez de 294, *p294*
balsa wood 330
balsam fir 21
bananas 320
Banff National Park *p27*, 41, *p41*
bank 46
Banneker, Benjamin 158, *p158*
Banting, Frederick G. 45, *p45*
Barbados 305
barrel cacti 82, *p82*
Barton, Clara 193–194, *p193*
Batista, Fulgencio 307
Battle of Little Bighorn 71
Battles:
  Alamo 175, *p175*
  Britain 242, *p242*
  Bull Run 189
  Bunker Hill 145, *p145*
  Concord 144
  Gettysburg 190, *p190*
  Lexington 144, *p144*
  New Orleans 174
  San Jacinto 176
  San Juan Hill *p216*, 217
  Saratoga 149
  Vicksburg 190
bauxite 300
Bay of Fundy 36, *p36*

Bay of Pigs 264
Beaver Indians 24
Belize 285, 288
Bell, Alexander Graham 209–210, *p210*
Bella Coola 88
Belmopan, Belize 288
Bering Strait 3, *p3*
Berkeley, Lord John 125
Berlin Wall 251, *p251*
Bermudas 296
Best, Charles H. 45, *p45*
Bethune, Mary McLeod 221, *p221*
Bible references used in text:
  Genesis 1:28 11
    7:17–21 73
    8:22 9
    9:6 153
    10:25 4
  Leviticus 25:10 147
  Psalm 72:8 26
  Proverbs 24:21 153
  Matthew 24:6 230
    25:21 168
  Luke 1:63 299
  John 17:3 118
  Acts 17:26 3
  Romans 2:11 260
    8:32 170
    13:1–7 153
  1 Thessalonians 5:18 115
  1 Timothy 2:1–2 153
    2:2 275
  1 Peter 2:13–16 153
Big Four 247
Big Room 81
Bill of Rights 156–157
Black Hills 68
Black History:
  individuals
    Allen, Richard 166
    Anderson, Marian 257
    Armistead, James 148
    Attucks, Crispus 141
    Banneker, Benjamin 158, *p158*
    Bethune, Mary McLeod 221, *p221*
    Brooke, Edward C. 258
    Burleigh, Harry T. 172

Carey, Lott 169–170
Carney, William Harvey 188
Carver, George Washington 196–197, *p196*
Chavis, John 171
Davis, Jr., Benjamin O. 246, *p246*
Davis, Sr., Benjamin O. 246
Douglass, Frederick 186
Ferguson, Catherine 171
George, David 37
Haynes, Lemuel 143, 170
Henson, Matthew 230
Jasper, John 170–171, *p170*
Johnson, James Weldon 172
King, Jr., Dr. Martin Luther 257–258, *p258*
Liele, George 166–167, 300
Matzeliger, Jan Ernst 212
Morgan, Garrett A. 212
Moseley-Braun, Carol 258
Parks, Rosa 257
Powell, General Colin 271, *p271*
Price, Mary Leontyne 172
Rillieux, Norbert 212
Robinson, Jackie 256–257, *p257*
Teague, Collin 169
Thomas, Justice Clarence 260–261, *p261*
Truth, Sojourner 183
Tubman, Harriet 183–184, *p183*
Washington, Booker T. 195–196, *p196*
Watts, Jr., J. C. 258
Weaver, Robert C. 258
Wheatley, Phillis 133, *p133*
Wilder, L. Douglas 258
Woods, Granville T. 212
Work, John Wesley Sr. 172

Index

topics
  African Baptist Missionary Society of Richmond 169
  Civil Rights Act (1964) 258
  civil rights movement 257–258
  desegregation 257
  educators 195–197, 221
  Emancipation Proclamation 188
  Fighting Red Tails 246
  Fisk Jubilee Singers 172, *p172*
  inventors 196–197, 212
  missions 37, 166–167, 169–170
  preachers 166–167, 169–171, 257–258
  statesmen 258, 260–261, 271
  slavery 111, 128, 133, 170–171, 182–184, 188, 192, 294, 334
  spirituals 171
  Tuskegee Institute 196, 246
  Underground Railroad 183
Blackfoot Indians 70
blockade 187
blubber 15
Blue-Backed Speller 164
Bogotá, Colombia 331–332
Bolívar, Simón 326, *p326*
Bolivia 316, 330–331
Bonaire 305
Bonaparte, Napoleon 172
Bonhomme Richard 150–151, *p151*
Boone, Daniel 160–161, *p161*
Boonesborough 161
Booth, John Wilkes 192
boreal forest (*see* taiga)
Bosnia 273
Boston 116, *p255*
Boston Massacre 141, *p141*
Boston Tea Party 141–142, *p142*
Boyle, Robert 300
Braddock, General Edward 138, *p139*
Bradford, William 114
Bradley, General Omar 247
Brainerd, David 61, 134
branded 200
Brant, Joseph 62, *p62*
Brasília, Brazil 336, 337
Brazil 316, 334–337
  cities 336–337
  geography 334
  history 334–335
  people 335–336
  resources and industry 335
Brazilian Highlands 316
Brewster, Elder 113
bristlecone pine 79
British Columbia 42–43
broadleaf trees 21–22
Brooke, Edward C. 258
browsing 76
Bryan, William Jennings 235, *p235*
Buck Island 303
Buenos Aires, Argentina 338
bullfights 284
burial mounds 57, *p57*
Bush, George H. W. 270–271, *p270*
Bush, George W. 274–275, *p275*

C

Cabot, John 31, 106
Cabral, Pedro Alvares 325
cacao bean 335
cacti 82
Calgary, Alberta 41
California 176, 178
California Gold Rush 177, *p177*
California redwood tree 86
Calvert, George 126
Camp David Peace Accords 266
camp meetings 166, *p167*
Campanius, John 60–61
Campbell, Ben Nighthorse 259
Canada 26–49, *p28*
  climate 45
  geography 26–30
  government 48–49
  history 31–34
  people 44–45
  provinces 35–43
  resources and industry 45–47, *p47*
  territories 43–44
Canada balsam 21
Canadarm 45, *p45*
Canadian National Tower (*see* CN Tower)
Canadian Rockies 30
Canadian Shield 27
Canadian Tulip Festival 39
candelilla 281
Cape Breton Island 36
Cape Horn 8
Caracas, Venezuela 332–333, *p333*
Carey, Lott 169–170
Carib Indians 292
Caribbean Sea 6, 277, 292, 296
Carlsbad Caverns 81, *p81*
Carnegie, Andrew 206–207
Carney, William Harvey 188
Carolinas 127–128
Carter, Jimmy 266, *p266*
Carteret, Sir George 125
Cartier, Jacques 32, *p32*
Cartwright, Peter 166, *p166*
Carver, George Washington 196–197, *p196*
Carver, John 112
Cascade Range 86
cassava 323
Castilian Spanish (*see* Spanish language)
Castro, Fidel 259, 307–311, *p307*, 313
Cayuga Indians 57
Cayuse Indians 91
Central America 6, *p7*, 276, *p278*, 285–291
  climate 286
  geography 285
  history 285–286
  people and nations 285, 288–291
  resources 286
  wildlife 286–287
Central Pacific Company 194
Central Powers 230
Challenger 268, *p269*
Champlain, Samuel de 32, *p32*, 33, 121
Chao, Elaine 259
Charles I, King 116
Charles Town 127
Charleston 127
Charlotte Amalie, U.S. Virgin Islands 303
Chavis, John 171
Cherokee Indians 58
Cheyenne Indians 70
Chichén Itzá 286
Chihuahuan Desert 78, 80–81, 281
Chile 316, 340
Chinook Indians 88
Chippewa Indians (*see* Ojibwa)
chocolate 278
Christ of the Andes 338
Christian school movement 263
Church of England 112
Churchill, Manitoba 40
Churchill, Sir Winston 247, *p247*
circuit-riding preachers 165–166
Citaltépetl 280
Civil Rights Act (1964) 258
Civil War 186–191
civil government 153
civil rights movement 257
Clark, Geoge Rogers 150
Clark, William 172

Index 355

Clermont 208, *p208*
Clinton, William ("Bill") 273–274, *p273*
CN Tower 39, *p39*
Coast Ranges 86
coconut palms 297
Cody, Buffalo Bill 201, *p201*
coffee 320, 331, *p331*, 335
Coke, Thomas 304
Colombia 316, 331–332
Colorado 176
Colorado Plateau 78, 79–80
Colorado River 74–75
Colt, Samuel 214
Columbia Plateau 78
Columbia River 75, 86
Columbus, Christopher 7, 31, 292–294, *p293*
Comanche Indians 70
Common House 113
Commonwealth of Independent States 272
Commonwealth of Nations 48
Communism 238–239, 250–251, 307–313
compromise 184
concentration camps 246, *p246*
Confederate 186
Confederate States of America 186
Congregational churches 120
Congress 155
conifers 21
Connecticut 119–120
conservative 263
Constitution, U.S. 153
Constitutional Convention 152–154
constitutional monarchy 48, 153
constitutional republic 155
containment 253
Cook, Captain James 34, *p34*, 215

Coolidge, Calvin 233–234, *p234*
Copan 289
coral reef 297, *p297*
Cordilleras 72, *p72*
Cornwallis, General Lord 151
Cortés, Hernando *p278*, 279
Costa Rica *p276*, 285, 288
cotton gin 182
coup 272
covered wagon 162
cow towns 200
Crater Lake 86, *p86*
Cree Indians 24
Creek Indians 58–59
creosote bushes 82
Croatoan 109
Crockett, Davy 175
Crow Indians 70
Cuba 216, 259, 264, 292, 306–310, 312–313
Cuban Missile Crisis 264
culture 5
Cumaná, Venezuela 332
Cumberland Gap 51, 161
Curaçao 305
curare 324
Curtis, Charles 259
Custer, General 71
Cuzco 324, *p325*
Cuzco, Peru 329
cyclone (see hurricanes)

D

D-Day 244
Dakota Indians 70
Danish West Indies (see Virgin Islands)
Dare, Virginia 108
Darwin, Charles 234–235
Davis, Jefferson 186
Davis, Jr., Benjamin O. 246, *p246*
Davis, Sr., Benjamin O. 246
De Shazer, Jacob 249

Death Valley 80
deciduous 22
Declaration of Independence 146–147, *p146*, 343
Delaware 122–123
Delaware Indians 59
democracy 153
Dempster Highway 43–44, *p43*
Devil's Island 333
Dewey, Admiral George 216
dictator 238
dictatorship 153
Discovery 109
District of Columbia 159
dog sleds 19
Dominica 304
Dominican Republic 300, 301
Dominion of Canada 34
Douglas fir 86
Douglas, Stephen A. 185
Douglass, Frederick 186
Dove 126, *p126*
drought 64
Dutch 122

E

Easter Island 318
Eastern United States 50–63, *p52*
Eastman, George 214
economy 254
Ecuador 316, 329–330
Edison, Thomas 210–211, *p210*
Edmonton, Alberta 41
Edwards, Jonathan 131–132
Eisenhower, Dwight D. 262, *p262*, 247
El Salvador 266, 285, 288, *p289*
electric light bulb 210–211
Eliot, John 60, *p60*, 117
Elizabeth I, Queen 107
Ellesmere Island 26

Elliot, Jim and Elisabeth 322, *p322*
Emancipation Proclamation 188
emeralds 331
England 121
equator 316
Ericson, Leif 31
Erie Canal 163–164, *p163*
Erik the Red 16
Eskimo 18, *p19*, 20
estancias 337
estuaries 297–298
Europe 2, 241, *p241*
Evans, James 40
Everglades 59
evergreens 21, *p22*
executive power 155

F

Falkland Islands 318, 339
fall line 52
Farewell Address 158
Fascist Party 239
fauna 73
fazendas 335
Ferdinand, Archduke 231, *p231*
Ferdinand, King of Spain, 293
Ferguson, Catherine 171
fiesta 284
Fighting Red Tails 246
Fillmore, President Millard 180
Finney, Charles 205, *p205*
First Amendment 157, 344
First Continental Congress 142
Fisk Jubilee Singers 172, *p172*
Flag Day 149
flatboat *p162*, 163
Flathead Indians (see Salish Indians)
flora 73
Florida 69
Ford, Gerald R. 265, *p265*
Ford, Henry 211

356 New World History & Geography

Index

Fort Christina 122
Fort Duquesne 138, *p139*
Fort le Boeuf 137
Fort McHenry 174
Fort Sumter 186
"forty-niners" 177
France 121
Franklin, Benjamin 133
free enterprise system 111
French and Indian War 33, 137–140, *p138*
French Guiana 316, 333
frigid zone 16
Fuchida, Mitsuo 249
Fulton, Robert 208
Fundamental Orders of Connecticut 120
fundamentalist 235

G

Gadsden Purchase 176
Galápagos Islands 318
gap 51
Garfield, James 203, *p203*
gauchos 337, *p338*
General Sherman Tree 87
geography 2
George III, King 140, *p140*
George, David 37
Georgia 128–130
Germany 239–240, 241–242
Geronimo 93
Gettysburg Address 191, 345
geysers 75
ghost town 178, *p178*
giant sequoia 87, *p87*
glacier 14–15
Glenn, John 262
Goble, Jonathan 180–181
Goddard, Robert H. 214, *p214*
Godspeed 109
Goforth, Jonathan 45
gold spike 195
Goodyear, Charles 214
Gorbachev, Mikhail 269

Gore, Al 274
Gorgas, Colonel William 290
government 261–262
Governor General 48
Gran Chaco 316
Grand Banks 46
Grand Canyon 75, 79, *p79*, 337
Grand Teton National Park *p73*
Grant, Ulysses S. 188–189, *p189, 191*
grazing 76
Great Awakening 131–134
Great Barrier Reef 337
Great Basin Desert 78–79
Great Bear Lake 30
Great Britain 242
Great Depression 236, *p236*
Great Divide 73–74
Greater Antilles 296
Great Lakes 29–30, *p29*
Great Plains 5
Great Salt Lake 79
Great Salt Lake Desert 79
Great Slave Lake 30
Great Smoky Mountains 51, *p51*
Great Society 264
Great White Fleet 228, 230
Greene, Nathanael 151
Greenland 6, 16
Green Mountain Boys 145
Grenada 267–268, *p268*, 304–305
Grenfell, Sir Wilfred 21, 35
Guadalajara, Mexico 283
Guadeloupe 304
Guam 217
Guanabara Bay 336, *p336*, 337
guano 84
Guantánamo Bay 307
Guatemala *p6*, 285, 288–289
Guatemala City, Guatemala 289
Guayaquil, Ecuador 330

Guiana Highlands 316
Gulf Coastal Plain 52, 53
Gulf of California 277
Gulf of Mexico 6, 69
Gulf of St. Lawrence 27
Gulf Stream 69
Guyana 316, 333

H

habitat 4
Haiti 273, 293, 300, 301
Hale, Nathan 148
Half Moon 121
Hall of Fame 225, *p225*
Hancock, John 147
hardwoods 22
harpoon 20, *p20*
Harris, Townsend 181
Hartford 120
Harvard College 118
Havana, Cuba 306, *p306*
Havasupai Indians 79–80
Hawaii 215–216
Haynes, Lemuel 143, 170
haystack prayer meeting 167
headwaters 74
Hells Canyon 78
hemlock 86
Henry, Patrick 143
Henson, Matthew 230
Hessians 146
Hickok, Wild Bill 201
hieroglyphics 286
Hirohito, Emperor 240
Hiroshima 245
Hispanic Americans 259
Hispaniola 292, 300
history 2
Hitler, Adolf 239–240, *p240*
hogan *p9*, 10
Holocaust 246
homeschool movement 274
Homestead Act 202
Honduras 285, 289, *p289*
Hooker, Thomas 120

Hopewell Indians 57
Hopi Indians 80, 92
hornbook 118, *p118*
hot springs 75
House of Burgesses 126
House of Commons 48
House of Representatives 155
Houston, General Sam 175–176
Howe, Elias 214
Hudson Bay 6, 27
Hudson Bay Company 33
Hudson, Henry 33, *p33*, 121
hurricanes 298
Huss, John 124
Hussein, Saddam 271

I

iceberg 15
Idaho 178, 179
igloos 19, *p19*
Iguaçú Falls 338
Illinois 161
immigrant 204, *p204*
Inauguration Day 157
Inca Indians 8, 324–325
Independence Day 146
Independence, Missouri 178
Indiana 161
Indians (*see also* American Indian tribes):
  culture
    clothing 10, 24, 278
    crafts 325
    customs and religion 70–71, 88–89, 277–278, 285–286, 323, 324
    education 9, 278, 325
    food 9, 24, 57, 278, 323–325
    housing 10, 24, 58, *p59*, 71, *p323*
    recreation 10, *p10*, 285
    religion 10–11, *p10*, 24–25
    travel 24

Index 357

individuals
    Atahualpa 325
    Brant, Joseph 62, *p62*
    Geronimo 93
    Joseph, Chief 91, *p91*
    Massasoit, Chief 59, 114
    Montezuma *p278*, 279
    Pocahontas *p124*, 125
    Rogers, Will 11
    Sacagawea 89
    Samoset 59, 114
    Sequoya 62–63, *p63*
    Sitting Bull 71, *p71*, 201, *p201*
    Squanto 114
    Tattamy 61
    Tecumseh 62, *p62*
    Thorpe, Jim 11
missionaries to
    Brainerd, David 61, 134
    Campanius, John 60–61
    Eliot, John 60, *p60*, 117
    Elliot, Jim and Elisabeth 322, *p322*
    Gardiner, Captain Allen 339
    Saint, Nate and Rachel 322
    Spalding, Henry and Eliza 90
    Whitman, Marcus and Narcissa 90
    Williams, Roger 61
industrial parks 255
"In God We Trust" 192–193
Inouye, Daniel Ken 259
Intermountain Region 78–81
Interstate Highway System 262
Inuit 18
Iqaluit, Nunavut 44
Iraq 271
ironclad 187
Iroquois League of Five Nations 57
Isabel, Princess 334
Isabela 293

Isabella, Queen of Spain, 293
Israel 252
Isthmus of Panama 277, 293
Isthmus of Tehuantepec 280
Itaipú Dam 335, *p335*
Italy 239
Iztaccíhuatl 280

J

Jackson, General Andrew 174
Jackson, Stonewall 189–190, *p189*
Jamaica 293, 300
James I, King 109
James River 109
Jamestown 109–111, *p111*
Japan 240, *p241*, 243–245
Jasper, John 170–171, *p170*
Jefferson, Thomas 146, 172
Johnson, Andrew 192
Johnson, Lyndon B. 264, *p264*
Jones, Casey 223
Jones, John Paul 150–151
Joseph, Chief 91, *p91*
Joshua tree *p81*, 82
judicial power 155, 156
Judson, Adoniram 167, 168, *p168*

K

Kai-shek, Chiang 247, 250–251, *p251*
kayak 20
Kennedy, John Fitzgerald 263–264, *p263*
Kentucky 161
Keres Indians 92
Key, Francis Scott 174
King Charles I 116
King George III 140, *p140*
King, Jr., Dr. Martin Luther 257–258, *p258*
Kingston, Jamaica 300

Klondike Gold Rush 43, *p43*
Korean War 252–253, *p252*
Kuhn, Isobel 45
Kuwait 271

L

La Paz, Bolivia 330
Lake Erie 29
Lake Huron 29
Lake Itasca 69
Lake Maracaibo 332
Lake Michigan 29
Lake Nicaragua 285
Lake Ontario 29
Lake Superior 29–30
Lake Titicaca 330–331, *p330*
Lake Winnipeg 40
Land of the Midnight Sun 16
land rush 202
Latin America 276
Latin-American Spanish (*see* Spanish language)
Lee, Robert E. 189, *p189*, 191
Leeward Islands 303–304
leggings 10
legislative power 155
Lenin, Nikolai 238
Leon, Juan Ponce de 106
Lesser Antilles 296, *p304*
Lewis, Meriwether 172
liberal 234, 263
Liberia 169
Liberty Bell 147, *p147*
lichen 17
Liele, George 166–167, 300
life expectancy 220
Lima, Peru 329
Lincoln, Abraham *p183*, 184–186, *p185*, 188
log cabins 122, *p122*
London Company 109
longhorns 200, *p200*
longhouses 58, *p58*

Lord Baltimore (*see* George Calvert)
Louisiana Purchase 172
Louisiana Territory 172
Lower California (*see* Baja California)
Loyalists 33–34
Lusitania 232

M

MacArthur, General Douglas 247–249, *p248*, 252–253
Machen, J. Gresham 235, *p235*
Machu Picchu 329, *p329*
Mackenzie River 30
Madeira River 321
Madison, Dolly 174
Madison, James 153, 174
Magellan, Ferdinand 294, 325–326
mail train 224
Maine 216
maize 9
Mammoth Cave 51
Mammoth Hot Springs 75
Managua, Nicaragua 289
Manaus, Brazil 336
mangroves 297
Manitoba 40
Marconi, Guglielmo 225
Maritime Provinces 35–37
Marshall, General George C. 247
Marshall, James 177
Martinez, Melquiades ("Mel") 259
Martinique *p6*, 293
Maryland 126–127
Mason, John 119
Massachusetts 116–118
Massachusetts Bay Colony 116
Massachusetts Bay Company 116
Massasoit, Chief 59, 114
Matos, Huber 260, *p260*
Matzeliger, Jan Ernst 212

358   *New World History & Geography*

Index

Maya Indians 6–7, 285–286, *p285*
Mayflower 112, *p113*
Mayflower Compact 112–113, *p113*
McCormick, Cyrus 199–200
McGuffey, William H. 164
"melting pot" 204
Merrimac 187, *p187*
Mesa Verde National Park *p92*
Mesabi Range 68
mesas 79
mestizos 282–283
Mexican Cession 176
Mexican Plateau 280–281
Mexican War 176
Mexico 6, 276, 277–284, *p278*
   climate 281
   geography 280–281
   government 284
   history 279–280
   people 277–278, 282–284
   resources and industry 281–282
   wildlife 281–282
Mexico City, Mexico 281, 283, *p283*
Meyer, F. B. 222, 235
Michigan 161
Middle America 276–277
Middle Colonies 121–125, *p121*
Middle East 2
Middle United States 64–71, *p66*
migration 2
Mills, Samuel J. 167
Mineta, Norman 259
Mink, Patsy Takemoto 259
Minnesota 161
minutemen 142
Mississippi River 6, 68–69
Missouri Compromise 184
Missouri River 68–69
Model T *p212*
modernist 234
Mohawk Indians 57, 58

Mojave Desert 78, 80
Mojave Indians 92
monarchy 153
Monitor 187, *p187*
Monroe, James 174
Monrovia 170
Montana 178
Monterrey, Mexico 283
Montevideo, Uruguay *p340*, 341
Montezuma *p278*, 279
Montgomery, Lucy Maud 35
Montreal 37, 38
Moody, Dwight L. 205, *p205*, 222
Moravians 124
Morgan, G. Campbell 222, 235
Morgan, Garrett A. 212
Morse Code 209
Morse, Samuel 208–209
Moseley-Braun, Carol 258
Mount Aconcagua 317
Mount Elbert 72
Mount Everest 337
Mount Logan 43
Mount McKinley 5–6
Mount Pelée 296, *p296*
Mount Rainier 86
Mount Rushmore 68, *p68*
Mount Shasta 86
Mount Whitney 80, 86
Mounties (*see* Royal Canadian Mounted Police)
mukluks 19
Mussolini, Benito 239, *p240*

N

Nagasaki 245
NASA 262
Nassau, Bahamas 301
National Socialism (*see* Nazi Party)
Native Americans (*see* Indians *and* American Indian tribes)
NATO 262
Navajo Indians 80, 92

Nazi Party 239–240
Netherlands Antilles 305
neutral nations 230
Nevada 176
New Amsterdam 121
New Brunswick 36, *p44*
New England Colonies 116–120, *p116*
New England Primer 118
New France 32
New Frontier 263
New Hampshire 119
New Jersey 124–125
New Mexico 176
New Netherland 121
New Orleans 172
New Sweden 122–123
New World 2
New York 121–122
New York City 122, 147, 157
Newfoundland (island) 26
Newfoundland (province) 35–36, *p35*
Nez Percé Indians 89, 91
Niagara Falls 29–30, *p29*
Nicaragua 266, 285, 289–290
Niña 292
Nisei 245, *p245*
Nixon, Richard M. 265, *p265*
nocturnal 84, 286
Nootka Indians 88
North America 2, 5, *p7*
North American Desert 78, *p81*
North Carolina 128
North Pole 14, 230
Northern Lights 337
Northwest Ordinance of 1787 161–162
Northwest Passage 31
Northwest Territories, Canada 43–44
Northwest Territory, U.S. 152, 161
Nova Scotia 36–37
Nunavut 44
nutmeg 304, *p305*

O

O'Connor, Sandra Day 268
O'Higgins, Bernardo 326
Oakley, Annie 201, *p201*
Obookiah, Henry 168–169
Of Plymouth Plantation 114
Oglethorpe, James 128–129, *p129*
Ohio 161, 162–163
Ohio River 69, 136
oil (*see* petroleum)
Ojibwa Indians 24, *p24*, 25
Oklahoma City 273, *p273*
Oklahoma Land Rush 202, *p202*
Old Faithful 75, *p75*
old-field school 130, *p130*
Ole' Deluder Satan Act 117
Omaha, Nebraska 194
Ona Indians 339
Oneida Indians 57
Onondaga Indians 57
one-room schoolhouse *p164*, 165
Ontario 38–39
Operation Desert Storm 270–271
orchids 321
Oregon 178, 179
Oregon Country 178
Oregon Territory 178
Oregon Trail 178, *p179*
Osler, Sir William 44–45
Ottawa 38–39, *p38*
Ottawa Indians 24
Ozarks 68

P

Pacific Coast 85–87
Pacific Ocean 294
Painted Desert 80
Palestine 252
Pampas 317, *p317*, 337, *p338*
pamperos 337

Index 359

Panama 285, 290–291
Panama Canal 228, 277, 290, *p290*
Panama City, Panama 291
paper birch 22
Papiamento 305
Paraguay 316, 340
Paraguay River 334
Paraná River 334, 335, *p335*
Paricutín 282, *p282*, 337
parkas 19
Parks, Rosa 257
Parliament 48
Patagonia 338–339
patriots 141
patroon system 121
Patton, George S. 247
Pearl Harbor 243–244, *p243*
Peary, Robert 230
Pedro II 334
Peleg 4
pemmican 24
Penn, William 123–124, *p123*
Pennsylvania 123–124
Pennsylvania Dutch 124
Perestroika 269
permafrost 16
Perry, Commodore Matthew 180, *180*
Persian Gulf War 270
Peru 316, 328–329
Petrified Forest National Park 80
petrified log *p81*
petroleum 207, 320, 332
Philadelphia 124, 152
Philippine Islands 216, 217
phonograph 210, *p210*
Pico Duarte 301
Piedmont Plateau 52
Pilgrims 112, *p112*
pimento 300, *p300*
piñata 284
pine forests 281

Pinta 292
pioneer 160
Pizarro, Francisco 325, 326
Plains Indians 70–71
plankton 15
plantations 127, *p128*
plaza 283
Pledge of Allegiance 222
Plymouth 113–115
Pocahontas *p124*, 125
polio vaccine 255
Polk, President James K. 176
polyps 297
poncho 284
ponderosa pine 73
Pony Express 194, *p194*
Popocatépetl *p277*, 280
Port Royal, Acadia 33
Port-au-Prince, Haiti 301
Potlatch 89
Potomac River 159
Powell, General Colin 271, *p271*
prairie 64
Prairie Provinces 40–41
Preamble to the Constitution 344
President (U.S.) 155
prickly pear 82
prime minister 48
Prince Edward Island 35, *p35*
progress 208
Promontory Point, Utah 195
Protestantism 276
Providence 118
pueblo 91
Pueblo Indians 91–92
Puerto Rico 217, 259, 293, 299–300, *p299*
Pullman, George 223
Pullman sleeping cars 223
Puritan churches (*see* Congregational churches)
Puritans 116

Q
Quakers 123
Québec (province) 37–38
Quebec Act 142
Quebec City, Québec 37–38, *p37*, 33
Quechua 325, 329
Queen Elizabeth I 107
Quito, Ecuador 329–330

R
radio 233, *p233*
railroad *p219*, 223–224
Raleigh, Sir Walter 107
Rangoon, Burma 168
Reagan Doctrine 267
Reagan Revolution 267
Reagan, Ronald 266–269, *p266*
reaper 199
reed boats *p330*, 331
representative democracy 153
representative government 126
Republic of China 251
republic 153
reservation 91, 199
Revere, Paul 143, *p143*
Rhode Island 118–119
Rice, Luther 168
Richmond, Virginia 191
Rights of Americans 344
Rillieux, Norbert 212
Rimmer, Dr. Harry 235
Rio de Janeiro, Brazil 336
Rio de la Plata 338
Rio Grande 176
Roanoke 107–109, *p109*
Robertson, James 40
Robinson, Jackie 256–257, *p257*
Rockefeller, John D. 207
Rocky Mountains 5, *p5*, 72
Roe vs. *Wade* 263
Rogers, Will 11, *p11*
Rolfe, John *p124*, 125

Roman Catholicism 276
Romance languages 279
Roosevelt 230
Roosevelt, Franklin D. 236, 242, *p242*, 247, *p247*
Roosevelt, Theodore 216, *p216*, 226–228, *p226*, 227, 228, 230
Ross, Betsy 149
Rough Riders 216–217
Royal Canadian Mounted Police 48–49, *p48*
Royal Colony 125
rubber 323
Russia 238, 268–269, 271–272

S
S.D.I (*see* Strategic Defense Initiative)
Sacagawea 89, 172, *p173*
Sacramento, California 194
sagebrush 79, *p81*, 82
saguaro cactus 80, *p81*
Salish Indians 91
Salk, Dr. Jonas 255
Samoset 59, 114
San José, Costa Rica 288
San Juan, Puerto Rico 299–300
San Martín, José de 326
San Salvador 292, 301
San Salvador, El Salvador 288
Santa Anna, General 175
Santa Maria 292
Santiago, Chile 340
Santo Domingo, Dominican Republic 301
São Paulo, Brazil 336
sapodilla 281, *p281*
Saskatchewan *p40*, 41
Savannah 129
Schwarzkopf, General Norman 271, *p271*
SEATO 262

history 106–275
indians 57–59, 70–71, 79–80, 88–93
population 218
wildlife 55–56, 65–67, 76–78, 83–84
Uruguay 316, 340–341
Uruguay River 334
Utah 176
Ute Indians 91

V

V-E Day 244
Valdivia, Pedro de 326
Valley Forge 149–150, p150
Valparaíso, Chile 340
Vancouver Island 27
Vancouver, British Columbia 42–43
Vancouver, Captain George 27, 34
Venezuela 316, 332–333
venison 56
Vespucci, Amerigo 325, p325
Veterans Day 233
Victoria Falls 337
Victoria Island 26
Victoria, British Columbia 42, p42
Vietnam War 264–265, p265
Vikings 31, p31
Virgin Islands 302–303, p302
Virgin Islands National Park 303
Virginia 107, 125–126
Volcán Antofalla 337
voodoo 301

W

Wampanoag 59
wampum 55, p55
War for Independence (American) 144–151
War of 1812 173–174
Warr, Lord De La 110, 111
Washington 178, 179
Washington, Booker T. 195–196, p196
Washington, D.C. 159
Washington, George 137, p137, 147, 148, p148, 150, 157–158
Watergate affair 265
Watts, Isaac 166
Watts, Jr., J. C. 258
Weaver, Robert C. 258
Webster, Noah 164
Wesley, Charles 166
Wesley, John 129, 165
West Indies 7, 292–313, p296
climate 298
geography 296–297
history 292–295
peoples and islands pp. 299–306
resources and industry 298
wildlife 297–298
Western Cordillera 30
Western Hemisphere 2, p7
Western United States 72–93, p74
Westinghouse, George 214
Wheatley, Phillis 133, p133
white sands 81
White, John 108, p109
Whitefield, George 130, 132–134, p132
Whitehorse, Yukon Territory 43
Whitewater Investigation 273
Whitman, Marcus and Narcissa 90, 178
Whitney, Eli 182
wickiups 92
wigwams 10
Wilder, L. Douglas 258
Wilderness Road 161
Wilhelm II, Kaiser 230
Williams, Roger 61, 118–119, p119
Williams, Samuel Wells 180
Williamsburg 126
Wilson, Woodrow 231, p231
Windward Islands 304–305
Winnipeg 40
Winthrop, Governor John 116–117, p117
Wisconsin 161
Woods, Granville T. 212
World Trade Center 273
World War I 230–233
World War II 230, 241–249, p244
Wright, Orville 212–213
Wright, Wilbur 212–213
Wyoming 176, 178

X–Z

Yahgan Indians 339
Yellowknife Indians 24
Yellowknife, Northwest Territories 43
Yellowstone Lake 75
Yellowstone National Park 75
York 39
Yorktown, Virginia 151
Yosemite Falls 87, p87
Yosemite National Park 87
Yosemite Valley 87
Yucatán Peninsula 6, 69, 280
yucca plant p81, 82
Yukon River 43
Yukon Territory 43
Zedong, Mao 251
Zimmerman Note 232
Zinzendorf, Count von 124, 302
Zuñi Indians 92

Index

Second Continental Congress 145
Second Great Awakening 165
selvas 321
Seminole Indians 59
Senate (Canada) 48
Senate (U.S.) 155
Seneca Indians 57
Separatists 112
Sequoia National Park 87
Sequoya 62–63, *p63*
serape 284
Serapis 150–151, *p151*
Seven Natural Wonders of the World 337
Seward, William H. 215
Shah of Iran 266
Shawnee Indians 58
Shepard, Jr., Alan B. 262
Sherman, General William T. 191
Shields, T. T. 45
Sholes, C. L. 214
shopping malls 255
Shoshone Indians 89
shot heard 'round the world 144
Sierra Madre Occidental 280
Sierra Madre Oriental 280
Sierra Nevada Range 86–87
siesta 283
Sioux Indians 70, *p70*
Sitting Bull 71, *p71*, 201, *p201*
skyscrapers 254–255
Smith, Captain John 110, *p110*
Smith, Gypsy 222, 235
Snake River 78
Society of Friends (*see* Quakers)
Somalia 273
sombrero 284
Sonoran Desert 78, 80, 281
South America 2, *p7*, 8, 293, 316–341, *p318*
climate 316

geography 316–318
history 324–327
nations 316, 328–341
people 323–324
religion 326–327
resources 320, 323
wildlife 318–320
South Carolina 127–128
South Georgia Islands 318, 339
Southern Colonies 125–130, *p125*
Soviet Union (*see* Russia)
space age 262
Spalding, Henry and Eliza 90
Spanish Armada 109
Spanish language 276, 279
Spanish-American War 216–217
spirituals 171
spruce 21
Squanto 114
St. Augustine 106
St. Croix 303
St. John 303
St. Lawrence River 27–28
St. Lawrence Seaway 27–29, 262
St. Lucia *p295*
St. Mary's City 126
St. Thomas 303
Stalin, Joseph 239, *p239*, 247, *p247*
Stamp Act 140–141
stampede 200
Standish, Captain Miles 113
"Star-Spangled Banner" 174, *p174*
"Star Wars" (*see* Strategic Defense Initiative)
Steamboat Geyser 75
steel 206
Stowe, Harriet Beecher 183
strait 3
Strait of Magellan 8, 318
Strategic Defense Initiative 269
straw market 301, *p301*
Stuyvesant, Peter 121, *p122*

suburbs 254
Sucre, Bolivia 330
Sugar Loaf Mountain 336, *p336*
sugar cane 298, *p298*
Sunday, Billy 205, *p205*, 222, 235
supermarkets 255
Supreme Court 155–156, 263
Suriname 316, 333
Susan Constant 109
Sutter, John 177
Sweden 122
syllabary 62, *p63*

T

taiga 21
Taiwan (*See* Republic of China)
tariffs 184
Tattamy 61
tax 140
Teague, Collin 169
technology 255
Tecumseh 62, *p62*
teddy bear 227
teepees 10
Tegucigalpa, Honduras 289
telegraph 208
telephones 225
television 256, *p256*
Tennessee River 69
Tenochtitlán 277–278
tepees 71, *p71*
territory 215
Tewas Indians 92
Texas 176
Thanksgiving 114–115, *p114*
Thatcher, Margaret 339
Thirteenth Amendment 188
Thomas, Justice Clarence 260–261, *p261*
Thomson, James 327
Thorpe, Jim 11, *p11*
Tidewater Region 52

Tierra del Fuego 8, 318, 339
timberline 14, *p14*
time line 106, 108, 136, 160, 182, 198, 218, 238, 254
Titanic 229, *p229*
Tlingit Indians 88
tobacco 125–126
Tobago 305
Tojo 240, *p240*
tomahawk 9
Toronto 38, 39
Torrey, R. A. 222, 235
tortillas 278, 283, *p283*
totem poles 88, *p88*
trade winds 298
transcontinental railroad 194
Treaty of Ghent 174
Treaty of Paris 151–152
Trenton 148
Trinidad 305
Tropic of Cancer 281
tropical forests 281
Truman, Harry S. 250
Truth, Sojourner 183
Tubman, Harriet 183–184, *p183*
tumbleweeds 64, *p65*
tundra 16, *p16*, 73
Tuskegee Institute 196
typhoon (*see* hurricanes)

U

u-boats 231–232, *p231*
umiak 20
Uncle Tom's Cabin 183
Underground Railroad 183
Union 186
Union Pacific Company 194
United Nations 250, *p250*
United States *p176*, *p187* (*see also* individual states)
geography 50–53, 64–65, 68–69, 72–75

Index 361